GLOBALIZATION, SPIRITUALITY, AND JUSTICE

THEOLOGY IN GLOBAL PERSPECTIVE SERIES

Peter C. Phan, General Editor
Ignacio Ellacuría Professor of Catholic Social Thought,
Georgetown University

The *Theology in Global Perspectives* series responds to the challenge to re-examine the foundational and doctrinal themes of Christianity in light of the new global reality. While traditional Catholic theology has assumed an essentially European or Western point of view, *Theology in Global Perspective* takes into account insights and experience of churches in Africa, Asia, Latin American, Oceania, as well as from Europe and North America. Noting the pervasiveness of changes brought about by science and technology, and growing concerns about the sustainability of Earth, it seeks to embody insights from studies in these areas as well.

Other books published in the series

Trinity: Nexus of the Mysteries of Christian Faith, Anne Hunt
Orders and Ministry: Leadership in the World Church, Kenan B. Osborne, O.F.M.
Eschatology and Hope, Anthony Kelly, C.Ss.R.
Spirituality and Mysticism: A Global View, James A. Wiseman
Meeting Mystery: Liturgy, Worship, Sacraments, Nathan D. Mitchell
Creation, Grace, and Redemption, Neil Ormerod
Globalization, Spirituality, and Justice: Navigating the Path to Peace, Daniel G. Groody, C.S.C.
Christianity and Science: Toward a Theology of Nature, John F. Haught
Ecclesiology for a Global Church: A People Called and Sent, Richard R. Gaillardetz
An Introduction to Theology in Global Perspective, Steven B. Bevans
The Christian Moral Life: Faithful Discipleship for a Global Society, Patricia Lamoureux and Paul J. Wadell
Christianity and the Political Order: Conflict, Cooptation, and Cooperation, Kenneth R. Himes, O.F.M.

THEOLOGY IN GLOBAL PERSPECTIVE SERIES

Peter C. Phan, General Editor

GLOBALIZATION, SPIRITUALITY, AND JUSTICE

Navigating the Path to Peace

REVISED EDITION

DANIEL G. GROODY

ORBIS BOOKS

Maryknoll, New York 10545

Founded in 1970, Orbis Books endeavors to publish works that enlighten the mind, nourish the spirit, and challenge the conscience. The publishing arm of the Maryknoll Fathers and Brothers, Orbis seeks to explore the global dimensions of the Christian faith and mission, to invite dialogue with diverse cultures and religious traditions, and to serve the cause of reconciliation and peace. The books published reflect the views of their authors and do not represent the official position of the Maryknoll Society. To learn more about Maryknoll and Orbis Books, please visit our website at www.maryknoll.org.

Library of Congress Cataloging in Publication Data

    Groody, Daniel G., 1964-
       Globalization, spirituality, and justice : navigating the path to peace / Daniel G. Groody.
         p. cm. — (Theology in global perspective series)
       Includes index.
       ISBN 978-1-57075-696-2 (pbk.)
       ISBN 978-1-62698-150-8 (rev. ed. pbk.)
       1. Globalization—Religious aspects—Catholic Church. 2. Christianity and justice—Catholic Church. 3. Catholic Church—Doctrines. I. Title.

    BX1795.G66G76 2007
    261.8—dc22

                    2006038214

*To my parents, Edward and Catherine,
who were the first to show me that
at the heart of spirituality and justice is love.*

If you have a marked preference for certain people . . . it should be for
the poorest, the most abandoned . . . the least gifted by nature. . . .
If you surround them with the most assiduous attention,
it is because their needs are greater,
and it is only justice to give more to those who have received less.

Basile Antoine Marie Moreau
Founder, the Congregation of Holy Cross

Contents

Figures and Tables

Abbreviations and Sources Used in This Work

Official Roman Catholic documents are cited by the common abbreviation in parentheses followed by a number. The number is the article or paragraph number referred to or quoted from that document. For example "(LG 11)" means *Lumen Gentium*, article 11. Most quotations of the documents of Vatican II are taken from the inclusive language version edited by Austin Flannery, O.P., *Vatican Council II*, 2 vols. (Northport, N.Y.: Costello, 1996-98). In some cases, especially where the translations offered more poetic expression, I have drawn from the Vatican documents online, which are available at http://www.vatican.va.

Most documents of Catholic Social Teaching are taken from David J. Shannon and Thomas A. O'Brien, eds., *Catholic Social Thought: The Documentary Heritage* (Maryknoll, N.Y.: Orbis Books, 1992).

For writings of the church fathers, and when drawing from the original languages, I have used the J.-P. Migne editions.

CA *Centesimus Annus*, Encyclical Letter of Pope John Paul II on the hundredth anniversary of *Rerum Novarum*, May 1, 1991.

CCC *Catechism of the Catholic Church*, 2nd ed. (English translation by various publishers). The 2nd Latin edition was promulgated on August 15, 1997, by Saint John Paul II in the apostolic letter *Laetamur Magnopere* (1st ed., promulgated October 11, 1992). Text available online at http://www.vatican.va.

CP *The Challenge of Peace: God's Promise and Our Response*, Pastoral Letter on War and Peace, National Conference of Catholic Bishops (US), May 3, 1986.

CSDC *Compendium of the Social Doctrine of the Church*, Pontifical Council for Justice and Peace (Vatican City: Libreria Editrice Vaticana, 2004).

DCE *Deus Caritas Est,* God Is Love, Encyclical Letter of Pope Benedict XVI, December 25, 2005.

DR *Divini Redemptoris*, On Atheistic Communism, Encyclical Letter of Pope Pius XI, March 19, 1937.

EA *Ecclesia in America*, The Encounter with the Living Jesus Christ: The Way to Conversion, Communion and Solidarity in America, Apostolic Exhortation of John Paul II, January 22, 1999.

EG *Evangelii Gaudium*, Apostolic exhortation of Pope Francis on the proclamation of the Gospel in today's world, November 24, 2013.

Since, as Saint Augustine has put it succinctly, sin is *aversio a Deo*—a turning away from God—and salvation is *conversio ad Deum*—a return to God. Or as Groody, adopting an arresting term, puts it, we must turn away from "money-theism" to monotheism, making the God of Jesus Christ and not Mammon the only true God.

Turning to God, however, requires turning to one's neighbors, especially those who are oppressed by injustice and poverty. Consequently, Groody devotes the first four chapters to a study of justice in the privileged sources of Christian thought, that is, the signs of the time, the Bible, early Christian writers, and the Magisterium. In a genuine spirit of interreligious dialogue he then seeks to enrich the Christian teaching on justice with the teachings of other religious traditions on the same theme. To put flesh and blood on these teachings, he turns our gaze to the "images of mercy, icons of justice" as models for our practice. The remaining three chapters deal with the links between justice on the one hand and theology, liturgy, and spirituality on the other.

Reading *Globalization, Spirituality, and Justice: Navigating the Path to Peace* is an unsettling, even discomforting, yet tremendously hopeful experience. At the least, like its author, one can no longer play a round of golf without glimpsing the invisible broken bodies littering the fairways and without being shocked by the questions of "what it means to be a Christian in a world of destitution and how to reconcile the differences between poverty and prosperity, slavery and freedom, misery and opportunity." Then, hopefully, like Groody, we will have the grace to sit beside the Saras of Grand Central Station and discover in their faces the God of our Lord Jesus Christ.

Preface

A number of years ago I was living and working in Latin America, and toward the end of my stay there I spent some time in Lima, Peru. Before my departure, a terrorist group called Sendero Luminoso announced its latest strategy to intimidate the people of the city. On the very day I was scheduled to leave, they were going to shut down the transportation infrastructure of Lima. I was able to change my flight to the preceding day and before heading off I attended to some pastoral responsibilities, one of which was to visit a jail on the edge of the city. The prison itself had only room for fifteen hundred inmates, but there were more than five thousand people crammed into this wretched place. Many were desperate *campesinos* from rural areas who, after coming to Lima in search of work, ended up stealing merely to survive. Amid outbreaks of cholera and other diseases, many people looked on with envy as they realized I was headed to the United States.

Hours after visiting this dismal prison, I boarded a plane for Miami. Since I arrived a day early, I decided to call on a college roommate and ask if he wanted to get together. When he came to pick me up at the airport, he asked if I wanted to play a round of golf. It had been a while since I had been back in the United States or even swung a golf club, but I willingly accepted his invitation. As we entered the gates of his country club, I felt the culture shock of being back home. Instead of overcrowded buses and packed trains, I was surrounded by Mercedeses, Lexuses, and Porsches of every shape and color. In place of dust and dirt, I found myself on manicured fairways. And in contrast to a world of scarcity, I found myself in a world of abundance. Going from a prison to a promised land in less than twelve hours brought into sharp contrast the two spheres that are part of the planet and the world I have lived in over the years. To be quite honest I very much enjoyed the round of golf that day. And the comfortableness of this environment was delightful. Yet a deeper part of me felt uncomfortable as I remembered the world I had just left. It raised many questions about what it means to be Christian in a world of destitution and how to reconcile the differences between poverty and prosperity, slavery and freedom, misery and opportunity.

This book is a reflection on how to think about poverty, justice, and liberation in light of Christian faith and within our current global context. It offers a theological reading of globalization and a global reading of theology. As I reflect on my own social location, I admit to writing as what Thomas Merton calls "a guilty bystander." I was raised in the suburbs of the northeast United States, grew up in a household of corporate America, and even for a time worked for one of the largest corporations in the world. For all practical purposes, I am a citizen of empire. For some, this history indeed might make me less credible as an author writing about global inequities, but for others I hope it will be an invitation to move beyond guilt and reflect on a different way to live and be in the world. This book flows from a faith that seeks understanding oriented toward a love that produces justice.

While personally I have greatly enjoyed the benefits of globalization, over time I began to realize that not only has it left many people behind but also it has left unanswered many important human questions. The hunger for something more than material prosperity, in part, prompted an interest in spirituality. For many years I engaged in extended retreats and meditations and found the thirty-day *Spiritual Exercises of St. Ignatius* one of the most formative and transformative experiences of my life. The more my spirituality developed, the more questions about social justice surfaced. As I became interested in social justice, I began to see that poverty in the world is connected to complex issues like globalization.

When the invitation came to write this book, I welcomed the opportunity because it gave me the chance to put into words decades of reflection on the subject. Although this book draws on years of study, it also arises out of my direct service with immigrants, orphans, the homeless, and many others who have helped me understand how to think about God in our contemporary context. Through all of these experiences I have learned to draw from any source of insight. I resist labels like liberal or conservative, since the issues of justice are common to all of us. Part of the challenge entails moving beyond the boxes we put each other in, which is why I draw on a range of sources that often are not considered together, such as Christianity and major world religions, Catholicism and Protestantism; figures such as Oscar Romero and Blessed Teresa, Jim Wallis and Charles Colson; as well as subjects such as liberation theology and church teaching, and social justice and the eucharist.

Above all, this is a book about relationships and the gift and challenge of living in right relationships. It seeks to examine the themes of poverty, spirituality, justice, and liberation in our contemporary world and the hope and guidance offered by the Christian tradition. While dialoguing with the disciplines of social science and major world religions, this book is primarily a work of Christian theology and a reflection on the meaning of the Gospel message for our complex era of global change. It covers a vast array of material spanning almost three thousand years of theological thought, whose sources range from early biblical texts to contemporary theological reflection. Synthesizing this large body of material into a concise and coherent volume presented constant challenges, and admittedly each chapter could easily be a book in itself. Yet with all the limitations, I have tried to examine the contribution of the Christian tradition to the process of globalization, and the contribution of globalization to a renewed understanding of theology.

To avoid the temptation of domesticating the message of the Gospel to more self-serving interpretations that legitimate the status quo and can even baptize social injustice, Christian theology seeks to understand the heart of the Gospel message by returning to its foundational sources. These sources help us understand God from different vantage points and help us examine what we believe, what we value, where we look for guidance, how we live with differences, who our models are, how we understand faith today, how we worship, and ultimately how we live a faith that does justice. Traditionally, these issues are investigated through various subdisciplines of theology, such as Scripture, patristic theology, moral theology, interreligious dialogue, hagiography, systematic theology, liturgy, and spirituality.

In the pages that follow we want to explore how each of these subdisciplines helps us reflect on God's challenge to us amidst this sea of change, and the attendant requirements of the human community for building a more just and humane society, one that liberates and elevates all the members of the global village. Each of the following subdisciplines of theology will be treated in a separate chapter, and each offers us an important coordinate in mapping out a journey toward justice:

- The Judeo-Christian Scriptures and biblical reflection
- The homilies and writings of the early church fathers
- Catholic social teaching and the documents of the magisterium
- Major world religions and ecumenical dialogue
- Extraordinary individuals and modern icons of faith and justice
- Contemporary theological reflection and liberation theology
- Liturgical worship and social transformation
- The spiritual journey and the challenge of justice

These chapters are meant to enlighten, empower, and guide the individual and collective journey of Christian faith. They are meant to help probe the deeper questions of life, particularly those human and spiritual questions that globalization has left largely unaddressed and unanswered.

While each of the chapters has its own particular methodology, each according to the nature of the primary source material, the work as a whole has a common methodological approach. Each chapter begins and ends with a narrative either from my own life or another source. In some way or another these narratives either encapsulate the substantive content of the chapter, summarize it, or provide important bridge material from the preceding chapter or to the subsequent chapter. The narrative passages help bind together the wide-ranging material into a more synthetic whole. In between these introductory and concluding narratives, I have framed the substantive theoretical content of each chapter.

In addition, the use of narratives and metaphors is an epistemological decision. I have tried to write in a way that is both intellectually sound and accessible to a broad range of readers. Because some of the deeper truths about human life can only be grasped analogically through story, I have tried to write in a way that both informs the mind and reaches the heart. Blaise Pascal said that the heart has its reasons which reason does not know, and here I have tried to probe the deeper sources of knowledge as it leads to understanding, understanding as it leads to wisdom, wisdom as it leads to action, action as it leads to right relationships, and right relationships as they lead to the realization of what it means to be human before God.

While the epistemology of the Enlightenment with its emphasis on reason has contributed much to the technological advancement and development of our current global economy, it is the epistemology of the heart that I believe merits further reflection. I believe that the deeper truths of human life must be perceived through the "eyes of the heart." More than simply the center of emotion and sentimentality, the heart is the domain of the deepest searching of human life. The heart is also the domain of spirituality. I define spirituality as how one lives out what one most values, and Christian spirituality as how one lives out what Jesus most values.[1] In other words, Christian spirituality in this book is about following Jesus and living out the values of the kingdom of God. Spirituality begins in the human heart, and it generates a community transformed by the love of God and others. Lived out in its personal and public dimensions, spirituality is the way in which the invisible heart of God is made visible to the world.

Putting people's personal and collective experience of God into written words is one of the great challenges of theology in general and this work in particular. In regard to language, I have tried to use inclusive language whenever possible, especially when speaking about horizontal relationships (men and women, rather than just men). The exception to this is when I quoted someone directly, such as the church fathers, John F. Kennedy, or Gandhi,

---

1. Among the many accepted definitions of spirituality, Sandra Schneiders names it as "the experience of conscious involvement in the project of life integration through self-transcendence toward the ultimate value one perceives" ("The Study of Christian Spirituality: The Contours and Dynamics of a Discipline," *Christian Spirituality Bulletin* 1 [Spring 1998]: 1, 3-12).

in which case I preserved the author's words exactly, even though I am aware of the problem of sexist language. Most of the Scripture texts cited are from the New American Bible, although I also draw on the New Revised Standard Version, especially when it offers an inclusive-language translation.

While this book is written in my own words, it is the fruit of a lifetime of conversation with great friends and colleagues. I have learned that books are best written in community, and this manuscript would not be what it is today without the support, encouragement, and countless critical comments from my friends and colleagues that helped develop it and make it better. Above all, I would like to thank my own religious community, the Congregation of Holy Cross, and my colleagues at the University of Notre Dame, particularly those in the Department of Theology, the Institute for Latino Studies, the Kellogg Institute for International Studies, the Graduate School, the Joan B. Kroc Institute for International Peace Studies, the Mendoza College of Business, and the Institute for Scholarship in the Liberal Arts of the College of Arts and Letters. I am also grateful for the generous support of the Faculty Research Program of the University of Notre Dame: the Rodney F. Ganey, Ph. D., Research Program, the NDVI Lilly Faculty Fellows Program, and the ATS/Lilly Theological Research Program. I am grateful to Bill and Colleen Ryan, Anita and Mario Valencia, Sr. Maria Gonzalez and the people of the Mexican American Cultural Center, Eugene and Denise Desimone, George Dilli, Macrina and Ed Hjerpe, Robert Van Kirk, Mark Nishan, Chad and Paula Tiedemann, Bob and Maureen Dee, and Bill and Gerri Groody, who helped provide the support and space to write this book. I also would like to thank my students at Notre Dame, from whom I learned much, and whose comments, questions, and feedback helped refine this manuscript.

Many colleagues provided invaluable critical feedback to every part of this work, and in particular I am grateful to John Cavadini, Gil Cardenes, Allert Brown-Gort, Doug Franson, Bill O'Neill, Jake Empereur, Lee Tavis, Jeffry Odell Korgen, Bill Purcell, Dan Philpot, Ernie Bartell, Jerry Powers, Kevin Seasoltz, Michael Driscoll, Maxwell Johnson, Nathan Mitchell, John Melloh, Matt Ashley, Mary Doak, Oliver Williams, Ken Belanger, Thomas Gallagher, Sr. Ozana, Jim Towey, Steve Warner, Bob Pelton, Mike Griffin, Rich Brown, Bob Nogosek, Tom Lemos, Jerry Baumbach, Jaleh Dashti-Gibson, Asma Afsaruddin, Brad Malkovsky, Paul Kollman, Bob Dowd, Kristin Shrader-Frechette, Walter Brueggemann, Peter Hinde, Andrew Felton, Mary Clemency, Janine Siegel, Anne Williams, Pheme Perkins, Wendy Wright, Branko Milanovic, David Loy, Andrew Hofer, Brian Daley, Jim Phalan, Desiree Zamora, Maria Ruvalcaba, Chris Bachner-Reimer, Elias Moo, and Andy Buechel.

I would like to thank Mignon Montpetit and Jenny Manier, two friends with gifted minds who became great companions on this journey of justice and met often with me in the revision of this manuscript. They were part of a larger journey with JustFaith Ministries, which also helped inspire this work. I am particularly grateful to Jack Jezreel, and Jay Freel-Landry, whose invitation to journey with a JustFaith group provided countless moments of insight into the journey of faith today. I want to thank all those from JustFaith who worked with me on this manuscript and helped me rethink justice from the "ground up," especially Jim Paladino, Laurie McGowan, Therese Sullivan Powers, and Jennifer Monahan.

I am also grateful to Robert Ellsberg, publisher, Orbis Books, Bill Burrows, and Peter Phan for their invitation to do this book and for their constant support through its writing. I would like to thank Gustavo Gutiérrez, Tim Matovina, and Virgilio Elizondo, whose support, friendship, and feedback helped bring this project to birth; to Liz and Mike Lafortune for their sacrifice, generosity, and countless hours of commitment to this work; to Terry Garza for her dedication and support of this work and that of the Center for Latino Spirituality and Culture; to Lisa Marie Belz, an emerging scholar in biblical studies, who provided not only precise, critical feedback but helped me integrate the best of scholarship with commitment to the grass roots; to Claudia Ramirez for her kind heart, generous spirit, and constant attention to details in this project; and finally to Mary J. Miller, whose precise mind, deep faith, and magnanimous work ethic helped develop and refine this book, and whose constant encouragement helped me see, in all my limitations and doubts, that it is a humble work about the kingdom of God in our midst.

Lastly, I would like to thank all those who are poor and broken in any way with whom I have had the chance to journey over the years as a fellow pilgrim of faith. In all humility, they have been some of my best teachers about God, and if in some small way this book helps to bring insight into God's love for the world, and God's love for the poor in particular, I am grateful.

1

A Gift of God, A Human Responsibility

The Global Community and
the Challenge of Justice

A GIFT OF GOD: THE PLANET IN GLOBAL PERSPECTIVE

An Over-view: A Global Picture of the Earth

ON SEPTEMBER 12, 1962, President John F. Kennedy delivered a visionary speech in which he laid down an unprecedented challenge: "We choose to go to the moon," he said. "We choose to go to the moon in this decade and do the other things, not because they are easy but because they are hard."[1] With these words the space program of the United States shifted into high gear, and its leaders took on the daunting challenge of navigating their way to the moon and making it safely back home. Six years after Kennedy's speech, three astronauts boarded Apollo 8, and a tower of fire boosted them at 24,000 miles per hour into the cosmic night. They were the first to break the gravitational umbilical cord with Mother Earth and enter the lunar orbit.

On Christmas Eve, 250,000 miles from home, the crew of Apollo 8 reached the dark side of the moon. As they passed above the shadows of the cold and lifeless terrain of the lunar surface, they glimpsed what no human beings had ever seen before: the earth rising over the moon's horizon. Beholding the world in this way inspired the astronauts to read the first words from of the Book of Genesis:

> In the beginning, God created the heaven and the earth, and the earth was without form, and void; and darkness was upon the face of the deep. And the Spirit of God moved upon the face of the waters. And God said, Let

---

1. Theodore C. Sorensen, Eric K. Sorensen, Stephen E. Sorensen, and Philip J. Sorensen, eds., *Let the Word Go Forth: The Speeches, Statements, and Writings of John F. Kennedy* (New York: Delacorte Press, 1988), 178. This speech in written and audio form is also available online at the JFK Library website, http://www.jfklibrary.org.

there be light: and there was light. And God saw the light and that it was good: and God divided the light from the darkness (Gn 1:1-4).[2]

Seeing the earth from space was a milestone of political will and scientific achievement, human understanding and global awareness, theological insight and divine contemplation.

Beholding our planet from space has enabled us to see our place in the universe in a new way. American astronaut Donald Williams noted, "For those who have seen the earth from space, and for the hundreds and perhaps thousands more who will, the experience most certainly changes your perspective. The things that we share in our world are far more valuable than those which divide us."[3] As he was orbiting the globe in the Space Shuttle, Saudi Arabian astronaut Sultan Bin Salmon al-Saud observed, "The first day, we pointed to our countries. Then we were pointing to our continents. By the fifth day we were aware of only one Earth." German cosmonaut Sigmund Jähn also said, "Before I flew I was already aware of how small and vulnerable our planet is; but only when I saw it from space, in all its ineffable beauty and fragility, did I realize that humankind's most urgent task is to cherish and preserve it for future generations." A gift of God, the earth is a precious, delicate, celestial jewel of breathtaking beauty with infinitely rich topographical, biological, and cultural diversity. A human responsibility, it is the place that we are called to care for and cultivate, and it is the context where we learn to live in relationship with each other. It is the cosmic home of over seven billion people.[4]

If the world as we know it today was proportionally reduced to a village of 100 people, 50 would be male and 50 would be female;[5] 61 would be Asian, 15 African, 10 European, and 14 from the Americas (North, South, Central, and Caribbean) and Oceania.[6] Drawing people together from many different cultures, languages, and religions, 14 in this village would speak, as their first language, Mandarin, 7 English, 7 Hindi, 6 Spanish, 4 Russian, 4 Arabic, 3 Bengali, 3 Portuguese, 2 Malay-Indonesian, 2 Japanese, and 1 German. The other 61 would speak Korean, French, Javanese, Urdu, and many other languages.[7] From a faith perspective, 33 would be Christian, 23 Muslim, 14

---

2. As quoted by astronauts from the King James Version.

3. Quotations in this paragraph are from Kevin Kelley, *The Home Planet* (Reading, Pa.: Addison-Wesley, 1988), 139, 82, 140.

4. The United Nations declared October 31, 2011, the birthdate of the world's seven billionth baby. See "As world passes 7 billion milestone, UN urges action to meet key challenges," available on the UN website at http://www.un.org.

5. Gender figures are from 2011. Available at http://en.worldstat.info/World.

6. Population by continents, from a 2014 estimate, can be found at http://www.worldatlas.com/geoquiz/thelist.htm.

7. Ibid. Also note, according to the *CIA World Factbook* (https://www.cia.gov), as of 2015, an

Hindu, 11 from other religions including Sikh, Jewish, and Baha'i, 10 non-religious, 7 Buddhist, and 2 atheists.[8]

An Under-view: The Problem of Poverty

While space exploration has given us an entirely new way of looking at our global home, new research has also enabled us to see with greater clarity not only the dark side of the moon but also the dark side of planet earth. Even as scientific advances have brought us closer to some of the remote places of outer space, socioeconomic studies show that the distance between the rich and the poor on earth is greater than ever. Looking at the world from the perspective of the economically underdeveloped gives us a very different picture of the earth. Statistical data and empirical trends, in particular, help us understand more accurately the problematic contours of our contemporary reality.

In our worldwide community of over seven billion people, the resources are unevenly distributed.[9] The disparity shows us that the collective wealth of the richest one percent of the people in the world is 65 times the total wealth of the poorest 50 percent of the world's population.[10] This global income gap has an impact on our global village of 100 people as well. Twelve people in our village are chronically undernourished.[11] Eleven people do not

---

estimated 7,100 languages were spoken in the world. Approximately 80 percent of these languages were spoken by fewer than 100,000 people.

8. Religion figures are from a 2010 *CIA World Factbook* estimate.

9. Some of the most significant studies on global poverty and global inequalities come from the United Nations and the World Bank. In particular see the annual *Human Development* and *World Development* reports: the *Human Development Report 2005: International Cooperation at a Crossroads* (New York: United Nations, 2005), *Inequality Predicament: Report on the World Social Situation 2005* (New York: United Nations, 2005), and the *World Development Report 2006: Equity and Development* (New York: Oxford University Press, 2005). See also Jeffrey Sachs, *The End of Poverty: Economic Possibilities for Our Time* (East Rutherford, N.J.: Penguin Press, 2005); Branko Milanovic, *Worlds Apart: Measuring International and Global Inequality* (Princeton, N.J.: Princeton University Press, 2005); and Bob Sutcliffe, *100 Ways of Seeing an Unequal World* (London: Zed Books, 2001).

10. Credit Suisse, "Global Wealth Report 2013" (Zurich: Credit Suisse, 2013); available at https://publications.credit-suisse.com, and Forbes's "The World's Billionaires," at http://www.forbes.com/billionaires/list/. A conservative estimate for 2010 finds that at least a third of all private financial wealth, and nearly half of all offshore wealth, is now owned by the world's richest 91,000 people—just 0.001 percent of the world's population. The next 51 percent of all wealth is owned by the next 8.4 million—just 0.14 percent of the world's population. See http://www.globalissues.org/article/26/poverty-facts-and-stats.

11. Food and Agriculture Organization of the United Nations, "The State of Food Insecurity in the World 2014," available at http://www.fao.org. The 2012–2014 estimate is that 805 million people worldwide are chronically undernourished. This figure is down 100 million over the last decade.

have access to clean drinking water,[12] and four people do not have access to adequate sanitation.[13] In the village of 100 people, twenty-three live in substandard housing and one is homeless.[14] Seventeen people in the village do not have access to electricity, and four rely on wood, crop waste, dung, and other biomass to cook with and heat their homes.[15] Sixteen people are unable to read,[16] and sixty remain unconnected to the Internet.[17] Seven will have a college degree.[18] Three people in our village are migrating.[19] Overall, seventeen exist on US$1.25 per day, and, in all, thirty-one struggle to live on two dollars a day or less.[20] A sobering seventy people in our global village of one

12. World Health Organization, "Water Fact Sheet," July 2014, available at http://www.who.int. In 2012, 89 percent of the world's population had access to an improved drinking-water source. Almost 4 billion people now get water through a piped connection; 2.3 billion access water through other improved sources including public taps, protected wells, and boreholes. 748 million people rely on unimproved sources, including 173 million who depend on surface water. See also *CIA World Factbook*.

13. World Health Organization, "Sanitation Fact Sheet," July 2014, available at http://www.who.int. In 2012, 64 percent of the world's population had access to improved sanitation facilities including flush toilets and covered latrines; 2.5 billion people still do not have access to these basic facilities. See also *CIA World Factbook*.

14. UN-Habitat, "State of the World's Cities 2010–2011, Cities for All: Bridging the Urban Divide," at http://sustainabledevelopment.un.org. A billion people—32 percent of the global urban population—live in urban slums.

15. National Geographic, "Five Surprising Facts about Energy Poverty," May 29, 2013; available at http://news.nationalgeographic.com.

16. *CIA World Factbook*. Almost three-quarters of the world's 775 million illiterate adults are found in only ten countries (in descending order: India, China, Pakistan, Bangladesh, Nigeria, Ethiopia, Egypt, Brazil, Indonesia, and the Democratic Republic of the Congo); of all the illiterate adults in the world, two-thirds are women; extremely low literacy rates are concentrated in South and West Asia and Sub-Saharan Africa (2010 estimate).

17. United Nations International Telecommunications Union, "Internet well on way to 3 billion users, UN telecom agency reports," available at http://www.un.org. Seventy-eight percent of people in developed countries are expected to have access to the Internet by the end of 2014, but in countries that are still developing, the percentage of connected users drops dramatically to 32 percent by the end of 2014.

18. Robert J. Barro and Jong-Wha Lee, "A New Data Set of Education Attainment in the World, 1950 - 2010," *Journal of Development Economics* 104 (April 2010): 184-198. Statistics cited in "College Graduates Spur Economic Growth: Chart of the Day" (May 2010), available at www.bloomberg.com.

19. United Nations Department of Economic and Social Affairs, "International Migration 2013," available at the United Nations website at http://www.un.org. In 2013, the number of international migrants worldwide reached 232 million, an increase of 57 million, or 33 percent, compared to 2000.

20. World Bank, "Poverty Overview," October 7, 2014, available on the World Bank website at http://www.worldbank.org. These estimates are from 2011 and are figured in so-called 2005 international dollars or PPP (purchasing power parity) dollars. Instead of simple exchange rates, PPP reflects a more accurate estimate of the standard of living in a country because it accounts better for the average living costs (mainly measured in food costs) in that country. For instance, with US$1, one can buy, on average, more food in India than in the United States. US$1.25 per day is a measure of extreme poverty, and US$2 per day is a common measurement of deep deprivation.

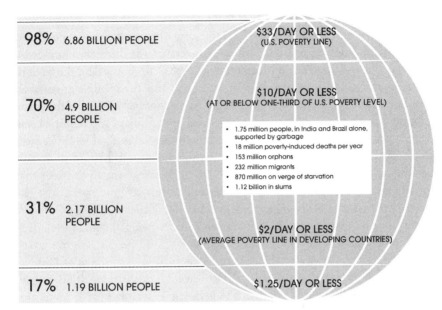

GLOBAL INCOME

FIGURE 1. An Economic Snapshot of the World[21]

hundred live on US\$10 per day or less.[22] In brief, as the World Bank describes it, two-thirds of the world population lives in poverty[23] (see fig. 1).

21. I am grateful to Branko Milanovic of the World Bank for his help in constructing this chart. These calculations are done in purchasing power parity dollars (see n. 20). For number of those supported by garbage, see Bharati Chaturvedi, "Mainstreaming Waste Pickers and the Informal Recycling Sector in the Municipal Solid Waste," *Handling and Management Rules 2000, A Discussion Paper,* and Maria Helena, Tarchi Crivellari, Sonia Dias, and André de Souza Pena, "Waste Pickers & Solid Waste Management" (2008), available on the WIEGO website at http://www.wiego.org; for number of poverty-induced deaths, see Thomas Pogge, "World Poverty and Human Rights," *Ethics & International Affairs* 19.1 (Spring 2005), also available at the EIA website, http://www.carnegiecouncil.org; for number of orphans, see "Children's Statistics," at the SOS Children's Villages USA website, http://www.sos-usa.org; for number of migrants, see "International Migration 2013," at http://www.un.org.pdf; for number of those on the verge of starvation, see "2015 World Hunger and Poverty Facts and Statistics," at http://www.worldhunger.org; for number of those living in slums, see "State of the World's Cities 2010–2011, Cities for All: Bridging the Urban Divide," at http://sustainabledevelopment.un.org; for U.S. poverty level, see "Poverty Guidelines," at http://aspe.hhs.gov.

22. Ernst & Young, "Hitting the Sweet Spot: The Growth of the Middle Class in Emerging Markets" (2013), 4; available on the Ernst & Young global website at http://www.ey.com.

23. The World Bank describes three degrees of poverty: extreme or absolute poverty, moderate poverty, and relative poverty. Extreme poverty means living on less than US\$1.25 per day. People in this category do not have enough to survive and lack the basic necessities of life; extreme poverty is "poverty that kills." More than eight million people worldwide die each year; 22,000 die each

While the bright side of reality is that in recent years the standard of living for more than half the world has actually gotten better, the dark side is that half of the global village still lives in dire poverty.[24] The difference in income between the richest and poorest countries was 3 to 1 in 1820, 11 to 1 in 1913, 35 to 1 in 1950, 44 to 1 in 1973, and 72 to 1 in 1992.[25] Recent research indicates that these trends continue to get worse, not better.[26] While the distribution of income is important in assessing global financial inequities, the distribution of wealth is also an important indicator (see table 1). Wealth is less equitably distributed worldwide than income, with half of all wealth held by only 2 percent of the world's adults.[27] It is staggering to consider that the richest 80 *individuals* on earth have, collectively, as much wealth as the assets of the poorest 3.5 billion people, or one-half of the world's population.[28] Since these 80 people, in a planet of over 7 billion people, equal only a tiny fraction of a person in our theoretical village of 100 people, we might say that a ring on the finger of the richest one person in our village of 100 has the same monetary value as the cumulative wealth of the poorest 50 people. It is worth noting that, if current trends continue, the richest 1 percent of the global population is soon expected to have at least a 50 percent share of the total global wealth. This means that, combined, "the richest 1 percent will own more than all the rest by 2016."[29] A cursory glimpse of the state of the world reveals that economic growth and income development have not advanced hand in hand with human development. As Nelson Mandela put it, "Massive poverty and obscene inequality are such terrible scourges of our times—times in which the world boasts breathtaking advances in science, technology, industry and wealth accumulation—that they have to rank alongside slavery and apartheid as social evils."[30]

---

day, because they are too poor to survive. Moderate poverty is defined as living on $1.25 to $2.00 per day. People in this category have just barely the basic needs of life. Relative poverty, defined as a household income below the national average, means a living standard below the common middle class. See www.worldbank.org and Sachs, *End of Poverty*, 20-24.

24. Sachs, *End of Poverty*, 19.

25. Angus Maddison, *Monitoring the World Economy: 1820-1992* (Paris: OECD, 1995); and idem, *The World Economy: A Millennial Perspective* (Paris: OECD, 2001).

26. See World Bank, *World Development Report 2006: Equity and Development*; Milanovic, *Worlds Apart;* and Glen Firebaugh, *The New Geography of Global Income Inequality* (Cambridge, Mass.: Harvard University Press, 2006).

27. "Winner Takes (Almost) All," in *The Economist*, December 7, 2006.

28. Oxfam International, "Even It Up: Richest 1% Will Own More Than All the Rest by 2016," January 19, 2015, at http://www.oxfam.org; and Oxfam International, "Wealth: Having It All and Wanting More," January 19, 2015, at http://www.oxfam.org.

29. Ibid.

30. *Human Development Report 2005: International Cooperation at a Crossroads*, 4.

TABLE 1. Global Wealth[31]

Percent of Global Population	Number of People	Individual Wealth
Bottom 50	3.5 billion	Less than $2161
Top 50	3.5 billion	At least $2161
Top 40	2.8 billion	At least $3517
Top 30	2.1 billion	At least $6318
Top 20	1.4 billion	At least $14,169
Top 10	700 million	At least $61,041
Top 5	350 million	At least $150,145
Top 1	70 million	At least $514,512

The continent most deeply entrenched in poverty is Africa. Nine of the ten poorest countries in the world are located in Africa. More than half of the people live in extreme poverty.[32] The poor countries have in many cases been made worse off by accumulating high levels of debt to multilateral institutions such as the International Monetary Fund. Although there has been some movement toward debt relief, in most places the poorer the country the more likely it is that the people paying the foreign debt never contracted the loans in the first place, nor received any of the benefits.[33] Poorer countries now spend at least twenty-five dollars in debt repayment for every one dollar they receive in new loans, making it all the more difficult to break the spiral of poverty.[34]

While poverty is widespread on continents like Africa, Asia, and Latin America, the wealthiest nation on earth has the widest gap between the rich

---

31. I am grateful to the World Institute for Development Economics Research (WIDER), a division of the United Nations University in Helsinki, for their groundbreaking study on worldwide wealth. This first of its kind study attempts to determine how wealth, as opposed to income, is distributed around the world, and is based on data from thirty-eight countries and extrapolations for the rest of the countries of the world in 2000. High income countries for which data was available included Britain, Sweden, Japan, and the United States. More populous, but poorer countries included China, India, and Indonesia. Income is defined as the flow of money that runs though an entity such as a household or a nation on a yearly basis. Wealth is the total assets an entity has accumulated over its lifetime to date, minus its liabilities. Financial assets include real estate, consumer durables, and even livestock, while liabilities include all debt. For more on this study, see "World Distribution of Household Wealth" available at www.wider.unu.edu. Note: WIDER has not updated this data since 2000.

32. See top ten poorest countries in the world as of 2014 at www.mapsofworld.com. See also Sachs, *End of Poverty*, 21.

33. See "Debt: The Facts," *New Internationalist* 312 (May 1999), available online at http://www.newint.org/issue312/contents.htm. For more on debt relief, see *Human Development Report 2005: International Cooperation at a Crossroads*, 89-90.

34. Based on World Bank data, and available at http://www.globalissues.org.

and the poor of any industrialized nation.[35] In the United States, many go to bed hungry and go without proper medical care, education, clothing, or housing.[36] One out of every seven Americans lives in poverty, and almost one out of every two American children experience episodic poverty at least two consecutive months of the year.[37] Overall, in the richest country of the world, there are more than 45 million people living in poverty, which is more than the entire population of Canada.[38]

Our analysis from "below" becomes even more challenging as we survey our collective spending patterns as a human family in relationship to basic human needs (see table 2, p. 9 below).[39]

According to these figures, the world spends slightly more than six times as much money on fragrances as it gives to developing countries in education aid.[40] The world spends almost as much money on toys and games as the "aggregate global extreme poverty gap," or the difference between the income of the extremely poor (those living on *less than* US$1.25 per day)

---

35. See the Catholic Campaign for Human Development at http://www.povertyusa.org/.

36. For more on poverty thresholds, see U.S. Census Bureau resources at http://www.census.gov/hhes/www/poverty/poverty.html, and the Institute for Research on Poverty at the University of Wisconsin in Madison at http://www.irp.wisc.edu/.

37. In 2013, the official poverty rate was 14.5 percent (see https://www.census.gov). "Nearly 44 percent of all US kids were in poverty for two or more months from 2009 to 2012, the Census Bureau reported." See Danielle Kurtzleben, "Why Child Poverty in the US May Be Much Worse Than You Realize," at http://www.vox.com.

38. In 2013, there were 45.3 million people living in poverty in the United States (see https://www.census.gov). The population of Canada in 2013 was just over 35 million people.

39. Richard Falk makes a distinction between "globalization from above" and "globalization from below." Globalization from above deals with initiatives undertaken by large organizations like governments, multinational corporations, or other major financial institutions, and globalization from below refers to initiatives taken by people directly concerned with protecting the environment, human rights, and development. Globalization from above is more profit and politically centered; globalization from below is more people-centered and directed toward the creation of a "global civil society." Richard Falk, "The Monotheistic Religions in the Era of Globalization," *Global Dialogue* 1, no. 1 (Summer 1999): 147.

40. In 2013 the global community of over 7 billion people collectively spent US$45 million on an aggregate of men's, women's, and unisex mass and premium fragrances. Also in 2013, more than 57 million children across the globe did not have access to primary education; many of them may never have the opportunity to set foot in a classroom. Aid to education dropped from US$6.2 billion in 2010 to US$5.8 billion in 2011, harming aid to basic education and putting at risk meeting the 2015 Millennium Development goal for education, but also hopes of extending global goals to include universal secondary education after 2015. For less than half of what was spent on fragrances in 2013, the worldwide community could have provided slightly more than triple the education aid given in 2010 (US$22.5 billion), which would have given many of the 57 million children who have never been to school the chance to start. See UNESCO, "Schooling for Millions of Children Jeopardized by Reductions in Aid," UIS Fact Sheet, June 2013, pages 1, 6; available at http://www.uis.unesco.org.

TABLE 2. Annual Global Priorities in Spending[41]

Spending Priorities	$U.S. Billions	Percentage of Global Military Spending
Fragrances[42]	45	2.6
Pet food, pet care products worldwide[43]	73	4.2
International development aid (ODA)[44]	135	7.7
Toys and games worldwide[45]	153	8.7
Narcotics worldwide[46]	380	21.75
Alcohol worldwide[47]	683	39.1
Tobacco worldwide[48]	783	44.8
Luxury market worldwide[49]	1800	103.0
Military spending worldwide[50]	1747	100

41. These figures reflect data collected for 2013 and are reported in billions of U.S. dollars. Historic regional/global values are the aggregation of local currency country data at current prices converted into the common currency using y-o-y exchange rates. The data for fragrances, pet food and products, toys and games, alcohol and wine, and cigarettes and tobacco products was collected on January 15, 2015, from *Euromonitor*, a subscriber only source, and is available upon request from the author.

42. Fragrances are defined as an aggregate of men's, women's, and unisex mass and premium fragrances.

43. The aggregation of dog and cat food, other pet food, and pet care products.

44. International development aid (ODA) measures the official state funds in developed countries that are sent to developing countries. More information on this report is available at the Organization for Economic Cooperation and Development (OECD) website. For 2013 figures, see "Aid to Developing Countries Rebounds in 2013 to Reach an All-Time High," www.oecd.org.

45. The aggregation of traditional toys and games and video games.

46. This figure measures world consumer markets for heroin and other opiates, marijuana, and amphetamines. See Edward Gresser, "World Drug Trade: $50 Billion?" (August 17, 2014), at http://progressive-economy.org.

47. Alcohol includes wine (the aggregation of still and sparkling light grape wines, fortified wine and vermouth, non-grape wine, fine and luxury wines, and Champagne), spirits (the aggregation of whiskey, brandy, cognac, white spirits, rum, tequila, liqueurs, and other spirits), cider/perry (cider is made from fermented apple juice; perry is made from fermented pear juice; both artisanal and industrial are included), and beer (the aggregation of lager, dark beer, stout, and non/low alcoholic beer).

48. The aggregate of cigarettes, cigars, cigarillos, and smoking tobacco such as pipe tobacco and roll-your-own tobacco. Nonsmoking tobacco such as snuff and chewing tobacco is not included.

49. Total annual sales of luxury goods such as apparel, cosmetics, watches, and jewelry, and luxury experiences such as private airline services and five-star restaurants. See Olivier Abtan, et al., "Shock of the New Chic: Dealing with New Complexity in the Business of Luxury" (Boston Consulting Group, January 2014), http://www.luxesf.com.

50. Sam Perlo-Freeman and Carina Solmirano, "Trends in World Military Expenditure, 2013" (SIPRI Fact Sheet) Stockholm International Peace Research Institute (SIPRI), April 2014, available at http://books.sipri.org. A pattern has been established in recent years whereby military

and the raise in income that would take them *up to* the $1.25 line.[51] The world spends fifteen and a half times more on luxury items and experiences than the money that would be needed to provide adequate sanitation for the 2.5 billion people across the globe who do not yet have this basic necessity.[52] Moreover, it is sobering to consider that the world spends nearly six times as much on tobacco as on international development aid.

The most troubling area of global expenditures is military spending. While militaries have responded to human disasters such as the 2004 tsunami in the Indian Ocean, which left 230,000 dead and millions homeless, in point of fact they do little to fight the war on poverty. Every hour 840 children die from poverty, hunger, easily preventable diseases and illnesses, and other related causes, which is the equivalent of a tsunami every eleven days.[53] Yet even the smallest reductions in military expenditures could dramatically affect human development.[54] For one day's global military spending, we could achieve universal coverage and fully scale-up malaria intervention around the world for one year.[55] For what we spend in two days on the military, we could provide twice UNICEF's 2013 total revenue to be used for supplies and ser-

---

spending has fallen in the West—that is, in North America, Western and Central Europe, and Oceania—while it has increased in other regions. This tendency was even more pronounced in 2013, with military spending increasing in every region and subregion outside the West.

51. According to the World Bank, the poorest 17 percent of the world's population, or 1.2 billion people, are extremely poor, living on less than US$1.25 per day. If the incomes of every extremely poor person were to rise to the $1.25 line, the aggregate increase in their income would need to total at least $169 billion dollars in 2005 PPP terms. This number is the aggregate extreme poverty gap. It is important to note that extreme poverty gap is the conceptual amount of direct additional income an average extremely poor person would need to get to $1.25 per day and is not indicative of the level of assistance required to close the gap. See World Bank, "The State of the Poor: Where Are the Poor and Where Are They Poorest?" (April 17, 2013), 4; available at http://www.worldbank.org. See also n. 20, above.

52. The cost to provide basic sanitation is estimated at US$115 billion per year to the Millennium Development Goals (MDG) target year of 2015. The expenditure is dominated by capital costs and only about 10 percent of the estimate is for operation and maintenance. See World Health Organization, "Global Costs and Benefits of Drinking Water Supply and Sanitation Interventions to Reach MDG Target and Universal Coverage" (Geneva: WHO, 2012), 3, 5-6; available at http://www.who.int.

53. Anup Shah, "Today Around 21,000 Children Died Around the World," *Global Issues* (September 24, 2011), http://www.globalissues.org.

54. The Stockholm International Peace Research Institute (SIPRI) is a reputable source for statistics on military spending. For recent trends, see the military expenditure chapter in *SIPRI Yearbook 2013*, http://www.sipri.org/yearbook/2013/03. For summary figures, see Anup Shah, "World Military Spending," June 30, 2013, www.globalissues.org. For example, in 2012 the U.S. was responsible for 39 percent of the total military spending in the world, followed by China (9.5% of world share), Russia (5.2%), the UK (3.5%), and Japan (3.4%).

55. It is estimated that US$5.1 billion is required annually to achieve universal coverage and fully scale-up malaria interventions around the world. UNICEF, "Malaria" (2014), http://www.unicef.org. As a global community, our military spending comes to US$4.8 billion per day (see table 2, above).

vices for vulnerable children worldwide.[56] For less than a week's global military spending, we could provide the US$29 billion per year that it will take to provide to everyone who does not yet have it access to both drinking water and improved sanitation.[57]

The loss of human potential due to poverty is especially serious when the global village as a whole is wealthy enough to do something about it. Because there is a direct connection between national security and human insecurity, the gross disparity between military budgets and human need is not only irresponsible, but the justification for this disparity is also ill conceived. As former military leader and Secretary of State Colin Powell noted, "The war on terror is bound up in the war on poverty."[58] The lack of resources and opportunities creates great social instability, and it is a fertile ground for desperate people to incite violence, if not terrorism. Jeffrey Sachs commented that if we "spent more time and money on mobilizing Weapons of Mass Salvation in addition to combating Weapons of Mass Destruction, we might actually get somewhere in making this planet a safer and more hospitable home."[59] Poverty and gross inequality throughout the world waste human potential, weaken the entire community, and put the whole human family at risk.[60] On the most basic level, development is a necessary condition for justice and peace, and the first step toward a safer world is to help those who are most in need.

While measured primarily in socioeconomic terms, poverty is a complex, multidimensional issue that affects people at all levels of their existence. As the World Bank notes, "Poverty is a pronounced deprivation in well-being. To be poor is to be hungry, to lack shelter and clothing, to be sick and not cared for, to be illiterate and not schooled." It means having limited choices and entails, as a woman from Latvia put it, "humiliation, the sense of being dependent and being forced to accept rudeness, insults, and indifference when we seek help."[61] The lack of opportunities and resources diminishes people's

---

56. UNICEF, "Our Story 2013," http://www.unicef.org. Total UNICEF revenue in 2013 was US$4.9 billion; two days of global military spending is slightly less than US$10 billion (see table 2, above).

57. World Health Organization, "Global Costs and Benefits of Drinking Water Supply and Sanitation Interventions to Reach MDG Target and Universal Coverage" (Geneva: WHO, 2012), 5-6, http://www.who.int. The capital costs of achieving the MDG goal for improved sanitation is estimated at US$23 billion per year; drinking water costs are US$6 billion per year (see table 2, above).

58. Sachs, *End of Poverty*, xvii. This quotation comes out of the introduction by Bono in this work.

59. The term "weapons of mass salvation" refers to vaccines, medicines, and food relief, among other aids to development. See http://www.globalpolicy.org/socecon/develop/2002/1024weapons.htm.

60. World Bank, *World Development Report 2006: Equity and Development*, 2.

61. World Bank, *World Development Report 2000/2001* (New York: Oxford University Press, 2001), 15, 3.

political, social, cultural, and economic freedom, and, amidst the anxiety for survival, it also forces many people to work multiple jobs, which strains, if not ruptures, relationships. It can break down people's sense of creativity, productivity, and even self-respect, diminishing their hope for better lives and dramatically reducing the capacity for human development.[62] Above all, to be poor means to be insignificant.[63]

An Inner-view: The Terrain of the Human Heart

How can we begin to interpret the genesis of the social discord and disorder that have resulted in such poverty? While the global inequities of today are rooted in the structural injustices in society, on a deeper level they are also integrally related to the disorders of the human heart. Perhaps even more daunting than trying to conquer the challenges of "outer space" is conquering the challenges of "inner space." The terrain of the human heart is an infinitely vast mystery, with unlimited capacity for good and for evil. "The earth provides enough to satisfy every man's need," Mahatma Gandhi noted, "but not every man's greed."[64] Correcting the disorders in society challenges us first to understand the terrain of the human heart, as noted in Vatican II's Pastoral Constitution on the Church in the Modern World, *Gaudium et Spes*:

> The truth is that the imbalances under which the modern world labors are linked with that more basic imbalance which is rooted in the heart of man ... [where] many elements wrestle with one another. Thus, on the one hand, as a creature he experiences his limitations in a multitude of ways; on the other he feels himself to be boundless in his desires and summoned to a higher life. Pulled by manifold attractions he is constantly forced to choose among them and renounce some. Indeed, as a weak and sinful being, he often does what he would not, and fails to do what he would. Hence he suffers from internal divisions, and from these flow so many and such great discords in society. (GS 10)

The current disorders of society begin with the disorders of the human heart, from which flow destructive choices that unravel relationships.

At the same time, the heart is the source from which flows the greatest values and aspirations of human life. More than simply the place of sentiment and feeling, the heart deals with inner wealth, with what people possess

---

62. United Nations, *Human Development Report 1999*, 16.

63. Gustavo Gutiérrez, "Memory and Prophecy," in *The Option for the Poor in Christian Theology*, ed. Daniel G. Groody (Notre Dame, Ind.: University of Notre Dame Press, 2007), 25-26.

64. Quoted in E. F. Schumacher, *Small Is Beautiful: Economics as if People Mattered* (New York: Harper & Row, 1975), 33.

inside themselves. It refers to the quality of people's characters, the endowment of their souls, and the treasure within them. The heart symbolizes the whole process of human understanding that can only be grasped from the depths of one's being, the place where the human and the divine intersect, that is, where one lives out one's spirituality. In other words, spirituality deals with the terrain of the human heart, with what one values, with how one lives out one's relationships, and in particular with how one responds to the most vulnerable members of the human family.

In the pages that follow we will explore the forces in the human heart that ultimately shape human society and the forces of human society that shape the human heart. We will do this by weaving together three different dimensions of our lives: (1) the over-view of reality and the dynamics of globalization (the terrain of our socioeconomic context), (2) the under-view of reality and the challenge of justice (the problem of poverty), and (3) the inner-view of reality and the dynamics of spirituality (the terrain of the human heart). We will look at globalization's impact on creation, justice's challenge to the forces of de-creation (or sin), and spirituality's movement toward the promise of re-creation. At the core of this reflection we will look primarily at the quality of our relationships, especially our relationship to the Creator, to other creatures, and to creation. From this relational structure, we will begin to construct a theological framework from which to examine the challenges and opportunities of globalization. This framework will offer us the beginnings of a "nautical map" that can help us sort out the respective values, priorities, and beliefs that influence our individual and collective decision making in order to help us better navigate the path to peace.

A HUMAN RESPONSIBILITY: THE MARKETPLACE IN GLOBAL PERSPECTIVE

The genesis of today's disordered economy is a complex and often contested conversation that goes well beyond the scope of this book.[65] However we understand its origins, the new global marketplace is transforming our world as never before. The current density of interactions between people and the rapid interchange of ideas, money, and trade makes this an entirely new era that has brought progress as well as regress, gains as well as losses, and new opportunities as well as new problems.[66]

---

65. For more on the history of globalization, see Michael Bordo, "Globalization in Historical Perspective," *Business Economics* (January 2002): 20-29.

66. While the drive for new market expansion has been a part of human civilization since earliest times, globalization as we know it today is a new chapter in human history. See Robert O.

Globalization has created possibilities for local, regional, and global integration, but it has also left waves of disintegration in its wake. It has given us
more and more of a free market, but it has unmasked human and structural
"unfreedoms" that contribute to making so few so wealthy while so many
remain so poor. It has given us new technology such as global positioning systems, which help us find our way in time and space, but in other ways it has
made us less able to find the ethical coordinates and the spiritual vision that
would help us navigate to a place of human solidarity. In order to understand
the assets and liabilities of our contemporary context, we need to examine
more carefully and critically the meaning and motor of globalization, the
premises and players that shape it, and ultimately the direction and destiny
that are defining where we are headed as a human family.

The Globalization of Civilization: A New Era of Integration and Dis-integration

Globalization means different things to different people.[67] To the political
scientist, it signifies a new internationalism. To the economist, it connotes
linking local, regional, and national financial networks. To the sociologist,
it entails the rich intersection of multiple societies and worldviews. To the
anthropologist, it implies the struggle for unique ethnic and cultural identities
amidst what has been called the "McDonaldization" or "Wal-Martification"
of world culture.[68] As Robert J. Schreiter puts it, "There is no one accepted
definition of globalization, nor is there consensus on its exact description.
Nearly all would agree, however, that it is about the increasingly interconnected character of the political, economic, and social life of the peoples of
this planet."[69] Civilization, as we know it, is undergoing an unprecedented
process of global transformation.

A key turning point in the globalization of civilization came at the end
of the cold war. By the second half of the twentieth century, the world was
characterized by one central feature: division. This division was symbolized

---

Keohane and Joseph S. Nye, Jr., "Globalization: What's New? What's Not? (And So What?)" *Foreign Policy* 118 (Spring 2000): 104-19.

67. The body of literature on globalization is immense, and for an extensive bibliography, see
the globalization website at Emory University, Atlanta, Georgia. Available online at http://www.
sociology.emory.edu/globalization.

68. George Ritzer, *The McDonaldization of Society*, rev. ed. (Thousand Oaks, Calif.: Pine Forge
Press, 2004), 1.

69. Robert J. Schreiter, *The New Catholicity: Theology between the Global and the Local* (Maryknoll, N.Y.: Orbis Books, 1997), 4-5.

by one landmark: the Berlin Wall.[70] It divided countries and cultures, friends and families, ideologies and theologies. It marked the dividing line between the east and the west, capitalism and communism, and more generally the empires of the United States and the Soviet Union. When the Berlin Wall crumbled in 1989, however, new possibilities for market expansion and cross-cultural interconnectedness were opened up.

The post–cold war era, in contrast, is characterized by a different central feature: integration. This integration is represented by one key symbol: the World Wide Web. The Internet has linked together constituencies of every sort, making the global community more interrelated than ever before. Developments in transportation, communications, and technology, coupled with the dismantling of trade barriers, have linked individuals and communities in a way that is faster, cheaper, and more efficient than in any previous generation. This current global business arena, trademarked as it is by liberalization, universalization, westernization, and modernization, now extends its reach across virtually every political border. As Thomas Friedman summarizes the situation,

> [I]n the broadest sense we have gone from an international system built around division and walls to a system increasingly built around integration and webs. In the Cold War we reached for the hotline, which was a symbol that we were all divided but at least two people were in charge—the leaders of the United States and the Soviet Union. In the globalization system we reach for the Internet, which is a symbol that we are all connected and nobody is quite in charge.[71]

Because no one is in charge—or at least no one in charge of major decisions claims to have any accountability for the welfare of the planet as a whole—it becomes less clear where we are going as a global village.

As the new centers of economic power, multinational corporations have become arguably the major driving force behind globalization. Of the world's one hundred largest economic entities, 40 are corporations and 60 are countries.[72] Royal Dutch Shell recorded 2012 revenues that exceeded the Gross Domestic Products (GDPs) of 171 countries, making it the 26th largest economic entity in the world. It ranks ahead of Argentina and Taiwan, despite employing only 90,000 people.[73] Even though corporations provide invaluable

---

70. Thomas L. Friedman, *Longitudes and Attitudes: The World in the Age of Terrorism* (New York: Anchor Books, 2003), 4.

71. Ibid.

72. See "Corporate Clout 2013: Time for Responsible Capitalism," http://www.globaltrends. com. These figures represent data from 2012.

73. Ibid.

assets to the process of globalization, this seismic economic shift away from nation-states to multinational businesses has significantly influenced political decisions.[74]

Because much of the global village (especially in the American sector) is increasingly influenced by the political agendas of business leaders, some wonder if some democratic countries should be called "corporatocracies." Some even wonder if elected officials should dress like NASCAR drivers and display more openly the emblems of corporate sponsors that finance cost-intensive campaigns. Such transparency would help explain the motivating factors behind those decisions by some government leaders which favor special interest groups even at the expense of the common good.

From the perspective of the entire human family, it remains to be seen whether this new era of globalization is positive or negative. Some see this time period as the greatest chapter yet in human history, especially those who have reaped the financial rewards of new and expanding markets and have hit the jackpot in this new "global casino."[75] Edwin A. Locke notes,

> The fact that free trade is now becoming truly global is one of the most important achievements in the history of [hu]mankind. If, in the end, it wins out over statism, global capitalism will bring about the greatest degree of prosperity and the greatest period of peaceful cooperation in world history.[76]

Others are not so optimistic about the current trends. Nobel Prize winner and former World Bank chief economist Joseph E. Stiglitz says, "The West has driven the globalization agenda, ensuring that it garners a disproportionate share of the benefits, at the expense of the developing world . . . The result was that some of the poorest countries in the world were actually made worse off."[77]

Whether one sees it as positive or negative, globalization is nonetheless an integral part of the world picture and an evolving part of human society. As Gustavo Gutiérrez notes,

> To be against globalization as such is like being against electricity. However, this cannot lead us to resign ourselves to the present order of things because

---

74. Ibid. Note that the biggest industry group in terms of size remains the energy majors, including Royal Dutch Shell in the number one slot, followed by ExxonMobil at number two. Combined, the revenues of the top five energy companies (Royal Dutch Shell, ExxonMobil, BP, Sinopec, and China National Petroleum) were the equivalent of 2.9% of global GDP in 2012.

75. Richard C. Longworth, *Global Squeeze: The Coming Crisis for First-World Nations* (New York: McGraw-Hill, 1998), 8.

76. Edwin A. Locke, "Anti-Globalization: The Left's Violent Assault on Global Prosperity," *Capitalism Magazine*, May 1, 2002, http://capitalismmagazine.com.

77. Joseph E. Stiglitz, *Globalization and Its Discontents* (New York: W. W. Norton, 2002), 7.

globalization as it is now being carried out exacerbates the unjust inequalities among different sectors of humanity and the social, economic, political, and cultural exclusion of a good portion of the world's population.[78]

To get at the root problems that contribute to the polarization of civilization, it is important to do a serious critical examination of the theoretical foundations of the current global economic system.

The Invisible Hand: The Free Market and the Struggle of Human Unfreedom

Much of society's unquestioned faith in the value of the capitalist system has its roots in the thinking of Scottish moral philosopher Adam Smith (1723-1790), whose book *The Wealth of Nations* (1776) is considered a foundational work in classical economics.[79] He wrote that the principle of self-interest guides individuals and facilitates human progress.[80] According to Smith, unencumbered pursuit of self-interest will result in the greatest happiness for the greatest number. What guides social progress, according to Smith, is the "invisible hand" or the natural market forces, which have given birth to the contemporary notion of the "free market." Today, the notion of the "invisible hand" is invoked to promote the unfettered pursuit of everything from science to economics.

The difficulty, as Larry Rasmussen points out, is that "[Smith] did not . . . envision a capitalist society. He envisioned a capitalist economy within a society held together by noncapitalist moral sentiments."[81] Smith had a religious vision of the world and saw the invisible hand as a way in which a benevolent God guides the universe. Smith understood that this hand operates within an ethical context, which values the dignity of the human person, the common good, and the promotion of a just society. He viewed self-interest with respect to a larger theocentric vision of life that ultimately had reference to other people and the well-being of the community as a whole. He knew that "no society can surely be flourishing and happy, of which the far greater part of the members are poor and miserable."[82] In order for an economy to be

---

78. Gustavo Gutiérrez, "Memory and Prophecy," in *The Option for the Poor in Christian Theology*, 32.

79. For more on this subject, see Ernesto Screpanti and Stefano Zamagni, *An Outline of the History of Economic Thought*, 2nd ed. (Oxford: Oxford University Press, 2005).

80. Adam Smith, *The Wealth of Nations* (1776; London: Everyman's Library, 1981), 12.

81. Larry L. Rasmussen, *Moral Fragments and Moral Community* (Minneapolis: Fortress Press, 1993), 41-42.

82. Adam Smith, *An Inquiry into the Nature and Causes of the Wealth of Nations*, ed. Edwin Cannan (Chicago: University of Chicago Press, 1976), 88.

stable, he held that all members of society should have at least the minimum necessary to live a dignified life and to appear in public without shame.

Smith's perception of the positive role of self-interest in developing an economy then needs to be distinguished from self-centeredness, which ignores or negatively influences the common good. While people in any generation are susceptible to the self-centeredness that results in disorder, today this self-centeredness is also structured into large, complex institutions that shape and direct financial systems and determine how resources are allocated. The problem with today's global economy is not capitalism per se but rather the abuses and excesses that flow from the capitalist system.[83]

In our own day and age, few areas are more off track than the worlds of sports, entertainment, and business. The excessive disparity between compensation of chief executive officers (CEOs) of major corporations, for example, and that of their workers is but one example of a system that has lost its way. In the early years of the third millennium, some CEO salaries are as much as 411 times that of the average worker, nearly ten times the 42-to-1 CEO-to-worker ratio in 1982.[84] By 2006, the CEOs of major corporations made annually, on average, $11.3 million. As these same corporations face financial pressures because of competition in the global economy, some CEOs and their corporate boards give themselves inordinate salaries and bonuses, some even after poor performance, laying off workers, and eliminating pension plans for many workers.[85] Whatever arguments can be made about the

---

83. Consider the case of Tyco Corporation's Dennis Kozlowski. After giving him $135 million in salary, stock options, and other compensation, paying for half of his wife's $2.1 million birthday party on the Italian island of Sardinia, and forgiving a loan of $25 million for art, antiques, and a $6,000 gold-and-burgundy shower curtain for his New York apartment, Tyco laid off 18,400 employees. Kozlowski was eventually convicted, which shows some measure of bringing corporate abuses into line, but excessive and indefensible compensation of corporate leaders alongside layoffs remains an accepted, unjust, and disordered part of the current global market. For more on the benefits and weaknesses of the capitalist system, see Raghuram Rajan and Luigi Zingales, *Saving Capitalism from the Capitalists* (London: Random House Business Books, 2003). See Scott Klinger, Chris Hartman, Sarah Anderson, John Cavanagh, and Holly Sklar, *Executive Excess 2002: CEOs Cook the Books, Skewer the Rest of Us* (Boston: Institute for Policy Studies, 2002), 2; Joel Bakan, *The Corporation: The Pathological Pursuit of Profit and Power* (New York: Simon & Schuster, 2004).

84. See Klinger et al., *Executive Excess 2002*, 1.

85. For example, Bruce Rohde, former chairman and CEO of ConAgra Foods, who retired in September 2005, received more than $45 million during his leadership and retired with a package worth over $20 million, even though during his watch share prices fell by 28 percent and the company cut 9,000 jobs. Hank McKinnell, CEO of Pfizer, was given over $79 million for five years of work, even though under his leadership stocks decreased in value by 40 percent. The company also guaranteed him a life pension valued at $6 million a year. Eleven CEOs for companies like Lucent Technologies, Home Depot, Hewlett-Packard, Wal-Mart, and others received a total of $865 million in 2004 and 2005 even though their shares collectively fell in value by $640 billion. Lee Raymond, who retired in December 2005 as CEO of oil giant Exxon, received $686 million in compensation from 1993 to 2005, even as oil prices increased. See Jill Rauh, *CEOs Awarded Millions as Companies Downsize*, June 10, 2006, available at the Education for Justice Web link at Center of

relative worth of corporate leaders in contributing to the solvency and profit-ability of a company, a virtually unquestioned system of disordered compensations has now become a normal and accepted part of corporate culture.

Even those thoroughly invested in the current global economy have begun to question its fundamental premises. Some people, like financier George Soros, have expressed their doubts about the current course of globalization and a naive faith in the invisible hand:

> Insofar as there is a dominant belief in our society today, it is a belief in the magic of the marketplace. The doctrine of laissez-faire capitalism holds that the common good is best served by the uninhibited pursuit of self-interest . . . unsure of what they stand for, people increasingly rely on money as the criterion of value . . . The cult of success has replaced a belief in principles. Society has lost its anchor.[86]

As we become conscious of the human "unfreedoms" that flow from the disorders of the human heart, we realize that the free market alone is insufficient to bring genuine human liberation and indeed may result in the opposite when it enslaves us in our inordinate desires. For this reason and many others, the strengths of the free-market system must also be evaluated alongside of weaknesses of human nature.

In our current predicament, we are losing sight of people in the pursuit of profit, responsibility in the face of new freedom, and the common good in the search for self-interest. As the United Nations summarizes this situation, "In our interconnected world, a future built on the foundation of mass poverty in the midst of plenty is economically inefficient, politically unsustainable and morally indefensible."[87] We have veered off course as a human family, and correcting today's abuses requires more than "market-logic" if we are to overcome the economic polarities that negatively affect the global village. The world as we know it today cries out for moral and spiritual wisdom that can help us navigate the path to peace.

The Wayward Ship: The Path to Peace and the Challenge of Navigation

Consolidating our reflection up to this point into a foundational analogy, we can say that, in this time of titanic change, we are becoming more aware

---

Concern website, www.coc.org (subscription required). See also Sarah Anderson, John Cavanagh, Chris Hartman, and Scott Klinger, *Executive Excess 2003: CEOs Win, Workers and Taxpayers Lose* (Boston: Institute for Policy Studies, 2003), 1.

86. George Soros, "The Capitalist Threat," *The Atlantic* 279, no. 2 (February 1997), 45-58, http://www.theatlantic.com.

87. *Human Development Report 2005: International Cooperation at a Crossroads*, 17.

that we are traveling together through the cosmos on a common ship. While a few passengers have first-class suites on the upper decks, the vast majority of the earth's inhabitants are slaving along in the steam room as the vessel moves forward. The economy is the engine that is driving the ship; technology is fueling it; communications is steering it. It is not clear, however, who the captain is, what nautical maps are being used, or where we are going as a human community. While we cling to a vague hope of a better world on the horizon, we also recognize that we could be shipwrecked on the icebergs of human greed if we stay on our current course. The whole patrimony of the earth and the well-being of the human race depend on how we steer our way through these uncharted waters.

While many of us feel overwhelmed, powerless, and even incapable of changing the current course of our ship, this era is also a time of immense opportunity. What President Kennedy said about the challenges of going to the moon could equally be applied to globalization and the challenges ahead:

> We set sail on this new sea because there is new knowledge to be gained, and new rights to be won, and they must be won and used for the progress of all people. For space science, like nuclear science and all technology, has no conscience of its own. Whether it will become a force for good or ill depends on man . . . [we must] decide whether this new ocean will be a sea of peace or a new terrifying theater of war. I do not say that we should or will go unprotected against the hostile misuse of space any more than we go unprotected against the hostile use of land or sea, but I do say that space can be explored and mastered without feeding the fires of war, without repeating the mistakes that man has made in extending his writ around this globe of ours.[88]

With the immense possibilities of the present moment, how are we to navigate the path to peace amidst the tides of injustice?

While some argue that the ship will navigate best if economic decisions are left in the hands of individuals who are free to pursue their own interest within political rules, serious analysis challenges this naive assumption, since it is the moral equivalent of venturing out into the open seas without any kind of navigational equipment. The work of government and nongovernmental agencies, such as the United Nations Millennium Development Goals (table 3), offer better markers that can begin to redirect our wayward ship. Progress has been made on many of the goals. Extreme poverty has been halved; malaria and tuberculosis targets will be reached if current trends continue; the drinking water goal was reached five years early; all developing regions

---

88. Sorensen et al., *Let the Word Go Forth*, 177-78.

have achieved or are close to achieving gender parity in primary education; and the political participation of women continues to increase. However, more work is needed in areas such as reducing hunger; reducing maternal mortality; increasing access to antiretroviral therapies; increasing access to improved sanitation, and increasing access to primary education, especially in conflict-affected regions.[89]

TABLE 3. United Nations Millennium Development Goals[90]

The United Nations has formulated eight Millennium Development Goals, which provide tangible benchmarks for measuring progress as a human community. These goals are:	
Goal 1	Eradicate extreme hunger and poverty. Cut by half the proportion of people living on less than $1 a day and in a state of malnutrition.
Goal 2	Achieve universal primary education. Ensure that all children are able to complete primary education.
Goal 3	Promote gender equality and empower women. Eliminate gender disparity in primary and secondary education.
Goal 4	Reduce child mortality. Cut the under-five death rate by two-thirds.
Goal 5	Improve maternal health. Reduce the maternal mortality rate by three-quarters.
Goal 6	Combat HIV/AIDS, malaria, and other diseases. Halt and begin to reverse HIV/AIDS and other diseases.
Goal 7	Ensure environmental sustainability. Cut by half the proportion of people without sustainable access to safe drinking water and sanitation.
Goal 8	Develop a global partnership for development. Reform aid and trade with equal treatment for the poorest countries.

In addition, scholars from various academic disciplines have helped identify and analyze the terrain and the obstacles before us, and some have even offered a course of action that would begin to steer us in the right direction.

---

89. *Millennium Development Goals Report 2014* provides an overview of progress and is available on the United Nations website, http://www.un.org. See especially pp. 4-5. See the data in chart form by specific goals by world regions at *Millennium Development Goals: 2014 Progress Chart*, http://www.un.org. It is important to note that meeting the 2015 Millennium Development Goals is a first step and that the post-2015 agenda is poised to carry on the work and "integrate the social, economic, and environmental dimensions of sustainable development."

90. For more on the Millennium Project, see http://www.unmillenniumproject.org.

While these historical, political, economic, social, and psychological studies of globalization have offered immense insight into the phenomenon of world-wide change, each one of these disciplines has its limitations. History helps us understand our place in the unfolding course of world events, but it cannot help us understand the contribution we are called to make to it. Politics helps us understand the relationships within and among nations, but it has not given us insight into the values needed to make us a better global village. Economics helps us understand the complexities of financial transactions, but it has virtually ignored the human costs that stem from current market systems. Sociology helps us grasp human behavior, but it has not helped us address the deeper disorders of the human heart that affect it. Psychology helps us understand our relationship with ourselves, but it has stopped short of helping us understand better our relationship with God.

Alongside developments in the social sciences, theology makes an important contribution to this process of globalization. Even though Christian theology has been used to legitimate some of the very structures and systems, such as colonization and even slavery, that have contributed to global imbalances, it is equally true that theology has also been a prophetic voice in denouncing abuses and announcing God's reign of justice. When done in a spirit of humility, as faith seeking understanding that generates knowledge born of love, theology offers reflection on what it means to be authentically human in the world.[91] For the theologian, globalization offers a new hope for human solidarity and interconnectedness, which coexist against the reemergence of age-old human constants like greed, selfishness, and sinfulness. Theology can also be understood as an intellectual discipline that offers to the human community a navigation system of the human heart that helps us find the way to life-giving relationships that are foundational to building a peaceful world.

Today, three of the most important tools for navigation are sonar, radar, and global positioning systems. Sonar helps map out the ocean depths; radar helps us identify obstacles on the ocean surface; and global positioning systems help us understand our location through satellite technology. Extending our foundational analogy even further, we can say that, like sonar, theology offers us insight to the world beneath the ocean surface by probing the deeper terrain of human nature in all its capacities for virtue and sin. Like radar, it offers us a picture of the world in front of us by examining how we interact with others and our environment. Like a global positioning system, it offers us insight into transcendent realities by helping interpret the signals from above that can help us find our way from within our own social locations.

---

91. I borrow these two insights from Thomas Aquinas and Bernard Lonergan, respectively.

The discipline of theology is closely related to the academic study of Christian spirituality. Christian spirituality draws from the same wells of inspiration as theology, but it also seeks to understand these truths in the light of the complexities of human experience. Spirituality deals with how human life takes shape in the experience of our relationships with God, others, ourselves, and creation. It probes who we are, what we value, how we interact, why we are here on earth, and ultimately where we are going as individuals and as a human community. Moreover, the academic study of Christian spirituality builds a bridge between theology and other academic disciplines.

As our society becomes more and more secularized, many people are particularly wary about mixing theology and spirituality not only with politics but also with science and social-scientific reflection. Yet Wernher von Braun, one of the engineers who designed the rockets used to send human beings to the moon, offered important insight into how these disciplines need each other:

> For me there is no real contradiction between the world of science and the world of religion. The two are dealing with two different things, but they are not in conflict with each other. Theologians are trying to describe the Creator; scientists are trying to describe His creation. Science and religion are not antagonists; on the contrary, they are sisters . . . While, through science, man tries to harness the forces of nature around him, through religion he tries to harness the forces of nature within him.[92]

The central focus of this book is to explore in more depth how Christian theological and spiritual reflection, rooted in the reality of poverty and in dialogue with other religious traditions and other academic disciplines, can help us understand better and respond to the challenge of justice and the call to build a more humane global village.

A CALL TO CONVERSION:
THEOLOGY IN GLOBAL PERSPECTIVE

The Theological Problem: "Money-theism"

Whether we are conscious of it or not, we are doing theology all of the time. What most threatens the global ship at this point in history is not whether one believes in God but rather in which god one believes. One's god is what one devotes one's heart to, what one most values and even sacrifices for. One of the

---

92. Ernst Stuhlinger and Frederick I. Ordway III, *Wernher von Braun, Crusader for Space: A Biographical Memoir*, rev. ed. (Malabar, Fla.: Krieger, 1995), 271.

most fundamental challenges human beings have faced throughout history, as we will see in the next chapter, is not atheism but idolatry. Because idolatry greatly contributes to today's social disorder, the path to peace is also a challenge to conversion. From a theological perspective conversion is not just about changing from one religion to another but more fundamentally moving from irresponsibility to responsibility in multiple areas of human life.[93]

In large part, the root cause of global injustice is anchored in a fundamental theological and anthropological error that has been referred to today as "money-theism."[94] Money-theism deals with the idolization of capital, expressed as the worship of the gods of the marketplace, and is often practiced through the rituals of the stock market and the liturgies of global capitalism. In this system people are measured in terms of their net worth, accumulated possessions, and incomes rather than their human worth, the quality of their character, and their spiritual depth. The value and worth of human beings have become more and more reduced to a "market fundamentalism," where the market alone defines what it means to be human.[95]

While money-theism is a temptation of the global marketplace, it also can infiltrate the church and Christian theology. When theology loses a sense of justice as a central reference point of the kingdom of God, it can easily become a hollow reflection on abstractions that have little connection to reality and little potential to transform the world or the human heart. Because Christian theology is about fidelity to the Gospel message within one's own life and times, every generation faces the challenge of identifying which theologies will ultimately lead to communion with God and others and rejecting those that will certainly divide us as a human family.

In order to understand better what contribution theology makes to the process of globalization, and in turn how globalization can help us rethink the meaning of theology, it helps, as a starting point, to reflect on what it means to be human before God.[96] In contrast to a global culture that understands salvation almost exclusively in terms of material and economic

---

93. I am particularly in debt to Donald Gelpi and his understanding of conversion as a movement from irresponsibility to responsibility, and his identification of five areas of conversion, namely, religious, intellectual, affective, moral, and social. See Donald Gelpi, *Committed Worship: A Sacramental Theology for Converting Christians*, 2 vols. (Collegeville, Minn.: Liturgical Press, 1993).

94. I am grateful to David R. Loy, who first gave me this insight into the concept of "money-theism." See "The West against the Rest? A Response to *The Clash of Civilizations*," on the website of the Transnational Foundation for Peace and Future Research, http://www.transnational.org.

95. Richard Falk, "The Monotheistic Religions in the Era of Globalization," *Global Dialogue* 1, no. 1 (Summer 1999): 148.

96. For more on biblical anthropology, see Michael D. Guinan, *To Be Human before God: Insights from Biblical Spirituality* (Collegeville, Minn.: Liturgical Press, 1994); Hans Walter Wolff, *Anthropology of the Old Testament* (Philadelphia: Fortress, 1974); and Leo G. Perdue, *Wisdom & Creation: The Theology of Wisdom Literature* (Nashville: Abingdon, 1994).

progress, Christian faith affirms that to be human means that one is made in the image and likeness of God (Gn 1:26-27). One of the primary tasks of Christian theology is to distinguish the God in whose image and likeness we are made from a god of our own making. Irrespective of one's station in life, one's possessions, and one's bank account, Christianity recognizes the fundamental dignity and infinite worth of each and every person. Moreover, in contrast to Western society's emphasis on the autonomous individual, Christianity sees each human life as profoundly interconnected with others in a series of overlapping relationships. The Christian Scriptures understand this interconnectedness not simply in terms of information transfer but in terms of "embeddedness." To be embedded means to belong to at least four sets of relationships: People are embedded into God, into self, into others, and into the natural world.[97] These relationships are central to the process of human fulfillment and global transformation.

The central question of free human beings is how to live these relationships in a way that generates life rather than death. As relationships move toward life, they bear fruit in order, peace, and justice. As they move toward death, they bear fruit in disorder, chaos, and injustice. Life is the integration of these relationships. Death is the dis-integration of these relationships. The goal of human life is to bring relationships into right order, for when this happens peace and justice result.

The long story of history reveals that we have repeatedly broken the bonds of these relationships and have brought chaos and disorder upon ourselves and the world around us. Traditionally, the rupturing of these relationships is known as sin. In the Scriptures, to sin is to deny reality, to break the covenantal relationship with God, and to refuse to live in right relationships with others to whom one is bound by covenant. Sin eventually leads to the breakdown of relationships, disorder in society, and social injustice. Because of sin humanity finds itself caught in destructive patterns from which it is unable to free itself, such as various forms of addiction, greed, selfishness, abuse, violence, and war. In the face of its own inner and outer poverty, humanity lives in a state of brokenness, a brokenness that calls out for healing, for deliverance, and ultimately for liberation from all that oppresses, dominates, and enslaves it.

---

97. The notion of social embeddedness also emerges in business ethics. Lee Tavis and Timothy Tavis state, "Capitalism is a highly productive and beneficial economic system if it functions efficiently, but in order to function efficiently it must be set within a context of social and moral institutions which both provide the necessary social infrastructure and act as moderators of the drive for profit and advantage. Without these institutions, unfettered capitalism will ultimately destroy its own underpinnings." Timothy M. Tavis and Lee A. Tavis, "The Person, the Market, and the Community," in *The Invisible Hand and the Common Good*, ed. Bernard Hodgson (New York: Springer, 2004), 330.

The Theological Center: The Paschal Mystery

"I am a believer in the idea of a super-story," writes Thomas Friedman, "the notion that we all carry around a big lens, a big framework, through which we look at the world, order events, and decide what is important and what is not."[98] For Friedman, this new lens is the new international system of globalization. Understanding the contours of this intricate system of globalization helps us begin to bring the complexity of our current situation into focus, but in and of itself it does not give us a framework through which to evaluate this system, to sort out its values, to critique its relative strengths and weaknesses, to interpret the changes, or even to clarify where the global ship is going.

From the perspective of Christian theology, the super-story is not simply the new international system of globalization but the larger story of human beings in relationship with God and each other. These relationships are at the heart of the Christian story. Christian theology affirms that this story took a decisive and definitive turn in the life of Jesus of Nazareth, whose life, death, and resurrection are *the* super-story and the defining revelation of who God is and what it means to be human. More than simply interpreting the Scriptures, then, the Scriptures interpret us.[99] They tell us who we are. They help us understand the divine–human interaction that underlies every story of every person in every time period. This story expresses itself in generosity and greed, life and death, meaning and meaninglessness, love and apathy, belonging and division, good and evil, justice and injustice. Scripture helps us understand that we are created in love by God, burdened by sin, yet wait in hope for the creation of a new heaven and a new earth (2 Cor 5:17; Is 65:17-25; Rv 21:1-4).

The starting point for our theological reflection—a reflection on justice and liberation in the context of worldwide poverty—is a firm grasp of the world as it is and a firm commitment to working for the world that the God of love wants for all creatures. Ignacio Ellacuría, who was martyred in El Salvador in 1989 because of his convictions about justice, believed that theological reflection should begin with a firm footing in historical "reality."[100] This is a theological statement, and his belief is that among the poor there is a greater theological "density" than elsewhere. The task of understanding "reality" adequately, however, leaves us with a complex set of hermeneutical,

---

98. Friedman, *Longitudes and Attitudes*, 3.

99. I am grateful to Sandra Schneiders for this insight.

100. See Ignacio Ellacuría, *Escritos Teológicos*, vol. 1 (San Salvador, El Salvador: UCA Editores, 2000), 187-218. See also Jon Sobrino, "La Teología y el 'Principio Liberación,'" in *Revista Latino-americana de Teología* 12 (Mayo-Agosto 1995): 115-40; and Michael E. Lee, "Liberation Theology's Transcendent Moment: The Work of Xavier Zubiri and Ignacio Ellacuría as Noncontrastive Discourse," *Journal of Religion* 83 (April 2003): 226-43; Kevin Burke and Robert Lassalle-Klein, *Love That Produces Hope: The Thought of Ignacio Ellacuría* (Collegeville, Minn.: Liturgical Press, 2006).

methodological, and practical challenges. Reality is defined in different ways by different people, and our perception of it is often greatly influenced by our social locations and vested interests in those locations.

For many people today, reality is greatly shaped by modern media, the visual imagination it engenders, and the underlying value system inherent in this imagination. Especially today when "reality television" has become a popular form of entertainment, it is particularly critical to reflect on what reality means. From the standpoint of Christian theological reflection, an adequate understanding of reality must foster a vision of life based on communion with God and community with each other. In contrast to our current world order, this means that reality must include the lives of the poor and, indeed, must start from there. Only when we begin with the excluded can we speak in terms of a society of mutual enrichment, interconnection, and interdependence that enhances the lives of all members of the human family. Christian theology asserts that any reality that in the end divides, degrades, and diminishes a significant part of the human community rather than unites, uplifts, and enriches it is contrary to the will of God.

For Ellacuría, reality begins not with the terms of free-market enterprise or mass media, but with the experience of those who are poor, marginalized, and victimized. Ellacuría understood reality, above all, as inhuman poverty, which results in the cruel and unjust death of the poor majority. He searched for his theological understanding among the poor of the world, whom he called the "people crucified in history."[101] He believed that the God of Life was to be found amidst those who are poor, and he encouraged people to keep their "eyes on the God of life, on the God of the poor, and not on the idols of death that devour the poor."[102] From this "under-view" perspective we want to read the story of Jesus of Nazareth and the paschal mystery and try to understand its meaning and significance for us today.

The Theological Imperative: Justice

In many respects, the Christian story addresses the problem of injustice and the challenge of justice.[103] Today, however, the word "justice" is so commonplace, particularly in activist and religious circles, that it has come to mean everything and nothing. For some, it conjures up images of picket lines and angry protestors. For others, the word "justice" evokes the image of a

---

101. Ignacio Ellacuría, "Función Liberadora de la Filosofía," *Estudios centro americanos* 435/436 (1985): 50.

102. For more on Ellacuría's thought, see Kevin Burke, *The Ground Beneath the Cross* (Washington, D.C.: Georgetown University Press, 2000).

103. Richard W. Gillett, *The New Globalization: Reclaiming the Lost Ground of Our Christian Social Tradition* (Cleveland, Oh.: Pilgrim Press, 2005).

blindfolded woman holding scales in one hand and a sword of retribution in the other. For still others, it evokes wronged victims having their day in court. Common to all these images of justice is some notion of vengeance or revenge. Whatever the debatable merits of these connotations, justice from a Christian perspective has an entirely different meaning.[104]

In Christian theology there are two principal notions of justice: internal justice and external justice. Internal justice deals with one's experience of justification or being put in right relationship with God through the saving work of Jesus Christ. External justice deals with the promotion of good works. Internal justice refers to God's activity within a person; external justice refers to one's response to God's grace. Internal justice relates to the first and the greatest command, to love the Lord God with all one's heart, soul, and mind (Mt 22:37-38). External justice relates to the second command to love one's neighbor as oneself (Mt 22:39). It seeks humanizing activity leading to right relationships with one's self, the community, its social structures, and finally to the environment itself.[105] God's justice, in other words, is not principally about vengeance or retribution but about restoring people to right relationship with God, themselves, others, and the environment. We will look more specifically at the biblical notion of justice in the next chapter, but for now I offer some initial thoughts on an overall framework of justice.

The Old Testament has a rich and nuanced meaning of the term "justice."[106] While there are many different ways in which the Scriptures speak about justice, the two principal expressions in the Old Testament are variations of the word *sedaqah* (used 523 times) and *mishpat* (used 422 times). *Sedaqah* is more than a legal term and is often translated as "righteousness," whereas *mishpat* refers to "justice or judgment."

Sedaqah encompasses many aspects of life, including the distribution of material necessities. As Gerhard von Rad notes, "There is no concept in the Old Testament with so central a significance for all relationships of human life as that of *sedaqah*" (justice/righteousness or upright relations).[107] How-

---

104. As John Donahue notes, "Though Yahweh punishes sinners there is no text in the Old Testament where [God's] justice is equated with vengeance on the sinner. Yahweh's justice is saving justice where punishment of the sinner is an integral part of restoration." "Biblical Perspectives on Justice," in *The Faith That Does Justice: Examining the Christian Sources for Social Change*, ed. John C. Haughey (New York: Paulist, 1977), 72.

105. This definition is drawn in part from an excellent article by Michael Crosby, "Justice," in *The New Dictionary of Catholic Spirituality*, ed. Michael Downey (Collegeville, Minn.: Liturgical Press, 1993), 597.

106. John R. Donahue, "The Bible and Catholic Social Teaching," in *Modern Catholic Social Teaching: Commentaries and Interpretations*, ed. Kenneth R. Himes (Washington, D.C.: Georgetown University Press, 2005), 9-40.

107. Gerhard von Rad, *Old Testament Theology*, trans. D. M. G. Stalker (New York: Harper & Bros., 1962), 370.

ever, lest the word *sedaqah* be associated with contemporary connotations of moral high-mindedness, spiritual superiority, or religious Puritanism, it more precisely has to do with relational interdependence and a profound attentiveness to the needs of others. In other words, *sedaqah* is integrally related not simply to personal righteousness but also to social righteousness.[108] Because justice is about relationship, there can be no harmony if there is no justice, and there can be no justice if there is not right relationship.[109] Justice is about fidelity to the demands of these relationships. It deals with how individuals, families, communities, as well as juridical, religious, and political authorities, interact with each other, with the most vulnerable members of society, and with the Covenant God.[110]

In the New Testament, Jesus brings the notions of *sedaqah* and *mishpat* to fulfillment and is revealed as the Justice of God, the one who reconciles the world to himself and restores people to right relationship. Even when he does not speak directly about justice, Jesus is constantly seeking to bring people into right relationships.[111] More than a peripheral dimension of Christian doctrine, this notion of God's desire to restore relationships through Christ is the foundation for social responsibility. As a corollary, the biblical notion of sin also gives a way of understanding the human potential for evil, which fractures relationships, disrupts the harmony of creation, and results in social disorder and injustice (Jas 1:13-15).

CHRISTIAN DISCIPLESHIP:
MAKING VISIBLE THE INVISIBLE HEART OF GOD

In summary, we stand at this great crossroads in history with vast and unexplored frontiers before us. Globalization is radically changing the way we understand ourselves, others, God, and the environment in which we live, and it presents the human community with unparalleled opportunities and possibilities, but also with unprecedented challenges and difficulties, especially in the face of widespread social injustice. Christian theology gives us a way of interpreting this time of change and helps us sort out the world we are creating through our individual and collective decisions. It challenges us

---

108. Donahue, "Bible and Catholic Social Teaching," 14.

109. For more on the theme of justice as right relationship, see J. L. Mays, "Justice Perspectives from the Prophetic Tradition," in *Prophecy in Israel: Search for an Identity*, ed. David L. Petersen (Philadelphia: Fortress Press, 1987), 144-58; and Donahue, "Biblical Perspectives on Justice," 68-112.

110. See "Righteousness in the OT," *Interpreter's Dictionary of the Bible* (Nashville: Abingdon, 1961), 80.

111. Walter Burghardt, "Worship and Justice Reunited," in *Liturgy and Justice: To Worship God in Spirit and Truth,* ed. Anne Y. Koester (Collegeville, Minn.: Liturgical Press, 2002), 37.

to reflect on whether these decisions enhance relationships or unravel them, whether they lead to harmony and order or discord and war, whether they will bring us into communion with God and others or polarize and divide us as a human family. As the gaps between the rich and the poor make us more aware of a *globalization of polarity*, in this book we want to examine more in depth what John Paul II refers to as a *globalization of solidarity* (EA 55).

Like navigating to the moon, finding our way in this time of complex change is demanding and costly. Yet, as Kennedy observed, all great and honorable actions are usually met with "great difficulties," but these in turn must be met and overcome "with answerable courage." Precisely in the context of the daunting challenges that lay ahead, Kennedy was able to say,

> We choose to go to the moon in this decade and do the other things, not because they are easy, but because they are hard, because that goal will serve to organize and measure the best of our energies and skills, because that challenge is one that we are willing to accept, one we are unwilling to postpone, and one which we intend to win, and the others, too.[112]

Justice and liberation are not simply about reordering the economy but about reordering the hearts of peoples. As noted by the United Nations, "People are the real wealth of nations," and at this point in history, what the global village most needs is not so much an unbridled belief in the invisible hand that guides the world economy but a renewed faith in the invisible heart of a God of Life.[113]

In the pages that follow, we will look at how Christian discipleship is the way that the invisible heart of God is made visible in the world. We will explore how the past speaks to the present, how the present helps us understand the message of the past in new and challenging ways, and how both can help us look toward a future of hopeful possibilities as we seek to look at theology in global perspective.

QUESTIONS FOR REFLECTION

1. What do you think are the positive aspects of globalization? What are its negative features?
2. What do you think is the contribution of theology to globalization? Globalization's contribution to theology?
3. How do you react to statistics on global poverty?
4. In what ways do you see the social injustice of today as related to the inner disorders of the human heart?

---

112. Sorensen et al., *Let the Word Go Forth*, 178.

113. The notion of the "invisible heart" comes from United Nations, but I have interpreted this idea in theological terms. *Human Development Report 1999*, 77.

5. What do you think are the major obstacles to achieving the Millennium Development Goals? What are the ramifications if they are not met?
6. What are structural injustices? Can you identify one?
7. What understanding of justice do you bring to these readings? How would you define it?
8. To what extent do those with more resources have moral obligations to help the poor? Why?
9. If you could be captain of the "global ship," what would you do to steer the human community in the right direction?

SUGGESTIONS FOR FURTHER READING AND STUDY

Bakan, Joel. *The Corporation: The Pathological Pursuit of Profit and Power.* New York: Simon & Schuster, 2004.

Dunning, John H. *Making Globalization Good.* New York: Oxford University Press, 2003.

Firebaugh, Glen. *The New Geography of Global Income Inequality.* Cambridge, Mass.: Harvard University Press, 2006.

Friedman, Thomas L. *Longitudes and Attitudes: The World in the Age of Terrorism.* New York: Anchor Books, 2003.

———. *The Lexus and the Olive Tree: Understanding Globalization.* New York: Farrar, Straus & Giroux, 1999.

Gillett, Robert W. *The New Globalization: Reclaiming the Lost Ground of Our Christian Social Tradition.* Cleveland, Oh.: Pilgrim, 2005.

Guinan, Michael D. *To Be Human before God: Insights from Biblical Spirituality.* Collegeville, Minn.: Liturgical Press, 1994.

Haughey, John C., ed. *The Faith That Does Justice: Examining the Christian Sources for Social Change.* New York: Paulist, 1977.

Hodgson, Bernard, ed. *The Invisible Hand and the Common Good.* New York: Springer, 2004.

Kammer, Fred. *Doing Faithjustice: An Introduction to Catholic Social Thought.* New York: Paulist, 2004.

Knitter, Paul F., and Chandra Muzaffar, eds. *Subverting Greed: Religious Perspectives on the Global Economy.* Maryknoll, N.Y.: Orbis Books, 2002.

Longworth, Richard C. *Global Squeeze: The Coming Crisis for First-World Nations.* New York: McGraw-Hill, 1998.

Milanovic, Branko. *Worlds Apart: Measuring International and Global Inequality.* Princeton, N.J.: Princeton University Press, 2005.

Rajan, Raghuram, and Luigi Zingales. *Saving Capitalism from the Capitalists.* London: Random House Business Books, 2003.

Rasmussen, Larry L. *Moral Fragments and Moral Community.* Minneapolis: Fortress, 1993.

Rifkin, Ira. *Spiritual Perspectives on Globalization: Making Sense of Economic and Cultural Upheaval.* Woodstock, Vt.: Skylight Paths, 2003.

Sachs, Jeffrey. *The End of Poverty: Economic Possibilities for Our Time.* East Ruther-ford, N.J.: Penguin, 2005.

Schreiter, Robert J. *The New Catholicity: Theology between the Global and the Local.* Maryknoll, N.Y.: Orbis Books, 1997.

Stiglitz, Joseph E. *Globalization and Its Discontents.* New York: W.W. Norton, 2002.

Sutcliffe, Bob. *100 Ways of Seeing an Unequal World.* London: Zed Books, 2001.

United Nations. *Human Development Report 2005: International Cooperation at a Crossroads.* New York: United Nations, 2005.

————. *Inequality Predicament: Report on the World Social Situation 2005.* New York: United Nations, 2005.

2

A Living Word, A Saving Narrative

Biblical Perspectives on Justice

Many years ago I was part of a group of seminary students in Chicago. We decided to do a study to find every biblical reference on one particular subject—the poor and oppressed. We searched the Scriptures for each mention of the subject and found, to our astonishment, that there are thousands of verses about the poor in the Bible ... The Bible, we discovered, was full of poor people. And even more startling to discover, God is portrayed throughout the Bible as the deliverer of the oppressed ...

One zealous seminarian in our group decided to try an experiment. He found an old Bible, took a pair of scissors, and then proceeded to cut out every single reference to the poor. It took him a very long time ... Amos ... Isaiah ... the prophets were all decimated ... In the New Testament, the young seminarian put his scissors to ... the Magnificat ... Matthew 25 about caring for "the least of these" ... Jesus' first sermon at Nazareth ... The Beatitudes ... The clear injunctions in the epistle of James not to treat the rich differently than the poor didn't survive the scissors, nor did the exhortation in John's letters that if we do not love our neighbor in need, we simply do not love God ... All of that and more was snipped right out of the Bible. When the seminarian was finished, that old Bible hung in threads. It wouldn't hold together; it fell apart in our hands. It was a Bible full of holes. I used to take the holey old Bible out with me to preach. I would hold it high above American congregations and say, "My friends, this is the American Bible—full of holes from all that we have cut out." Protestants, Catholics, evangelicals, Jews, liberals, and conservatives—we all hold Bibles that are full of holes ... In America and throughout the Western world, we have responded to all that the Scriptures say about the poor by pretending it just isn't there. We have cut the poor out of the Bible.[1]

---

1. Jim Wallis, *The Soul of Politics: A Practical and Prophetic Vision for Change* (Maryknoll, N.Y.: Orbis Books, 1994), 149-50.

G OD'S CONCERN FOR THE POOR and oppressed is one of the most central themes of the Bible. In the New Testament one out of every sixteen verses is about the poor. In the Gospels, the number is one out of every ten; in Luke's Gospel it is one out of every seven, and in James, one out of every five.[2] From a Christian perspective, whenever a community ceases to care for the most vulnerable members of society, its spiritual integrity falls apart.

THE BIBLE AND THE SOCIAL LOCATION OF THE POOR

As we begin to explore what the Scriptures say about the poor, it is also important to examine what the poor say about the Scriptures. Many parts of the Bible speak not only *about* the poor but are written as good news *for* the poor. Consequently, the poor themselves have something important to say about the meaning of these sacred texts.

While biblical interpretation is greatly enhanced by biblical scholarship and reflection on the lived experience of Christian faith, many scholars are becoming increasingly conscious of how social location also shapes our understanding of the Scriptures. Where and how we live affects what we see and how we understand, and the social location of the poor in many ways enables them to see truths in the Bible, and therefore in human life, that others in more prosperous social locations might miss or ignore alto-gether.[3] This is not to romanticize the poor, since poverty itself does not guarantee a better grasp of the biblical message. Nor does poverty make one immune from errors of fundamentalism, reductionism, anti-intellectualism, sensationalism, privatization, and other extremes in biblical interpretation. It does mean, however, that when the Bible is read from the perspective of the marginalized and excluded, one can more readily perceive God's active and gratuitous concern for all people and especially the least of society. As Monika Hellwig explains,

> [T]he poor and oppressed suffer the consequences of sin and sinfulness in the world in the most obvious and immediately painful way. For this reason their whole existence disposes them to look for redemption and attunes them to listening for any message of hope. For this reason also, they are in the best position to discern whether the hope held out is an authentic answer to the human dilemma or not.[4]

---

2. Ibid., 149.

3. Monika Hellwig, "Good News to the Poor: Do They Understand It Better?" in *Tracing the Spirit: Communities, Social Action and Theological Reflection*, ed. James E. Hug (New York: Paulist, 1983), 122–48.

4. Ibid., 131. Walter Brueggemann notes that the more primitive one is socioeconomically, the

As we read the Bible from the perspective of the poor we can more readily discern that the God of the Scriptures reaches out to people in pain, not because of merit but because of mercy, not because they are more virtuous but because they are more vulnerable, and not because the poor are good but because God is good.

A NARRATIVE APPROACH TO SCRIPTURE AND HUMAN LIBERATION

While we can approach the theme of justice and human liberation in the Bible from many different perspectives, our focus here is to explore the theme within the world of the text itself, that is, the narrative content of the Scriptures. Like a rich, pictorial tapestry, the Bible is woven together by different theological threads that portray God's action in history and God's love for the world. It is beyond the scope of this book to look at these theological threads in detail, but rather we will examine the most prominent thematic strands of poverty, justice, and human liberation and how they fit into the overarching story lines of the Scriptures. While other works examine in greater depth these various biblical theologies and their historical context, here we will examine how the major narrative strands of Scripture, or meta-narratives, can help us understand the challenging gift of living in right relationship with God, others, ourselves, and creation.[5]

In the Scriptures we can identify five interrelated meta-narratives: (1) the Narrative of the Empire, which deals with the human capacity to create kingdoms that dominate and oppress; (2) the Narrative of the Poor, which concerns itself with the ones who are dominated and oppressed; (3) the Narrative of Yahweh, which deals with how God creates and seeks to liberate human beings made in the image and likeness of God; (4) the Narrative of Idolatry, which concerns itself with how people attempt to create God in their own disordered image and likeness and consequently enslave themselves through sinful choices; and (5) the Narrative of the Gospel—the central narrative of the Christian Scriptures—which proclaims a new kingdom that promises

---

easier it is to believe the rhetoric of divine agency and see divine action ("Prophetic Faith at the Edge of the Abyss," class notes, Notre Dame, Ind., July 12, 2006, 19).

5. See Joseph A. Fitzmyer, "What Do the Scriptures Say about Justice?" in *Jesuit Education 21: Conference Proceedings on the Future of Jesuit Higher Education, 25-29 June 1999*, ed. Martin R. Tripole (Philadelphia: Saint Joseph's University Press, 2000), 98-112. See also Moshe Weinfeld, "'Justice and Righteousness'—The Expression and Its Meaning," in *Justice and Righteousness: Biblical Themes and Their Influence*, ed. Henning Graf Reventlow and Yair Hoffman (Sheffield: JSOT Press, 1992), 229-46.

freedom and liberation from all human empires, all human sinfulness, all idolatry, and all poverty and oppression. These narratives open up possibilities for a new imagination and, crowned by the Narrative of the Gospel, have the potential to transform our personal and collective narratives.[6] The Passover Narrative not only integrates these narratives but also challenges us to "pass-over" from the stories that govern the current world dis-order to those that offer hope for a more ordered and humane society.

THE NARRATIVE OF THE EMPIRE

In the Bible, Egypt is the first in a series of empires, including Assyria, Babylon, Persia, Greece, and Rome, that embody power structures that benefit the elite, enslave the poor, and dominate the weak. The notion of empire often describes political entities, but it is not limited to them. Symbolically, the empire represents any power that arrogates to itself the power that belongs to God alone, or any group or institution that subjugates the poor and needy for its own advantage.

We are introduced to the abuses of Egypt's imperial power in Exodus 1. The reigning pharaoh instigates injustice by violating the proper ordering of relationships and unjustly enslaving and dominating the poor for his own imperialistic ambitions:

> Accordingly, taskmasters were set over the Israelites to oppress them with forced labor. Thus they had to build for Pharaoh the supply cities of Pithom and Rameses. Yet the more they were oppressed, the more they multiplied and spread. The Egyptians, then, dreaded the Israelites and reduced them to cruel slavery, making life bitter for them with hard work in mortar and brick and all kinds of field work—the whole cruel fate of slaves. (Ex 1:11-14)

When the labor needed for construction projects exceeded what could be provided by domestic workers and prisoners of war, state policies for build-

---

6. Walter Brueggemann, "That the World May Be Redescribed," *Interpretation* 54, no. 4 (2002): 359-67; idem, *The Prophetic Imagination*, 2nd ed. (Minneapolis: Fortress, 2001). Imagination here is not the world of fantasy; it is the world from which people make ethical decisions that shape their character. For more on imagination and epistemology, see Garrett Green, *Theology, Hermeneutics and Imagination: The Crisis of Interpretation at the End of Modernity* (Cambridge: Cambridge University Press, 2000). For an important text in Old Testament study that deals with how public speech and text create alternative worlds, see Phyllis Trible, *God and the Rhetoric of Sexuality* (Philadelphia: Fortress, 1978). See also Michael Goldberg, *Jews and Christians: Getting Their Stories Straight* (Nashville: Abingdon, 1985), 14. For more on the exodus as an "orienting experience," see Irving Greenberg's "Judaism and History: Historical Events and Religious Change," in *Perspectives in Jewish Learning*, vol. 1, ed. Stanley Kazan and Nathaniel Stampfer (Chicago: Spertus College Press, 1977).

ing projects allowed for the enlistment of immigrants, the vulnerable, and foreign laborers.[7] Such policies enabled the leaders of the empire to exploit the poor, a sin that caused those who were oppressed to cry out to God (Ex 5:22-23). The abusive practices of the empire set it on a collision course with Yahweh, who chooses the poor and empowers the lowly, beginning with the Israelites in Egypt (Ex 6:1-8).

The word Egypt (*mitsrayim*) literally means "double straits" (a reference to upper and lower straits that form the territory of Egypt through which the Nile flows), "narrow places," or "narrow confinement."[8] In Exodus 2:20 we read, "I, the Lord, am your God, who brought you out of the land of Egypt, that place of slavery." Beyond the literal reading of the word *mitsrayim*, the subsequent figurative interpretations are striking. Israel was not only delivered from a geographical place but also from a narrow way of thinking. Specifically, Yahweh delivered Israel from the place of slavery *and* the empire mentality. At Sinai, liberation from the empire means something more comprehensive than simply *taking off* the shackles of Egypt. It means *taking on* a new mind-set, adopting a new way of looking at the world, living out a different narrative in one's personal and communal life, and ultimately learning to love as God loves.

The implications of living out of this new narrative are made clear in Leviticus 11:45: "Since I, the Lord, brought you up *from the land of Egypt* that I might be your God, you shall be holy, because I am holy." Holiness demands a way of thinking and a way of life that is different from that of the empire. Otherwise, when the tables are reversed and Israel comes to power in the promised land, it runs the risk of living out of the Narrative of the Empire and enacting the same abusive practices on others as Egypt imposed on them. Throughout the centuries, rabbinic wisdom has taught that it was far easier to take Israel out of Egypt than to take Egypt out of Israel; in other

---

7. Brick making under Pharaoh meant physical as well as economic violence. In Exodus, Pharaoh's ambitious building projects influenced him to force the Israelites to produce bricks needed for these structures, and their daily quotas kept them from attending to their own livelihood. The work itself was physically taxing, and when they did not meet their quotas, supervisors beat and humiliated them (Ex 5:6-8, 14-15), but even if they met their quota, they still suffered impoverishment. See Laurel A. Dykstra, *Set Them Free: The Other Side of Exodus* (Maryknoll, N.Y.: Orbis Books, 2002), 65; and Walter Brueggemann, "Pharaoh as Vassal: A Study of a Political Metaphor," *Catholic Biblical Quarterly* 57, no. 1 (January 1995): 27-51.

8. I am grateful to Lisa Marie Belz for this suggestion. The Hebrew letters for "Egypt" are those found in Ps 116:3 "the snare (literally "the oppressive confinement" or "narrow straits") of Sheol . . ."; and Ps 118:5 "out of my 'distress' (literally 'strait,' 'narrow confinement,' 'tight place') I called on the Lord." There is an exact match between the unvocalized Hebrew "Egypt" and "narrow straits" as it is spelled in Lam 1:3: "All her persecutors come upon her where she is narrowly confined." The author of Lamentations is clearly using a play on words here between "narrow confinements" and Egypt. See also Dykstra, *Set Them Free*, 58.

words, it was simpler to take Israel out of the empire than to take the Empire Narrative out of Israel.

The Narrative of the Empire not only is apparent outside Israel's ranks, but also creeps into its own spirit and soul, emerging in its desire for a king. Kingship seduces Israel into the Narrative of the Empire and makes it susceptible to the vices of imperialism, nationalism, slavery, militarism, and elitism, leading to slavery and oppression.[9] We see Yahweh's total rejection of the empire mentality in 1 Samuel 8:6-22, where the connections between the Egyptian empire and Israelite kingship are apparent [as noted by the indications in brackets]:

> Samuel was displeased when they asked for a king to judge them. He prayed to the Lord, however, who said in answer: "Grant the people's every request. It is not you they reject, they are rejecting me as their king. As they have treated me constantly from the day I brought them up from Egypt to this day, deserting me and worshiping strange gods, so do they treat you too. Now grant their request; but at the same time, warn them solemnly and inform them of the rights of the king who will rule them." Samuel delivered the message of the Lord in full to those who were asking him for a king. He told them: "The rights of the king who will rule you will be as follows: He will take your sons and assign them to his chariots and horses, and they will run before his chariot [IMPERIALISM]. He will also appoint from among them his commanders of groups of a thousand and of a hundred soldiers [NATIONALISM]. He will set them to do his plowing and his harvesting [SLAVERY], and to make his implements of war and the equipment of his chariots [MILITARISM]. He will use your daughters as ointment-makers, as cooks, and as bakers. He will take the best of your fields, vineyards, and olive groves, and give them to his officials [ELITISM]. He will tithe your crops and your vineyards, and give the revenue to his eunuchs and his slaves. He will take your male and female servants, as well as your best oxen and your asses, and use them to do his work. He will tithe your flocks and you yourselves will become his slaves. When this takes place, you will complain against the king whom you have chosen, but on that day the Lord will not answer you." The people, however, refused to listen to Samuel's warning and said, "Not so! There must be a king over us. We too must be like the other nations, with a king to rule us and to lead us in warfare and fight our battles." When Samuel had listened to all the people had to say, he repeated it to the Lord, who then said to him, "Grant their request and appoint a king to rule them."

---

9. For more on empire, see R. S. Sugirtharaja, *The Bible and Empire: Postcolonial Explorations* (Cambridge: Cambridge University Press, 2005); and Jim Garrison, *America as Empire: Global Leader or Rogue Power* (San Francisco: Berrett-Koehler, 2004).

The problem with kingship is that it leads Israel back to Egypt all over again and tries to set individuals, communities, and nations above God, who alone is the sovereign ruler of creation.[10] Amid the disordering of relationships, people's judgment about reality becomes skewed. When this happens it is not uncommon for people to be scandalized by what matters little and not scandalized by what matters most. The desert and exile are places where Israel is given an opportunity to restructure its imagination about power, relationships, and ultimately who will rule over the people. In leaving Egypt behind, the desert sojourn was the place for Israel to begin again even though so few were able to reimagine their world in new categories.[11]

THE NARRATIVE OF THE POOR

The Narrative of the Poor takes shape most often around those who are the victims of society's greed, exploitation, and manipulation, that is, those who suffer the consequences of empire. Although the Old Testament uses various words to denote the poor, all refer in some way to those who lack economic resources and material goods, and who experience political and legal powerlessness and oppression.[12] Some scholars believe that the term "Hebrew" itself (*Apiru, Habiru*) referred originally to a social class of poor and marginalized people in Canaan,[13] and much of the Old Testament is about their story.[14]

---

10. See Walter Brueggemann, *Solomon: Israel's Ironic Icon of Human Achievement* (Columbia: University of South Carolina Press, 2005), 126-28. Solomon is *pharaoh* in Israel and employs some of the economic and labor practices of Egyptian governance.

11. Ten of the twelve spies sent by Moses to explore the land of Canaan were able to convince the entire Israelite community not to take possession of and dwell in the land as God had instructed them to do, because they feared the inhabitants of the land and did not believe that they could be victorious over them. Only Joshua and Caleb believed God that the people could overcome and possess the land that God was giving them. Only they were able to reimagine their community in terms of God's gracious gifts (Nm 13:1-2, 17-33; 14:1-9, 26-38).

12. The Old Testament uses the words *dal* ("low, weak, downtrodden"); *ani* ("afflicted, oppressed, wretched"); *muk* ("low, oppressed"); *ebyon* ("wanting, needy, deprived"); *yarash* ("dispossessed"); and finally *rush* ("destitute"). W. R. Domeris, *Journal of Theology for Southern Africa* 57, no. 1 (1986): 57-61.

13. Richard J. Sklba, *Pre-exilic Prophecy: Words of Warning, Dreams of Hope, Spirituality of Pre-exilic Prophets*, Message of Biblical Spirituality 3 (Collegeville, Minn.: Liturgical Press, 1990), 71.

14. While there were undoubtedly many poor Hebrews, those who are named and whose stories we have in the early Old Testament record were not poor. Consider Noah, who had resources enough to build and outfit the ark (Gn 6:13-16); Abraham and Lot, who had so much livestock and so many servants that the land could not support both families so they had to separate (Gn 13); Jacob and Esau, who both had great wealth when they reunited as evidenced by the gifts that Jacob offered to Esau and Esau's response (Gn 32:13-16; 33:1-11); Joseph, who became rich and powerful in Egypt (Gn 41:39-43); the eleven remaining sons of Jacob, of whom there are no indications of poverty since they were able twice to buy grain in Egypt during a famine (Gn 42:1-2; 43:1-2); and the Israelites, who initially were not slaves in Egypt and became exceedingly numerous (Ex 1:7). It

Only later did the term "Hebrew" refer to a specific religious and cultural identity.[15] Frequently the poor were small farmers, day laborers, construction workers, beggars, debt slaves, and village dwellers,[16] and the most vulnerable of these were widows, orphans, and strangers. From the scriptural evidence, God is the defender, protector, and liberator of the poor, and God commands those who follow him to do likewise for those who are weak and defenseless (Ex 22:21-22; Dt 15:7; Pss 82:3-4; 103:6; 140:12; 146:7).

In the Narrative of the Poor, there is no indication that God's action on behalf of the poor is because of any intrinsic merit or moral worthiness on Israel's part. In fact, God's action in favor of the poor, as seen in the story of the exodus, continually challenges posterity to create a just society that reflects Yahweh's own love for those who are vulnerable. Once the Israelites are liberated from their own bondage in Egypt, God enjoins them to live out his gratuitous mercy by showing mercy to others, and this mercy is evidenced economically by canceling debts during the year of release (Dt 15:1-5). The Scriptures clearly indicate that poverty is an inhuman condition and contrary to the will of a loving God.

Obedience to God requires setting up societal structures to eradicate poverty in Israel. This is something that Leviticus 25 proposes to do with laws on land tenure. The jubilee year also promised restoration of land, which had been lost through debt, back to the original family of ownership. The biblical presumption is that poverty is eradicable and that it is incumbent on the privileged to respond compassionately to those who find themselves in a situation of poverty. As Leviticus 25 demonstrates, the task of any real compassion for the poor is to develop structures that will protect, not exploit them. Just as Yahweh reached out to Israel in its poverty, Yahweh commands future generations to remember and reach out to the poor, the oppressed, and the stranger (Ex 23:9). The exodus event is so significant in the Narrative of the Poor (Ex 3:10, 12, 16-17; 6:6, 13, 26; 7:4-5) that Israelites are repeatedly urged to remember it as foundational to their identity as God's chosen people (Ex 16:32; 20:2; 23:9; 29:46; 32:7-8, 11-12; Lv 25:38; Dt 5:6; 6:12; and others). Such memory will also become the basis for social responsibility and social justice.

---

is expressly because the Israelites became so numerous in Egypt that they were seen as a threat and were taken into bondage as slaves (Ex 1:9-11). It is at this point in their history that we may more accurately say that the Israelites as a people were poor and oppressed.

15. While there is still considerable debate, many scholars believe that the Hebrews are the people called *Habiru* in the tablets found at Tell al-Amarinah, Egypt (from about 1400 B.C.), found in 1887, and the Amarna letters, which refer to the *Habiru.*

16. J. David Pleins, "Poverty" (Old Testament), in D. N. Freedman, ed., *The Anchor Bible Dictionary,* electronic ed. (New York: Doubleday, 1996).

As Israel becomes more prosperous, it often forgets its own history, and as a consequence, forgets those in human need. When this happens, the prophets speak out in Yahweh's own name and denounce those who crush, deprive, destroy, and oppress the poor (Is 3:14-15; 32:6-7; Am 4:1; 8:4). These prophets hear the suffering of God's people while the rest of society mutes it or cannot hear it amid their activity and prosperity. When David commits adultery with Bathsheba and later kills her husband to cover his sin, the prophet Nathan tells King David a parable about a rich man who steals from a poor man, making clear to David that he has trampled on the rights of the less powerful (2 Sm 12:1-14). When King Ahab and his wife Jezebel take advantage of Naboth in order to annex his coveted vineyard, the prophet Elijah pronounces God's judgment on him for his abuse of power and his exploitation of the poor (1 Kgs 21:1-29). When the widow in Elisha's day runs out of resources to sustain her family, he miraculously multiplies her supply of oil so that she can pay off the debt she owes to her creditor and thereby avoid the enslavement of her two sons (2 Kgs 4:1-7). In the Narrative of the Poor, Israel's prophets fight to protect the rights of the vulnerable, especially in the face of civil, economic, or even religious authorities who try to deny them.

Amos (ca. 760-750 b.c.) rebukes those who live easy and comfortable lives and feast on rich banquets while the poor of the land languish in hunger (Am 8:4-5). He rails against those with summer and winter homes while many of their covenanted family live in slums (Am 3:15). He denounces those who sell the poor and needy for a pair of sandals (Am 2:6; 8:6), and those who trample on the heads of the poor and deny justice to the oppressed (Am 2:7). He rejects the hollow religion of those whose injustice renders their worship useless (Am 5:21). Amos proclaims instead a whole new society shaped not by the status quo but by a prophetic imagination, where "justice roll[s] down like waters and righteousness like an ever-flowing stream" (Am 5:24). By speaking of justice and righteousness in terms of water and flowing streams, on which Israel depended for productive crops, Amos effectively says that without justice, Israel's life would be a totally barren landscape; without concern for the poor the people of God are spiritually dead.[17]

---

17. John R. Donahue, "Biblical Perspectives on Justice," in *The Faith That Does Justice: Examining the Christian Sources for Social Change,* ed. John C. Haughey, Woodstock Studies 2 (New York: Paulist, 1977), 75. See also Roy L. Honeycutt, "Amos," in Trent C. Butler, ed., *Holman Bible Dictionary* (Nashville: Holman, 1991), 46-47. The ministry of Amos took place at a time when Israelite society was experiencing the inevitable decay that characterizes misdirected prosperity. This could be traced to corrupt religious structures and material prosperity, which Israelites often interpreted as a sign of divine favor. Excessive luxury and self-indulgence were clearly manifest (1:6ff.; 4:1ff.; 5:10ff.; 6:1ff.; 8:4ff.). Exploitation of the poor occurred throughout the land (2:6; 3:10; 4:1; 5:11; 8:4-6). Justice was distorted, and the dynamism of personal religious experience gave way to the superficiality of institutional religion as demonstrated in the conflict between Amos and Amaziah,

Like Amos, Isaiah of Jerusalem (740-701 B.C.) also sees injustice first-hand. He denounces those who become wealthy at the expense of the poor (Is 3:14-15), and rebukes the princes for being "greedy for presents and eager for bribes, show[ing] no justice to the orphan, and the widow's cause never reach[ing] them" (Is 1:23). In Israel, and in the ancient Near East in general, the king is obligated to protect the poor and the weak. Isaiah tries to awaken people to those who are suffering, even while their own avarice makes them more and more deaf. In Isaiah 58, thought by many scholars to have been written nearly two centuries after Isaiah of Jerusalem, we read how the Narrative of the Poor continues to remain central in the prophetic imagination as this text equates right worship with right practice:

> This, rather, is the fasting that I wish:
>   releasing those bound unjustly,
>   untying the thongs of the yoke;
> Setting free the oppressed,
>   breaking every yoke;
> Sharing your bread with the hungry,
>   sheltering the oppressed and the homeless;
> Clothing the naked when you see them,
>   and not turning your back on your own.
> If you remove from your midst oppression,
>   false accusation and malicious speech;
> If you bestow your bread on the hungry
>   and satisfy the afflicted;
> Then light shall rise for you in the darkness,
>   and the gloom shall become for you like midday.
>   (Is 58:6-7, 9b-10)

As the prophets of Israel repeatedly insist, without attending to the rights and needs of the poor, people cannot truly know God nor render to God true worship. Jeremiah reiterates that knowledge of the Lord is not an intellectual exercise but obedience expressed through active commitment to those who suffer (Jer 21:12; 22:3, 15-16).

THE NARRATIVE OF YAHWEH

The Narrative of Yahweh is integrally related to the Narrative of the Empire and the Narrative of the Poor. In the face of the empire, Yahweh's insistence

---

the priest of Bethel (7:10ff.). See also D. N. Premnath, *Eighth Century Prophets: A Social Analysis* (St. Louis, Mo.: Chalice, 2003).

on divine sovereignty is not a manifestation of an empty lust for power. As Walter Brueggemann notes,

> The reason for Yahweh's challenge of sovereignty in the text is a substantive one. Changed sovereignty bespeaks changed policy, reflective of the intention of the new *imperium*. And of course this narrative leaves us in no doubt concerning the substantive element in the new policy: it is "Let my people go." It concerns the release of the community of slaves from the abusive labor policies of Pharaoh.[18]

While Pharaoh's commands are all about production and commodity (Ex 5—making bricks), the Narrative of Yahweh, particularly as it is expressed in the Ten Commandments (Ex 20; Dt 5), is about relationships and neighborliness. In contrast to the empire, Yahweh elevates the humble, empowers the lowly, and emancipates the poor.

The most significant metaphor Israel uses in describing its relationship to Yahweh, and certainly the most central in understanding the biblical notion of justice, is that of covenant. A covenant (Hebrew *berit*) is a binding agreement between two parties that results in a new relationship. The goal of the covenant is right relationships, which produce life, justice, and peace.

In the Scriptures two dominant covenant trajectories developed, the first one stems from Yahweh's covenant with Abraham (Gn 15:1-18; 17:1-14) and David (2 Sm 7:1-17), and the second flows from the Mosaic covenant (Ex 19-24). The Abrahamic/Davidic covenant is an unbreakable agreement, but the Mosaic covenant can be severed by disobedience; the first stresses God's commitment to Israel, and the second emphasizes Israel's responsibility to God.[19] As Raymond Brown notes, "While the covenants of divine commitment gave Israel confidence, the covenants of human responsibility gave Israel a conscience."[20]

The gift and responsibility of the covenant entail a vertical change expressed as right worship rather than idol worship and a horizontal change expressed as right social behavior rather than social injustice. While Pharaoh's way of organizing public power leads to death, God's way leads to life and the flourishing of relationships. To follow the covenant means life; to break it means death. The choice is always a life-and-death issue, and the community must

---

18. Brueggemann, "Pharaoh as Vassal," 27-51.

19. See, however, Ps 89:20-37, where the Davidic covenant seems to be conditional upon obedience, but the unconditional, steadfast love of Yahweh for David's line is reasserted. In Ps 89:38ff. Yahweh seems to break off the covenant with David, but here we see in the end of Book III of the Psalms a movement away from a human king to the divine king in Book IV (Psalm 90-106). Brueggemann, *Solomon*, 58-59, 219.

20. Raymond E. Brown, *The Book of Deuteronomy*, Reading Guide 10 (Collegeville, Minn.: Liturgical Press, 1965).

make that choice repeatedly (Dt 30:15-20). New behavior is expected to flow out of new life and concern for others as a response to Yahweh's concern for Israel. In gratitude for Yahweh's gift of a new life, Israel is to show care for strangers and aliens (Dt 15:1-11). When Israel forgets its social responsibilities, the prophets invoke the images of the Mosaic covenant (Mi 6:6-8 and Hos 6:6-7). Jeremiah promises as well a new heart and a new covenant that will not be broken (Jer 31:33, with allusions in Ez 11:19; 36:25-27).

Through the covenant and in various other ways, the Narrative of Yahweh reveals God's desire to enter into relationship with people. Moses experiences Yahweh's presence on a mountain in the wilderness (Ex 3:1-4:17), Elijah in a "still, small voice" on Mt. Horeb (1 Kgs 19:9-12), Isaiah in the Jerusalem Temple (Is 6:1-13), and Paul on a highway to Damascus (Acts 9:1-9, 17-19). Israel collectively experienced Yahweh in a pillar of cloud and a pillar of fire (Ex 13:21-22). These are but a few examples of the relationship that God established with people, both individually and communally.

Israel's relationship with Yahweh also takes shape around its relationship with the poor. Israel promotes an active concern for the poor not because it is a good social-welfare philosophy but because this concept is rooted in the nature of God, who hears the cries of people in pain.[21] After a description of the oppression, harsh labor, and slavery of the Israelites (Ex 1:14), we read in Exodus,

> But the Lord said, "I have witnessed the affliction of my people in Egypt and have heard their cry of complaint against their slave drivers, so I know well what they are suffering. Therefore I have come down to rescue them from the hands of the Egyptians and lead them out of that land into a good and spacious land . . . So indeed the cry of the Israelites has reached me, and I have truly noted that the Egyptians are oppressing them." (Ex 3:7-9)

The Narrative of Yahweh reveals a God of absolute fidelity who frees people from bondage and calls people into new, transformative relationships. Instead of economic exploitation and social degradation, instead of slavery and oppression, instead of making bricks and worshiping Pharaoh, Yahweh held out a different vision of life. In contrast to human beings who seek to dominate, control, and impose their own will at the cost of the distress, hardship, and even death of the powerless, the Scriptures present a new narrative shaped by the God of Justice, who brings life, well-being, and wholeness,

---

21. That God hears and responds to his people in pain is a common theme throughout the Old Testament. For an example of God responding to an individual, see 1 Sm 1:1-20 for the story of the birth of Samuel to barren Hannah. For another example of God responding to his people collectively, see Neh 1-2:8 for the story of Nehemiah returning to Jerusalem to rebuild the city walls.

especially to those negatively affected by the self-serving interests of the empire.[22] The Narrative of Yahweh in particular confronts human beings with a decision about which narrative will govern their lives. Ultimately it is a decision to allow God alone to reign over one's life and direct one's destiny. As Joshua exclaims:

> Now, therefore, fear the Lord and serve him completely and sincerely. Cast out the gods your fathers worshiped beyond the River and in Egypt, and serve the Lord. If it does not please you to serve the Lord, decide today whom you will serve, the gods your fathers served beyond the River or the gods of the Amorites in whose country you are dwelling. As for me and my household, we will serve the Lord. (Jos 24:14-15)

Choosing life rather than death will remain the ongoing challenge of God's people, especially as they struggle with the seductions of idolatry.

THE NARRATIVE OF IDOLATRY

The Narrative of Idolatry is one important key to understanding the story of Israel and, more generally, the human story. It reveals the endless capacity of human beings to disrupt the proper and just order of relationships by breaking from Yahweh's covenant and following false gods. The problem for the Israelites is that they move from faith in Yahweh, who liberates them from Egypt, to faith in idols that ultimately enslave them. Idols are gods who can be manipulated and controlled, gods who gratify but also dehumanize, who allure with false promises, and who ultimately unravel the bonds of human relationships. As one of the recurring themes in Scripture, idolatry unmasks the enduring human tendency to make God into our own image and likeness rather than to conform ourselves to God's image and likeness. This is precisely the temptation of the empire, which would seek to subordinate Yahweh fully to the purpose of the king.[23]

We see in the Book of Judges the habitual pattern of Israel's propensity toward idolatry. While Israel begins its relationship with Yahweh in a place of rest and restoration, Judges brings out the cycle of Israel's recurring infidelity in the context of God's enduring fidelity. The consequence of worshiping other gods made Israel vulnerable to its enemies, and therefore Israel's own misguided decisions become instruments of the people's self-destruction.

---

22. Richard J. Clifford, "Justice in the Bible," in *Jesuit Education 21: Conference Proceedings on the Future of Jesuit Higher Education, 25-29 June 1999*, ed. Martin R. Tripole (Philadelphia: St. Joseph's University Press, 2000), 113-16. See also Norbert Lohfink, *Option for the Poor: The Basic Principles of Liberation Theology in the Light of the Bible* (Berkeley, Calif.: Bibal, 1995).

23. Brueggemann, *Prophetic Imagination*, 28.

Eventually they are delivered into the hands of oppressors who plunder and enslave them until they cry out to Yahweh in repentance and remorse. God raises up judges to deliver them, and through their repentance and God's gratuity, they are restored again to right relationship. Unfortunately, peace never lasts for long:

> Even when the Lord raised up judges to deliver them from the power of their despoilers, they did not listen to their judges, but abandoned themselves to the worship of other gods. They were quick to stray from the way their fathers had taken, and did not follow their example of obedience to the commandments of the Lord. Whenever the Lord raised up judges for them, he would be with the judge and save them from the power of their enemies as long as the judge lived; it was thus the Lord took pity on their distressful cries of affliction under their oppressors. But when the judge died, they would relapse and do worse than their fathers, following other gods in service and worship, relinquishing none of their evil practices or stubborn conduct. (Jgs 2:16-19)

This cycle (see fig. 2) repeats itself at least six times in the 350 years of judges, and each time the scriptural account gives the cause: "Because [or 'again'] the Israelites offended the Lord . . ." (Jgs 3:7, 12; 4:1; 6:1; 10:6; 13:1), and "all people did what was right in their own eyes" (Jgs 21:25 NRSV).

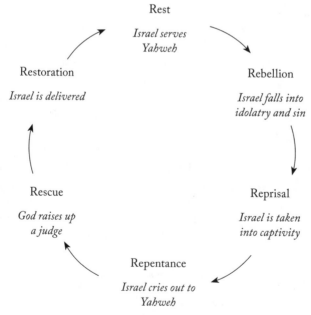

FIGURE 2. The Cycle of Idolatry

The cycle illustrates that it is not so much a matter of *whether* one believes in God or not, but rather in *which* god one believes.[24] As Fred Kammer observes, "Culturally . . . [for Israel] it was far more natural to reshape God than to be atheists, to create gods who were compatible with their own evolving sense of themselves as owners and property holders, gods whose worship and allegiance would not disturb those status rights . . . They were not the jealous God Yahweh who stubbornly insisted on an intimate relationship with a chosen people, who wanted hearts, not sacrifices."[25]

The cycle of idolatry begins with rest and restoration, when the Creator and the creature live in right relationship with each other. In this state Israel sees who it is before God, a steward of creation, blessed by God, drawn into community, and entrusted with caring for the earth. It is a time of prosperity, a time of right order and shared goods, a time of peace, a time when those who harvest the land also take care of the poor among them. It is a time when justice reigns. Even if Israel never actually achieved this just community life, the Scriptures still challenge the people to imitate the justice that they themselves received (Neh 5; Is 61; Jer 34:8-22).

As people work hard on the land, and as they become owners of it, they begin to lose a sense of their role as stewards. As possessions increase, self-centeredness creeps in, followed by rebellion. The more Israel rebels against Yahweh, the more wealth becomes a god of its own. In the process Israel forgets the poor, as the seduction of prosperity lures them into a spiritual amnesia. Israel forgets where it came from and to whom it belongs. As Kammer observes, "The forgetting of the *anawim* [the poor] was a critical sign of a more profound memory loss: forgetting Yahweh."[26] As noted in Deuteronomy,

> Be careful not to forget the Lord, your God, by neglecting his commandments and decrees and statutes which I enjoin on you today: lest, when you have eaten your fill, and have built fine houses and lived in them, and have increased your herds and flocks, your silver and gold, and all your property, you then become haughty of heart and unmindful of the Lord, your God, who brought you out of the land of Egypt, that place of slavery; who guided you through the vast and terrible desert with its saraph serpents and scorpions, its parched and waterless ground; who brought forth water for you from the flinty rock. (Dt 8:11-15)

---

24. The term "atheist" was first used by Cambridge Greek professor Sir John Cheke in 1540 when translating Plutarch's *On Superstition* into Latin. The atheist thinks there are no gods. See Michael J. Buckley, *At the Origins of Modern Atheism* (New Haven: Yale University Press, 1987), 9. Of course Israel was not atheist, nor were any communities in the ancient world. Israel was idolatrous, falling repeatedly away from Yahweh in favor of the gods of their own making or choosing.

25. Fred Kammer, *Doing Faithjustice*, rev. ed. (New York: Paulist, 2004), 30-31.

26. Ibid., 29.

Indeed, with penetrating insight, the biblical writer cautions against the delusion of the comfortable, that is, making even of oneself an idol to be worshiped and believing oneself to be the source of one's blessings:

> Otherwise, you might say to yourselves, "It is my own power and the strength of my own hand that has obtained for me this wealth." Remember then, it is the Lord, your God, who gives you the power to acquire wealth, by fulfilling, as he has now done, the covenant which he swore to your fathers. (Dt 8:17-18)

To forget Yahweh is to forget the source of life and all blessing. For this reason, Deuteronomy sternly warns that the logical outcome of idolatry is self-destruction:

> But if you forget the Lord, your God, and follow other gods, serving and worshiping them, I forewarn you this day that you will perish utterly. Like the nations which the Lord destroys before you, so shall you too perish for not heeding the voice of the Lord, your God. (Dt 8:19-20)

Despite the repeated warnings of the judges and prophets, Israel often preferred gods intimately connected with financial prospects, gods who legitimized greed, exploitative commercial practices, and neglect of the poor. No longer feeling constrained by the demands of the covenant with Yahweh, they followed gods that did not require integrity, honest conduct, or compassion for the needy and powerless. Worshiping Baal, for example, Ahab and Jezebel could justify theft, exploitation, and numerous murders (1 Kgs 16:29-21:29).

As there is more to Egypt than the designation of a physical place, there is also more to the Canaanites than an ethnic people. The origin of the name "Canaan" is disputed, but some scholars believe that "Canaan" comes from the word for reddish-purple. The Hebrew form of Canaan is taken from a Hurrian word meaning "belonging to the land of red-purple."[27] From the fourteenth century B.C., Canaan designated that country where "Canaanite" or Phoenician traders exchanged their goods for a most important commercial product, a red-purple coloring, which came from murex mollusks of coastal Palestine and was used for dying fabric. Purple was an aesthetic color of fine cloth, a color that arguably could have symbolically connoted the marketplace.[28] If this is true, it is plausible that there was a connection between the historical people who inhabited this land and the marketplace. In time the name Canaanite became associated with

---

27. Merrill F. Unger, "Canaan, Canaanites," *The New Unger's Bible Dictionary* (Chicago: Moody Press, 1988), 202.

28. Michael Astour, "The Origin of the Terms 'Canaan,' 'Phoenician,' and 'Purple,'" *Journal of Near Eastern Studies* 24 (1965): 346-50.

commerce.[29] In Luke, for example, the rich man who ignores the poor beggar Lazarus dresses in purple garments (Lk 16:19), and more than merely a literary observation, this is a further indication of his affluence and prosperity.

The biblical diatribe against the Canaanites and the command to "destroy all their stone figures and molten images" (Nm 33:51-52), then, was railing not simply against a group of people but against a market-materialism mindset. As they approached the land of Canaan, Yahweh said to Israel, "Do not defile the land in which you live and in the midst of which I dwell; for I am the Lord who dwells in the midst of the Israelites" (Nm 35:34). It is as if Yahweh warns Israel of the seductive power of the marketplace and rebukes any form of syncretistic utilitarianism that would marry Yahweh with the gods of commerce (Dt 20:16-18).

The Canaanites symbolize those people who practice a way that is governed by the pursuit of commodity. The gods of the marketplace are the gods that lead to a self-seeking autonomy that sees the self as the source of life rather than as a receptive creative agent of God's divine power. These gods have a seductive power precisely because they are associated with gods of the market. The fertility gods who impregnate the earth help crops grow, which in turn increases profit. Fertility gods convey the idea that human beings have within themselves the seeds of generativity. The seductive lie is that if we contain the seeds, then we can be autonomous and can divest ourselves of our relationships with others. Such autonomy is the antithesis of the covenant. The recurring temptation of the Israelites is that they believe they can live independently of their interconnectedness with Yahweh and others. Without Yahweh humans inevitably self-destruct, which returns Israel not only to Egypt but to exile, making Israel once again vulnerable to the forces of chaos. The Narrative of Idolatry gives us a way of seeing how sin creeps into human culture, how it takes roots in a community, and how it eats away at the people's relationship with Yahweh like a cancer.

THE NARRATIVE OF THE GOSPEL

The opening accounts of the New Testament begin with a clash between empire and Gospel, between the reign of Caesar Augustus and the reign

---

29. I am grateful to Walter Brueggemann for this insight. See also Norman Gottwald, *The Politics of Ancient Israel* (Louisville, Ky.: Westminster John Knox, 2001); and Norman Gottwald, *The Tribes of Yahweh: A Sociology of the Religion of Liberated Israel, 1250-1050 BCE* (1979; repr. London: Sheffield Academic Press, 1999). Note that various Old Testament references shed light on Yahweh's attitude toward traders and marketplace commerce. Among them, see Jb 41:6; Is 2:6-8; Ez 16:29; 17:4; Hos 12:7; Zep 1:11. Each of these indicates negative traits or ends of those involved in commerce: arrogance, dishonesty, insatiable greed, and eventual ruin.

of God, between a king who seeks to save his own power even at the cost of others' lives (Mt 2:16), and the king who lays down his own power so he might save the lives of all who are open to his reign (Mt 20:28; Mk 10:45). At the heart of the Narrative of the Gospel is Jesus Christ. Through his life, death, and resurrection, God subverts the power of the empire, destroys idols which oppose the God of Life, brings good news to the poor, reveals the undying love of Yahweh, and proclaims a new kingdom of truth and life, of holiness and grace, of justice, love, and peace. The Narrative of the Gospel not only gives flesh to the liberating story of the Scriptures but it is *the* defining Narrative of Christian faith.

In his book *Galilean Journey*, Virgilio Elizondo summarizes the Gospel story around three central aspects of Jesus' life: his beginnings in Galilee, his destination in Jerusalem, and the consummation of his life in the resurrection. These experiences of Jesus give rise to what Elizondo calls the Galilean Principle, the Jerusalem Principle, and the Resurrection Principle.[30] Each of these principles brings out a different dimension of the Gospel Narrative as it applies to our lives today. The Galilean Principle deals with Jesus' identification with those who are marginalized; the Jerusalem Principle with his confrontation of evil; and the Resurrection Principle with God's power to create new life.

According to Elizondo, the fact that Jesus is born in a stable in Bethlehem and takes up his residence and ministry in Galilee is more than a geographical note recorded by the evangelists. Rather, it is the beginning of the good news, especially for those who are poor and excluded in any way. Jesus' entry into the world challenges the way the world normally thinks about power, authority, and greatness, especially for someone of divine origin. His humble birth (Lk 2:6-7), the angelic announcement to lowly shepherds rather than to people of social rank (Lk 2:8-12, 15, 20), and the offering by his parents of doves rather than a lamb at his presentation in the Temple (Lv 12:6-8; Lk 2:24), are all part of an early Christian tradition which held that Jesus was born of poor parents. This news is liberating for all in human need precisely because it reveals God's solidarity with them and his final authority over all the forces that threaten them.

Not only is Jesus born among the poor, but he reaches out to those in Galilee. While the political power resided in Rome, the intellectual power in Athens, and the religious power in Jerusalem, Galilee was the center of nowhere even though it was the crossroads to everywhere. Galileans were considered insignificant people by those who held civil and religious power.

---

30. Virgilio Elizondo, *Galilean Journey: The Mexican-American Promise* (Maryknoll, N.Y.: Orbis Books, 2000).

They were poor peasants, farmers, or lower-class workers. Even carpenters were considered inferior. As Elizondo notes,

> Galilee was the home of the simple people—that is, of the people of the land, a hardworking people, marginated and oppressed regardless of who was in power or what system of power was in effect. They were the ones who were left out and exploited by everyone else. They shared the fate of other peoples living on the margins of "better" civilizations. Nobody looks for leadership from or has high expectations of those who live in the sticks . . .[31]

In living and ministering in Galilee, Jesus becomes associated with a rejected group of people. In becoming a Galilean Jew, God in Jesus becomes a "reject" of the world so that in his very body he will reveal the lie of the world that degrades human beings. From this social location he undermines all the world's categories, which deprecate and dehumanize, rejecting the idols which classify or segregate human beings based on social labels such as superior or inferior, rich or poor, worthy or unworthy. Instead, Jesus reveals the truth that all human beings have an essential, inalienable dignity given by God. Moreover, in taking up his ministry in Galilee, Jesus bases his authority not on worldly power of any kind but on a new relationship with God and others. From Galilee he announces this new relationship, and a new kingdom, among a people who are the most excluded from virtually every worldly kingdom.

Jesus in Galilee reaches out to all who are rejected in any way and offers them the good news that God does not exclude them and that they too are invited into the kingdom. In his universal and all-embracing love, Jesus rejects rejection because rejection and exclusion of others are the great sin of the world, the very power basis of the empire. His ministry among outcasts is an expression of God's love, which manifests itself through a downward mobility, as Paul expresses in his letter to the Philippians:

Have among yourselves the same attitude that is also yours in Christ Jesus,

> who, though he was in the form of God,
>   did not regard equality with God
>   as something to be grasped.
> Rather, he emptied himself,
>   taking the form of a slave,
>   coming in human likeness;
> and found human in appearance,
>   he humbled himself,

---

31. Ibid., 52.

becoming obedient to death,
even death on a cross. (Phil 2:5-8)

Undeterred by the labels and stereotypes of his day, Jesus reaches out to those whom the world discards. He not only reaches out to them, but, in this inversion of the value structure of the empire and the revelation of a new value structure of the kingdom, Jesus declares that through the poor revelation and salvation will come to everyone (Mt 19:16-24; Mk 10:17-25; Lk 4:18-19; 11:37-41; 12:33-34; 14:12-14; 18:18-25; 19:8-9; Jas 2:2-6a). Finding his true identity and strength in his unquestioned intimacy with God—as do many of the poor—Jesus offers to everyone an invitation to that same divine friendship, which is expressed especially in his practice of table fellowship.

Jesus' table fellowship with sinners and with the poor symbolizes the all-inclusiveness of his ministry. As John Meier observes:

> In the eyes of the stringently pious, Jesus' table fellowship with the ritually or morally unclean communicated uncleanness to Jesus himself. Jesus, of course, saw it the other way round: he was communicating salvation to religious outcasts. His meals with sinners and the disreputable were celebrations of the lost being found, of God's eschatological mercy reaching out and embracing the prodigal son returning home (see, e.g., Mk 2:13-17; Lk 15:1-32). His banquets with sinful Israelites were a preparation and foretaste of the coming banquet in the kingdom of God—a metaphor that appears in various sayings and parables (see, e.g., Mk 2:19; Lk 13:28-29 par; 14:15-24 par). Thus, the Last Supper does not stand in splendid isolation. It is instead quite literally the "last" of a whole series of meals symbolizing the final feast in the kingdom of God. There is therefore nothing strange about Jesus' holding a special, symbolic meal with his disciples (especially if he sensed his approaching arrest or death) or about his connecting the meal with the coming kingdom of God.[32]

What is tasted in table fellowship is the joy of sharing, which is further developed in the kingdom of God that Jesus proclaims.

Because of a love that rejects evil, Jesus welcomes all to the table and resists the temptations that seek to pervert his kingdom into the ways of the empire (Mt 4:1-11; Mk 1:13; Lk 4:2-13). Whereas the kingdom of the empire expresses itself in an elitism that excludes the poor from its privileges, Jesus proclaims a new kind of kingdom and, quoting Isaiah, reveals that his whole ministry takes shape around the Narrative of the Poor:

---

32. John P. Meier, *Mentor, Message, and Miracles*, vol. 2 of *A Marginal Jew: Rethinking the Historical Jesus* (New York: Doubleday, 1994), 303.

> The Spirit of the Lord is upon me,
>> because he has anointed me
>> to bring glad tidings to the poor.
> He has sent me to proclaim liberty to captives
>> and recovery of sight to the blind,
>> to let the oppressed go free. (Lk 4:18)

Appearing more than a hundred times in the Gospel Narrative, the kingdom of God redefines what kingship means in the Old Testament and presents God as the Lord of all creation who reestablishes his reign in human hearts. This kingdom reveals God's salvation and the fulfillment of Israel's hope (Lk 2:29-32). One does not enter it by natural birth or by human merit, but one receives it as a gift of God (Jn 1:12-13; 3:3-5). Some accept this invitation and persevere amidst the challenges of discipleship. Some accept it for a while and then turn away. Others reject it altogether (Mt 13:3-23; Mk 4:1-20; Lk 8:4-15). While it is a gratuitous gift received in faith, this kingdom demands certain behaviors, attitudes, and dispositions. The Beatitudes offer a descriptive picture of the qualities of those who internalize the Gospel Narrative. They help people reimagine what it means to be blessed by God (Mt 5:3-12; Lk 6:20-23) and move toward discipleship, which is characterized by an openness to the will of God, compassion, meekness, mercy, purity of heart, nonviolence and peacemaking, and perseverance in persecution.

Reversing the value system of the empire and the quest for personal gain, rank, and reputation, Jesus embodies the Beatitudes in life-giving service to others, which is expressed symbolically in the washing of his disciples' feet. This humble act is both an example for his disciples and a foreshadowing of the cleansing and liberating effect that his life-saving death will accomplish (Jn 13:1-17; 19:30). Jesus reveals that human greatness ultimately is measured by service to others in self-giving love. In the simple gesture of taking up the basin and the towel, Jesus reveals the great contrast between the way of the empire and the way of the Gospel, between the love of power and the power of love, and between the passion of humans to become God and the passion of God to become human.

The reign of God, then, is one of radical inclusion, expressed in Jesus' welcome of all people, especially those whom the world rejects. Yet because the religious and political authorities have clear divisions between the clean and unclean, the included and the excluded, the worthy and the unworthy (Mt 9:11; 11:19; 21:31-32; Mk 2:15-16; Lk 5:29-30; 7:28-29, 43; 15:1), they reject Jesus. The Galilean Principle, then, is about the one who rejects rejection by welcoming all, but is subsequently rejected by those at the heart of the empire.

The Jerusalem Principle deals with Jesus' decision to confront the sin of the world, which in part takes shape in the structures and authorities that oppress people. Jesus destroys the lie of the world that some people are better than others, seeking to bring out the humanity and dignity of each person created in the image and likeness of God. In challenging the forces of darkness, the laws that protect the powerful, and the false gods who legitimate and perpetuate inequity, Jesus poses a threat to the status quo, and for this he was crucified. Even on the cross, the cruelest of punishments left for those who sought to subvert the empire, Jesus expresses his solidarity with those at the bottom of society, revealing, above all, that not even hatred, violence, and rejection can break God's unconditional love for us and that the evil of disorder in the world will not extinguish the order of God's compassion for his people.

While the intention of the empire is to destroy Jesus and make his ministry end in total failure, the Resurrection Principle deals with God's power to bring about new creation, even amidst the injustice—and victory—of the cross. The resurrection signals God's vindication of Jesus and points to his way as *the* way. This event establishes Jesus as the Justice of God, the Lord of this new kingdom of life, and demolishes the legitimacy of the structures that reject Jesus, even though unjust structures will continue to exist until the new kingdom comes in its fullness. In the new kingdom, ushered in by the resurrection, a new way is opened to live in a world still encumbered by the unjust structures of the empire. Instead of the categories and labels of social location, those who enter into the reign of God can live in community with one another, and within the new communitarian structure can care for one another (Acts 2:42-47; Gal 3:26-28).

Empowered by the resurrected Lord, the first disciples reiterate the connection between the wealth of the Gospel and the poor of the world (2 Cor 8:9). Because one empire will replace another until Christ's kingdom comes in its fullness, the task of the Christian community is to create an alternative way to live, move, and be in the world. Even when the early church faced doctrinal controversies within its own ranks, Paul reiterated that one priority is clear: to be mindful of the poor (Gal 2:10), to take up collections for the poor (2 Cor 8-9), and to alleviate poverty (Rom 15:25-27; 1 Cor 16:1-4; 2 Cor 8). James indicates that care for the poor is the faithful response to the message of the Gospel:

> If a brother or sister has nothing to wear and has no food for the day, and one of you says to them, "Go in peace, keep warm, and eat well," but you do not give them the necessities of the body, what good is it? So also faith of itself, if it does not have works, is dead. (Jas 2:15-17)

In the New Testament, the Narrative of the Gospel comes together with the Narrative of the Poor in the final judgment in Matthew's account (Mt 25:31-46). Here the criteria for inheriting the kingdom of God are laid out:

> For I was hungry and you gave me food, I was thirsty and you gave me drink, a stranger and you welcomed me, naked and you clothed me, ill and you cared for me, in prison and you visited me. (Mt 25:35-36)

Following the separation of the righteous from the unrighteous, Jesus lays out the heart of the Gospel message: "Whatever you did for one of the least of these who are members of my family, you did for me" (Mt 25:40).[33] In the second part of this scene, the unrighteous are punished, not because they did not know the commandments but because they did not recognize where the demands of those commandments were to be met in the world.[34] As John Donahue reminds us, "The doing of justice is not the application of religious faith, but its substance; without it, God remains unknown."[35] Christ's kingship and presence are hidden among the downtrodden and disfigured of the world. Even while the empire sees the poor as unvalued, unworthy, and unwanted, Jesus sees the poor not as "other" but as brothers and sisters who are part of his own body. He offers a new way to live in interconnectedness and solidarity, sharing joy and sorrow, caring for each other's needs, loving our neighbors as ourselves (Mt 22:34-40; Mk 12:28-34; Lk 10:25-37). It is precisely because of the way Jesus sees the poor that we know,

> God's heart has a special place for the poor, so much so that he himself "became poor" (2 Cor 8:9). The entire history of our redemption is marked by the presence of the poor . . . When he began to preach the Kingdom, crowds of the dispossessed followed him, illustrating his words: "The Spirit of the Lord is upon me, because he has anointed me to preach good news to the poor" (Lk 4:18). He assured those burdened by sorrow and crushed by poverty that God has a special place for them in his heart: "Blessed are you poor, yours is the kingdom of God" (Lk 6:20); he made himself one of them: "I was hungry and you gave me food to eat", and he taught them that mercy towards all of these is the key to heaven (cf. Mt 25:5ff.). (EG 197)

---

33. For more on different ways in which Mt 25:31-46 has been interpreted throughout history, see John Donahue, "The 'Parable' of the Sheep and the Goats: A Challenge to Christian Ethics," *Theological Studies* 41, no. 1 (March 1986): 3-31.

34. Donahue, "Biblical Perspectives on Justice," 105.

35. Ibid., 76.

PASSOVER: THE INTEGRATING NARRATIVE

Remembering the Biblical Story: Justice and the Passover Narrative

As we look at both the Old and New Testaments, the Passover Narrative integrates all the other narratives. We will explore more fully the significance of the Passover in chapter 8 on liturgy and justice, but here the focus is its connection to the entirety of the Scriptures. Although the Passover Narrative specifically refers to God's deliverance of the Hebrews from their poverty and oppression (Ex 12ff.), more generally Passover reveals God's action in history on behalf of the most vulnerable (the Narrative of the Poor), God's commitment to human liberation (the Narrative of the Empire), God's expectation of right worship (the Narrative of Idolatry), God's enduring fidelity (the Narrative of Yahweh), and ultimately God's promise of a new kingdom and a new creation (the Narrative the Gospel).

These words from a second-century Easter homily by Saint Melito of Sardis begin to bring out the connection between the central story of Jesus and the integrating story of the Passover:

> He is the Passover of our salvation. It is he who suffered much in many . . .
> It is he who in Abel was slain, in Isaac was bound, in Jacob was a wanderer, in Joseph was sold, in Moses was cast out, in the lamb was sacrificed, in David was persecuted, in the prophets was dishonored. It is he who in the virgin was incarnated, who on the tree was suspended, who in the earth was interred, who from the dead was awakened, who to highest heaven was elevated.[36]

The Passover Narrative is most fully expressed in Jesus' Passover from death to life, celebrated in the eucharist. To remember Jesus in the eucharist is to remember God's saving deeds in history. It is also to remember Jesus' preference for those considered the least and most insignificant in society. In the eucharist, Jesus becomes the Passover bread (Jn 6:33, 35) and lamb (1 Cor 5:7), and when Christians break bread, they proclaim the death of the Lord until he comes again and brings to fulfillment the kingdom of God (1 Cor 11:26). In the breaking of the bread, Christians celebrate how God was broken open and shared his life with others, bringing healing and redemption to the world. At the same time, the breaking of the bread is about the brokenness of the body of Christ in the suffering of all people in our world today. The eucharist invites us to enter with Christ into the brokenness of human life, trusting that the God who raised Jesus from the dead will bring about

---

36. Saint Melito of Sardis, *On the Passover*, trans. Richard C. White (Lexington, Ky.: Lexington Theological Seminary Library, 1976), 37-38.

new relationships and new creation as we learn to give our lives in service to others, as nourishment to those in need, as bread for the world. In the end, the Passover Narrative expressed in the eucharist is a call to move with Jesus from death to life.

Transforming the Human Story:
Conversion as a Narrative Pass-over

While there is a tendency to give finality to these biblical accounts and to see them as a completed book, a closed canon, the New Testament ends on a note of openness, "Come, Lord Jesus" (Rv 22:20). Because it is an open-ended narrative, those who read and hear the Scriptures are drawn into the drama and are asked how their personal and communal stories interface with these biblical narratives. The Bible is not just a historical or literary document but an inspired text that calls for personal and communal narrative engagement, an engagement that leads to conversion and transformation.

The process of conversion—of choosing to live out a different story and live out a different set of values than those of the empire—can be understood as narrative "pass-over," in which one moves from one life-defining narrative to another. More than the substitution of one narrative for another, however, it is the exchange of an enslaving narrative for a liberating one. Because all people, whether conscious of it or not, are living out of a personal and communal narrative, the Scriptural narratives help us reevaluate the prepackaged values that come to us from society and popular media, including the false gospels that promise superficial redemption through more luxurious cars, bigger houses, or stronger drugs. The task of discipleship entails discerning which of these narratives enslave us and which help us become truly free, all the while knowing that final liberation will come only at our own resurrection.

However one may view his personal history and politics, the story of Charles Colson merits further reflection as an example of Narrative pass-over. He spent most of his life in politics living according to the Narrative of the Empire. As an aide to Richard Nixon, he was ruthless in his approach to his political enemies and was known as the White House "hatchet man." So thoroughly engrossed was Colson in the Narrative of the Empire that even the media in the 1970s said he was "incapable of humanitarian thought."[37]

Colson admitted that he had no faith in God but only in his imperialistic ambitions, yet during the fallout of Watergate a friend introduced him to the Narrative of the Gospel through C. S. Lewis's book *Mere Christianity* and

---

37. Prison Fellowship Ministries, *About Charles W. Colson*, available at http://www.pfm.org.

the Gospel of John. On August 12, 1973, Colson experienced Narrative pass-over. As his friend read to him Lewis's chapter on pride, Colson thought,

> Of course I had not known God. *How could I? I* had been concerned with myself. *I* had done this and that. *I* had achieved, *I* had succeeded and *I* had given God none of the credit, never once thanking Him for any of His gifts to me. I had never thought of anything being "immeasurably superior" to myself. Or if I had in fleeting moments thought about the infinite power of God, I had not related Him to my life.[38]

In his car on the way home that night he began to sob uncontrollably. In his own mind, the Narrative of the Empire and its hollow promises collapsed, and he opened himself to something bigger that would speak to the ache in his heart. He pleaded and offered himself to God saying, "Take me, take me," admitting to himself that it was not much of an offer.[39] For the first time he realized he was not alone, and he could begin to live out a new life story. It was the beginning of a lifelong transformation for Colson. When Colson's passing over from the Narrative of the Empire to the Narrative of the Gospel became public, the *Boston Globe* reported, "If Mr. Colson can repent from his sins, there just has to be hope for everybody."[40]

After serving a seven-month prison term for his role in Watergate, Colson founded Prison Fellowship Ministries in 1976, which, in collaboration with churches of all confessions and denominations, has become the world's largest outreach to prisoners, ex-prisoners, crime victims, and their families.[41] Colson visited prisons throughout the United States and the world and built a movement working with more than forty thousand prison ministry volunteers in one hundred countries that continues even after his death in 2012.

While not everyone experiences changes in their lives as dramatic as those of Charles Colson, his life names the enduring challenge to discover those narratives which ultimately make us more human as they put us in touch with transformative spiritual realities. While some go through the process of Narrative pass-over in more gradual ways, all are called to discover through the Scriptures the mysteries of creation, sin, and redemption which bring to fulfillment the promise of new creation. In naming the truth about God and about human life, the narratives of the Scriptures invite us to wait in hope to pass over from slavery to freedom, from injustice to justice, from death to life. In the next chapter we will look at what the first generations of Christians

---

38. Charles W. Colson, *Born Again* (Old Tappan, N.J.: Chosen Books, 1976), 114.
39. Ibid., 117.
40. Ibid., 167.
41. Prison Fellowship Ministries, *About Charles W. Colson*, available at http://www.pfm.org.

said about wealth, poverty, and justice, and how they struggled to make the Narrative of the Gospel their own.

QUESTIONS FOR REFLECTION

1. To what extent is idolatry present in the world today? Where do you see it at work?
2. Is it possible to understand the Scriptures if one is not in touch with the poor? Why or why not?
3. Why is it important to read the Bible from the perspective of the poor?
4. What institutions today have you seen that manifest characteristics of the empire?
5. What happens to a people when they forget their key narratives?
6. What does it mean to say that Scripture gives us an "alternative imagination"?
7. How do you think your social location affects the way you read the Scriptures?
8. Discuss this statement: "In the economy of the empire, people are scandalized by what matters little and not scandalized by what matters most."
9. What is most scandalous to you about the world situation of today?

SUGGESTIONS FOR FURTHER READING AND STUDY

Bennett, Harold V. *Injustice Made Legal.* Grand Rapids: Eerdmans, 2002.

Birch, Bruce C. *Let Justice Roll: The Old Testament, Ethics and the Christian Life.* Louisville, Ky.: Westminster John Knox, 1991.

———. *What Does the Lord Require? The Old Testament Call to Social Witness.* Philadelphia: Westminster, 1985.

Brueggemann, Walter. *The Prophetic Imagination,* 2nd ed. Minneapolis: Fortress, 2001.

———. *Solomon: Israel's Ironic Icon of Human Achievement.* Columbia: University of South Carolina Press, 2005.

———. *Theology of the Old Testament: Testimony, Dispute, Advocacy.* Minneapolis: Fortress, 1997.

Ceresko, Anthony B. *Introduction to the Old Testament: A Liberation Perspective.* Maryknoll, N.Y.: Orbis Books, 1992.

Croatto, J. Severino. *Exodus: A Hermeneutics of Freedom.* Maryknoll, N.Y.: Orbis Books, 1981.

Donahue, John R. "The Bible and Catholic Social Teaching." In *Modern Catholic Social Teaching Commentaries and Interpretations,* edited by Kenneth R. Himes. Washington, D.C.: Georgetown University Press, 2005.

———. "Biblical Perspectives on Justice." In *The Faith That Does Justice: Examining the Christian Sources for Social Change,* edited by John C. Haughey, Woodstock Studies 2. New York: Paulist, 1977.

———. *What Does the Lord Require? A Bibliographical Essay on the Bible and Social Justice.* St. Louis, Mo.: Institute of Jesuit Sources, 2000.

Dykstra, Laurel. *Set Them Free: The Other Side of Exodus*. Maryknoll, N.Y.: Orbis Books, 2002.

Elizondo, Virgilio. *Galilean Journey: The Mexican-American Promise*. Maryknoll, N.Y.: Orbis Books, 2000.

Epsztein, León. *Social Justice in the Ancient Near East and the People of the Bible*. London: SCM, 1986.

Fitzmyer, Joseph A. "What Do the Scriptures Say about Justice?" In *Jesuit Education 21: Conference Proceedings on the Future of Jesuit Higher Education, 25-29 June 1999*, edited by Martin R. Tripole. Philadelphia: Saint Joseph's University Press, 2000.

Goldberg, Michael. *Jews and Christians: Getting Their Stories Straight*. Nashville: Abingdon, 1985.

Gottwald, Norman. *The Politics of Ancient Israel*. Louisville, Ky.: Westminster John Knox Press, 2001.

———. *The Tribes of Yahweh: A Sociology of the Religion of Liberated Israel, 1250-1050 BCE*. 1979. Reprint. London: Sheffield Academic Press, 1999.

Grassi, Joseph A. *Informing the Future: Social Justice in the New Testament*. New York: Paulist, 2003.

Hofman Y., and H. Reventlow. *Justice and Righteousness: Biblical Themes and Their Influence*, Journal for the Study of the Old Testament Supplement 137. Sheffield: JSOT Press, 1992.

Hoppe, Leslie J. *There Shall Be No Poor among You*. Nashville: Abingdon, 2004.

Kammer, Fred. *Doing Faithjustice*, rev. ed. New York: Paulist, 2004.

Lohfink, Norbert. *Option for the Poor: The Basic Principle of Liberation Theology in the Light of the Bible*. Berkeley, Calif.: Bibal, 1995.

Mott, Stephen C. *Biblical Ethics and Social Change*. New York, NY: Oxford University Press, 1982.

Pleins, J. David. *The Social Visions of the Hebrew Bible: A Theological Introduction*. Louisville, Ky.: Westminster John Knox, 2001.

Premnath, D. N. *Eighth Century Prophets: A Social Analysis*. St. Louis, Mo.: Chalice, 2003.

Sklba, Richard J. *Pre-exilic Prophecy: Words of Warning, Dreams of Hope, Spirituality of Pre-exilic Prophets*, Message of Biblical Spirituality 3. Collegeville, Minn.: Liturgical Press, 1990.

Swartley, William M. *Israel's Scripture Traditions and the Synoptic Gospels: Story Shaping Story*. Peabody, Mass.: Hendrickson, 1994.

Walsh, J. P. M., *The Mighty from Their Thrones: Power in Biblical Tradition*. Eugene, Ore.: Wipf & Stock, 2004.

3

An Ancient Message,
A Contemporary Meaning

Justice and the Early Church

Do you want to honor Christ's body? Then do not scorn him in his nakedness, nor honor him here in the church with silken garments while neglecting him outside where he is cold and naked. For he who said: This is my body, and made it so by his words, also said: You saw me hungry and did not feed me, and inasmuch as you did not do it for one of these, the least of my brothers, you did not do it for me. What we do here in the church requires a pure heart, not special garments; what we do outside requires great dedication . . . For God does not want golden vessels but golden hearts . . . Of what use is it to weigh down Christ's table with golden cups, when he himself is dying of hunger? First, fill him when he is hungry; then use the means you have left to adorn his table. Will you have a golden cup made but not give a cup of water? What is the use of providing the table with cloths woven of gold thread, and not providing Christ himself with the clothes he needs . . . Do not, therefore, adorn the church and ignore your afflicted brother, for he is the most precious temple of all.[1]

JOHN CHRYSOSTOM NOTED THAT in the early days of the church the priests used chalices of wood and had hearts of gold. In his own day and age, he lamented that they use chalices of gold and have hearts of wood. Even as he directed his words to the church leaders of his day, his words were also addressed to all who profess faith in the risen Lord, challenging them to model their lives on the life of Christ and the witness of the first Christians. The apostles were rich, he said, not because of their money or possessions but because of their spiritual wealth and charitable deeds.[2]

---

1. John Chrysostom, *Homily 50 on the Gospel of Matthew*, PG 58:508-509; *The Homilies of St. John Chrysostom, Archbishop of Constantinople, On the Gospel of Matthew*, trans. Part II, Homily XXVI-LVIII (Oxford: James Parker & Company, 1879), 686. This particular translation is taken from *Liturgy of the Hours*, vol. 4 (New York: Catholic Book Publishing Company, 1975), 182-83.

2. *Nicene and Post-Nicene Fathers*, First Series, vol. 10, *Chrysostom: Homilies on the Gospel of Saint*

John Chrysostom (ca. 350-407), patriarch of Constantinople, was well known for his excellent preaching. He devoted his substantial income to the construction of hospitals and to alleviating the suffering of the poor, always preaching on the moral obligation to those in need, particularly in his *Homilies on Matthew.* The topic was so frequent in his sermons that he was often known as "Saint John the Almsgiver."

Chrysostom's words highlight the persistent presence of the poor and the demand they make on Christian conscience. The struggle to meet this demand in light of the challenge of the Gospel comes out especially in the theological reflections of early church writers like Chrysostom and other church fathers.[3] They wrote from extremely diverse cultural settings, social locations, and time periods, and they held different views on civil obligations, church–state relationships, and even war and peace.[4] While their ideas cannot easily be harmonized into a monolithic body of thought, they do show substantial agreement on the issues of poverty, liberation, and justice, which we want to explore here in more detail.[5]

In the first chapter we noted that reality is an important starting point for theological reflection. In this chapter we want to look at how the church's tradition of preaching and its articulation of doctrine help us interpret that reality. While the previous chapter on the Bible and justice weaves together various thematic strands that form the tapestry of Scripture, this chapter

---

Matthew, ed. Philip Schaff, trans. George Prevost (Peabody, Mass.: Hendrickson, 1999), "The Gospel of St. Matthew, Homily L," 313.

3. For the sake of the flow of this chapter, whenever I have quoted directly from an English translation of the fathers of the church, I have changed both the sexist language and the old English expressions (thou, thee, etc.). For more biographical information on the early church fathers, see Everett Ferguson, ed., *Encyclopedia of Early Christianity*, 2nd ed., 2 vols. (New York: Garland, 1997); Joseph F. Kelly, *The Concise Dictionary of Early Christianity* (Collegeville, Minn.: Liturgical Press, 1992); Johannes Quasten, ed., *Patrology*, vols. 1-3 (Utrecht/Antwerp: Spectrum Publishers, 1966); Angelo di Berardino, ed., *Patrology*, vol. 4 (Westminster, Md.: Christian Classics, 1986); and *New Catholic Encyclopedia*, ed. editorial staff of Catholic University of America, 2nd ed., 15 vols. (New York: Thomson-Gale, 2002).

4. For a good introductory article on this subject, see Peter C. Phan, "Fathers of the Church, Influence of," in *The New Dictionary of Catholic Social Thought*, ed. J. A. Dwyer (Collegeville, Minn.: Liturgical Press, 1994), 388. See also William J. Walsh and John P. Langan, "Patristic Social Consciousness: The Church and the Poor" in *The Faith That Does Justice: Power in Biblical Tradition*, ed. John C. Haughey, Woodstock Studies 2 (New York: Paulist, 1977). I am also very grateful for the book *Justicia y Explotación en la Tradición Cristiana Antigua*, ed. Juan Leuridan (Lima: Centro de Estudios y Publicaciones [CEP], 1973).

5. For more of early church thought on poverty and justice, see Charles Avila, *Ownership: Early Christian Teaching* (Maryknoll, N.Y.: Orbis Books, 1983); Justo L. González, *Faith and Wealth* (San Francisco: Harper & Row, 1990); Peter C. Phan, *Social Thought: Message of the Fathers of the Church* 20 (Wilmington, Del.: Michael Glazier, 1984); Susan R. Holman, *The Hungry Are Dying: Beggars and Bishops in Roman Cappadocia* (New York: Oxford University Press, 2001).

stitches together a patristic patchwork of early church reflections into a theological quilt on wealth, poverty, and discipleship. While each square in this quilt has its own unique integrity, in that each writer should be understood in his own life, times, and theology, we can also sew together some underlying themes by bringing out what these early writers shared in common.

While others have written more about the historical context of the church fathers and their message, our focus here is to look at how these ancient texts help name a truth about human experience that can assist us in claiming that reality in our own day. The power of reading these early church writers is hearing them speak from their own generation an enduring message that stands the test of time for all generations. They flesh out the narratives of the Scriptures and challenge their hearers to make the Gospel Narrative the substance of their own personal narratives. As the proclivities of our global culture tend to what is new and innovative, which often limits our perceptual horizon to the latest fad and novelty, these early church writers tap into deeper currents of spirituality, which help us understand better the liberating message of the Gospel.

The church fathers are divided into two groups: Latin (West) and Greek (East), and they lived between the end of the apostolic age (ca. A.D. 100) and the death of Pope Gregory the Great in the West (d. 604) and John Damascene in the East (d. 749). They include figures such as Clement of Alexandria, Basil the Great, Gregory of Nazianzus, Gregory of Nyssa, John Chrysostom, Ambrose of Milan, Augustine of Hippo, Leo the Great, Gregory the Great, and others. Through homilies, letters, treatises, biographies, histories, apologies, scriptural commentaries, liturgical texts, apothegms, songs, poems, journals, and other literary forms, they forged some of the earliest doctrines about Christian faith and discipleship in the first centuries of Christianity.

TRINITY AND SOCIETY: AN INTEGRAL RELATIONSHIP

Central to the early writings and the doctrinal development of the church is the notion of the Trinity, which emerged as the early church tried to think through the roles of the Father, the Son, and the Spirit in the mystery of salvation.[6] One of the terms the early church writers introduced to understand how the three persons of the Trinity relate to one another is the core idea of *perichoresis*.[7] While this notion was formally articulated in the fourth century,

---

6. For an excellent overview of trinitarian theology, see Anne Hunt, *Trinity: Nexus of the Mysteries of Christian Faith*, Theology in Global Perspective (Maryknoll, N.Y.: Orbis Books, 2005).

7. I am particularly indebted to Leonardo Boff for this insight into Trinity, society, and

today it can offer us a way of interpreting these texts and a model for human relationships. It can also provide a foundation from which to understand a faith that seeks justice.

First articulated by the Cappadocian fathers Basil the Great, Gregory of Nyssa, and Gregory of Nazianzus (and John Damascene some four centuries later in the early Greek-speaking church), the word "perichoresis" is a Greek term that is a combination of two words *peri* (around) and *chōreō* (to dance), which means "to exchange places" or "to dance around."[8] It is philosophical, analogical, and metaphorical language that sees the trinitarian relationship as a divine dance. In this dance the individual identities of the Father, the Son, and the Holy Spirit are each maintained, but their relationship with one another is characterized by an in-dwelling love that expresses itself through total mutuality, reciprocity, and interpenetration of and with each other (Jn 14:10-11). Their love is expressed through the complete gift of self and total reception of the other. In other words, the Trinity is a divine dance of three persons who so totally love one another and so totally offer themselves to one another and so totally receive one another that they become one with each other. As the prototype of the perfect society, this understanding of the Trinity offers us a model of social communion for the world. Through participation in the divine mystery, Christians in faith and through the Spirit seek to create a society that conforms to this life-giving and love-generating dance.[9]

Perichoresis, then, is a way of understanding God's invitation to humanity to join the dance of intimacy with the Trinity, to move outward toward others in love and to realize our fundamental interconnectedness with one another. While God invites all to enter into this divine dance, we recognize that we have choices about whether or not we want to take God's hand. We must make decisions about how closely we want God to dance with us and how much we want God to be the lead partner. Reading the texts of these patristic writers is a way of learning the steps of this dance and of learning how to listen to the music of the Spirit so that, as God works his love in us, our lives become graced events as God's life unfolds within each one of us.

---

perichoresis. See Leonardo Boff, *Trinity and Society* (Maryknoll, N.Y.: Orbis Books, 1988), 11ff. See also Catherine Mowry LaCugna, *God for Us: The Trinity & Christian Life* (New York: HarperCollins, 1992), 270-71.

8. Various scholars, for example, Gerald O'Collins, maintain that perichoresis does not mean "to dance around" and that the Greek will not support this definition. Instead, he says, it means "cyclical movement," the being-in-one-another of the Trinity. In a unique "coinherence" or mutual interpenetration, each of the trinitarian persons is transparent to, and permeated by, the other two. While we differ on the exact translation of the term perichoresis, and even whether it functions metaphorically or philosophically, we both agree on the notion of the interpenetration of each member of the Trinity to the others. Gerald O'Collins, *The Tripersonal God: Understanding and Interpreting the Trinity* (New York: Paulist, 1999), 132.

9. Boff, *Trinity and Society*, 11.

ESTABLISHING A FRAMEWORK FOR ONE'S
PERSONAL NARRATIVE

For many of the church fathers, social justice involves a tripartite understanding of relationships: understanding one's relationship with one's Creator, understanding oneself as a creature, and understanding creation properly. The fathers took it for granted that people often find themselves lost and disoriented, without purpose or meaning in their lives. They realized that both original and personal sin have weakened our capacity to evaluate and discern, and ultimately make life-giving choices. Dependent on the tangible and the visible, and even impatient with things spiritual, people often settle for the framework offered by the world around them, without ever critically examining it or testing its relative adequacy. In the face of the nontangible yet more important spiritual realities, the fathers offer both a compass and a map to help people navigate their way through competitive forces that pull on them.

The church fathers believe that the framework that shapes the life of a Christian must be nothing other than the life of Christ. This framework asserts itself against those frameworks in every generation that would suggest that life consists in the endless accumulation of goods, the maximization of profit, the ambitious rise to power, and other forms of idolatry that directly contradict the Narrative of the Gospel. They encourage and challenge their hearers to construct a Christian vision of the world that transforms the way they think about their lives, their resources, and the commonly and even uncritically accepted norms of their particular cultures.

> *Ambrose* (ca. 339-397) was a theologian and bishop of Milan, Italy. He wrote frequently against the moral shortcomings of his day, particularly the greed of the wealthy in his *Homily on Tobit* and *On the Story of Naboth*. He is well known for having given to the poor all the worldly wealth he had accumulated before his consecration.

The Christian life, by its very nature, is God and other oriented. To keep first in one's mind the love of God and the needs of others is the heart of love and an expression of justice. Ambrose notes, "No virtue produces more abundant benefits than . . . justice, which is more concerned with others than with itself, neglecting its own advantages, and preferring the common good."[10] Elsewhere, Ambrose explains:

---

10. Ambrose, chapter 3 of *The Paradise*, PL 14:298; Saint Ambrose, *Hexameron, Paradise, and Cain and Abel*, trans. John J. Savage (New York: Fathers of the Church, 1961), 288.

If, then, any one wishes to please all, he must strive in everything to do, not what is useful for one's self, but what is useful for many, as also Paul strove to do. For this is "to be conformed to the image of Christ" . . . For Christ our Lord, though He was in the form of God, emptied Himself so as to take on Himself human form, which He wished to enrich with the virtue of His works.[11]

As a substantive commentary on biblical revelation, the patristic reflections on the Scriptures give us an unfolding sense of what it means to establish an adequate vision of one's life in the midst of the challenges of a disordered world.

> *Gregory of Nazianzus* (ca. 330-390) was a close friend of Saint Basil's and briefly patriarch of Constantinople before civil and ecclesiastical in-fighting forced his resignation. His most famous works are his five *Theological Orations,* which helped clarify Christian belief in the Trinity. In addition to these, he gave a number of other orations, many of which developed his ideas on justice, particularly the fourteenth, *On Love for the Poor,* which was prompted by his meeting with several lepers.

Understanding God as Creator

Patristic literature appeals above all to reason and Scripture as a way of helping people understand who we are as human beings before a loving Creator. Gregory of Nazianzus makes it clear that a Christian vision of the world must establish God as the Lord of Creation and the ruler of one's life:

Recognize the source of your existence, of your breath of life, your understanding, your knowledge of God (itself the greatest of all gifts), your hope of gaining the heavenly kingdom, equality of honor with the angels . . . Where did you obtain all these things? From whom? Or, to speak of lesser matters, that is, the visible world around us, who gave you to see the beauty of heaven, the sun in its course, the orb of the moon, the countless stars and the harmony and order? . . . Who gave you rain, husbandry, food, the arts, dwellings, laws, governments, a civilized mode of life, friendly converse with your fellow man? . . . Who made you lord and king of everything on

---

11. Ambrose, *On the Duties of the Clergy,* PL 15; see also the English translation in *Nicene and Post-Nicene Fathers,* Second Series, vol. 10, *Ambrose: Select Works and Letters,* ed. Philip Schaff and Henry Wace, trans. H. De Romestin (Peabody, Mass.: Hendrickson, 1994), pp. 69-70, book 3, chap. 3, par. 15.

earth? Who, without listing them individually, endowed you with all the things that lift humans above the rest of creation?[12]

Understanding God as the author of creation is one of the building blocks of a Christian vision of the world. Other implications flow from this understanding, such as the gift of creation, the primacy of the love of God, the equality of people, and interconnectedness of all creatures.

> *Basil the Great* (ca. 330-379) was bishop of Caesarea in Asia Minor and wrote the communal rule that still guides Eastern Christian monasticism. He established many homes for the poor and sick in the areas under his episcopal authority and constantly encouraged an ascetical life of detachment from material wealth and riches. In particular, when a major famine hit Cappadocia in 368, he used his inheritance to help others; he summoned others to a spirit of solidarity, which helped prevent disastrous starvation.

Not only do humans benefit from a benevolent Creator, but patristic literature illustrates that all of creation itself is good. It also brings out that human beings are summoned by the Creator to be stewards of the earth. As Basil notes,

> We must say first that no possession if it had been bad in itself would have been created by God. "For every creature of God" it says "is good and nothing is to be rejected" (1 Tim 4:4). Secondly, that the commandment of the Lord instructed us not to cast away possessions as evil and avoid them, but to administer them as stewards. And a man is condemned, not absolutely because he has them but because he had wrong thoughts concerning them, or used them badly.[13]

Not only are human beings and the earth a creative expression of divine love, but God wills that creatures enjoy all of creation as a gift and that they care for it wisely. Pope Leo the Great in one of his sermons establishes that all that is seen and unseen comes as a gift from God:

> For not only are spiritual riches and heavenly gifts received from God, but earthly and material possessions also proceed from His bounty, that He may be justified in requiring an account of those things which He has not

---

12. Gregory Nazianzus, *Oration 14 On Love for the Poor*, PG; see also Saint Gregory of Nazianzus, *Select Orations*, trans. Martha Vinson (Washington, D.C.: Catholic University of America Press, 2003), 55-56.

13. Basil, *Short Rules*, PG 31:1145; see also *The Ascetic Works of Saint Basil*, trans. W. K. L. Clarke (New York: Macmillan, 1925), 264-65.

so much put into our possession as committed to our stewardship . . . God's gifts, therefore, we must use properly and wisely, lest the material for good work should become an occasion of sin.[14]

Throughout many of their writings, the church fathers bring out that God is the Creator of all, that all God creates is good, and that God wills all human beings to share in God's creation.

> Leo the Great (d. 461) was pope from 440 to 461. He is best known for his sermons and the christological work in his tome, which was particularly important for the Council of Chalcedon in 451. Through his moral persuasiveness he put himself on the front line of danger and persuaded Attila the Hun not to attack Rome, saving countless lives.

Understanding Oneself as a Creature

The church fathers also reiterate that the gift of creation should lead us to love God above all created things. God deserves primacy in our lives not only because God is Creator but because only God can satisfy the deepest longings of human beings. Orienting one's life to God is intrinsic to the inner structures of human life, as eloquently articulated in the oft-quoted phrase from Augustine, "You arouse us to take joy in praising you, for you have made us for yourself, and our heart is restless until it rests in you."[15]

> Clement of Alexandria (ca. 150-ca. 220) was most likely the head of a catechetical school in Alexandria, though little is known of his life. Most of his writings are attempts to reconcile Christianity and Greek philosophy, but his sermon *Who Is the Rich Man That Is Saved?* discusses many issues of social justice.

Without acknowledging God as the source and destiny of all human yearning, one easily frustrates the proper order of relationships, attempting to satisfy one's longing for the Creator with other gods, idols, people, or possessions. Such displacement inevitably leads to unhappiness, division, disorder, and chaos, as Clement of Alexandria observes:

---

14. Leo the Great, *Sermon X, On the Collections*, chapter 1, PL 54:164; see also the English translation in *Nicene and Post-Nicene Fathers*, Second Series, vol. 12, *Leo the Great, Gregory the Great*, ed. Philip Schaff and Henry Wace, trans. Charles Lett Feltoe (Peabody, Mass.: Hendrickson, 1994), "Sermon X, On the Collections," 120.

15. Augustine, *The Confessions of St. Augustine*, trans. John K. Ryan (New York: Doubleday, 1960), 43.

"Seek first the kingdom of heaven, and all these things shall be added unto you." [Lk 12:31] . . . God brought our race into communion by first imparting what was His own, when He gave His own Word, common to all, and made all things for all. All things therefore are common, and not for the rich to appropriate an undue share. That expression, therefore, "I possess, and possess in abundance: why then should I not enjoy?" is suitable neither to human beings, nor to society. But more worthy of love is that: "I have: why should I not give to those who need?" For such a one—one who fulfils the command, "You shall love your neighbor as yourself"—is perfect.[16]

Clement and others bring out that we come to understand who we are as creatures only in light of our relationship to our Creator and only as we open ourselves to our neighbors in need.

Because of the paternity of God and the gratuity of his gifts, all human beings share a common bond by virtue of their link to a common Creator. Moreover, as Ambrose points out, understanding oneself as a creature entails understanding that all are created equally in the eyes of God:

The earth was established as common [patrimony] for all, for both rich and poor alike. Why do you arrogate for yourselves alone, you who are rich, exclusive right to the land? No one is rich by nature, for nature begets everyone as poor. Indeed, we are neither born with garments nor are we begotten with gold and silver. Naked and needy, in want of food, clothing, and drink, are we first brought forth into the light of day; naked does the earth receive those whom it had brought forth; it knows not how to enclose within the tomb the expansive boundaries of one's estates [or] the excessive extremes of one's possessions.[17]

Lactantius (ca. 240-ca. 320) was employed in the court of Diocletian before he converted and was forced out, but was recalled after the Peace of Constantine to tutor the new emperor's son. Known mostly as a rhetorician, he did work in theology, particularly in *The Divine Institute*, the fifth book of which is an entire treatise on justice, which he identifies as the most important virtue for society.

The church fathers reiterate that social and economic distinctions mean nothing before God. They believe there is an inherent democracy of human

---

16. Clement of Alexandria, *The Instructor*, book II, chap. III, PG 8:542. *The Ante-Nicene Fathers*, ed. Alexander Roberts and James Donaldson (American Reprint of Edinburgh Edition; Grand Rapids: Eerdmans, 2001), 2:268.

17. Ambrose, *On the Story of Naboth*, PL 14:731B.

creation in that all share the same status before God. If any distinctions can be made, they are measured by the quality of the heart and not by the quantity of one's assets. Lactantius makes a similar observation when he says,

> Justice . . . is equity . . . If all have the same Father, by an equal right we are all children. No one is poor in the sight of God, but he who is without justice; no one is rich, but he who is full of virtues; no one, in short, is excellent, but he who has been good and innocent; no one is most renowned, but he who has abundantly performed works of mercy; no one is most perfect, but he who has filled all the steps of virtue . . . For where all are not equally matched, there is not equity; and inequality of itself excludes justice, the whole force of which consists in this, that it makes those equal who have by an equal lot arrived at the condition of this life.[18]

In addition Basil, drawing on a metaphor used by Paul, observes that our common origin in the gift of a common Creator should lead us to recognize our common bonds with each other:

> None of us is self-sufficient even as regards bodily needs, but we need one another's help in getting what is necessary. For just as the foot has certain powers but lacks others, and without the help of the other limbs neither finds its own strength sufficient for endurance nor has the support of what is lacking . . . since God the Creator ordained that we need one another, as it is written, (1 Cor 12:12-26), in order that we may be linked with one another.[19]

John Chrysostom is emphatic about illustrating our interconnectedness:

> If you enjoy [wealth] alone, you too have lost it: for you will not reap its reward . . . As . . . it is a vice in the stomach to retain the food and not to distribute it, (for it is injurious to the whole body,) so it is a vice in those that are rich to keep to themselves what they have. For this destroys both themselves and others. Again, the eye receives all the light: but it does not itself alone retain it, but enlightens the entire body. For it is not its nature to keep it to itself, so long as it is an eye. Again, the nostrils are sensible of perfume; but they do not keep it all to themselves, but transmit it to the brain, and affect the stomach with a sweet savor, and by their means refresh the entire person. The feet alone walk; but they move not away themselves only, but transfer also the whole body. In like manner do you, whatsoever

---

18. Lactantius, *Divine Institutes* 5.15, *On Justice* PL 6:598; *The Ante-Nicene Fathers*, ed. Alexander Roberts and James Donaldson (American Reprint of Edinburgh Edition; Grand Rapids: Eerdmans, 2001), 7:150-51.

19. Basil; *Rule #7 of the Longer Rules*, PG 31:915; see also *Ascetic Works of Saint Basil*, 163.

you have been entrusted with, keep it not for yourself alone, since you are doing harm to the whole and to yourself more than all . . . For in every thing to give and receive is the principle of numerous blessings: in seeds, in scholars, in arts. For if people desire to keep their arts to themselves, they subvert both themselves and the whole course of things.[20]

Basil is even more direct,

To the hungry belongs the bread that you keep. To the naked belongs the clothing that you store in your closet. To the barefoot belongs the footwear that rots in your house. To the needy belongs the cash that you hide away. In short, you could have provided assistance to all those whom you treated unjustly.[21]

The divine perichoresis at the heart of creation reveals the fundamental calling of all human beings to create a community of radical sharing and mutual interdependence. In contrast to a society that prizes individualism and self-sufficiency, and where the winner takes all, the Christian vision of reality brings out that all beings have their origin in sharing. We come to realize that what is done to one is done to all: when any are losing, all are affected; when any are deprived, all suffer; and when any are empowered, all benefit.

Understanding Creation in a Proper Way

The church fathers regularly dispelled any superficial notion that wealth is a sign of God's blessing intended only for the benefit of one's family and friends. Quite the opposite is true; they challenged those with resources to create a bigger and less self-interested vision of their lives that included especially their brothers or sisters in need. In contrast to some prevailing philosophies of their day, the fathers relativized any notion of private property in light of the universalization of all goods. Because everything comes from God, they believed that all is to be shared equitably, without some enjoying abundance while others lack the means with which to sustain themselves. Chrysostom insists that the disparities between the haves and the have-nots are not at all part of the divine intention for humankind:

God in the beginning made not one man rich, and another poor. Nor did He afterwards take and show to one treasures of gold, and deny to the other

---

20. John Chrysostom, *Homily 10 on 1st Corinthians*, PG 61:86-87; English translation in *Nicene and Post-Nicene Fathers*, First Series, vol. 12, *Chrysostom*, trans. Talbot W. Chambers (Peabody, Mass.: Hendrickson, 1999), 57.

21. Basil, *Homily on the text: I will Destroy my Granaries*, PG 31:277-78.

the right of searching for it: but He left the earth free to all alike. Why then, if it is common, have you so many acres of land, while your neighbor has not a portion of it? It was transmitted to me by my father. And by whom to him? By his forefathers. But you must go back and find the original owner.[22]

Chrysostom's understanding of this Christian framework entailed that faith in a common God meant common property,

But is not this an evil, that you alone should have the Lord's property, that you alone should enjoy what is common? Is not "the earth God's, and the fullness thereof?" If then our possessions belong to one common Lord, they belong also to our fellow-servants. The possessions of one Lord are all common.[23]

Even while the Scriptures help to illuminate this ideal, Ambrose points out the human tendency to do just the opposite, that is, instead of dancing with God and sharing with others, we prefer to dance alone to the tune of our own self-interest:

[We] regard common property as personal property. But nothing is personal property since nothing can be ours for ever . . . Why do you value your wealth so much? Remember that God meant you to share the fruit of the earth with the rest of the animals. The birds of heaven make no special claims for themselves. Because they are never envious of others, they always have enough.[24]

Cyril of Alexandria (ca. 376-444) was patriarch of Alexandria and a leading theologian of his day, particularly in his work on Christology, which was very influential at the Council of Ephesus in 431. These works also have a strong spiritual core, however, particularly focusing on the image of God in human persons, from which flows human dignity that must be respected and treated with justice.

Cyril of Alexandria goes even further to say that greed for excess wealth goes against what it means to be a creature of God,

Let us therefore be faithful with this earthly wealth, which is something lowly, even minimal and of no value, since it so easily slips away, and let

22. John Chrysostom, *Homily 12 on First Timothy*, PG 62:563; English translation in *Nicene and Post-Nicene Fathers*, First Series, vol. 13, *Chrysostom*, trans. Gross Alexander (Peabody, Mass.: Hendrickson, 1999), 447.

23. Ibid., 448.

24. Ambrose, *Commentary of St. Ambrose on The Gospel according to St. Luke,* trans. Ide M. Ni Riain (Dublin: Elo Press, 2001), 228-29.

us not usurp for ourselves what has been given to us for our brothers and sisters, who have the same needs as we do, so that we do not make wealth to be something unjust by holding on to what belongs to another. It does not belong to us, first of all, because we have brought nothing with us into this world, and secondly, because it truly belongs to the poor. In this way what is our own will be entrusted to us, the true and lasting wealth which is godly and spiritual. Indeed, to possess wealth is naturally foreign to every human being.[25]

Alluding to the first temptation of Adam and Eve (Gn 3:1-7), they also warn that money, power, and fame can eclipse one's self-understanding and lure delusions of grandeur.

Private property, for many of the fathers, is at best an ambivalent blessing. They believe that human beings can never be more than provisional, temporary owners of any of the world's goods.[26] Because our ownership of anything is transitory, John Chrysostom warns that

Wealth is not a possession, it is not property; it is a loan for use. For when you die, willingly or unwillingly, all that you have goes to others, and they again give it up to others, and they again to others. For we are all sojourners; and the tenant of the house is more truly perchance the owner of it, for the owner dies, and the tenant lives, and still enjoys the house.[27]

Chysostom named the common and persistent human deception to believe that one has ownership of anything in any permanent or absolute sense. When speaking to the people of Antioch, he said, "I have often smiled, when reading wills that said, let such a man have the ownership of these fields, or of this house, and another the use thereof. For we all have the use, but no man has the ownership."[28]

> *Asterius of Amasea* (d. ca. 410) was a bishop and lesser-known Cappadocian father who wrote praising the martyrs and condemning paganism. Among his extant homilies, the subject of morality is common, giving practical advice to his congregations.

---

25. Cyril of Alexandria, *On the Gospel of Matthew*, PG 72:816.

26. For an excellent source on John Chrysostom on poverty and justice, see Saint John Chrysostom, *On Wealth and Poverty*, trans. Catharine P. Roth (Crestwood, N.Y.: St. Vladimir's Seminary Press, 1984).

27. John Chrysostom, *Homily 11 on 1 Timothy*, PG 62:556; English translation in *Nicene and Post-Nicene Fathers*, First Series, vol. 13, *Chrysostom*, trans. Gross Alexander (Peabody, Mass.: Hendrickson, 1999), 443.

28. John Chrysostom, *Homily 2, To the People of Antioch*, PG 49:42; see also *The Homilies of St. John Chrysostom, Archbishop of Constantinople, On the Statues, or To the People of Antioch* (Oxford: John Henry Parker, 1842), 104.

Like Chrysostom, his contemporary, Bishop Asterius of Amasea, also tries to cut through the deceptions of ownership when he writes,

> Many times I have spoken with you in my homilies about a lie which insidiously takes shape in the minds of human beings, a lie that multiplies sins and diminishes the good deeds that each of us ought to practice as citizens. This lie [we tell ourselves] is to think that we possess as owners and lords those things given to us for our use in life. Because we hold on tightly to this lie, we fight violently, make war, press charges, [and] go to whatever extreme to cling to the material things as if they were essential goods.[29]

An excessive emphasis on ownership separates people from community and ultimately leads them to sin, not only against God but against others who cry out in need.

> *Augustine* (354-430) is one of the greatest theologians in the history of the Western church, writing during the tumultuous period of the fall of the western Roman empire. In addition to his two most famous works, the *Confessions* and *City of God,* Augustine dealt with the themes of justice repeatedly in his numerous biblical commentaries and sermons.

What ultimately distorts human perceptions of reality is not the goods of the earth but greed. For Augustine, sin meant being turned in on oneself, one's eyes blinded by the "swelling tumor" of pride. Sin cuts in on the dance between God and human beings. Basing their teaching on Scripture, the church fathers understood that, although created for freedom, human beings not only bear the wounds of original sin but they make sinful, self-centered choices. Not only is this doctrine of inherited and personal sin an integral part of Christian revelation, but it has great hermeneutical value in helping us understand human nature.[30] The fathers understood that while human beings are called to worship God, they often worship creation; instead of orienting themselves toward the God who created them, they make a god out of created things; instead of understanding the earth as common patrimony, human-kind turns in on itself and insists on inventing distinctions between what is common and what is private. Chrysostom condemns the divisions that result from human greed because they pervert the divine designs of justice:

> And observe, that concerning things that are common there is no contention, but all is peaceable. But when one attempts to possess for oneself anything,

---

29. Asterius, *Homily 2, On the Wicked Supervisor,* PG 40:180.
30. John Paul II, *Centesimus Annus* 25.

to make it one's own, then contention is introduced, as if nature herself were indignant, that when God brings us together in every way, we are eager to divide and separate ourselves by appropriating things, and by using those cold words "mine and yours."[31]

Chrysostom recognized too that human beings can often go so far off track that they will sell the treasure of their divine birthright for useless, created things:

> Tell me not then of the abundance of [rich people's] possessions, but consider how great loss the lovers of this abundance undergo in . . . losing Heaven . . . [It is] . . . as if any one after being cast out of the highest honor in kings' courts, having a dung heap, were to pride himself on that. For the storing up of money differs nothing from that, or rather that is even the better. For that is serviceable both for husbandry, and for heating a bath, and for other such uses, but the buried gold for none of these things . . . Unless he uses it rightly; countless evils at least spring from them.[32]

Beyond personal sin, however, John Chrysostom notes that sin is part of the fabric of society that further deforms a fallen world. Accordingly, people instinctively assign ultimate value to arbitrary, even transitory things, leading them to live out of narrative frameworks that go counter to that of the Gospel Narrative. Such frameworks often "drug" people into settling for superficial appearances rather than searching for qualities that are more valuable and enduring:

> Is a pearl beautiful? Yet consider, it is but sea water, and was once cast away in the bosom of the deep. Are gold and silver beautiful? Yet they were and are but dust and ashes. Are silken vestments beautiful? Yet they are nothing but the spinning of worms. This beauty is but in opinion, in human prejudice, not in the nature of the things . . . We are everywhere under the influence of covetousness and opinion . . . a thing is valued for its rarity, and not for its nature . . . But let us recover from this intoxication, let us fix our view upon that which is truly beautiful, beautiful in its own nature, upon godliness and righteousness; that we may obtain the promised blessings, through the grace and loving kindness of Jesus Christ our Lord.[33]

---

31. John Chrysostom, *Homily 12 on First Timothy*, PG 62:564; English translation in *Nicene and Post-Nicene Fathers*, First Series, vol. 13, 448.

32. John Chrysostom, *Homily 63 on the Gospel of Matthew*, PG 58:608; English translation in *Nicene and Post-Nicene Fathers*, First Series, vol. 10, 391.

33. John Chrysostom, *Homily 17 on First Timothy*, PG 62:596; English translation in *Nicene and Post-Nicene Fathers*, First Series, vol. 13, 470.

Many of the church fathers also believed that human beings commit some of the worst injustices in judging other human beings by categories other than those of the Gospel. Gregory of Nazianzus brings out the degrading depths to which human beings have descended and the height to which they are ultimately called:

> Our human family has been so fragmented that we are now alienated from one another with a variety of labels, and greed has hacked away at the nobility of our nature to the point of arrogating even the legal process, the right arm of the power of government. But as for you, I ask you to look to that original egalitarian status, not the latter-day discrimination; not the law of the tyrant, but that of the Creator. Help nature as much as you can; honor your ancient freedom; cultivate your self-worth; draw a veil over the ignominy of our race; treat sickness; alleviate need: the healthy person, the need of the sick; the rich person, the need of the poor; the person who has not stumbled, the one who lies fallen and crushed; the one full of spirit, the one discouraged; the one who enjoys prosperity, the one who toils in adversity.[34]

Above all else, the fathers insist on seeing the inherent beauty and dignity of all human beings, as God-given gifts, that are often obscured because of social prejudices.

CHALLENGING THE IDOLATRY OF WEALTH

In general, the church fathers were against not wealth but the self-serving accumulation of wealth. They recognized that idolatry is not just a challenge of biblical times but an ongoing human challenge in every generation. Because riches—like other good things in our lives—have an almost magnetic capacity to attract self-centered motives, they can become idolatrous and can work against the creative purposes and other-oriented designs of the soul. Often the social mores of society nurture and cultivate these selfish motives, and the patristic literature names how riches, power, and fame can lure people into seductive frameworks that ultimately rupture the proper order of relationships. Much of the teachings of these writers sought to bring people back to reality, back to the music of the Spirit, back to the basic dance steps of God, back to a sense of justice expressed in rightly ordered relation-

---

34. Gregory Nazianzus, *Oration 14 On Love for the Poor*, PG 35:891; Saint Gregory of Nazianzus, *Select Orations*, trans. Martha Vinson, Fathers of the Church 107 (Washington, D.C.: Catholic University of America Press, 2003), 58-59.

ships. They wanted their hearers to recognize the snares, illusions, and seductions of wealth that lure people away from the dance floor and into the cold, dark alleys of isolation.

The Snare of Wealth

Much of the patristic literature addresses how—when people set their minds and hearts on physical rather than spiritual riches, when their frame of reference centers them not on the love of God but on the love of capital gain, and when the accumulation of possessions becomes a more consuming concern than the works of justice and mercy—the god of money takes possession of them and directs their lives in very deliberate ways. Drawing on Scripture and his own empirical observations, Chrysostom brings out the core of the problem:

> For the "love of money is the root of all evils" (1 Tm 6:10). Hence come fightings, and enmities and wars; hence emulations, and railings, and suspicions, and insults; hence murders, and thefts, and violations of sepulchers . . . And all the evils that you may find, whether in the house or in the market-place, or in the courts of law, or in the senate, or in the king's palace, or in any other place whatsoever, it is from this that you will find they all spring. For this evil it is, this assuredly, which fills all places with blood and murder, this lights up the flame of hell, this makes cities as wretchedly off as a wilderness, yes, even much worse.[35]

> *Gregory of Nyssa* (ca. 335-ca.395) was the brother of Saint Basil and bishop of Nyssa in Cappadocia. He was highly influential in the development of Trinitarian thought, particularly in his *Against Eunomius* and his important role in the First Council of Constantinople in 381. Many of his surviving sermons deal with the treatment of the poor.

Greed breaks communion and seduces people to the lowest form of human behavior. Gregory of Nyssa warns people against fanning the consuming fires of avarice, which not only deprives the poor but dehumanizes the rich:

> The poor, indeed, are our brothers and sisters . . . If one wanted to take possession of everything and exclude his brothers and sisters of even the third or fifth part [of their inheritance], such a one would be a cruel tyrant,

---

35. John Chrysostom, *Homily 11 on the Epistle to the Romans*, PG 60:491; English translation in *Nicene and Post-Nicene Fathers*, First Series, vol. 11 (Peabody, Mass.: Hendrickson, 1999), 414.

an implacable savage, an insatiable beast who wanted the best of the banquet for himself alone; or rather, he would be the most savage of the beasts themselves. Even a wolf allows another wolf a share of the prey it devours, and many dogs feed together upon one carcass. Yet the insatiably greedy never allow any other human being to have a share in their wealth. Let a moderate table be enough for you. Do not throw yourself into the sea of unbridled consumption. Unbearable is the shipwreck that will overwhelm you, for not only would you be torn by rocks hidden below water, but you would rush headlong into the dark depths from which no one having fallen has ever escaped.[36]

As Basil illustrates, greed is an all-consuming god that demands unrelenting obedience:

What will you reply to the Judge, you who dress up walls [with adornments] but let human beings go naked? You who, adorning horses, look away from your brother in rags? You who, allowing your bread to grow stale, do not feed the hungry? You who, burying your gold, look down upon the poor who choke in poverty's tight grip? And if you have a wife at home who also loves wealth, the sickness is doubled since she becomes inflamed over luxuries, increases her love of sickening pleasures, injects herself with the sting of superfluous desires, while imagining certain rocks to be like pearls, emeralds, and hyacinths. She uses gold for everything, and joins evil with bad taste. Her desire for these objects is not a passing one but grows into an obsession night and day. Next, a swarm of flatterers who applaud her desires, gathering together goldsmiths, those that supply extravagant perfumes, merchants, and interior decorators. With her constant demands, the woman does not allow her husband to breathe. There is not sufficient wealth for feminine fancies, even if they flowed from the rivers. Women ask for perfume from Barbarian lands as if it were common oil from the market, and coral, abalone, and exotic fruit, more even than sheep's wool. Gold embedded with precious stones serves them as ornaments for the forehead or the neck; one uses it as a belt, another ties her hands and feet with it. For women who love gold enjoy having their hands cuffed, as long as the cuff be of gold. When, therefore, will one care for one's soul when enslaved by these feminine desires? Torments and surges sink the decaying ship; and so the wicked dispositions of women sink the weak souls of their husbands.[37]

Despite the obvious sexism of this passage, if Basil were writing today, he would undoubtedly rail against the vanities of men who squander their

---

36. Gregory of Nyssa, *On Loving the Poor*, PG 46:465-66.
37. Basil, *Homily against the Rich*, PG 31:287-90.

wealth on fancy sports cars, diamond-studded watches, or expensive sport-ing events and the like. He would even be harsher on corporate leaders of any gender who are more attuned to corporate profit than the just treatment of their employees, and any others who subvert the common good for selfish gain, perverting the natural law with disordered self-interest.

The church fathers would not limit their diatribes only to abuses in the secular, socioeconomic, and political sphere. Many spoke out not only against the wealthy but also against church leaders. After Constantine (274-327) established Christianity as the favored religion of the Roman empire (325), the church believed in many ways that it had conquered the world. Yet the concern of the church fathers was that the world of affluence, privilege, and prestige was reconquering the church.[38] In other words, as the church became part of the empire, the empire became part of the church. The lack of spiritual depth manifested itself in part through clergy, who spent more time worrying about the liturgical rubrics and ornaments of the church than its larger mission to the world. As Chrysostom adds,

> For indeed the saying, "Sell your goods, and give to the poor, and come and follow me," (Mt 19:21) might be seasonably addressed to the prelates of the church with respect to the property of the church. For in any other way it is not possible to follow Him as we ought, not being freed from all grosser and more worldly care . . . But now the priests of God . . . who are invited to the very inmost shrines of the heavens, and who enter into the true holy of holies, take upon ourselves the cares of tradesmen and retail dealers. Hence great neglect of the Scriptures, and remissness in prayers, and indifference about all the other duties; for it is not possible to be split into the two things with due zeal.[39]

The early church writers consistently tried to make the connection between liturgy and justice.

Theodoret of Cyrus (ca. 393-ca. 465) was a Syrian bishop who, in addition to preaching, helped create the infrastructure of the region for all people by contributing to the finances needed to build aqueducts and bridges. His theological expertise was primarily in the debates over the nature of Christ, but he also worked on moral matters in some of his more systematic writings and homilies.

---

38. Frederic William Farrar, *Gathering Clouds: A Tale of the Days of St. John Chrysostom* (London: Longmans, Green and Co., 1906), 47.

39. John Chrysostom, *Homily 85 On the Gospel of Matthew*, PG 58:762-63; English translation in *Nicene and Post-Nicene Fathers*, First Series, vol. 10, 510.

They also bring out that wealth can give one an exaggerated and illusory sense of self importance. As Theodoret of Cyrus explains:

> How could wealth be the definition of happiness and the foundation of good fortune if it is the means by which wicked men become supercilious and puffed up, strutting through the marketplace on horseback or in carriages, despising others in so far as it is seemly for them to look down on them, wronging, grasping, appropriating what does not belong to them, coveting what is unbecoming, taking their neighbors' belongings, enjoying other people's good fortune, trading on the misfortunes of the poor, and so on?[40]

Even in the days of these writers, the wealthy went to such extremes in their spending that it could hardly be considered rational. We read in Clement of Alexandria's sarcastic diatribes against those who use their wealth for foolish, even stupid amenities:

> For silly are they who, from greed, take delight in what they have hoarded up. "He that gathers wages," it is said, "gathers into a bag with holes." Such is he who gathers corn and shuts it up; and he who gives to no one, becomes poorer . . . It is a farce, and a thing to make one laugh outright, for men to bring in silver urinals and crystal vases de nuit, as they usher in their counselors, and for silly rich women to get gold receptacles for excrements made; so that being rich, they cannot even ease themselves except in a superb way. I would that in their whole life they deemed gold fit for dung . . .[41]

Throughout their writings, the church fathers repeatedly insist upon shaking people from the intoxicating drug of riches, urging them to discover instead the genuine freedom that comes from living in tune with reality and the promises of the Gospel.

The Cost of Wealth

The church fathers often wanted their hearers to grow in wisdom and understanding as they reflected on the cost of wealth, especially to the soul. They recognize that when wealth is unshared it can take possession of a person to such an extent that it absorbs all of one's energy and attention, to the point

---

40. Theodoret, *Discourse 6 On Providence*, PG 83:646; English translation, *Theodoret of Cyrus On Divine Providence*, trans. Thomas Halton (New York: Newman Press, 1988), 74.

41. Clement of Alexandria, *The Instructor*, book II, chap. III, PG 8:437; *Ante-Nicene Fathers*, 2:248.

that one has no time for God or good works. Worshiping creation rather than the Creator makes people calloused to the needs of others. Ambrose notes that one of the costs of wealth is the inability to see in the poor an image of one's very self:

> The swollen pride and cancerous growth of the rich have their own way of revealing themselves. These people forget their human condition and think that they are superior to nature. In the wretched state of the poor they actually find something to season their pleasures. They laugh at the poor, insult the disadvantaged, and diminish the very ones on whom any decent person would have pity.[42]

These writers continually seek to lead people away from the Narrative of the Empire and into the freedom offered them as children of God according to the Narrative of the Gospel, as Chrysostom reminds his hearers:

> For a dreadful, a dreadful thing is the love of money; it disables both eyes and ears, and makes people worse to deal with than a wild beast, allowing a person to consider neither conscience, nor friendship, nor fellowship, nor the salvation of his own soul, but having withdrawn them at once from all these things, like some harsh mistress, it makes those captured by it its slaves . . . it persuades them even to be grateful for it; and the more they become enslaved, the more does their pleasure increase; and in this way especially the malady becomes incurable, in this way the monster becomes hard to conquer.[43]

Inordinate attachment to wealth results in sins not only of commission but also of omission by refusing to help those who cry out for help. The real cost of riches is that it blinds one from doing anything in the face of one's neighbor in need, which, as Chrysostom points out, is a sure sign of spiritual death:

> Terrible is the burden of these words: the Lord of all and Creator says, "I was hungry, and you did not give me something to eat" (Mt 25:42). What soul would not be touched by this, even should it in fact be made of stone? Your Lord goes about hungry, and you treat yourself to luxuries—and not only this abuse, but also the fact that, in our luxury, you manage to ignore him, not that he wants much more than only a scrap of bread to alleviate his hunger. Yet, while he goes about frozen with the cold, you pay him no attention in your silken garments, and instead of showing compassion

---

42. Ambrose, *Book 8 On the Gospel of Luke*, PL 15:1860; see also Ambrose, *Commentary of St. Ambrose on The Gospel according to St. Luke*, trans. Ide M. Ni Riain (Dublin: Elo Press), 274.

43. John Chrysostom, *Homily 65 On the Gospel of John*, PG 59:363; English translation in *Nicene and Post-Nicene Fathers*, First Series, vol. 14 (Peabody, Mass.: Hendrickson, 1999), 243.

you pass by heedlessly. What pardon does this deserve? Accordingly, let us not make this the object of our concern, to seek in every way possible to acquire more possessions, but consider how to dispose of them properly by alleviating the need of those found wanting, lest we lose those goods that last forever . . .[44]

The Corrupting Influence of Wealth

The church fathers admonished their hearers to beware of the corrupting influence of greed, which divides rather than unites, corrupts rather than redeems, enslaves rather than frees, scatters rather than reconciles. Greed above all takes a toll on relationships, as Basil points out:

> Because of wealth, relatives act as if they do not know their family of origin; brothers look upon each other with murderous intent; because of wealth, deserts breed murderers; the seas, pirates; the cities, corrupt professionals. Who is the father of lies, the architect of false accusations? Who breeds perjury? Is it not wealth and the eagerness to acquire it? What is to become of you, oh people? Who has, with such treachery, transformed your possessions into something to be used against you? "These are all means which work together towards one's livelihood," [you say]. Has not money, then, become an instrument of evil?[45]

Ironically, as Ambrose observes, sometimes wealth is inversely proportional to generosity,

> Oh rich ones, such are your kindnesses! The less you give, the more you demand. Such is your humanity that you plunder even as you pretend to give aid! Even a poor person is for you a fruitful means of acquiring profit. In their need, you subject the poor to high interest loans, compelling them to pay what they do not have. You truly are merciful, enslaving for yourself the poor whom you free from bondage to another! They who have not even life's basic necessities are forced to pay exorbitant fees and high interest. Is there anything more oppressive? The poor ask for medicine and you offer poison; they beg for bread and you stretch out a sword; they appeal for

---

44. John Chrysostom, *Homily 50 on Genesis*, PG 54:450; English translation, St. John Chrysostom, *Homilies on Genesis 46-67,* trans. Robert C. Hill (Washington, D.C.: Catholic University of America Press, 1992), 54-55.

45. "These are all means which work together towards one's livelihood" can also be translated "while in reality, all of these forms of exploitation only collude against life itself." Basil, *Homily against the Rich*, PG 31:297-98.

freedom and you impose servitude; they implore you to absolve them of their bondage to you and you twist more tightly the hideous knot of the noose.[46]

Basil condemns ill-gotten and ill-used affluence, confirming that it causes one to lose touch with what it means to be a creature. If the right of possessing gold belongs to anyone, Ambrose argues that usually it belongs to the poor, who are the ones who risk their lives and expend their labor mining for what enriches others, not themselves:

> By the needy is gold acquired yet to the needy is it denied. The needy toil and labor to seek out and find what they will never be permitted to possess.[47]

Zeno of Verona (ca. 300-ca. 380) was bishop of Verona, Italy. Very little is known of his life, including whether or not he was martyred (some list him as a martyr, others as a confessor). We do have, however, several homilies attributed to him, largely against the Arians, but also encouraging his people to live moral lives dedicated to justice and charity.

Zeno of Verona here speaks about how sometimes laws were put in place to protect the powerful, and how the most serious of sins was the exploitation of the most vulnerable,[48]

> Avarice . . . is the enemy of justice. Because of avarice, the granaries of some are full of wheat while the stomachs of many are empty. Because of avarice, the price of a product increases with its scarcity. Avarice is the cause of fraud, perjury, robbery, conflicts, and war; each day wealth is sought at the moaning of others. The confiscation of goods is habitually called "industry;" the appetite for others' goods is prodded on attentively with the most heated arguments under the pretext of self-defense, so that whoever is defenseless, although innocent, will lose through the legal system whatever they have, which is worse than any violence. For that which is taken by force one day will be recovered while that which is taken by protection of the law cannot be recovered. Let whosoever wishes to boast of this injustice do so; however, let it be known that more miserable than the miserably poor is the one who becomes rich through the misery of others.[49]

---

46. Ambrose, *On the Book of Tobias*, PL 14:800.
47. Ambrose, *On the Story of Naboth*, PL 14:783.
48. For an interesting interpretation on this topic, see Harold V. Bennett, *Injustice Made Legal* (Grand Rapids: Eerdmans, 2002).
49. Zeno of Verona, *Treatise 3 On Justice*, PL 11:286.

Ironically, as many of these church fathers point out, while many seek to become something through their money, it often undoes them; instead of finding themselves through the accumulation of possessions, they often end up losing themselves. Instead of getting more in touch with reality, they live in a fantasy world of their own illusions, disconnected from the true sources of happiness that can be found only in love emanating from a right relationship with God and others.

FOLLOWING THE WAY OF CHRIST

The church fathers relativized, and even ridiculed, everything in light of the surpassing gift of Christ. Their primary concern was discipleship. Their motive was not to make rich or powerful people feel guilty but to liberate people from the status quo, which baptized the injustices of their own day and age. While they did not conceive of the possibility of radically changing unjust structures and institutions, they did seek to awaken people to the immense responsibility that the resources entrusted to them demanded, following the scriptural directive, "Much will be required of the person entrusted with much, and still more will be demanded of the person entrusted with more" (Lk 12:48b).

True Possessions Are in Heaven

Conforming their lives to Christ was the central concern of the fathers, which has direct implications for how people understand and use their goods and possessions. Their words were both deconstructive and constructive, descriptive and prescriptive, as they hold forth a compelling vision of Christian life and virtue and cut through the erroneous framework of their time. In many respects much of their reflection on poverty and justice is an extended meditation on the passage, "Do not store up for yourselves treasures on earth, where moth and decay destroy, and thieves break in and steal. But store up treasures in heaven, where neither moth nor decay destroys, nor thieves break in and steal" (Mt 6:19-20). They were interested in helping people judge wisely the things of earth and to love the things of heaven (Col 3:1-2).[50] As Clement of Alexandria put it, "wisdom is not bought with coin of earth, nor is it sold in the market-place, but in heaven. And it is sold for true coin, the immortal Word, the regal gold."[51]

---

50. These words are also part of the Roman Catholic Sacramentary and are part of the liturgical prayers of the church. National Conference of Catholic Bishops, *The Sacramentary* (New York: Catholic Book Publishing, 1985), 11.

51. Clement of Alexandria, *The Instructor*, book II, chap. III, PG 8:437. *The Ante-Nicene Fathers*, 2.248.

Chrysostom points out that it is senseless to settle for earthly ambitions when far greater heavenly awards await us,

> Only the virtues of the soul are properly our own, as alms-giving and charity. Worldly goods, even by those without, were called external things, because they are without us. But let us make them internal. For we cannot take our wealth with us, when we depart from here, but we can take our charities. But let us rather send them before us, that they may prepare for us an abode in the eternal mansions. (Lk 16:9)[52]

Discipleship means making space for the Lord amidst the many ways we are pressured to crowd him out of our lives. As Augustine observed,

> Many people, however, have no interest in making a place for the Lord; they seek their own interests, love their own possessions, rejoice in their own power, and are greedy for private property. Anyone who wants to make a place for the Lord must take the opposite line. He or she should rejoice not in what is privately owned but in what is common to all. That is what the first Christians did by making their private goods common. But did they thereby lose what they had owned? No, and I will tell you why not. If all things had remained private property, each person would have owned only what belonged to him or her individually; but when each person turned over his personal things to common ownership, he came to own what had belonged to others as well.[53]

When one does not know how to make room for the Lord and the poor, one is not a master of his wealth but its slave.

> Cyprian (ca. 205-258) was the bishop of Carthage and a great theologian from Christian North Africa during a time of intense persecution and confusion. He was born a wealthy pagan, and after his conversion he sold his vast estates and gave most of the proceeds to the needy. He also wrote some pastoral treatises on the need for equity in society, particularly in the wake of devastating barbarian invasions, called *On the Morality* and *On Works and Alms*.

In their quest to live lives of true freedom, many of the fathers looked to the first generation of Christians for how rightly to understand their possessions: "The community of believers was of one heart and mind, and no one

---

52. John Chrysostom, *Homily 11 On 1 Timothy*, PG 62:556. English translation in *Nicene and Post-Nicene Fathers*, First Series, vol. 13, trans. Gross Alexander (Peabody, Mass.: Hendrickson, 1999), 443.

53. Maria Boulding, *The Works of Saint Augustine: A Translation for the 21st Century* III/20, ed. Boniface Ramsey (Hyde Park, N.Y.: New City Press, 2004), 158-59.

claimed that any of his possessions was his own, but they had everything in common" (Acts 4:32). They believe that another cost of wealth is that it weakens the spirit. In the midst of persecution in third-century Carthage, Cyprian laments the failure of Christians to conform to the standards and ideals lived by the earliest Christian community described in Acts:

> But amongst us, that unity of mind has weakened in proportion as the generosity of our charity has crumbled away. In those days, they would sell their houses and estates and lay up to themselves treasure in heaven by giving money to the Apostles for distribution to those in need. But now, we do not even give tithes on our patrimony, and whereas Our Lord tells us to sell, we buy instead and accumulate. To such an extent has active faith withered among us, to such an extent have our people lost their old steadfastness in belief. That is why Our Lord says in his Gospel, with an eye on our times: "When the Son of man comes, will he find faith on the earth?" (Lk 18:8). We see what He foretold happening before our eyes. As to fear of God, or sense of justice, or charity, or good works—faith inspires us to none of them.[54]

True wealth consists not in the accumulation of goods, but in their distribution to others in need, not in cultivating one's bank account but in cultivating one's heart, not in having more but in being more. Echoing Jesus' own warning against gaining a world of possessions but losing one's soul, Chrysostom posed the following questions:

> What benefit is it to a man who has gained money but has not gained virtue? Why do you take others' possessions and lose your own? "I have," he says, "fruitful land." What of it? You do not have a fruitful soul. "I have slaves." But you do not have virtue. "I have clothing." But you have not obtained piety. You have what belongs to another, but you do not have what is your own. If someone gives you a deposit of money in trust, I cannot call you rich, can I? No. Why not? Because you have another's money. For this is a deposit; I wish it were only a deposit, and not a sum added to your punishment.[55]

Summarizing the centrality of spiritual growth and magnanimity, Ambrose counsels the following: "What you should give the needy is to your advantage; what diminishes, increases for you. He who feeds the poor,

---

54. Saint Cyprian, *The Unity of the Catholic Church*, ed. Johannes Quasten and Joseph Plumpe, Ancient Christian Writers (Westminster, Md.: Newman Press, 1957), 66-67.

55. John Chrysostom, *Sermon 6 On Lazarus and the Rich Man*, PG 48:1039; see also Saint John Chrysostom, *On Wealth and Poverty*, 116.

helps himself and has benefits. Mercy is planted on earth and germinates in heaven."[56]

Simple Life Is Freeing

Many early church writers believed that one of the ways of setting one's heart on the higher gifts entailed denying oneself some of the lesser gifts. They believed that a simple life is freeing. The fathers sometimes noted that the more people feed their desires, the more they want, and the fathers believed that paradoxically only by putting a restraint on our desires can we ever really know true Christian freedom. Like Chrysostom, Gregory of Nyssa stresses the importance of distinguishing needs from wants:

> So we say to God: give us bread. Not delicacies or riches, nor magnificent purple robes, golden ornaments, precious stones, or silver dishes. Nor do we ask Him for landed estates, or military commands, or political leadership. We pray neither for herds of horses and oxen or other cattle in great numbers, nor for a host of slaves. We do not say, give us a prominent position in assemblies or monuments and statues raised to us, nor silken robes and musicians at meals, nor any other thing by which the soul is estranged from the thought of God and higher things; no—but only bread![57]

As John Chrysostom reminds us in his sermons on repentance and reform, excess in anything cripples the spirit. In fact, as Chrysostom explains, having more becomes as much of a hindrance to the spiritual journey as wearing an over-sized sandal:

> What is beyond our wants, is superfluous and useless. Put on a sandal which is larger than your foot! You will not endure it; for it is a hindrance to the step. Thus also a house larger than necessity requires, is an impediment to your progress towards heaven. Do you wish to build large and splendid houses? I forbid it not; but let it be not upon the earth! Build yourself tabernacles in heaven, and such that you may be able to receive others— tabernacles that shall never be dissolved! Why are you mad about fleeting things; and things that must be left here? Nothing is more fallacious than wealth. Today it is for you; tomorrow it is against you.[58]

---

56. Ambrose, *On the Story of Naboth*, PL 14: 783.

57. Gregory of Nyssa, *Sermon 4 On The Lord's Prayer*, PG 44:1169; see also *St. Gregory of Nyssa: The Lord's Prayer, the Beatitudes*, trans. Hilda C. Graef (London: Newman Press, 1954), 63-64.

58. John Chrysostom, *Homily 2: To the People of Antioch*, PG 49:41; see also *The Homilies of St. John Chrysostom, Archbishop of Constantinople; On the Statues, or To the People of Antioch*, 104.

Voluntary Poverty Liberates

The most radical expression of self-denial at the service of these deeper heavenly desires expresses itself in voluntary poverty. Nonetheless, unless such renunciation achieves a deeper freedom of spirit and takes shape within the larger framework of imitating Christ, the renunciation entailed in voluntary poverty is superficial. As Basil cautions:

> Poverty is not always praiseworthy, but only that which is practiced intentionally according to the evangelical aim. Many are poor in their resources, but very grasping in their intention; poverty does not save these; on the contrary, their intention condemns them. Accordingly, not he who is poor is by all means blessed, but he who has considered the command of Christ better than the treasures of the world.[59]

The opposite is also true. John Chrysostom warns:

> The very heathens disbelieve the things that we say, since our doings, not our sayings, are the demonstration which they are willing to receive from us; and when they see us building ourselves fine houses, and laying out gardens and baths, and buying fields, they are not willing to believe that we are preparing for another sort of residence away from our city.[60]

Excess wealth enjoyed by Christians in a world of misery is a counter-witness to the Gospel, but above all, at the heart of poverty, according to the Gospel, is a spirit of love that claims Christ as the greatest treasure of life.

WEALTH AND WISDOM: A GOLDEN HEART AND HEAVENLY RICHES

While the church fathers acknowledge that the world we live in is messy and complex, they hold out the vision that Christian life offers an alternative to the empire and a different way of living and being in the world. They know that the kingdom of God in its fullness is beyond us, but they reiterate that it begins now and it should be reflected in the way Christians live their lives. They call people to reread life, not according to what the world is but according to who God is. When we do this we see that we are part of a common

---

59. Basil, *Homily on Psalm 33*, PG 29:361 (incorrectly referenced as 561 in Migne translation). See also *Saint Basil Exegetic Homilies*, trans. Agnes Clare Way (Washington, D.C.: Catholic University of America Press, 1963), 255-56.

60. Chrysostom, *Homily 12 On the Gospel of Matthew*, PG 56:697; English translation in *Nicene and Post-Nicene Fathers*, First Series, vol. 10, 79.

body of Christ that connects us to one another and by implication calls us to care for one another.

The church fathers help us see better the integral relationship between the Holy Trinity and the human family, between Christian faith and social justice, and between God's invitation to dance and our response. They urge their hearers to grow in wisdom by keeping these truths in mind: God is Lord, life is finite, and ultimately all of us will be judged by how we live our lives and use what is entrusted to us. They did not hesitate to emphasize that the disorder in this world will be reversed: the sorrowful will be comforted, the excluded welcomed, and the poor blessed. In the end, they reiterate that the divine economy greatly contrasts with the present order of things, and as Ambrose reminds us, death is the great equalizer:

> [At the time of death] a narrow plot is more than enough for rich and poor alike, and the earth, which did not contain the desire of the rich when alive, now totally holds the rich person captive in death. Nature, therefore, knows not how to distinguish between rich and poor when we are born; it knows not how to so discriminate when we die.[61]

In the end, as Chrysostom explains, the great tragedy of life is when riches result in exploiting others and in breaking down relationships rather than helping people and making the world better.

> The body of the rich man has been given to the earth, but the sight of his great monuments does not allow the memory of his greed to be buried with him. All who pass by, upon contemplating the greatness and wealth of the rich man's splendid house, will not cease to say, either to themselves or to their neighbor: "With how many tears was this house built! How many children lost their fathers [in its construction], and are left behind in abject poverty? How many widows were exploited, and how many laborers were robbed of their daily wages?" Therefore, everything happens the other way around for you: you wanted to enjoy glory while you lived, yet even after death, you do not rid yourself of accusers. The house carrying your name carved on its façade makes countless witnesses, even of those who never saw you alive, to cast blame upon you.[62]

Lamenting the missed opportunities to do good, Ambrose indicted those who keep their wealth only for themselves:

> Expensive ornaments fill you with delight while others have not [even] bread [with which to fill their empty stomachs] . . . As you put on costly

---

61. Ambrose, *On the Story of Naboth*, PL 14:731B.
62. John Chrysostom, *Homily on Psalm 48*, PG 55:516-17.

adornments, how terrible—oh rich one—is the judgment which you likewise put upon yourself! Exploited, the people starve, and you close your granaries! The people cry out in despair, and you toy with your jeweled ring. Oh unhappy one, in whose power it is to save from death the lives of so many and to have not the will to do so! Just the jewel of your ring could preserve the lives of the entire population.[63]

Zeno of Verona adds, "If you sold one of your jewels, and distributed its price among the poor, you would know by the needs met of how many sufferings your ornament is worth."[64]

Even though these sayings of the church fathers carry an ancient message, they have a contemporary meaning. They perceptively name some of the indicting and liberating truths about human life that all people in every generation face as we seek to understand the challenge of living in responsible relationship with God, others, and creation. In a time closer to our own, the movie *Schindler's List* is the story of how one man used his business and his resources to save Jews who were threatened with extermination at the hands of the Nazis. At the end of the movie Schindler is surrounded by some of the people he helped during the war. He breaks down in tears during his farewell speech as he realizes how many more people he could have saved if he had had more money, or if he had spent it more wisely, or if he had started caring sooner. Even while he saved over eleven hundred people from certain death and even risked his own life in the process, he felt he did not do enough and could have helped more people. Like the teachings of the church fathers, Schindler's life shows that tragedy, in the end, is not discovering that one could have done more good, but in discovering that one had the opportunity to do good yet did nothing. Many never realize how their resources could have been used to help others until it is too late. The early church writers emphasize that what matters in the end are people, not things; the treasure of heaven, not the wealth of earth; a golden heart, not golden riches. Chrysostom sums up the message this way:

If it is possible for you, remember everything I have said. If you cannot remember everything . . . I beg you, remember this without fail, that not to share our own wealth with the poor is theft from the poor and deprivation of their means of life; we do not possess our own wealth but theirs.[65]

---

63. Ambrose, *On the Story of Naboth*, PL 14:784.

64. Zeno of Verona, *On Justice*, PL 11:287.

65. John Chrysostom, *Sermon 2 on Lazarus and the Rich Man*, PG 48:991; see also Saint John Chrysostom, *On Wealth and Poverty*, 54–55.

QUESTIONS FOR REFLECTION

1. What passages of the early church fathers are most striking to you? Why?
2. What common threads in human experience do the church fathers name? In what ways do their words help us claim what is true in our own times?
3. What does the "universal destination of all goods" mean? In what ways is the notion of private property beneficial and detrimental?
4. Have you observed situations in which riches can be dangerous?
5. How do we know when our possessions own us, rather than the other way around?
6. How would you distinguish ownership from stewardship?
7. If social and economic distinctions mean nothing to God, why do they mean so much to human beings?
8. Can a Christian be rich and faithful at the same time? Explain.
9. Are the sayings of the church fathers suitable only for Christians, or do they have more universal appeal?
10. Why is it valuable to study these writings? What significance does it have for our own lives?

SUGGESTIONS FOR FURTHER READING AND STUDY

Avila, Charles. *Ownership: Early Christian Teaching.* Maryknoll, N.Y.: Orbis Books, 1983.

Bennett, Harold V. *Injustice Made Legal.* Grand Rapids: Eerdmans, 2002.

Boff, Leonardo. *Trinity and Society.* Maryknoll, N.Y.: Orbis Books, 1988.

Chrysostom, John. *On Wealth and Poverty.* Translated by Catharine P. Roth. Crestwood, N.Y.: St. Vladimir's Seminary Press, 1984.

Evans, G. R., ed. *The First Christian Theologians.* Malden, Mass.: Blackwell, 2004.

Frend, W. H. C. *The Early Church.* Minneapolis: Fortress, 1982.

González, Justo L. *Faith and Wealth.* San Francisco: Harper & Row, 1990.

Harmless, William. *Desert Christians.* New York: Oxford University Press, 2004.

Holman, Susan R. *The Hungry Are Dying: Beggars and Bishops in Roman Cappadocia.* New York: Oxford University Press, 2001.

Hunt, Anne. *Trinity: Nexus of the Mysteries of Christian Faith.* Theology in Global Perspective. Maryknoll, N.Y.: Orbis Books, 2005.

LaCugna, Catherine Mowry. *God for Us: The Trinity & Christian Life.* New York: HarperCollins, 1992.

O'Collins, Gerald. *The Tripersonal God: Understanding and Interpreting the Trinity.* New York: Paulist, 1999.

Phan, Peter C. *Social Thought.* Message of the Fathers of the Church 20. Wilmington, Del.: Michael Glazier, 1984.

Richardson, Cyril, ed. *Early Christian Fathers.* New York: Simon & Schuster, 1996.

4

A God of Life, A Civilization of Love

Catholic Social Teaching

On a dangerous sea coast where shipwrecks often occur, there was once a crude little life-saving station. The building was just a hut, and there was only one boat, but the few devoted members kept a constant watch over the sea, and with no thought for themselves went out day and night tirelessly searching for the lost. Many lives were saved by this wonderful little station, so that it became famous. Some of those who were saved and various others in the surrounding area wanted to become associated with the station and give of their time and money and effort for the support of its work. New boats were bought and new crews were trained. The little life-saving station grew.

Some of the members of the life-saving station were unhappy that the building was so crude and poorly equipped. They felt that a more comfortable place should be provided as the first refuge of those saved from the sea. They replaced the emergency cots with beds and put better furniture in the enlarged building. Now the life-saving station became a popular gathering place for its members, and they decorated it beautifully and furnished it exquisitely because they used it as a sort of club. Fewer members were now interested in going to sea on life-saving missions, so they hired life-boat crews to do this work. The life-saving motif still prevailed in this club's decorations and there was a special room where the club initiations were held. About this time, a large ship was wrecked off the coast, and the hired crews brought in boatloads of cold, wet, and half-drowned people. They were dirty and sick and some of them had black skin and some had yellow skin. The beautiful new club was in chaos. So the property committee immediately had a shower built outside the club where victims of shipwreck could be cleaned up before coming inside.

At the next meeting, there was a split in the club membership. Most of the members wanted to stop the club's life-saving activities as being unpleasant and a hindrance to the normal social life of the club. Some members insisted upon life-saving as their primary purpose and pointed out that they were still called a life-saving station. But they were finally voted down and told that if they wanted to save the lives of all the various kinds of people who were shipwrecked in those waters, they could begin their own life-saving station down the coast. They did.

As the years went by, the new station experienced the same changes that had occurred in the old. It evolved into a club, and yet another life-saving station was founded. History continued to repeat itself, and if you visit that sea coast today, you will find a number of exclusive clubs along that shore. Shipwrecks are frequent in those waters, but most of the people drown![1]

IN IMITATION OF CHRIST, the church's central task has always been "to seek and to save what was lost" (Lk 19:10). This challenge has always been at the heart of the Gospel message. Even though globalization has brought about some measure of human progress, many people today are still drowning at sea in the undercurrent of war, oppression, poverty, greed, abuse, drugs, fear, racism, meaninglessness, materialism, and many other perennial problems. Amidst these challenges, the church's mission remains constant: to reach out to people who are shipwrecked in any way, to proclaim the God of Life, and to build a civilization of love.

Part of the difficulty in fulfilling this mission, however, involves not only the problems at sea but also the problems at the rescue stations. Institutional limitations, alongside the personal and collective failures of the church, can create a thick fog of suspicion in people's minds that obscures the perception of the Gospel message. The ancient maxim *Ecclesia semper reformanda* means that the church, which is made up of fallible human beings, must be in a state of constant reformation in order to give more authentic witness to the light of Christ. Especially amidst the troubled waters of our times, it is good to take a step back from the scandals, corruption, and sins of the church in order to remember and reflect upon its central purpose.

One way to understand the church's mission is to study its social teachings. While the two previous chapters examined the Christian vision of justice in light of biblical and patristic sources, in this chapter we will look more specifically at some of the principles that guide and govern that vision. These principles, drawn in large part from biblical and patristic wisdom, offer a systematic understanding of what the church believes (orthodoxy) and how it lives out what it believes (orthopraxy), particularly in the exercise of charity and justice. After some foundational considerations, we will examine the

---

1. The original text, to which I have made slight modification, is from Theodore O. Wedel, "Evangelism: The Mission of the Church to Those Outside Her Life," *Ecumenical Review* 6, no. 1 (1953): 24.

core content of Catholic social teaching as it presents the social demands of Christian faith in a God of Life. Understanding Catholic social teaching in light of a God of Life, and using it as an acronymic framework for its major themes, offers us a valuable moral compass, which can assist us as we seek to navigate our way through the troubled waters of our own day and age.

CATHOLIC SOCIAL TEACHING: AN ETHICAL FOUNDATION FOR GLOBAL TRANSFORMATION

In general terms, Catholic social teaching refers to all the principles, concepts, ideas, theories, and doctrines that deal with human life and society as it has evolved over time since the days of the early church.[2] Catholic social teaching seeks to challenge those dimensions of society that diminish people's relationships with God, others, the environment, and themselves and to promote those factors that enhance these relationships. Catholic social teaching is not, however, a fixed, unchanging body of doctrine but a developmental understanding of the church's social mission in a dynamically changing world. While it draws heavily on theology, it also bases its reflection on philosophy, economics, sociology, and other social sciences. By linking theology with the academic disciplines, Catholic social teaching seeks to understand better the challenges of the current world and to provide an ethical foundation for global transformation.

In more specific terms modern Catholic social teaching refers to contemporary church and papal documents and encyclicals that address the social problems of today's world (tables 4 and 5). Although Benedict XIV (1740-1758) began issuing papal encyclicals in the eighteenth century,[3] most scholars agree that this era of modern Catholic social teaching began with the publication of Pope Leo XIII's *Rerum Novarum* in 1891.[4] This document

---

2. Kenneth R. Himes, ed., *Modern Catholic Social Teaching: Commentaries and Interpretations* (Washington, D.C.: Georgetown University Press, 2005). For an introduction to the topic of Catholic social teaching, see also Himes, *Responses to 101 Questions on Catholic Social Teaching* (New York: Paulist, 2001). I would like to thank Ken Himes and Jeffry Odell Korgen for their helpful comments on this chapter. I am especially grateful to Liz Murdock LaFortune for sharing her wisdom and insight as an experienced educator in Catholic social teaching and helping shape this chapter into its current form.

3. Michael Schuck, *That They Be One: The Social Teaching of the Papal Encyclicals 1740-1849* (Washington, D.C.: Georgetown University Press, 1991).

4. For more on the topic of Catholic social teaching in contemporary times, see David J. Shannon and Thomas A. O'Brien, *Catholic Social Thought: The Documentary Heritage* (Maryknoll, N.Y.: Orbis Books, 1992); Philip S. Land, *Catholic Social Teaching* (Chicago: Loyola University Press, 1994); Charles E. Curran, *Catholic Social Teaching, 1891-Present* (Washington, D.C.: Georgetown University Press, 2002); and Joe Holland, *Modern Catholic Social Teaching: The Popes Confront the Industrial Age 1740-1958* (Mahwah, N.J.: Paulist, 2003).

created a "seismic shift" in Catholic teaching by placing the church in solidarity not with the economic and political elite of society but with the working class and the poor.[5] Catholic social teaching recognizes that many today
are poor not because of laziness but because of a system of structures, policies,
and institutions that greatly diminish their options and keep them in poverty.

TABLE 4. Catholic Social Teaching at a Glance: Documents of the Universal Church

Documents of the Universal Church[6]				
Year	Document	Author	Context	Key Concept
1891	*Rerum Novarum* On the Condition of Labor	Pope Leo XIII	A new working class after the Industrial Revolution	Human dignity
1931	*Quadragesimo Anno* The Reconstruction of the Social Order	Pope Pius XI	After the Great Depression; rise of dictatorships in Europe	Subsidiarity
1961	*Mater et Magistra* Christianity and Social Progress	Pope John XXIII	Growing technological development alongside terrible poverty in Asia, Africa, and Latin America	Internationalization
1963	*Pacem in Terris* Peace on Earth	Pope John XXIII	The cold war; building of the Berlin Wall; Cuban missile crisis	Human rights
1965	*Gaudium et Spes* The Church in the Modern World	Vatican II	Cold war and the arms race	Signs of the times
1967	*Populorum Progressio* The Development of Peoples	Pope Paul VI	Vietnam War; African nations fighting for independence	Development
1971	*Octogesima Adveniens* A Call to Action	Pope Paul VI	Worldwide recession; new political reform movements	Political action

---

5. Edward DeBerri and James E. Hug, *Catholic Social Teaching: Our Best Kept Secret*, 4th ed.
(Maryknoll, N.Y.: Orbis Books, 2003).

6. While there is some variation in regard to which documents are considered part of the body
of modern Catholic social teaching, these are some of the most commonly cited documents. Most
of these documents are available online at http://www.vatican.va and http://www.cctwincities.org/
CatholicSocialTeaching. Some elements of this table are drawn from "Busy Christian's Guide to
Catholic Social Teaching" at U.S. Catholic, February 25, 2009, http://www.uscatholic.org.

Documents of the Universal Church (*continued*)				
Year	Document	Author	Context	Key Concept
1971	*Justitia in Mundo* Justice in the World	Synod of Bishops	Political turmoil around the world	Justice
1975	*Evangelii Nuntiandi* Evangelization in the Modern World	Pope Paul VI	Problems of atheism, consumerism, secularism, hedonism, indifference	Evangelization
1981	*Laborem Exercens* On Human Work	Pope John Paul II	Rise in power of multinational corporations; unemployment and exploitation of workers	Work
1987	*Sollicitudo Rei Socialis* On Social Concern	Pope John Paul II	Increasingly heavy debt in underdeveloped countries; unemployment	Underdevelopment, structural sin
1990	*Redemptoris Missio* The Missionary Activity of the Church	Pope John Paul II	Meaninglessness and confusion; rethinking of mission in contemporary world	Mission
1991	*Centesimus Annus* The Centenary	Pope John Paul II	The needs of the poor are still not met	A new world order
1992	*The Catechism of the Catholic Church*		Need for systematic understanding of the basic teachings of the church	Human communion
1995	*Evangelium Vitae* The Gospel of Life	Pope John Paul II	Abortion; death penalty; euthanasia: challenge of "culture of death"	Life
2004	*Compendium of the Social Doctrine of the Church*	Pontifical Justice and Peace Commission	Need for systematic understanding of social teaching of the church	Human solidarity
2009	*Caritas in Veritate* Charity in Truth	Pope Benedict XVI	Need for a godly approach to the development of peoples	Human development in charity and truth
2013	*Evangelii Gaudium* The Joy of the Gospel	Pope Francis	Prevalence of complacent consumerism and blunted conscience in the modern world	Renewed personal encounter with Jesus Christ resulting in restored dignity to creation

The universal message of modern Catholic social teaching is directed to all nations and all peoples, and it is concerned with all aspects of the human being and the full human development of every person (PP 42). It is addressed not only to Roman Catholics but also to other ecclesial communities, other religions, and all people of good will.[7] Its purpose is not to organize society but to challenge, guide, and form the conscience of the human community as it seeks a new social order (CSDC 81). Catholic social teaching sees the process of transformation as integral to its mission of evangelization (SRS 41), which it understands not as proselytism but as a way of helping people, under the light of the Gospel, to relate to each other in life-giving ways. "Action on behalf of justice and participation in the transformation of the world," note the bishops in *Justice in the World*, "fully appear to us as a constitutive dimension of the preaching of the Gospel, or, in other words, of the Church's mission for the redemption of the human race and its liberation from every oppressive situation" (JW 6).

UNDERSTANDING CHARITY AND JUSTICE

In modern Catholic social teaching, and among those who comment on it, there is significant discussion regarding the relationship between charity and justice. It is a distinction that has evolved over time and a necessary one as we consider what is needed for social change. To some people, there is a sharp difference between these two terms whereby charity involves working to meet the immediate needs of others through direct service and direct aid to the poor, while justice involves institutional change and transforming unjust social structures. This line of reasoning seeks to bring out that personal acts of charity alone do not suffice to meet the demands of justice.[8]

The problem with this perspective, however, is that it reduces Christian charity primarily to almsgiving. Charity includes almsgiving but it involves much more. In Catholic social teaching, Christian charity (*agapē*) is a more comprehensive term that is at the core of the Gospel message and is what makes justice possible (CCC 1889). It is not so much distinct from justice,

---

7. John XXIII first began speaking of Catholic social teaching in terms of addressing all people of good will and not simply Catholics in *Pacem in Terris* (1963). See United States Catholic Conference, *Sharing Catholic Social Teaching: Challenges and Directions* (Washington, D.C.: United States Catholic Conference, 1998), for further discussion on the role of Catholic social teaching in Catholic education.

8. For commentaries on the encyclical and the proper roles of charity and justice, see Richard Ryscavage, "Bringing Back Charity," *America* 194, no. 9 (March 13, 2006): 14-16; and Thomas Massaro, "Don't Forget Justice," *America* 194, no. 9 (March 13, 2006): 18-20. See also Office for Social Justice, "Charity and Justice" (St. Paul, Minn.: Catholic Charities), a comparison chart available at http://www.cctwincities.org/document.doc?id=124.

but rather the fundamental virtue that underlies and animates the practice of justice. In other words, charity is that which is given out of love. Justice, though closely related, pertains to what each person is entitled to as a human being. Charity is "the theological virtue by which we love God above all things . . . and our neighbor as ourselves" (CCC 1822), and justice is "the moral virtue that consists in the . . . will to give their due to God and neighbor" (CCC 1807). As an expression of charity, justice begins with attention to the needs and rights of each person, but it also extends to working for social structures within larger social networks and institutions that foster life (CSDC 208).

Pope Benedict XVI in his first encyclical, *Deus Caritas Est* (26f.), speaks about "social charity" (DCE 29). He writes that the Christian call to charitable actions is born out of love, but "[l]ove . . . needs to be organized if it is to be an ordered service to the community" (DCE 20). Social charity, he notes, is directed toward the transformation of the social order, even though the state and the church have different roles in this process:

> The Church cannot and must not take upon herself the political battle to bring about the most just society possible. She cannot and must not replace the State. Yet at the same time, she cannot and must not remain on the sidelines in the fight for justice. She has to play her part through rational argument and she has to reawaken the spiritual energy without which justice, which always demands sacrifice, cannot prevail and prosper. A just society must be the achievement of politics, not of the Church. Yet the promotion of justice through efforts to bring about openness of mind and will to the demands of the common good is something which concerns the Church deeply. (DCE 28)

The social mission of the church, then, expresses itself in terms of liberating the oppressed, calling to conversion the oppressors, and eliminating the structures of oppression. Challenging the sources of injustice, however, can create controversy and conflict, especially among those who benefit from these same structures.

The following story also helps clarify how charity must be expressed both in terms of direct aid and in terms of justice:

> Once upon a time, there was a town that was built just beyond the bend of a large river. One day some of the children from the town were playing beside the river when they noticed three bodies floating in the water. They ran for help and the townsfolk quickly pulled the bodies out of the river. One body was dead so they buried it. One was alive, but quite ill, so they put that person into the hospital. The third turned out to be a healthy child,

who they then placed with a family who cared for it and who took it to school. From that day on, every day a number of bodies came floating down the river and, every day, the good people of the town would pull them out and tend to them—taking the sick to hospitals, placing the children with families, and burying those who were dead. This went on for years; each day brought its quota of bodies and the townsfolk not only came to expect a number of bodies each day but also worked at developing more elaborate systems for picking them out of the river and tending to them. Some of the townsfolk became quite generous in tending to these bodies and a few extraordinary ones even gave up their jobs so that they could tend to this concern full-time. And the town itself felt a certain healthy pride in its generosity. However, during all these years and despite all that generosity and effort, nobody thought to go up the river, beyond the bend that hid from their sight what was above them, and find out why, daily, those bodies came floating down the river.[9]

While charity expressed as direct aid begins with caring for the bodies that float down the river, charity expressed as justice also leads to transforming the social structures that cause bodies to flow down the river in the first place.

One area where bodies regularly float down the river is along the U.S. border with Mexico. In addition to the canals, the bodies of undocumented immigrants are found in the mountains and deserts, where people die in their efforts to enter the United States to find work. In response to this problem, the bishops of Mexico and the United States have spoken out against the deaths of thousands along their border. While they urge individuals, communities, and governments to meet the immediate needs of immigrants and their families, they also challenge the global economic system that precipitates their migration in the first place and the political policies that compel them to travel into dangerous territory.[10] In the area of immigration reform as well as other areas, the church's commitment to social justice comes from the conviction that liberation begins now, in this world, on this earth, even while the church waits in hope for the time when all relationships will be made right when Christ comes again at the end of time.

---

9. Ronald Rolheiser, *The Holy Longing: The Search for a Christian Spirituality* (New York: Doubleday, 1999), 168.

10. See in particular the joint statement, United States Conference of Catholic Bishops and Conferencia del Espiscopado Mexicano, *Strangers No Longer: Together on the Journey of Hope: A Pastoral Letter Concerning Migration from the Catholic Bishops of Mexico and the United States* (Washington, D.C.: United States Conference of Catholic Bishops, 2003), available at http://www.usccb.org. See also Daniel G. Groody, *Border of Death, Valley of Life: An Immigrant Journey of Heart and Spirit* (Lanham, Md.: Rowman & Littlefield, 2002).

THREE DIMENSIONS OF SOCIAL JUSTICE

While it recognizes the need and function of civil and criminal law, Catholic social teaching understands justice more broadly than simply in juridical terms. Because unjust laws that benefit the powerful and exclude the weak can become legalized in a disordered world, Catholic social teaching makes certain distinctions when speaking about social justice.[11] Drawing on a rich intellectual tradition, especially that of Thomas Aquinas and later philosophical reflection, Catholic social teaching distinguishes three primary dimensions of social justice: commutative justice, contributive justice, and distributive justice (fig. 3).[12]

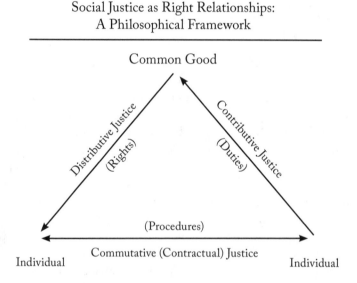

Social Justice as Right Relationships:
A Philosophical Framework

Common Good

Distributive Justice (Rights)

Contributive Justice (Duties)

(Procedures)

Individual   Commutative (Contractual) Justice   Individual

FIGURE 3. Social Justice as Right Relationships: A Philosophical Framework[13]

Commutative justice. Commutative or contractual justice deals with relationships between individuals, groups, and classes. This aspect of justice is the basic building block of society in that it deals with how individuals enter into relationship and agreements with each other. Commutative justice involves

---

11. For more on this topic, see Harold V. Bennett, *Injustice Made Legal: Deuteronomic Law and the Plight of Widows, Strangers, and Orphans in Ancient Israel* (Grand Rapids: Eerdmans, 2002).

12. Thomas Aquinas, *Summa Theologica*, II-II, 61, 5.

13. This diagram draws in part from the fine resources available on Catholic social teaching from the Office for Social Justice, St. Paul-Minneapolis, http://www.cctwincities.org. I am also grateful to Bill O'Neill, S.J., for his insights in developing it further with respect to rights, duties, procedures, and human dignity.

the give-and-take that is part of these relationships and the benefits and responsibilities that go with them. It seeks to ensure that human dignity and social responsibility are the basis of all economic transactions, contracts, and promises, recognizing that employers have an obligation to their workers to provide humane working conditions and to pay fair wages, and workers owe employers conscientious and diligent work in exchange for these fair wages (EJA 69).

Contributive justice. While commutative justice deals with the relationship of individuals with each other, contributive justice deals with an individual's relationship to society as a whole. It challenges those who take unfair advantage of a system in the name of claiming their rights without any reference to their responsibilities to a larger, collective body of society. Contributive justice recognizes the responsibility of individuals to the common good, which means that people have a duty to look out not only for their own welfare but also for that of others. Part of this obligation is fulfilled through participation in the civic life of a community, including paying taxes and voting.

Distributive justice. While individuals have a responsibility to the common good, the larger society has an obligation to individuals and groups as well. Distributive justice deals with the society's duty to the individual. It pertains to the relationship of the whole to the parts, and seeks to provide the minimum material resources that are necessary for individuals to have a humane and dignified life. As members of a human community, individuals have a right to have their basic needs met unless absolute scarcity makes this impossible. Distributive justice seeks the well-being of all members of a community, which means one's basic rights must be safeguarded and protected. It also puts special emphasis on protecting society's weaker members, advocating a greater solidarity with the poor.

Bringing commutative, contributive, and distributive justice together into one conceptual whole, social justice deals with how a society is organized and how its individuals and institutions are ordered and interact with each other.[14] At the core of social justice is a respect for each person's human dignity and an overall commitment to the common good. When such conditions are present, people have what is needed to grow into the realization of who they are called to be before God within the human community.

---

14. The term "social justice" came into being with Pius XI in his encyclicals *Quadragesimo Anno* (QA) in 1931 and his *Divini Redemptoris* (DR) in 1937. Philip Land, "Social Justice," in *The New Dictionary of Theology*, ed. Joseph A. Komonchak, Mary Collins, and Dermot A. Lane (Collegeville, Minn.: Liturgical Press, 1989), 548.

A GOD OF LIFE: A MATRIX FOR UNDERSTANDING
CATHOLIC SOCIAL TEACHING

Modern Catholic social teaching is a relatively large body of material, put together over a long period of time, written by various authors who used a variety of methodologies and addressed different social problems. All of these documents, however, draw their fundamental inspiration from one primary source: a common faith in Jesus Christ who reveals a God of Life. Many of the social problems addressed in *Rerum Novarum* in 1891 still exist today; some have even gotten worse. Moreover, many of the ethical concerns outlined by Leo XIII are sadly the same ones reiterated by John Paul II a century later.

Even though Catholic social teaching comprises a diverse body of teaching, as a whole we can identify discernible themes that remain relatively constant. Throughout the years, scholars have tried in various ways to synthesize this teaching into a systematic whole. Some have identified from seven to twenty themes that run through the documents. These treatments have been useful in identifying certain focal points of Catholic social teaching, but they have come up short in identifying a unifying thread that binds them all together. Building on these works, however, I would like to offer an overall matrix through which to connect these themes.

All of modern Catholic social teaching in one way or another speaks about A GOD OF LIFE who challenges the human community to build a civilization of love. If we look at A GOD OF LIFE as an acronymic matrix and an outline for this section, we can identify ten themes in Catholic social teaching:

1. A   analysis of social reality

2. G   gratuity of God
3. O   ordering of society toward the common good
4. D   dignity of the human person

5. O   option for the poor
6. F   freedom as rights and responsibilities

7. L   life as a sacred gift
8. I   involvement of all people in creation of a new social order
9. F   family of blood and family of humankind
10. E   environment and ecological stewardship

While we can identify other themes in Catholic social teaching, these arguably are the most important, and here we will explore these themes in more detail.

A GOD OF LIFE
Analysis of Social Reality

Catholic social teaching starts with the reality of the pressing social questions of each day and age and then analyzes them under the light of the Gospel.[15] These questions deal with work, family, war, racism, poverty, immigration, euthanasia, nuclear weapons, the economy, medical care, scientific research, politics, culture, abortion, capital punishment, the environment, and other areas that touch on human life, human dignity, and the common good. Catholic social teaching asks what demands such issues make on the human conscience, what values must be promoted, and what actions must be taken in order to achieve a just, ordered, and peaceful world. This analysis is a two-edged sword: on the one side, it critically assesses the negative dimensions of society that diminish ourselves, dehumanize others, and degrade the environment; on the other, it promotes the positive forces in society that dignify, humanize, and sustain the delicate bonds that unite us all as a human family.

The task of analysis begins with an accurate description of the world as it is and then asks, what kind of world God wants, what kind of society humans need, and what kind of system the environment can sustain. In analyzing the "signs of the times," modern Catholic social teaching seeks to understand what the Narrative of the Gospel says to a global society marked, especially in the West, by advanced industrial capitalism. While Catholic social teaching recognizes the positive dimensions of capitalism, it also asserts that the capitalist system has limits, and, if undisciplined and unchecked by moral parameters, it will diminish if not destroy the integrity of the human community.

Catholic social teaching analyzes the social order on global and local levels through documents addressed to the universal and regional church (tables 4 and 5). The documents addressed to the universal church offer the broad theological contours and moral principles derived from its faith in a God of Life and shed light on the major social questions of the world. The documents addressed to the regional churches deal with how these universal principles are appropriated and adapted, and they are further elaborated upon through various talks, speeches, and papers of individual church leaders. The *Compendium of the Social Doctrine of the Church* (CSDC) published in 2004 by the Pontifical Council for Justice and Peace synthesizes many of the teachings of the universal and regional church and marks a step forward in presenting a systematic understanding of Catholic social teaching. Together these documents seek to communicate what this teaching means within the specific challenges on state, national, and continental levels (SRS 9; OA 4).

---

15. For more on the method of social analysis in Catholic social teaching, see Joe Holland and Peter Henriot, *Social Analysis: Linking Faith and Justice* (Maryknoll, N.Y.: Orbis Books, 2003).

TABLE 5. Catholic Social Teaching at a Glance: Documents of the Regional Churches

Documents of Regional Churches[16]				
Year	Document	Author	Context	Key Concept
North America				
1979	Brothers and Sisters to Us	U.S. Bishops	Political freedom but racial and social inequity	Racial equality
1983	The Challenge of Peace: God's Promise and Our Response	U.S. Bishops	Cold war; nuclear arms race	Nuclear disarmament
1984	The Hispanic Presence: Challenge and Commitment	U.S. Bishops	Increased immigration; exponential growth in Latino population	Multiculturalism
1986	Economic Justice for All	U.S. Bishops	33 million poor in 1986 and 8 million unemployed in the U.S.	Economic justice
1986	To the Ends of the Earth	U.S. Bishops	Contamination of air, water, land; ozone depletion	Environmental stewardship
1991	Renewing the Earth: An Invitation to Reflection and Action on the Environment in Light of Catholic Social Teaching	U.S. Bishops	Environmental crisis; burden on the poor	Natural ecology; social ecology
1993	The Harvest of Justice Is Sown in Peace	U.S. Bishops	International injustice; regional wars; arms trade	Peacemaking
1996	The Struggle against Poverty: A Sign of Hope in Our World	Canadian Bishops	Economic disparity in the world	Development
1999	Ecclesia in America	Pope John Paul II	Economic polarization between North America and Central and South America	Globalization of solidarity

---

16. For a collection of summaries of Catholic social teaching documents, see DeBerri and Hug, *Catholic Social Teaching*; Terence McGoldrick, "Episcopal Conferences Worldwide on Catholic Social Teaching," *Theological Studies* 59, no. 1 (1998): 22-50.

	Documents of the Regional Churches (*continued*)			
Year	Document	Author	Context	Key Concept
North America (continued)				
2000	Responsibility, Rehabilitation, and Restoration: A Catholic Perspective on Crime and Criminal Justice	U.S. Bishops	Increasing crime	Human dignity applies to victim and offender; alternatives to current criminal justice models
2001	Global Climate Change: A Plea for Dialogue, Prudence and the Common Good	U.S. Bishops	Climate change	Stewardship; economic initiative
2003	Strangers No Longer: Together on a Journey of Hope	U.S./Mexican Bishops	Restrictive immigration policies; increased deaths at border	Justice and immigration
2003	For I Was Hungry and You Gave Me Food	U.S. Bishops	Concentration of power; globalization	Food, farmers, and farm workers
2005	A Culture of Life and the Penalty of Death	U.S. Bishops	25th year after Bishops called for ending the death penalty	Renewed call for an end to the death penalty
2009	Respecting the Just Rights of Workers: Guidance and Options for Catholic Health Care and Unions	U.S. Bishops	Follow up to original document, "A Fair and Just Workplace"	CST shapes actions of unions and management in assuring workers free and fair representation in the workplace
Central and Latin America[17]				
1968	The Medellín Conference Documents	Latin American Episcopal Conference	Vatican II; greater consciousness of poverty and its causes	Vatican II reforms in Latin America
1979	The Puebla Conference Documents	Latin American Episcopal Conference	John Paul II's visit to Mexico, affirming Medellín	Option for the poor
2002	The People of God Journeying in Central America	Central American Bishops	Free trade agreements	Solidarity

---

17. These documents are published in various texts and are available at the Spring Hill College Theological Library website, http://www.shc.edu/theolibrary/cstdocs.htm.

Documents of the Regional Churches (*continued*)				
Year	Document	Author	Context	Key Concept
Central and Latin America (continued)				
2002	Ethical and Gospel Imperatives for Overcoming Dire Poverty and Hunger	Brazilian Bishops	Social inequality; globalization	Human dignity
2007	Aparecida	Latin American Episcopal Conference	Fifth General Conference of the Latin American and Caribbean Bishops' Conferences	Challenges and demands necessitated by a new social and political turbulence
Africa[18]				
1981	Justice and Evangelization in Africa	Africa and Madagascar Episcopal Conferences (SECAM)	Foreign intervention; unjust distribution of resources	Education; participation
1992	The Future Is Ours	Zambian Bishops	1991 elections; economic need	Responsibility; accountability
1995	Ecclesia in Africa	Pope John Paul II	Massive poverty; Africa marginalized in global economy	Evangelization
1999	Economic Justice in South Africa	Southern African Bishops	Second democratic elections in South Africa	Christian economic values
2000	Christ Is Our Peace	African Bishops	Ethnic wars; racism; slavery; migration in Africa	Reconciliation; peace
2005	Be Not Afraid	Kenyan Bishops	Proposed new constitution for Kenya	Duty to vote; condemnation of violence
2005	Give Hope to Our People	Zambian Bishops	Review of Zambian Constitution	Dialogue; peace
Asia[19]				
1974	Evangelization in Modern Day Asia	Asian Bishops	Industrialization; secularization	Signs of the times

18. Information on these documents is available at the Center of Concern website, http://www.coc.org, and at Symposium of Episcopal Conferences of Africa and Madagascar (SECAM), http://www.secam-sceam.org. See also Association of Member Episcopal Conferences in East Africa, http://amecea.org.

19. Information on the Federation of Asian Bishops' Conferences is available at http://www.fabc.org.

Documents of the Regional Churches (*continued*)				
Year	Document	Author	Context	Key Concept
Asia (continued)				
1990	Journeying Together toward the Third Millennium	Asian Bishops	Collapse of the Berlin Wall	Solidarity
2000	A Renewed Church in Asia: A Mission of Love and Service	Asian Bishops	Renewal of church in Asia	Globalization
2002	Towards a Culture of Peace in the 21st Century: Our Responses as Christians to Social Advocacy	Asian Bishops	Globalization	Tasks ahead for peace and nonviolence
2011	Global Warming and Climate Change and Its Impact on Asia: Challenges and the Response of the Church	Asian Bishops	Climate change	Environmental stewardship
Australia[20]				
1998	A Milestone for the Human Family	Australian Bishops	50th anniversary of Declaration on Human Rights	Human rights and duties
2008	A Rich Young Nation: The Challenge of Affluence and Poverty in Australia	Australian Bishops	Affluence in Australia	Overcoming increasing polarization of society; human solidarity
2011	Building Bridges, Not Walls: Prisons and the Justice System	Australian Bishops	Rising prison population in Australia	Constructive alternatives to imprisonment; rehabilitation of prisoners
2013	Lazarus at Our Gate: A Critical Moment in the Fight against World Poverty	Australian Bishops	Assessing progress of MDGs just prior to 2015 target year	Renewed vision to combat world poverty

---

20. See Australia Catholic Bishops Conference's website, http://www.catholic.org.au.

Documents of the Regional Churches (*continued*)				
Year	Document	Author	Context	Key Concept
Europe[21]				
1996	The Common Good and the Catholic Church's Social Teaching	Bishops of England and Wales	Pessimism; upcoming elections	Democracy; human rights
2005	Towards the Common Good	Bishops of Ireland	Globalization of Irish economy; disparity in who benefits	Success; responsibility to the common good
2008	Mission to Migrants	Bishops of England and Wales	Increasing migration	Cultural and spiritual patrimony of migrants and how they enrich the church
2010	Meeting God in Friend and Stranger	Bishops of England and Wales	Increasing religious diversity	Interreligious dialogue
2010	Choosing the Common Good	Bishops of England and Wales	General election of 2010	Highlights key themes of CST

As it analyzes the cultural, political, economic, social, and religious structures that govern the development of civilization, Catholic social teaching addresses the problems that impede development, such as hunger, illiteracy, inadequate health care, poor sanitation, environmental contamination, corruption, political and economic instability, and inadequate social infrastructures (PP 56-61). Catholic social teaching denounces these maladies as contrary to the will of the God of Life. At the same time, it announces the will of this same God through its commitment to peace, justice, and human rights (RM 42).

A GOD OF LIFE
Gratuity of God

If analysis begins with reality, then Christian theology begins with God's gratuity. The gratuity of God means that all is a gift: all that we are, all that we own, all that we live in, and all those to whom we belong. In contrast to a society that more and more sees life in terms of self-generating accomplishments and hard-won possessions, Catholic social teaching believes that

---

21. See Catholic Bishops' of England and Wales websites, http://www.catholic-ew.org.uk and http://www.cctwincities.org.

everything flows as a gift of love from a God of Life. From the beginning, man and woman, created in the image and likeness of God (Gn 1:26-27), are called to embody visibly God's gratuity in a garden of life, where human beings are tasked with the work of cultivating the land and being stewards of the goods of the earth (CSDC 26). Catholic social teaching recognizes that God's gratuity is an unmerited gift, but it also makes demands on us as we seek to live and love as God does (Jn 13:34).

Catholic social teaching bases its ethical principles on the belief that God's gratuity is manifested especially in the gift of God's Son, who comes to earth not because of human merit but because of God's own desire to offer new life and to heal a broken world. Unless one sees God's gratuity as the starting point for ethical reflection, personal and social morality can be perceived as a set of arbitrary rules and regulations set forth by a policing God or a rigid and imposing church leadership. Personal and social morality flow above all from God's a priori free gift *of life* and free gift *of self*, and morality flows as a response to love, from a desire to give as one has been given to, to love as one has been loved, to conform one's life according to the Life-Giver. To follow Jesus, then, means patterning one's life on God's graciousness and mercy, of loving others without condition, of seeing one's connection to a common human family that is created by a God of Life, burdened by sin, but redeemed by love. It is only from the gratuitous love of God revealed in Jesus Christ that the church even begins to speak of social justice and a new morality.

A G**O**D OF LIFE
Ordering Society toward the Common Good

For each human being truly to develop as God intends, Catholic social teaching speaks about the imperative of ordering society according to the common good of all peoples.[22] Catholic social teaching sees the common good as the sum total of the social conditions that enable individual people and groups more fully and readily to reach human fulfillment through the just ordering of society (GS 26, 74).

The first encyclical of modern Catholic social teaching to take up the theme of a just ordering of society was Pope Leo XIII's *Rerum Novarum*. Written in 1891 in the context of the exploitation of workers during the Industrial Revolution, this document offered a vision of society based on a humane understanding of work, the right to own property, the principle of

---

22. Todd David Whitmore, "Catholic Social Teaching: Starting with the Common Good," in *Living the Catholic Social Tradition: Cases and Commentary*, ed. Kathleen Maas Weigert and Alexia K. Kelly (New York: Sheed & Ward, 2005), 59.

collaboration (instead of class conflict), the dignity of the poor, the rights of the weak, the obligation of the rich, the establishment of justice, and the right to unionize.[23] Forty years later, after the Depression and economic crisis of 1929, Pope Pius XI published *Quadragesimo Anno*. As economic polarities began to worsen around the globe, the document stressed that capital must cooperate with labor and not exploit it (QA 23). One hundred years after *Rerum Novarum*, recognizing that the current global economy still had not met the needs of the poor, in 1991 Saint John Paul II wrote *Centesimus Annus* in order to look at the common good with respect to the needs of the whole human family (CA 58).

One of the fundamental ways in which society must be ordered is according to economic justice. It measures the health of an economy not in terms of financial metrics like Gross National Product or stock prices, but in terms of how the economy affects the quality of life in the community as a whole (EJA Intro 14). It states that an ordered economy must be shaped by three questions: What does the economy do *for* people? What does it do *to* people? And how do *people* participate in it (EJA 1)? Most of all, it puts a strong emphasis on what impact the economy has on the poor.[24] It argues that the world's resources should be shared equitably, that the rights of workers ought to be respected, that economic decisions (and those who make them) must be more accountable to the common good, and, in brief, that the economy be made for human beings and not human beings for the economy.

Meeting the demands of the common good and the requirements of distributive justice challenges the lifestyles, policies, and social institutions that negatively influence the poor (EJA Intro 16). Catholic social teaching seeks the transformation of policies and systems created by individual and collective acts of selfishness, which become institutionalized (and even legalized) in society and contribute to underdevelopment and the degradation of the poor (SRS 36). As they examined social structures in light of the common good, the U.S. bishops noted, "Decisions must be judged in light of what they do *for* the poor, what they do *to* the poor, and what they enable the poor to do *for themselves*" (EJA 24).

The struggle for a more ordered society is also directly related to the search for peace, and therefore much of Catholic social teaching is built around the vision of a peaceful society.[25] Peace is an important dimension of Catholic

---

23. Congregation for Catholic Education, *Guidelines for the Study and Teaching of the Church's Social Doctrine in the Formation of Priests* (Washington, D.C.: Office of Publishing and Promotion Services, United States Catholic Conference, 1989), 20.

24. John Houck and Oliver F. Williams, eds., *Catholic Social Teaching and the United States Economy* (Washington, D.C.: University Press of America, 1984).

25. For more on Catholic social teaching and peace, see National Conference of Catholic Bishops (U.S.), *The Challenge of Peace: God's Promise and Our Response* (Washington, D.C.: United States

social teaching, but a thorough treatment of it goes beyond the scope of this chapter. Here it is enough to note that peace is the fruit of justice and is integrally related to the development and empowerment of poor people and poor countries (CA 5). Much more than the absence of war or the balance of power between enemies, peace is the result of a rightly ordered society and ultimately is a gift that flows from the God of Life (CP 68).

A GO**D** OF LIFE
Dignity of the Human Person

A society is ordered, according to Catholic social teaching, when it is structured and functions not according to the maximization of profit, the needs of a nation, or the greed of the disordered human heart but, beyond all else, according to the intrinsic worth, freedom, and dignity of every human person (GS 26). Catholic social teaching believes that human beings, created in the image and likeness of God (Gn 1:26-27), have by their very existence an inherent value, worth, and distinction. This means that God is present in every person, regardless of his or her race, nation, sex, origin, orientation, culture, or economic standing. Catholic social teaching asserts that all human beings must see within every person both a reflection of God and a mirror of themselves, and must honor and respect this dignity as a divine gift (GS 26-27).

Catholic social teaching pays particular attention to those in society whose dignity is diminished, denied, or damaged, or those who, when they are no longer deemed useful, are rejected and discarded, or those who are dehumanized in their jobs. Many workers today feel alienated in their work, as if they are no more than a disposable cog in a massive industrial machine, with no creative connection to their labor and no promise of meaningful work.[26] Catholic social teaching advocates in particular for those whom society discards as unproductive, upholding the rights of the poor, the elderly, the sick, and others who are vulnerable. In giving voice to the God of Life, the church believes that a central dimension of its mission is to promote the dignity of every person and to speak out when the poor, the least, and the weak are most threatened.[27]

Catholic Conference, 1983) and *The Harvest of Justice is Sown in Peace: A Reflection of the National Conference of Bishops on the Tenth Anniversary of the Challenge of Peace* (Washington, D.C.: United States Catholic Conference, 1994).

26. John Paul II, "Address at General Audience" May 1, 1991 (*L'Osservatore Romano*, English Edition, May 6, 1991), 3.

27. John Paul II, *Christifideles Laici*, Apostolic Exhortation on the Vocation and the Mission

A GOD OF LIFE
Option for the Poor

In light of the vast disparity between rich and poor nations and rich and poor people, one of the principal means through which the church defends human dignity is by giving priority to the needs of the poor. Rooted in the Beatitudes, the poverty of Jesus, and his attention to those in need, the option for the poor expresses the church's commitment to stand alongside those whom society dismisses as insignificant, and to work with them for their integral liberation and human development. The option for the poor is woven through all of modern Catholic social teaching and particularly the writings of John Paul II:

> This is an option, or a special form of primacy in the exercise of Christian charity, to which the whole tradition of the Church bears witness . . . [G]iven the worldwide dimension which the social question has assumed, this love of preference for the poor, and the decisions which it inspires . . . cannot but embrace the immense multitudes of the hungry, the needy, the homeless, those without medical care and, above all, those without hope of a better future. (SRS 42)

This option includes a commitment not only to people but also to cultures whose very existence is endangered by the process of globalization.

The option for the poor is also a way of empowering all people to participate in the common good, which begins by responding to the needs of all, especially those with the greatest need (EJA Intro 16). It requires reaching out to those who are weak in any way, speaking for the voiceless, defending the defenseless (EJA Intro 16), and empowering them to be agents in the making of their own destiny. The option for the poor is also a way of reminding us that, as children of a common Creator, we are all responsible for each other (SRS 38). It seeks to give expression, in part, to the eschatological promises of the kingdom of God, where those now excluded will find a place at the table of the common banquet (SRS 33, PP 47).

John Paul II said that this option means that "[t]he needs of the poor must take priority over the desires of the rich; the rights of workers over the maximization of profits; the preservation of the environment over uncontrolled industrial expansion; the production to meet social needs over production for military purposes."[28] It affirms that the single most important criterion of the health of a society is how it treats its most vulnerable members and how it

---

of the Lay Faithful in the Church and in the World (Washington, D.C.: Office of Publishing and Promotion Services, United States Catholic Conference, 1989), 37.

    28. John Paul II, "Address on Christian Unity in a Technological Age" (Toronto, September 14, 1984), *Origins* 14, no. 16 (October 4, 1984): 249, 5.

responds to the needs of the poor through its public policies (EJA 123). This theme of the option for the poor will be explored in more depth in chapter 7 on liberation theology.

A GOD OF LIFE
F reedom as Rights and Responsibilities

Above all, Catholic social teaching is not about rules, regulations, or burdensome instruction but about genuine, spiritual freedom. This freedom has two central dimensions: freedom *from* sin and freedom *for* love. More than simply freedom to do whatever one wants without outside interference, such freedom seeks to safeguard human dignity by protecting human beings against the burden of oppression and exploitation. At the same time it summons people, who are endowed by God with a free will, to carry the weight of human duty by contributing to the common good through service to others. This response, shaped by Christian faith, is other-oriented, and Catholic social teaching regards self-gift and self-sacrifice as the highest expression of the liberated heart.

In the language of Catholic social teaching, such freedom is spoken of in terms of fundamental rights and fundamental responsibilities. Freedom means that human beings are endowed with certain inherent, inviolable, inalienable, and universal rights (PT 9).[29] These rights involve the fulfillment of basic material needs and the protection of certain relationships. They include the right of people to "choose their state of life and set up a family, the right to education, work, to their good name, to respect, to proper knowledge, the right to act according to the dictates of conscience and to safeguard their privacy, and rightful freedom, including freedom of religion" (GS 26). These rights ensure that people have access to adequate food, clothing, housing, medical care, schooling, work, and social services, all of which are necessary in order to live dignified lives.

Alongside these fundamental rights, Catholic social teaching also speaks about incumbent responsibilities and duties to the common good. That is to say, rights and responsibilities go hand and hand in Catholic social teaching. As John XXIII observed, "To claim one's rights and ignore one's duties, or only half fulfill them, is like building a house with one hand and tearing it down with the other" (PT 30).

The fundamental rights involve not only civil, political, cultural, and social rights, but also economic rights (EJA Intro 17), which include the right to private property. Catholic social teaching acknowledges that private prop-

---

29. For more on rights and responsibilities, see David Hollenbach, *Claims in Conflict*, Woodstock Studies 4 (New York: Paulist, 1979).

erty can be an incentive to productivity and a way of administering society in an efficient way, but it does not consider it an unrestricted right, since the goods of the earth are meant for the benefit of all and so that all peoples may develop.[30] John Paul II puts it in this way: "Private property, in fact, is under a 'social mortgage,' which means that it has an intrinsically social function, based upon and justified precisely by the principle of the universal destination of goods" (SRS 42). In other words, private property is a right in Catholic social teaching, but it is not an absolute right, since we are not the final owners of any property, and there is a communal dimension even to all that we consider "private." *Gaudium et Spes* even goes so far as to say that persons in extreme need "are entitled to take what they need from the riches of others" (GS 69). To deny the exigencies of distributive justice with a mistaken belief that God "blesses" a privileged few while neglecting the masses of poor people in the world is tantamount to heresy.

In our contemporary global culture, as economic interests often take priority over all other concerns, Catholic social teaching brings the primacy of rights to the forefront of decision making. In its concern for the common good, it eschews those mentalities and practices of hoarding and accumulating personal fortunes while the rest of the world suffers in misery. While Catholic social teaching sees the value of wealth creation through markets and incentives, wealth creation is described as only a means, setting the conditions for possible human flourishing. Accordingly, economic efficiency is not an end in itself but only has value in the context of communitarian and egalitarian values of an overarching vision of the common good.[31] Catholic social teaching underscores the belief that with increased power comes increased accountability, with great wealth comes great responsibility, and with human rights come human duties.

A GOD OF LIFE
Life as a Sacred Gift

Catholic social teaching weaves the golden thread of the sacredness of human life through all of its major documents. This idea appears more than thir-

---

30. Some philosophers today make a distinction between strong rights and weak rights. Strong rights, like rights to life, are inviolable and essential to human dignity and security. Weak rights, like rights to property, are important to individuals but are subject to the needs of the common welfare and can be modified or revoked, if common needs are greater. See R. Dworkin, *Taking Rights Seriously* (Cambridge, Mass.: Harvard University Press, 1977), 267-79.

31. Oliver F. Williams, "Catholic Social Teaching: A Moral Compass for the Next Millennium," *Review of Business* 19, no. 1 (Fall 1997): 15-21. An example of how this approach might influence multinational pharmaceutical companies is discussed in Oliver F. Williams, "The UN Global Compact: The Challenge and the Promise," *Business Ethics Quarterly* 14, no. 4 (2004): 755-74.

teen hundred times in the documents to the universal church. Catholic social teaching gives expression to the value of human life in all of its stages, in all of its dimensions, in all of its manifestations. To affirm the sacrosanct value of all life does not mean that Catholic social teaching denies the reality of death, but rather that all human beings are endowed with a biological and spiritual gift that must be honored and respected.

Catholic social teaching also affirms that this life is brought to a completely new level through the life, death, and resurrection of Christ, who brings new creation and gives new life: "I came so that they might have life and have it more abundantly" (Jn 10:10). This does not mean that Catholic social teaching is interested only in the spiritual life of peoples or even just prolongation of biological life, but rather in a quality of life that reflects the designs of a provident God who desires the full and integral development of each person in community. In defending, promoting, and cultivating life, Catholic social teaching is concerned with life in this world, life in the next, and the relationship between the two.

In some statements, Catholic social teaching weaves this golden thread of life into a single piece of theological clothing called the "seamless garment."[32] The "garment" is a direct allusion to Jesus' crucifixion, when the Roman soldiers divided and distributed his garments and gambled over them (Mt 27:28, 35). This "garment" also gives symbolic expression to Jesus' solidarity with those who suffer unjustly and are sentenced to death in one form or another. Catholic social teaching reiterates that life should not be torn apart in any form, possessed or disposed of in any way by any authority.

The notion of the seamless garment also affirms that there is a consistent ethic of life from conception to death that runs through all social problems, "from womb to tomb." Catholic social teaching actively promotes "a culture of life," while at the same time it denounces a "culture of death," especially as it is manifested in murder, genocide, abortion, torture, subhuman living conditions, arbitrary imprisonment, war, racism, deportation, slavery, prostitution, the selling and exploitation of women and children, disgraceful working conditions, sexism, poverty, euthanasia, capital punishment, life-threatening pollution and other such evils (EV 3, 40, 56ff.; EA 63; EJA 179).

Beneath the denunciation of all these evils is the affirmation that human life must be the fundamental criterion against which all economic, political, social, and cultural progress is measured. In arguing for this consistent ethic of life, and while admitting certain distinctions, Catholic social teach-

---

32. Cardinal Joseph Bernardin was the first to introduce this notion of the "seamless garment." For a copy of this text, see "A Consistent Ethic of Life: Continuing the Dialogue" (William Wade Lecture Series, St. Louis University, St. Louis, Missouri, March 11, 1984), available at http://priests forlife.org.

ing affirms that one cannot be against one injustice and yet for another. As Martin Luther King, Jr., once observed, "[I]njustice anywhere is a threat to justice everywhere."[33] The church, for example, recognizes that both abortion and capital punishment tear at the very fabric of life to which the church gives witness. Even while the analysis of abortion and capital punishment may differ, in the end the argument against them comes to the same place by defending life, regardless of any moral precondition. It recognizes that destructive actions not only harm, hurt, or injure the victims, but they also degrade, diminish, and dehumanize those who inflict injury. A civilization of love cannot exist without being firmly grounded in a respect for life.

A GOD OF LIFE
Involvement of All People in Creation of a New Social Order

While Catholic social teaching notes that one of the primary functions of government is to protect the rights of individuals, a primary responsibility of individuals is to contribute to the progress of the human community. Catholic social teaching emphasizes that all people must become involved in the construction of a new social order, even if they do so in differing capacities. This means that justice must be worked out on all levels of society, from the most local to the most global, from the family to the highest echelons of government.

As globalization puts more and more decisions into the hands of high-level political and economic leaders, and more people feel left out of the economic, social, and political forces that dominate their lives, the notion of involvement becomes increasingly important. Excluding people from participation goes against the grain of the social nature and communal vocation of human beings (EJA 78). The social vision of Catholic social teaching maintains that individuals and their families do not exist for the state, but vice versa.

Sometimes Catholic social teaching speaks about involvement and participation in terms of "subsidiarity." Originally coined in 1931 by Pope Pius XI in *Quadragesimo Anno*, "subsidiarity" comes from the Latin word "assistance." Subsidiarity means that the exercise of power should be made by the smallest possible and most local units of society (QA 79). Catholic social teaching recognizes that some tasks should be handled at the local level and others at larger, more national levels. Believing that most often the best decisions are made at the local level, closest to the people who will be most affected

---

33. Martin Luther King, Jr., *A Testament of Hope: The Essential Writings and Speeches of Martin Luther King, Jr.*, ed. James M. Washington (New York: HarperCollins, 1986), 147.

by them, subsidiarity means handing decision making downward to smaller entities. It can also mean moving it upward to larger entities, even to transnational bodies, if this better serves the common good and protects the rights of people.[34] Subsidiarity, in this sense, becomes a corrective against the concentration of power and resources in the hands of a privileged elite. It helps put limits on government and keeps it from assuming totalitarian control over smaller constituencies, such as individuals, families, and local organizations, in ways that would render them powerless.

Catholic social teaching sees responsible citizenship as a virtue and involvement in the political process as a moral obligation.[35] The United States Bishops remind Catholics, "Every voice matters in the public forum. Every vote counts. Every act of responsible citizenship is an exercise of significant individual power."[36] At the very least, voting is the most basic way of participation, and therefore failure to vote is a moral failure (CCC 2240). A God of Life challenges *all* to be involved in building a civilization of love.

A GOD OF LIFE
Family of Blood and Family of Humankind

As relational creatures, we cannot come to know who we are and what we are meant to become unless we understand to whom we belong. Catholic social teaching understands the family as the primary network of relationships in which a person develops and therefore is the most fundamental cell of society and the church (PT 16; LG 11). In a time when there is a greater emphasis on individual competition and market productivity—both of which take their toll on human relationships—Catholic social teaching devotes a great deal of attention to the promotion and protection of family life. Catholic social teaching is thoroughly concerned with every aspect of society that negatively impacts family relationships, and it challenges those forces that threaten the ties between family members (EJA 93). It recognizes that the future of the planet is integrally related to the relative health of family life (GS 47), and consequently it advocates for the protection of the marriage bond, living wages, medical care, housing, religious liberties, and even the right to migrate when necessary (FC 46).

---

34. Catholic Bishops' Conference of England and Wales, *The Common Good and the Catholic Church's Social Teaching* (London: Catholic Bishops' Conference of England and Wales, 1996), 22.

35. United States Conference of Catholic Bishops, *Faithful Citizenship: A Catholic Call to Political Responsibility* (Washington, D.C.: United States Conference of Catholic Bishops, 2003).

36. United States Conference of Catholic Bishops, *Living the Gospel of Life: A Challenge to American Catholics* (Washington, D.C.: United States Conference of Catholic Bishops, 1998), 34.

Beyond any national, social, cultural, racial, economic, and ideological differences, Catholic social teaching understands one's personal family is an integral part of a larger global human family. This notion is closely connected to both the theme of the option for the poor and the theme of human solidarity. Solidarity is a form of friendship and social charity that binds together all members of the human family.[37] John Paul II argued that solidarity is profoundly linked to a more global sense of responsibility, and he warned against equating it with a "feeling of vague compassion or shallow distress at the misfortunes of so many people, both near and far. On the contrary, it is a firm and persevering determination to commit oneself to the common good, that is to say, to the good of all and of each individual, because we are all really responsible for all" (SRS 38).

Racism and xenophobic attitudes are the antithesis of solidarity and only further alienate people from each other and blind us from seeing our connection to a God of Life and to each other. The church denounces as contrary to the movement toward a civilization of love any attitude or policy that discriminates against the weak, handicapped, infirmed, elderly, immigrants, children, homeless, foreigners, or those from different denominations or religions. John Paul II believed that human beings enslaved by attitudes of racial prejudice and ethnic animosity live in a moral bankruptcy and that their only recourse to ethical solvency is human solidarity.[38]

Concern for the family of humankind means responding to human hunger, misery, and poverty. Because we share a fundamental interconnectedness with each other, not only does indifference to the suffering of others deprive the poor, but it also diminishes the rich. As long as glaring economic and social imbalances persist, peace is impossible (MM 157).

A GOD OF LIFE
Environment and Ecological Stewardship

Care for creation extends not only to our brothers and sisters but also to the environment itself.[39] Catholic social teaching addresses not only issues of the human environment that pertain to the family and the ordering of society, but also issues of the natural environment that pertain to the care

---

37. Pontifical Council for Justice and Peace, "Contribution to World Conference Against Racism, Racial Discrimination, Xenophobia and Related Intolerance," Durban, August 31-September 7, 2001, *Origins* 31, no. 15 (September 20, 2001): 266, 15.

38. John Paul II, "Homily at Germiston Racecourse," Johannesburg, South Africa, September 17, 1995.

39. John Paul II, *The Ecological Crisis: A Common Responsibility* (Washington, D.C.: United States Conference of Catholic Bishops, 1990), 16.

of the earth. Catholic social teaching defines ecological stewardship as "the ability to exercise moral responsibility to care for the environment,"[40] and it implies protecting the environment and intelligently using resources necessary for what humans need today while at the same time conserving these resources and safeguarding them for future generations. In other words, ecological stewardship is a way of protecting our earthly home, safeguarding its resources, and extending solidarity to those who come after us.[41]

Catholic social teaching asserts that we have reached a "critical point" with the environment.[42] The collective decisions that chart our current course have resulted in the contamination of the earth through air, water, and ground pollution, as well as new illnesses, climate change, the erosion of the ozone layer, the destruction of rain forests, the extinction of species, the depletion or near exhaustion of nonrenewable resources, and the imminent threat of nuclear annihilation. Such problems put the entire human family at risk (QA 21). It is sobering to consider that if the environment goes, nothing else will matter, for we will no longer be a global home in which any human life can survive.

Care of the earth is also connected to concern for the poor, not only because the earth is "mother" but also because the poor, in the places they are forced to live, more often suffer the effects of contamination, toxic wastes, and even ecological disasters. In December 1984, for example, more than eight thousand residents of Bhopal, India, died after an industrial accident at a Union Carbide pesticide plant.[43] Beyond the catastrophic human costs, this accident created an ecological calamity that is still felt today; its contaminated wastes are yet to be cleaned up. Moreover, the poor feel the brunt of natural disasters as well. As seen in Hurricanes Katrina and Rita in the United States in 2005, the poor are frequently the ones who are left behind, many because they do not have the finances or options to leave endangered areas.

The ecological problem is integrally related to the problem of consumerism, which devours the resources of the earth in an excessive and disordered way (CA 37). Industrialization has fueled unprecedented consumption patterns that are ecologically unsustainable. They are based more on a desire to

---

40. Ibid.

41. United States Conference of Catholic Bishops, *Global Climate Change: A Plea for Dialogue, Prudence and the Common Good* (Washington, D.C.: United States Conference of Catholic Bishops, 2001), 3.

42. John Paul II, "Address of John Paul II to Conference on Environment and Health," March 24, 1997 (*L'Osservatore Romano*, English Edition, April 9, 1997), 2.

43. For more on the option for the poor and the environment, see Stephen Bede Scharper, "Option for the Poor and Option for the Earth: Toward a Sustainable Solidarity," in *The Option for the Poor beyond Theology*, ed. Daniel G. Groody and Gustavo Gutiérrez (Notre Dame, Ind.: University of Notre Dame Press, 2014), 97-119.

have and to enjoy rather than on a desire to be and to grow (CA 37). Only when a spirit of solidarity, sacrifice, and restraint shapes our common quest for a better world will human beings realize the call to renew the earth as a faithful response to a God of Life.

"A GLOBALIZATION OF SOLIDARITY"

Catholic social teaching neither naively condemns the process of globalization nor uncritically embraces it. Rather it seeks to discern both its positive and negative dimensions as the church journeys toward a horizon of hope with faith and trust in a God of Life. It recognizes the positive dimensions in drawing together countries, economies, cultures, and ways of life with fresh approaches and a growing recognition of the interdependence of the human family and the international community.[44] At the same time, it sees that the social problems of today now have a worldwide dimension and have reached a new magnitude never before seen in human history. In light of the current global challenges, it offers an invaluable set of ethical coordinates that can help steer the ship of globalization in the right direction.

From the beginning of his pontificate, Pope Francis has made Catholic social teaching central to his apostolic vision. Not only does he witness to a life of simplicity and evangelical poverty, but he has articulated from the beginning that the church must go to the margins to work for justice and to address the disorders of globalization that cause widespread poverty. The first trip he took outside of the Vatican was to the small Italian island of Lampedusa where thousands of refugees have drowned in their search for protection, security, and a dignified life. In a mass celebrated on the island, the altar and the chalice were crafted from a refugee boat, and in front of the lectern was a ship's wheel. In that homily he reminds us of the first questions God asks, "Where are you?" (Gn 3:9), and "Where is your brother . . . [whose] blood cries out to me from the ground?" (4:9-10), and then specifically addressed what he calls the "globalization of indifference,"[45] an increasingly occurring phenomenon where we desensitize ourselves to the suffering of others, become used to it, and lose a sense of the gift and responsibility related to our common bonds. In *Evangelii Gaudium*, Francis expresses the Gospel message at the heart of his social vision:

> To sustain a lifestyle which excludes others . . . a globalization of indifference has developed. Almost without being aware of it, we end up being incapable

---

44. Pontifical Council for Justice and Peace, "Contribution to World Conference Against Racism," 2.

45. Pope Francis, *Homily at Lampedusa*, July 8, 2013; available at the Vatican website, www.vatican.va.

of feeling compassion at the outcry of the poor, weeping for other people's pain, and feeling a need to help them, as though all this were someone else's responsibility and not our own. (EG 54)

Whatever else in human society changes because of the whole process of globalization, the moral vision of Catholic social teaching will continue to rest on the foundation of human dignity, solidarity, and subsidiarity (EA 55). Whatever else globalization means to the development of some parts of the world and in particular to some individuals who benefit from it, Catholic social teaching will continue to evaluate the results in terms of how the current structures of society help create a more just social order, how they help the poor, how they contribute to the international common good, and how they foster genuine development.[46] Whatever else emerges on the economic, political, and social horizon, Catholic social teaching will continue to measure progress as "a globalization without marginalization,"[47] or as John Paul II called it, a "globalization of solidarity" (EA 55).

Building a Civilization of Love

To advance a "globalization of solidarity" means, in Paul VI's words, "building a civilization of love." One manifestation of this civilization became evident after a tsunami hit South Asia on December 26, 2004, leaving more than 230,000 dead and millions homeless. After this tragedy, individuals and organizations from around the world offered donations and collective resources in response to the catastrophe. One family from Texas offered their life savings of $25,000 to alleviate the pain of these people. Some organizations gave millions of dollars in aid to meet the massive human need. The globalization of institutions, networks, and systems that make this kind of relief possible offer unprecedented potential for doing good and addressing the pressing areas of human need and suffering around the world.

While such offers of direct assistance are noteworthy, every hour approximately 840 children die of preventable diseases,[48] which is equivalent to a 2004 tsunami every eleven days.[49] The ignorance and indifference to these people and other such injustices indicate that there is indeed much work that

---

46. John Paul II, "Peace on Earth to Those Whom God Loves," Message for the 2000 World Day of Peace, *Origins* 29, no. 28 (December 23, 1999): 453, 14.

47. John Paul II, "From the Justice of Each Comes Peace for All," Message for the 1998 World Day of Peace, *Origins* 27, no. 28 (January 1, 1998): 468, 3.

48. Anup Shah, "Today Around 21,000 Children Died Around the World," *Global Issues*, September 24, 2011, http://www.globalissues.org.

49. *Human Development Report 2005: International Cooperation at a Crossroads* (New York: United Nations, 2005), 1.

still needs to be done. The drowning of human beings in social ills of every kind makes incredible demands on human conscience, whose pressing needs cannot help but call to conversion all individuals and all institutions in the world, all of whom share a common responsibility to serve a world in distress. For the church to be a credible, prophetic voice in a world of injustice, it must first embody that which it hopes to realize in a global society (JW 40). Even when its own witness is imperfect, however, Catholic social teaching ultimately seeks to give expression to something greater than itself: that present among us is a God of Life, who offers us a path to healing and transformation as we commit ourselves to building up a civilization of love.

QUESTIONS FOR REFLECTION

1. Catholic social teaching is often referred to as the church's best kept secret. Why is it a secret and what keeps it from being better known?
2. As you analyze reality from your own social location, what principles of Catholic social teaching are most pertinent and relevant?
3. Discuss this statement: "If the environment goes, nothing else will matter, for we will no longer have a global home in which any human life can survive."
4. Some people argue that the Catholic Church has no authority and should have no role in political matters. What is your opinion?
5. What imbalances in society does Catholic social teaching seek to address?
6. List some concrete examples from your own experience that would distinguish charity from justice.
7. In what ways have you seen injustices of society made legal?
8. What are the positive dimensions of capitalism? Its pitfalls?
9. Why is progress in the current global system not measured against the value of life?
10. In what ways could the economy become more centered around people and not just profit?
11. In what ways has the church itself not lived up to the principles of Catholic social teaching?
12. Discuss this statement: "Action on behalf of justice is a constitutive part of preaching the Gospel."

SUGGESTIONS FOR FURTHER READING AND STUDY

Curran, Charles E. *Catholic Social Teaching, 1891-Present.* Washington, D.C.: Georgetown University Press, 2002.

DeBerri, Edward, and James E. Hug. *Catholic Social Teaching: Our Best Kept Secret.* 4th ed. Maryknoll, N.Y.: Orbis Books, 2003.

Dwyer, Judith, ed. *The New Dictionary of Catholic Social Thought.* Collegeville, Minn.: Liturgical Press, 1994.

Groody, Daniel G. *Border of Death, Valley of Life: An Immigrant Journey of Heart and Spirit.* Lanham, Md.: Rowman & Littlefield, 2002.

Groody, Daniel G., ed. *The Option for the Poor in Christian Theology.* Notre Dame, Ind.: University of Notre Dame Press, 2007.

Groody, Daniel G., and Gioacchino Campese, eds. *A Promised Land, A Perilous Journey.* Notre Dame, Ind.: University of Notre Dame Press, 2008.

Groody, Daniel G., and Gustavo Gutiérrez, eds. *The Option for the Poor beyond Theology.* Notre Dame, Ind.: University of Notre Dame Press, 2014.

Himes, Kenneth R. *Responses to 101 Questions on Catholic Social Teaching.* New York: Paulist Press, 2001.

———, ed. *Modern Catholic Social Teaching: Commentaries and Interpretations.* Washington, D.C.: Georgetown University Press, 2005.

Holland, Joe. *Modern Catholic Social Teaching: The Popes Confront the Industrial Age 1740-1958.* Mahwah, N.J.: Paulist, 2003.

Holland, Joe, and Peter Henriot. *Social Analysis: Linking Faith and Justice.* Maryknoll, N.Y.: Orbis Books, 1983.

Kammer, Fred. *Doing Faith Justice: An Introduction to Catholic Social Thought.* New York: Paulist, 1991.

Korgen, Jeffry Odell. *My Lord and My God: Engaging Catholics in Social Ministry.* New York: Paulist, 2006.

Land, Philip S. *Catholic Social Teaching.* Chicago: Loyola University Press, 1994.

Mich, Marvin L. Krier. *Catholic Social Teaching and Movements.* Mystic, Conn.: Twenty-Third Publications, 1998.

Pontifical Council for Justice and Peace. *Compendium of the Social Doctrine of the Church.* Vatican City: Libreria Editrice Vaticana, 2004.

Schuck, Michael. *That They Be One: The Social Teaching of the Papal Encyclicals 1740-1849.* Washington, D.C.: Georgetown University Press, 1991.

Shannon, David J., and Thomas A. O'Brien. *Catholic Social Thought: The Documentary Heritage.* Maryknoll, N.Y.: Orbis Books, 1992.

Weigert, Kathleen Maas, and Alexia K. Kelly, eds. *Living the Catholic Social Tradition: Cases and Commentary.* New York: Sheed & Ward, 2005.

5

A Common Humanity, A Different Creed

Justice and Non-Christian Religions

THE GODS MUST BE CRAZY is a controversial movie about the misadventures of Xi N'gao, a Junt-wasi tribesman from the African Kalahari Desert. The film begins by describing the life of the primitive bush natives of Africa, "the little people," who live in rural areas far from the developed urban world. Though the narrator never uses the word "globalization," these indigenous people are portrayed as living in one of the few places left on the earth that is untouched by the cultural, technological, economic, social, and even religious upheaval of the new world era.

This tribe lives in an area that looks like paradise, even though no such place actually exists. Giraffes, elephants, and other wildlife coexist with the community and live together in peace and harmony. One unique characteristic of the people is that they have no sense of private property. They claim nothing as their own, sharing everything in common and gathering only what is needed to support themselves. Portrayed as the most contented and gentle people in the world, they have no crime, punishment, violence, laws, police, judges, rulers, or bosses. They believe that the gods put only good and helpful things on the earth for them to use, and that nothing is bad or evil, provided one knows how to use the things of the earth.

After painting a utopian picture of the bush people, the movie abruptly shifts gears and moves six hundred miles to the south, to the "civilized world" of the big city. Everyone is rushing to work, frenetically moving from place to place, competing in industry, and laboring to keep pace with the modern world. Instead of adapting themselves to the natural world, people adapt themselves to the self-created world of the city. Instead of nature, we see roads, power lines, and heavy machinery. Instead of peace, we see discord, dissension, and division. Instead of harmony, we see stress, strain, and the busyness of life in global society.

The "uncivilized" world of the primitive Junt-wasi tribe and the "civilized" world of contemporary city dwellers first encounter each other one day when a small airplane flies over the area where the bush people live. The pilot throws a Coke bottle out the window which lands in the middle of the tribe. It is a curious gift from the sky, and Xi wonders why the gods have sent it. The bush people think it is the strangest and most beautiful thing they have ever seen. They are very curious about it, and it fascinates them. They cure snake skins with the Coke bottle, make music with it, and even produce art with it. Every day they discover a new use for the Coke bottle. They think it is the most functional thing the gods have ever given them, a real labor-saving device.

In time, however, the people begin to think that the gods had been careless because they sent only one bottle. Now, for the first time, the bush people do not want to share something because they have only one. Suddenly, everybody needs the Coke bottle most of the time. A thing they never had before becomes a necessity, which stirs up many unfamiliar emotions; selfishness, possessiveness, jealousy, hatred, and violence begin to infect the tribe. The Coke bottle eventually disrupts the harmony of the whole community. After seeing the negative effect it has on the people, Xi is angry with the gods, so he throws the bottle up in the sky and tries to give it back to them. After several unsuccessful attempts, Xi tries to take the bottle to the ends of the earth in order to get rid of it, and the rest of the movie chronicles this complex encounter between the beliefs and customs of the old world and the new world. Though arguably simplistic and romantic in its presentation of this African tribe, the movie is also a satirical critique of contemporary society, raising numerous questions about whether what the Western world calls "progress" has actually advanced the overall well-being of the global village. The clash of worlds in the film is a microcosm of the clash between tradition and modernity, between Western civilization and indigenous cultures, and between religion and globalization.

In this chapter we want to look more at the relationship between globalization and organized religious beliefs. So far we have considered how the Judeo-Christian tradition can help steer the ship of globalization in the right direction, but here we will examine what insight other major religions offer to assist people in navigating the path to peace. Given the scope, magnitude, and complexity of these world religions, this is a difficult task, not only because of the wide range of belief systems, and even sometimes the creedal variance within each religion, but also because the nuances are not easily grasped by those outside the tradition. While a detailed exploration of the major world religions goes beyond the scope of this chapter, our purpose here is to find some of the common ethical elements among several of the major religions that can offer a humanizing and liberating dimension to the globalization process and help counterbalance the major socioeconomic forces that govern it. First we will look at the Parliament of the World's Religions, which has tried to identify the ethical nucleus of all the major world religions. Then we will explore some of the central creeds, Scriptures, and theological and philosophical concepts of five of these religions, namely, Islam, Hinduism, Buddhism, the Bahá'í faith, and African indigenous religions. Lastly we will look at how these religions, while remaining true to their own unique traditions, can help create a new consciousness and greater human solidarity with the entire human family.

GLOBALIZATION AND A GLOBAL ETHIC

The Council for a Parliament of the World's Religions (CPWR) is an organization whose stated purpose is "to cultivate harmony among the world's religious and spiritual communities and foster their engagement with the world and its other guiding institutions in order to achieve a peaceful, just, and sustainable world."[1] Originally organized in 1893 and reconvened in 1988, it has become one of the major forums of interreligious dialogue throughout the world.[2] CPWR published in 1993 the groundbreaking document *Declaration Toward a Global Ethic*,[3] which speaks of "the ethical common ground shared by the world's religious and spiritual traditions."[4]

The document begins by saying, "The world is in agony,"[5] a fundamental crisis caused by the global economy, global ecology, and global politics. It is in agony because of war, environmental degradation, hunger, social disarray, violence, and the total disregard for justice: "The lack of a grand vision, the tangle of unresolved problems, political paralysis, mediocre political leadership with little insight or foresight, and in general too little sense for the commonweal are seen everywhere: too many old answers to new challenges." While it does offer simple solutions to complex problems, it suggests that the world's major religions can provide a moral foundation or a global ethic that can facilitate a "better individual and global order." This global ethic does not mean "a global ideology or a single unified religion beyond all existing

---

1. The Council for a Parliament of the World's Religions was organized in part as a centennial celebration of the 1893 World's Parliament of Religions, held in Chicago in conjunction with the Columbian Exposition. See Council for a Parliament of the World's Religions, http://www.parliamentofreligions.org.

2. Ibid.

3. Council for a Parliament of the World's Religions, *Declaration Toward a Global Ethic*, available at http://www.parliamentofreligions.org.

4. Ibid.

5. Ibid., 2.

religions, and certainly not the domination of one religion over all others." Rather, a global ethic means "a fundamental consensus on binding values, irrevocable standards and [fundamental moral values or] personal attitudes." "Without such a fundamental consensus on an ethic," the document states, "sooner or later every community will be threatened by chaos or dictatorship and individuals will despair."[6] Before looking specifically at this ethical nucleus, we want to examine here the way five major religions approach the themes of justice and human liberation.

ISLAM

Although the tragedies of September 11, 2001, suicide bombers, and other examples of Islamic fanaticism have tainted people's perceptions of this tradition, Islam contains profound human and religious teachings, has a rich spiritual history, and has much to contribute to a global ethic. The name *Islam* is related to the Arabic word *salam*, meaning peace.[7] As a religion, it began around fourteen hundred years ago, and its followers are called Muslims, which means "the one who surrenders to the will of God."[8] The leading figure in Islam is the prophet Muhammad (570-632), who is considered by Muslims to be a descendant of Ishmael, Abraham's first son. Islam accordingly has historical and theological affinities with both Judaism and Christianity, but it seeks to correct what it perceives as incongruities in Judeo-Christian religion as it historically developed. Islam holds out a purified religion of Abraham that opens up for all humanity the path to God.

Islam is a global religion with a global mission that promotes the globalization of ethical values. Fauzi Najjar believes that there is a three-tiered division in Islamic thought concerning globalization, ranging from "those who reject it as the 'highest stage of imperialism' and a 'cultural invasion,'" to those who welcome globalization, and finally to those who call for "finding an appropriate form of globalization compatible with the national and cultural interests of the people."[9]

---

6. Ibid., 4, 6.
7. For an important overview of all the major world religions with respect to justice, see Ira Rifkin, *Spiritual Perspectives on Globalization: Making Sense of Economic and Cultural Upheaval* (Woodstock, Vt.: Skylight Paths, 2002).
8. For a good introduction to Islam, see John L. Esposito, *Islam: The Straight Path* (Oxford: Oxford University Press, 1998).
9. Fauzi Najjar, "The Arabs, Islam, and Globalization," *Middle East Policy Council*, 2005, http://www.policyinnovations.org.

At its core, Islam shares a deep concern for social justice.[10] Consequently, it challenges some of the inherent values of global capitalism.[11] Anti-Western Muslims are not against globalization per se, but against the Western secularization that propagates materialism, greed, and selfishness and undermines values that are important to Islam, such as benevolence, justice, moderation, humility, honesty, and forgiveness.[12] Muslims are bound in duty to support any organization, group, or even other religion that promotes these values.

The Islamic Scriptures, or the Qur'an (meaning "recitation" and "reading"), provide the basic doctrine of the religion as well as core ethical guidelines that govern family life, law and order, ethics, dress, and religious observances. While there are different ways of interpreting these guidelines, Islamic faith revolves around five key pillars in its creed: (1) the pillar of *shahadah*, or the Muslim profession of faith, which is repeated several times daily in order to center the thoughts on the primacy of God in one's life; (2) the pillar of *salah*, or ritual worship, which Muslims observe five times a day at dawn, midday, afternoon, evening, and night; (3) the pillar of *sawm*, or fasting, during the month of Ramadan, for spiritual growth, piety, and identification with the poor; (4) the pillar of *zakat*, or almsgiving, which is an obligatory tax on the wealthy used to help the poor and the sick; and (5) the pillar of *haj*, or pilgrimage to Mecca (Saudi Arabia), which should be done at least once in a lifetime, if financially and physically feasible.

These pillars shape the Islamic worldview, where God is involved in everything, not just spiritual matters, and where public and private morality are part of a unified whole (Qur'an 22:64). Islam believes that God breathes his spirit into human beings, making them "vicegerents" (*khalifa*) on earth who must choose between good and evil. As vicegerents, humans have been entrusted with custodianship of the earth and its resources. To guide them God sent messengers like the Prophet Muhammad, who was the last of the great prophets. Such prophets speak of accountability for one's actions, which will result in reward and punishment, according to certain ethical principles. Muslims teach not only that Allah is merciful, but also that he is just and will

---

10. David R. Loy, "The West against the Rest," in *The Twenty-first Century Confronts Its Gods: Globalization, Technology, and War*, ed. David J. Hawkin (Albany: State University of New York Press, 2004), 97-102.

11. Ameer Ali, "Globalization and Greed: A Muslim Perspective," in *Subverting Greed: Religious Perspectives on the Global Economy*, ed. Paul F. Knitter and Chandra Muzaffar (Maryknoll, N.Y.: Orbis Books, 2003), 144.

12. For more on Islam's rejection of Westernization, not globalization per se, see Jacques Waardenburg, "Reflections on the West," in *Islamic Thought in the Twentieth Century*, ed. Suha Taji-Farouki and Basheer M. Nafi (New York: I. B. Tauris, 2004), 195-222; and Mona Maisami, "Islam and Globalization," *The Fountain* 43 (July-September 2003).

judge people harshly if they do not accept personal and collective responsibility for the less fortunate.[13]

As indicated by various parts of the Qur'an, justice is the cornerstone of Islamic life and faith: "True piety is this: to believe in God, and the Last Day, the angels, the Book, and the Prophets, to give of one's goods, however cherished, to kinsmen, and orphans, the needy, the traveler, beggars, and to ransom the slave, to perform the prayer, to pay the alms" (Qur'an 2:177); "Stand out firmly for justice, as witnesses to Allah, even as against yourselves or your parents, or your kin" (Qur'an 4:135); "Take no life, which God has made sacred, except by way of justice and law . . . And approach not the property of the orphan, except to improve it, until he attains the age of maturity. Give full measure and weight, in justice . . . And if you give your word, do it justice, even if a near relative is concerned; and fulfill your obligations before God" (Qur'an 6:151-53); "Give just measure and cause no loss by fraud and weigh with scales true and upright" (Qur'an 26:181-82); "Woe to (those) who pile wealth and lay it by, thinking that his wealth would make him last" (Qur'an 104:1-3); "And there are those who bury gold and silver and spend it not in the way of God: announce to them a most grievous penalty" (Qur'an 9:34).

In contrast to the neoliberal models that shape globalization, Islam does not believe in unlimited freedom or unbridled pursuit of economic self-interest. Islam shows organized restraints and has inherent counterbalances that challenge human greed through such doctrines as *halal* (that which is permitted), *haram* (that which is disallowed), and *akhira* (the hereafter). These principles have direct implications for how human beings create economic systems and measure progress, favoring in the end an economy that serves human beings, not vice versa.[14]

Muhammad himself was a merchant, skilled in the affairs of commerce, so in general Islam is not against commerce but against unbridled greed and a materialism that results in social inequities and the neglect of the poor and the needy.[15] Islamic faith has come up with strict guidelines that govern economic activities and shape how economic systems develop.[16] To prevent

---

13. Loy, "The West against the Rest," 97-102.

14. Ali, "Globalization and Greed," 152.

15. Some scholars argue that Islam forbids commerce and economic relations with non-Islamic states. Umar Ibrahim Vadillo and Fazlun M. Khalid write that "Islamic law defines the boundaries within which trade and business are just. Economics defines the boundaries within which trade and business will be more efficient. Islamic law and economics are two totally different approaches to seeing things which in their turn create two different ways of life." These scholars conclude that there is no such thing as Islamic economics because it goes against Islamic principles. Fazlun M. Khalid and Umar Ibrahim Vadillo, "Trade and Commerce in Islam," in *Islam and Ecology*, ed. Fazlun Khalid and Joanne O'Brien (New York: Cassell, 1992), 69-86.

16. The specific rules, prohibitions, requirements, and models of an Islamic economic system are the subject of much study. For more on an Islamic economic ethic, see Khalid and Vadillo,

the exploitation of those in financial distress, the Qur'an prohibits charging interest on loans (*riba*, "usury"). In theory this doctrine keeps any Muslim from taking unfair advantage of the vulnerable, and, combined with the principle of *zakat*, it reveals a profound respect for economic justice and fair and equitable behavior. The task of a Muslim is not to escape from the world but to work within history for the establishment of better relations among peoples.[17] As Karen Armstrong notes,

> Social justice [is] the crucial virtue of Islam. Muslims were commanded as their first duty to build a community (*ummah*) characterized by practical compassion, in which there was a fair distribution of wealth. This was far more important than any doctrinal teaching about God. In fact the Qur'an has a negative view of theological speculation, which it calls *zannah*, self-indulgent whimsy about ineffable matters that nobody can ascertain one way or another. It seemed pointless to argue about such abstruse dogmas; far more crucial was the effort (*jihad*) to live in the way God had intended for human beings. The political and social welfare of the *ummah* would have sacramental value for Muslims.[18]

The negative reaction against globalization stems from the belief that free-market profiteering is destructive of human community and promotes a counterethic to that which is at the heart of Islam. While such an ethic does not justify belligerent acts of terrorism, it does provide a critique of a society that has deified economic progress and made the economy an end in itself rather than a means. As Hatem Bazian observes,

> Globalization would be great if done right, if it were just. It is not that everyone has to become a Muslim, but there are certain Islamic values that are also universal, that every religion recognizes as consistent with righteous living . . . The globalization of righteous values is inherently Islamic, and is what the world needs. Globalism is God's plan.[19]

"Trade and Commerce in Islam," 69-86; Timu Kuran, *The Religious Undercurrents of Muslim Economic Grievances*, available at http://essays.ssrc.org/sept11/essays/kuran.htm; Rodney Wilson, "The Development of Islamic Economics: Theory and Practice," in *Islamic Thought in the Twentieth Century*, ed. Suha Taji-Farouki and Basheer M. Nafi (New York: I. B. Tauris, 2004), 195-221; Marcus Noland and Howard Pack, "Islam, Globalization, and Economic Performance in the Middle East," *International Economics Policy Briefs* (2004), available at http://www.iie.com.

17. Karen Armstrong, *Islam: A Short History* (New York: Modern Library, 2000), xi.

18. Ibid., 6. Armstrong's position concerning the virtue of social justice in Islam is contested by others, including Ann Elizabeth Mayer, who writes, "Many Muslim countries have entered reservations to provisions in human rights conventions guaranteeing, for instance, women's equality or freedom of religion on the grounds that these conflict with Islamic law." See Ann Elizabeth Mayer, "Islamic Law and Human Rights: Conundrums and Equivocations," in *Religion and Human Rights: Competing Claims?* ed. Carrie Gustafson and Peter Juviler (New York: M. E. Sharpe, 1999), 177.

19. Quoted in Rifkin, *Spiritual Perspectives on Globalization*, 43-44.

Islam seeks to be faithful to God's will in history through a profound respect of others and by helping make people generous, altruistic, just, and socially responsible. It sees poverty not as divinely sanctioned but rather as the result of human greed and avarice.[20] Unbridled economic expansion that fosters greed flies in the face of a religion that believes that each person must give beyond his or her direct needs for human and material development. Islam believes in a provident God, and when people live by God's commands and order their lives accordingly, there is more than enough for everybody.

HINDUISM

Hinduism is one of the oldest religious traditions of the world, dating back to 1500 B.C., and refers to a family of religious belief systems that have their origin in India. The word "Hindu" derives from the Sanskrit word *sindhu*, or river (specifically the Indus River, which flows from Tibet through Kashmir and Pakistan). Today as many as one billion people are Hindus, and 94 percent live in India, with much smaller numbers in Malaysia and Sri Lanka.[21]

As Ira Rifkin observes,

One approaches Hinduism much like the blind man approaches an elephant; the subject is so vast that conclusions can vary widely depending upon the part touched first. Of all the major faiths, Hinduism is the toughest to categorize, the most elastic in its authority, the most diverse in its range of accepted beliefs and practices.[22]

Hinduism has an unlimited number of deities and multiple paths to ultimate truth. It is difficult to assess the contribution that Hinduism offers to the process of globalization because there are some dimensions that support it and others that challenge the process. Moreover, because Hinduism tends toward what is otherworldly, some do not feel compelled to make any response to current challenges posed by globalization in this world apart from continuing their spiritual practices.[23]

Hindus define themselves as those who believe in Vedas or who follow the way (*dharma*) of the four classes (*varnas*) or four stages of life (*ashramas*). They believe in a single, supreme God (Brahman) worshiped through many gods,

---

20. Ibrahim Warde, *Islamic Finance in the Global Economy* (Edinburgh: Edinburgh University Press, 2000), 43.

21. Conrad Hackett and Joseph Naylor, "Many Religions Heavily Concentrated in One or Two Countries" (Pew Research Center, August 27, 2014), http://www.pewresearch.org.

22. Rifkin, *Spiritual Perspectives on Globalization*, 63.

23. See David Frawley, *Hinduism and the Clash of Civilizations* (New Delhi: Voice of India, 2001).

and rebirth (karma). There are three principal deities, one who is creator (Brahma), one who is preserver (Vishnu), and one who is destroyer (Shiva). The Scriptures are known as the *Bhagavad Gita*, as well as *Brahmanas, Sutras*, and *Aranyakas*, and among the teachings found in these sacred books, Hindus believe that the gods travel to earth, protect the poor and vulnerable, and restore order.

Vedic Hinduism recognizes four basic human needs or goals: (1) *dharma*; (2) *artha*; (3) *kama*; and (4) *moksha*. *Dharma* has to do with living in right relationship, in harmony, with oneself, with society, and with God. The principle of *dharma* has to do with rationality, duty, justice, peace, truthfulness, compassion, nonviolence, humanity, spirituality, tolerance, service to others, ethics, and philanthropy.[24] To violate *dharma* is to invite chaos. *Kama* has to do with the human need for pleasure, sexual and otherwise.[25] It is closely related to *artha*, or the accumulation of wealth. *Artha* is part of the design of human life that leads to commercial exchange and building up community; as long as it is guided by *dharma*, it is a blessing.[26] *Moksha* deals with the highest human ideal, which is human liberation. Of all these desires, this fourth goal of spiritual freedom supersedes all the rest and is considered the most important.[27] For more than four thousand years, Hindu sages have taught that *moksha* is the pinnacle of human enlightenment.

What flows from *moksha* is self-gift, or other-oriented service, as noted in the *Bhagavad Gita*:

Every selfless act, *arjuna*, is born from Brahman, the eternal, infinite godhead. He is present in every act of service. All life turns on his law . . . Whoever violates it, indulging his senses for his own pleasure and ignoring the needs of others, has wasted his life. But those who realize the

---

24. S. Cromwell Crawford defines the root of *dharma* to mean "to hold," asserting that the term "signifies that which upholds or emboldens law, custom, and religion, and it is very much analogous to the concept of 'Natural Law' in Christian ethics." S. Cromwell Crawford, "Hindu Ethics for Modern Life," in *World Religions and Global Ethics*, ed. S. Cromwell Crawford (New York: Paragon House, 1989), 5. Roy W. Perrett echoes Crawford's assertion, identifying dharma as "a system of obligations and prohibitions enshrined in the legal and religious texts" which "guarantees the harmonious evolution of the universe." Roy W. Perrett, *Hindu Ethics: A Philosophical Study* (Honolulu: University of Hawaii Press, 1998), 50.

25. The Hindu search for and praise of pleasure has often been misunderstood. Perrett writes that "the type of pleasure that is truly valuable is that in accordance with the demands of dharma" (*Hindu Ethics*, 60).

26. S. Cromwell Crawford, *The Evolution of Hindu Ethical Ideals* (Calcutta: Firma K. L. Mukhopadhyay, 1974), 206.

27. Sarah Jhingran discusses in detail how the search for liberation as spiritual freedom is at the heart of Hindu morality and ethics. Sarah Jhingran, *Aspects of Hindu Morality* (Delhi: Motilal Banarsidass, 1989), chap. 4.

Self are always satisfied. Having found the source of joy and fulfillment they no longer seek happiness from the external world. They have nothing to gain or lose by any action; neither people nor things can affect their security. Strive constantly to serve the welfare of the world for by devotion to selfless work one attains the supreme goal of life. Do your work with the welfare of others in mind. True sustenance is in service, and through it a man or woman reaches the eternal Brahman. But those who do not seek to serve are without a home in this world. (*Baghavad Gita*, chaps. 3 and 4)

Hinduism's contribution to a global ethic rests not only on how it understands God but on how it understands the human person. It sees one impediment to justice as the inability to handle wisely the dynamics of human desire. Hinduism recognizes that there is a place for pleasure in every human life, but it also recognizes how overindulgence in human desire can easily derail people and ruin them. For Hinduism, what is more important than the desire for possessions is the longing for self-realization. In other words, instead of seeking to *have* more, Hinduism calls people to *be* more. Possessions become evil when they possess the possessor. Human liberation results not from the quest for self-fulfillment of one's desires but from the gift of self for the good of others. This notion of magnanimity is brought out in a story told by the late Anthony de Mello, who frequently drew on the wisdom of Hindu thought and culture:

The *sannyasi*[28] had reached the outskirts of the village and settled down under a tree for the night when a villager came running up to him and said, "The stone! The stone! Give me the precious stone!" "What stone?" asked the *sannyasi*. "Last night the Lord Shiva appeared to me in a dream," said the villager, "and told me that if I went to the outskirts of the village at dusk I should find a *sannyasi* who would give me a precious stone that would make me rich forever." The *sannyasi* rummaged in his bag and pulled out a stone. "He probably meant this one," he said, as he handed the stone over to the villager. "I found it on a forest path some days ago. You can certainly have it." The man looked at the stone in wonder. It was a diamond. Probably the largest diamond in the whole world for it was as large as a man's head. He took the diamond and walked away. All night he tossed about in bed, unable to sleep. The next day at the crack of dawn he woke the *sannyasi* and said, "Give me the wealth that makes it possible for you to give this diamond away so easily."[29]

---

28. In Hindu religion, a *sannyasi* is a wandering mendicant and ascetic.
29. Anthony de Mello, *The Song of the Bird* (Anand, India: Gujarat Sahitya Prakash, 1982), 182-83.

In Hinduism, indulgence in desires brings fog; discipline and mortification bring light. In drawing people beyond the pleasures of the sensory world, Hinduism seeks to help people transcend human cravings and realize a more enduring satisfaction in spiritual enlightenment. As Huston Smith adds,

> Pleasure, success and duty are not what we really want, the Hindus say; what we really want is to be, to know, and to be happy. No one wants to die, to be in the dark about things, or to be miserable. Pleasure, success and duty are only approximations of what we really want; they are apertures through which our true wants come through to us [which are] liberation from everything that distances us from infinite being, infinite awareness, and infinite bliss.[30]

The Laws of Manu, an ancient Hindu text written almost four thousand years ago says, "Desire is never extinguished by the enjoyment of desired objects; it only grows stronger like a fire [fed] with clarified butter" (2:94). Because globalization is shaped predominantly by the forces of economics, and these are in turn fueled by consumption, a global culture of consumerism not only induces human greed but it also dehumanizes the rich while at the same time depriving the poor of a just share in the world's riches.

Quoting an ancient aphorism, former Indian state legislator Swami Agnivesh says, "The sea has limits but human desire has none."[31] Hindu religion recognizes that every generation has trouble reigning in desire, but it cautions against a society that fosters consumption patterns that enslave people and make greed their master. Restraint lies at the core of Hindu ethics, and liberation comes from progressive renunciation.[32] As Agnivesh adds: "In the global economy, the monster of greed threatens to enjoy a longer leash and farther reach . . . In that sense, globalization has unleashed the dogs of greed in poorer societies of the world."[33] Hinduism also sees how unrestrained consumption has consequences for the natural world, and its strong environmental ethic stems from its cosmic understanding of life.[34] The Vedas speak about *Mata bhoomih, putroham prithivyah*, meaning that the earth is our mother and we are all her children.

Hinduism, in accord with other great religious traditions, fosters the belief in *vasudhaiva kudumbhakom*, which means, "the whole world is one family."

---

30. Huston Smith, *The Illustrated World's Religions: A Guide to Our Wisdom Traditions*, 2nd ed. (New York: HarperSanFrancisco, 1995), 18.

31. Ibid., 53.

32. S. Cromwell Crawford, "Hindu Ethics for Modern Life," in *World Religions and Global Ethics*, ed. Crawford, 31.

33. Swami Agnivesh, "Religious Conscience and the Global Economy: An Eastern Perspective on Sociospiritual Activism," in *Subverting Greed*, ed. Knitter and Muzaffar, 46-47.

34. Crawford, "Hindu Ethics for Modern Life," 30.

Some Hindu teachings are based on *aparigraha,* or "non-acquisitiveness," which is central to the search for inner harmony, and they also foster a vision of life based on *varnashrama dharma. Varna* means "to choose," and it advocates the choice of a mission in life beyond any desire for material acquisition. This doctrine teaches that every person must choose among one of three missions in life: the mission to overcome ignorance, the mission to overcome injustice, or the mission to overcome inadequacy. It rests firmly on the belief in a supreme God who owns all and entrusts the gifts of the earth to human beings but also calls them to care for others.

BUDDHISM

Buddhism is based on the teachings of Siddhartha Gautama, or the Buddha, from the sixth century B.C. He was not a god or a savior but a great teacher who opened up a pathway to enlightenment. Often understood more as a philosophy than a religion, Buddhism has gained widespread acceptance and is widely practiced in Asia with approximately 500 million followers.[35] As with Hinduism, it is difficult to speak in terms of a monolithic Buddhist religion or to assess the impact of globalization on Buddhism. Some adherents reject globalization; others embrace it; still others are seeking to influence the shape and future direction of Buddhism and to address some of the problems caused by globalization.[36] On the whole, however, social justice has not been a central part of the Buddhist tradition. Largely because of the influence of the West and of the Abrahamic faiths and their prophetic concerns, however, Buddhism in some circles has begun to take a more socially committed direction.

At the core of Buddhism is the belief in four noble truths: (1) Life is suffering *(dukkha).* (2) The reason for suffering is attachment or craving *(tanha).* (3) Elimination of suffering is possible through a transformed mind *(nirvana).* And (4) the formula for the elimination of suffering is the Eightfold Path *(magga).* The Eightfold Path is a middle ground between excessive self-indulgence (hedonism) and excessive self-denial (asceticism). This path is based on highly interdependent principles that lead to growth in knowledge,

---

35. Hackett and Naylor, "Many Religions Heavily Concentrated in One or Two Countries." In 2014, the worldwide estimate of the number of Buddhists was 488 million.

36. I am very grateful to David Loy and Jim Phalan for their helpful comments on this section. For more on social justice and Buddhism, see Fred Eppsteiner, *The Path of Compassion: Writings on Socially Engaged Buddhism* (Berkeley, Calif.: Parallax Press, 1988). See also David Loy, "The Religion of the Market," *Journal of the American Academy of Religion* 65, no. 2 (Summer 1997): 275-90; John H. Dunning, *Making Globalization Good* (New York: Oxford University Press, 2003); and David R. Loy, *The Great Awakening: A Buddhist Social Theory* (Boston: Wisdom, 2003).

wisdom, and ethical living. They are right view, right intention, right speech, right action, right livelihood, right effort, right mindfulness, and right concentration.

The ultimate goal of Buddhism is to attain enlightenment, a state in which one sees reality as it truly is and has overcome greed, hatred, and ignorance. Buddhism seeks to wake up individuals caught up in the sleep of delusion, in the confidence that in waking up individuals it may wake up humanity. Buddhism has much to offer to a world in search of reality beyond the illusions and seductions of contemporary culture. Much of global culture that gives primacy to monetary concerns and material acquisition runs counter to much of what Buddhism values, especially family, community, spiritual values, and meaningful work.[37]

The Buddha sought to provide a pathway to the higher aspirations of the human heart that lead to human liberation. Traditional Buddhism does not speak about social justice in the same way the Abrahamic religions do, but it does not ignore the problem of poverty in the world either, and there are certain points of analogy in Buddhism that can serve as the starting point for dialogue with other religious traditions and for establishing a common global ethic.[38]

Buddhism does see that part of the solution to the world's injustice lies in *dana,* or generosity.[39] As David Loy notes, "*Dana* is the most important concept in Buddhist thinking about society and economics, because it is the main way our non-attachment is cultivated and demonstrated. We are called upon to show compassion to those who need our help."[40] Buddhism, as a pathway to virtue, highlights the primacy of generosity, because it believes that society breaks apart when people fail to fulfill the obligation of *dana*. Generosity is also one of the primary means through which an unjust society redistributes the goods of the earth to those deprived of them. The challenges posed by globalization and its widespread economic polarities, however, have required many Buddhists to realize that *dana*, if it is to correct the imbalances of glo-

---

37. Helen Norberg-Hodge, "Buddhism in the Global Economy," in *Local Futures: Institute for Ecology and Culture*, April 30, 2010, http://www.localfutures.org.

38. For more on Buddhist ethics, see Sallie B. King, *Being Benevolence: The Social Ethics of Engaged Buddhism* (Honolulu: University of Hawaii Press, 2005); Gunapala Dharmasiri, *Fundamentals of Buddhist Ethics* (Honolulu: University of Hawaii Press, 1988); Lily de Silva, "The Scope and Contemporary Significance of the Five Precepts," in *Buddhist Ethics and Modern Society*, ed. Charles Wei-hsun Fu and Sandra A. Wawrytko (Westport, Conn.: Greenwood, 1991), 143-58; and Peter Harvey, *An Introduction to Buddhist Ethics* (Cambridge: Cambridge University Press, 2000).

39. David R. Loy, "Pave the Planet or Wear Shoes? A Buddhist Perspective on Greed and Globalization," in *Subverting Greed*, ed. Knitter and Muzaffar, 63.

40. Ibid.

balization, must not simply be about almsgiving but about justice, which is closely tied to the notion of righteousness.[41]

Buddhism sees human nature as having both unwholesome and wholesome traits.[42] The process of liberation requires one to nurture wholesome traits even while the unwholesome traits exist. Traditionally, the lotus flower symbolizes and gives expression to this twofold dimension of human nature: the flower is rooted in the mud at the bottom of the pond but blooms upward.[43] The mud of life or its three poisons are greed (*lobha*), ill will (*doha*), and delusion (*moha*). In contrast, human life blooms through the counterparts of generosity (*dana*), loving-kindness (*metta*), and wisdom (*prajna*). Buddhism accepts that people have both wholesome and unwholesome traits in our nature, but it seeks to cultivate the wholesome while it works to root out the unwholesome. This has many implications for the current global system insofar as it asks probing questions about the values and motivations that are implicit in economic relationships, and therefore which should be encouraged and which discouraged. Buddhism, overall, values high moral character, self-sacrifice, honesty, integrity, impartiality, simple lifestyle, nonviolence, patience, detachment, and internal freedom. It also believes that individual spiritual growth promotes the development of community.

Many Buddhists believe that the problem with the global consumer culture is not that it is bad but that it is delusional. Like other major religions, Buddhism believes that there is much more involved in the process of self-realization than the satisfaction of material hungers. Because our lives are interconnected, Buddhism recognizes that we cannot live only for ourselves and disregard others who make our lives possible. Buddhism aims to provide a remedy for deep-rooted egoism, which negatively affects ourselves and the community by cutting through the lies, deceptions, and seductions of a fleeting world.[44] It believes that liberation comes only when people grasp reality correctly.

Buddhism also advocates for detachment so that people can distinguish truly between genuine needs and superfluous wants. Part of understanding the nature of the world entails understanding the nature of oneself.[45] Buddhism sees that "the greatest wealth is contentment," *santutthi paramam*

---

41. See Padmasiri de Silva, *Buddhism, Ethics and Society: The Conflicts and Dilemmas of Our Time* (Victoria: Monash University Press, 2002).

42. Loy, "Pave the Planet or Wear Shoes? A Buddhist Perspective on Greed and Globalization," in *Subverting Greed*, ed. Knitter and Muzaffar, 67.

43. Ibid.

44. Alfred Bloom, "Globalization and Buddhism," available at Sin Dharma Net, http://www.shindharmanet.com.

45. Loy, "Pave the Planet or Wear Shoes?" 59.

dhanam (Dhammapada 204).[46] Buddhism also challenges religious practices that are concerned with external observances but do not work at the greater challenge of purifying the heart and mind. Those religions that believe that human beings are born into fixed social caste systems that separate the rich from the poor, men from women, and that lead to the denial of basic human rights, human justice, and human dignity must also be purified if they are to lead to true human enlightenment. In its best form, Buddhism is a path to the purification of mind that leads to a right relationship with reality.

Two of the most notable Buddhist spokespersons on the contemporary world stage are the Dalai Lama and Thich Nhat Hanh. Not only do they provide a witness to the spiritual and transcendent dimensions of human life, but also they bring out our mutual interdependence on each other and on all creation. The Dalai Lama believes that internal development, or the meditative practices that lead one to turn inward, have direct implications for external development.[47] Thich Nhat Hanh calls this "interbeing," which rejects absolute autonomy and isolated individualism. The individual is ultimately interconnected in the community; what is done to the one is done to everyone, and what benefits one benefits all, provided compassion and generosity are fostered. As the Dalai Lama notes,

> A stock-market crash on one side of the globe can have a direct effect on the economies of countries on the other. Similarly, our technological achievements are now such that our activities have an unambiguous effect on the natural environment. And the very size of our population means that we cannot any longer afford to ignore others' interests . . . In view of this, I am convinced that it is essential that we cultivate a sense of what I call universal responsibility.[48]

Buddhism's sense of the interconnected nature of all reality helps remind human beings of these relationships and the consequences of violating them. Because all life is interconnected, actions have consequences that can positively or negatively affect these relationships. As David R. Loy sees it, "The most important point, from a Buddhist perspective, is that our economic emphasis on competition, individual gain, and private possession encourages the development of ill will rather than loving kindness. A society where people do not feel that they benefit from sharing with each other has already begun to break down."[49]

---

46. Ibid.
47. King, *Being Benevolence*, 358.
48. Dalai Lama, *Ethics for the New Millennium* (New York: Riverhead Books, 1999), 161-62.
49. Loy, "Pave the Planet or Wear Shoes?" 103.

Thich Nhat Hahn uses the phrase "engaged Buddhism" to speak about those Buddhist adherents who are socially engaged and are responding to the challenges of globalization and enacting Buddhist social conscience.[50] While the goal of Buddhists and others committed to social justice may be the same, the tactics and approaches can differ from other social activists. For Thich Nhat Hahn, engaged Buddhism means that "when faced with immense suffering, Buddhists must take action and engage their society," stepping beyond the ancient tradition of nirvana-seeking meditation, and confronting those responsible for profound suffering.[51] As Sybille Scholz, the former executive director of the Buddhist Peace Fellowship in Berkeley, California, observed,

> We're the ones who protest quietly . . . Holding up signs and making noise is like spitting in the wind. You impact no one because you are dismissed for your aggressiveness. And, besides, it makes you a more aggressive person, which just feeds into more aggressive action the next time you decide to protest. We try to be quiet. Silence allows space for listening. It opens up a space for dialogue that can be trusted.[52]

Buddhism puts priority on human persons and not simply on human progress that is measured by technological or material benchmarks. Engaged Buddhists believe that inner transformation and social action are integral parts of the same spiritual path.[53] In a world where more and more people are defined by the quantity of their possessions and the extent of their material riches, Buddhism, in contrast, prizes being over having, people over profit, and interconnectedness over individualism.

THE BAHÁ'Í FAITH

The Bahá'í faith is the youngest of the major world religions, and it is the one that most sees globalization as part of God's master plan, where humanity is being drawn into a single race that will be united into one global society.[54] Its founder, Bahá'u'lláh (1817-1892), is regarded as the most recent in the line of

---

50. Rifkin, *Spiritual Perspectives on Globalization*, 105.

51. John L. Esposito, Darrell J. Fasching, and Todd Lewis, "Buddhism: Ways to Nirvana," in *World Religions Today* (New York: Oxford University Press, 2002), 357.

52. Rifkin, *Spiritual Perspectives on Globalization*, 106. I am also grateful to Jaleh Dashti-Gibson for her insightful comments on this section.

53. Joseph Kornfield and Jack Goldstein, *Seeking the Heart of Wisdom* (Boston: Shambhala, 1987).

54. For more on Bahá'í faith, see the official international website at http://www.bahai.org.

messengers of God, in company with Abraham, Moses, Buddha, Zoroaster, Christ, and Muhammad. Bahá'í has members in 235 countries and territories throughout the world from over twenty-one hundred ethnic, racial, and tribal groups that number some five million worldwide. It believes that humanity is a single people with a common destiny. According to the Bahá'í faith, the principal challenge facing the peoples of the earth is to accept the fact of their oneness and to assist the processes of unification.[55]

Bahá'u'lláh believed the earth to be but one country, with humankind as its citizens, and each day we come closer to the unification of a global society. Even while respecting the principle of subsidiarity, the Bahá'í faith sees globalization as a part of God's plan of salvation because humanity is gradually evolving to a future where there will be one world language, one world parliament, one executive body, one world tribunal, one world force for maintaining order, and one world metropolis that will function as a global nerve center.[56] The historical forces now at work, according to Bahá'u'lláh, are beginning to break down traditional barriers of race, class, creed, and nation, which eventually will result in the birth of a universal civilization.[57]

This new civilization calls for the creation of a just, peaceful, and prosperous society that fosters cooperation, trust, and a genuine concern for others. It promotes key principles that the adherents believe will facilitate genuine progress: (1) oneness, whereby there is a common God, a common humanity, and a common faith; (2) inclusion, whereby all forms of prejudice are eradicated; (3) equality, whereby men and women are equal in all aspects of human society; (4) truth, whereby science and religious truths are in harmony with each other; (5) education, whereby children throughout the world can receive schooling; (6) language, whereby all learn a common world idiom in addition to their native tongue; (7) peace, whereby a world governing body oversees the common good;[58] (8) justice, which eliminates the extremes of wealth and poverty; and (9) openness, whereby people are free to investigate and search for truth.

While recognizing the immense potential of globalization to unite the human community, the Bahá'í faith recognizes the socioeconomic dispari-

55. See Holly Hanson Vick, *Social and Economic Development: A Bahá'í Approach* (Oxford: George Ronald, 1989).

56. See Charles Lerche, ed., *Emergence: Dimensions of a New World Order* (London: Baha'i Publishing Trust, 1991); and Firuz Kazemzadeh, "A Review of Our Global Neighborhood," *World Order* 27, no. 3 (Summer 1996): 43-47.

57. See also Farhad Sabetan, "An Exploration into the Political Economy of Global Prosperity," *Journal of Baha'i Studies* 7, no. 4 (June-September 1997): 43-68.

58. See especially The Universal House of Justice, *The Promise of World Peace: To the Peoples of the World* (Australia: Baha'i Publications, 1986), available online at http://www.bahaiteachings.org; and Jaleh Dashti-Gibson, "Understanding Post-Cold War Collective Sanctions," *World Order* 27, no. 3 (Summer 1996): 34-48.

ties caused by the current economic system.[59] One of the central dimensions of the vision of Bahá'u'lláh is justice.[60] He believed that the answer to the world's problems lies in a profound change of heart and mind that can come about only through religion. The Bahá'í faith also sees that part of the root problem comes from a profound misunderstanding of human nature. The Bahá'í faith believes that a "fundamental redefinition of human relationships is called for . . . among human beings themselves, between human beings and nature, between the individual and society, and between the members of society and its institutions."[61] While recognizing that the fundamentals of the economy have a divine dimension, the Bahá'í faith sees that humanity as a whole suffers from a disease that manifests itself in a lack of love and a lack of altruism.[62] Bahá'u'lláh saw economic injustice as a moral evil contrary to the will of God, and he warned the rich of "the midnight sighing of the poor, lest heedlessness lead them into the path of destruction, and deprive them of the Tree of Wealth." He also said "the poor in your midst are My trust; you must guard My trust, and be not intent only on your own ease."[63]

The Bahá'í faith believes that people must care not only for the poor but also for the environment.[64] The human and material resources of the earth must be used for the benefit of all over the long term and not for the advantage of the few in the short term. This can be done only if the fundamental principle of organized economic activity is cooperation. Bahá'u'lláh compared the world to the human body. Just as no cell exists independently of the body, so no human being can live independently of the human community to which he or she belongs. Nonetheless, each cell and each person has his or her own characteristics, so the Bahá'í faith is not looking for uniformity as much as unity, a unity that presupposes diversity.[65] The body, at the same time, is more than the sum total of its parts. The ultimate function of this unified body is called not only biological self-maintenance but self-awareness or consciousness.

---

59. For more on Bahá'í faith and the economy, see Mary Fish, "Economic Prosperity: A Global Imperative," *Journal of Baha'i Studies* 7, no. 3 (March-June 1997): 1-16.

60. For perspective on Bahá'í faith and justice, see "Abolition of Extremes of Poverty and Wealth," http://bahaiteachings.org.

61. *The Prosperity of Humankind* (Wilmette, Ill.: Bahá'í Publishing Trust, 2005), section III; also available online at http://www.bahaiteachings.org.

62. See "Abolition of Extremes of Poverty and Wealth."

63. Bahá'u'lláh, *The Hidden Words* (Wilmette, Ill.: Bahá'í Publishing Trust, 1985), 39, 41 (translation slightly changed).

64. For more on the environment in light of a global ethic, see Roxanne Lalonde, "University in Diversity: A Conceptual Framework for a Global Ethic of Environmental Sustainability," *Journal of Baha'i Studies* 6, no. 3 (September-December 1994): 39-73.

65. Bahá'í International Community, "The Prosperity of Humankind" (Haifa, Israel: Bahá'í International Community Office of Public Information, 1995), section I. See http://www.bahai.org/article-1-7-4-1.html.

Only from within this framework of cooperation does the Bahá'í faith believe in the concept of private property and private economic initiative. It does not believe that all should have the same income because of differences in talents, capacities, and relative value to society, which deserve different compensations. But it does say that all individuals should have a basic income that provides for essential needs while at the same time limiting income of others that would lead to excessive wealth. When people bring their spiritual ideals together with their practical decisions, then justice is truly possible.

In January 1995, the Bahá'í leadership released a statement, in preparation for the United Nations World Summit for Social Development in Copenhagen, that examines prevailing attitudes and practices in social and economic development.[66] Called "The Prosperity of Humankind," this document looks at what is happening in the world because of globalization, where it is taking us, and who is taking us there. This document recognizes that the current changes in society posed by globalization require an overhaul of how we think about policies, resources, planning, methods, organization, social structures, social justice, and even human nature itself. The document asks in a probing way why spirituality has not been more central to the process of globalization:

> Why, then, have spiritual issues facing humanity not been central to the development discourse? Why have most of the priorities—indeed most of the underlying assumptions—of the international development agenda been determined so far by materialistic world views to which only small minorities of the earth's population subscribe?[67]

At its core, this document recognizes that the current economic crisis is caused in large part because of the inability of humanity to define itself in terms of its fundamental spiritual dimensions. Many people in contemporary society instead define themselves in material terms, which has contributed largely to the widespread economic polarization and artificial distinctions between developing and developed countries. In order for all people to assume responsibility for a collective destiny, the Bahá'í faith believes that there must be a "consciousness of the oneness of humankind."

The document states that justice must be the central value that shapes the developing global community. Bahá'u'lláh said that justice is "the best beloved of all things" because it enables people to see things with their own eyes and to be fair-minded and equitable in their dealings with others. The Bahá'í faith understands justice on two levels. On the individual level, jus-

---

66. Ibid., section II.
67. Ibid., section IV.

tice means seeing things correctly and accurately distinguishing truth from falsehood. On the group level, justice functions like a compass that guides collective decision-making: "To the extent that justice becomes a guiding concern of human interaction, a consultative climate is encouraged that permits options to be examined dispassionately and appropriate courses of action selected."[68]

The document also notes that justice extends to the realm of culture, and in this sense it advocates for the safeguarding of legitimate diversity of cultures. It believes that every person has the right "to expect that those cultural conditions essential to his or her identity enjoy the protection of national and international law."[69] As the document notes,

> Much like the role played by the gene pool in the biological life of humankind and its environment, the immense wealth of cultural diversity achieved over thousands of years is vital to the social and economic development of a human race experiencing its collective coming-of-age. It represents a heritage that must be permitted to bear its fruit in a global civilization. On the one hand, cultural expressions need to be protected from suffocation by the materialistic influences currently holding sway. On the other, cultures must be enabled to interact with one another in ever-changing patterns of civilization, free of manipulation for partisan political ends.[70]

The Bahá'í faith, in summary, says that humanity is coming of age, the inhabitants of the earth are a single people, justice should be its ruling principle of social organization, and the world can be humanized through a rigorous pursuit of scientific and religious truth. This requires a radical rethinking of concepts that currently govern the way human beings live and move in the world. One of the visible expressions of justice is consultation, which among other things, enables people to transcend their own perspective and be open to a collective wisdom. According to Bahá'u'lláh, "No man can attain his true station except through his justice. No power can exist except through unity. No welfare and no well-being can be attained except through consultation."[71]

While the Bahá'í faith would regard much of the process of globalization as part of the unfolding of God's will, it would also say that currently humanity is technologically advancing but spiritually underdeveloped. It recognizes that the best of scientific and technological resources should be used to their

---

68. Ibid., section II.
69. Ibid.
70. Ibid.
71. Ibid., section III.

fullest extent, but these resources should especially be used to address the great ills of society such as poverty. In this sense, the Bahá'í faith says that in this process of globalization, "what is required of the peoples of the world is a measure of faith and resolve to match the enormous energies with which the Creator of all things has endowed this spiritual springtime of the race."[72]

AFRICAN INDIGENOUS RELIGIONS

Africa is the second largest continent in the world, and, with an area of nearly twelve million square miles, it is so vast that all of China, the United States (including Alaska), and Europe would fit into its borders. Not only is it the earliest recorded place of human existence, but Africa has more than twenty-one hundred languages and three thousand ethnic groups.[73] More than fifty modern nations currently occupy the African continent, and each has its own unique history, customs, and beliefs.[74] Its societal groups vary from itinerants to villagers, from tribes to urbanized communities, and, like its physical geography—which ranges from rain forest to inhospitable desert and almost everything in between—the spiritual landscape of Africa is diverse, complex, and fascinating.

Eighty percent of Africans today are Muslims or Christians, yet Africans had diverse and historically dynamic religious traditions and practices before their encounter with the religions of the book. Generalizing about what might be called these indigenous religions is difficult. Not only did they take a variety of forms, but they have also been shaped by encounters with other religious traditions in recent centuries, making it hard to characterize African religions under one name, to study them on their own, or to identify them by a common set of rubrics.[75] Despite the diversity and the impossibility of identifying some "pure" form of such traditions today, some basic commonalities exist and some generalizations can be made about their distinguishing features. These same themes also contribute to our reflection on a global ethic.

Many scholars argue that the overarching principle in African indigenous religions is that life flows as a sacred gift from a loving Creator God. Creation

---

72. Ibid., sections V, VII.

73. Ifi Amadiume, "Igbo and African Religious Perspectives on Religious Conscience and the Global Economy," in *Subverting Greed*, ed. Knitter and Muzaffar, 16.

74. *Merriam-Webster's Encyclopedia of World Religions*, ed. Wendy Doniger, (Springfield, Mass.: Merriam-Webster, 1999), 17.

75. *The Oxford Dictionary of World Religions*, ed. John Bowker (Oxford: Oxford University Press, 1997), 25-26.

and life go hand in hand, and life is considered the supreme treasure that should be reverenced, enhanced, sustained, and safeguarded.[76] Many African religions have complex ceremonies surrounding birth and death, rituals that celebrate, nurture, and protect life, especially when challenged by sickness, age, or division.

Closely related to the ethic of life is the centrality of relationships, particularly the family. In contrast to Western proclivities toward individual autonomy, Africans tend to understand themselves first as social creatures. They value their ties of kinship and family life, clan and community. To be human from the perspective of African indigenous religions means becoming active and participating members in a common network of relationships.

Indigenous African religions believe that, in the end, life is measured by the quality of one's relationship with the Creator, other people, creatures, and the created environment. Laurenti Magesa notes that, "not only is the view of the universe at the service, so to speak, of the formation and execution of good relationships, but relationships make possible the continuing existence of the universe."[77] Because humans are built for each other, they have a fundamental responsibility to each other:

> What falls on one, falls on all, [and the ethical consequence is that] we must repair every breach of harmony, every wound and lesion. We must demand reparation for ourselves because we are not merely ourselves, and for others because they are also ourselves.[78]

In this framework, refusal to share is morally wrong because it weakens the bonds of the human family, and it destroys the bonds needed to form community.

This community involves not only those who are living but also ancestors and those yet to be born. In contrast to those areas of the world where some of the unborn are unwanted and many of the elderly are considered a burden rather than a gift to the community, this witness is a promising contribution to a global ethic. African indigenous religions believe that the ancestors remain full members of the community, even after they die. Their lives are considered a heritage to the living, and many Africans believe they continue to influence the events of their families from beyond the visible

---

76. Chris Nwaka Egbulem, "African Spirituality," in *The New Dictionary of Catholic Spirituality*, ed. Michael Downey (Collegeville, Minn.: Liturgical Press, 1993), 18.

77. Laurenti Magesa, *African Religion: The Moral Traditions of Abundant Life* (Maryknoll, N.Y.: Orbis Books, 1997), 64.

78. Harvey Sindima, "Community of Life: Ecological Theology in African Perspective," in *Liberating Life: Contemporary Approaches to Ecological Theology*, ed. Charles Birch, William Eikan, and Jay McDaniel (Maryknoll, N.Y.: Orbis Books, 1990), 145-46.

world. In a similar way elders are often distinguished by the function they perform for the community—herbalist, rain-asker, diviner, medium, prayer leader, prophet—and are the leaders, teachers, counselors, and moral guides for the people.[79]

This ethic of life extends not only to the elderly and the deceased ancestors but also those yet-to-be-born. While not yet actively involved in the community, these too are members of the community in their potentiality. As a consequence they must not be wronged in any way by the living, nor should they be denied the opportunity to participate fully in the life of the community.[80] African indigenous religions have a strong sense of the common good and a strong sense of our interconnectedness as human beings. As John Mbiti has summed up the African ethic, "I am, because we are; and since we are, therefore I am."[81]

Because relationships are so important, African indigenous religions value the dignity of each and every human person. If any lack dignity, the entire community is diminished. Dignity means that there is practical evidence of abundant life and absence of want—wealth in crops, animals, and children— as well as the absence of disease and other social afflictions. This dignity of life is brought out in the conduct that promotes generosity, communion, right judgment, forgiveness, impartiality, and integrity.[82] It is especially demanded of the community leaders, who are held to a higher standard of behavior. The leaders are expected to keep peace and maintain relationships without physical coercion, and to do everything possible to prevent hostilities without the shedding of blood, which is abominable.[83] Treating every person with respect is another tenet common to African religions, and respectful behavior toward all prevents one from being "haunted" in this world and tormented in the next.

African culture, arguably stemming from the influence of its religious traditions, puts a high premium on the virtue of hospitality. The gift of shared food around the table creates a place where family relationships and friendships are forged and where community develops. Sharing food and conversation not only creates strong bonds of relationship, but it is more difficult to create division among those with whom one has broken bread, or to ignore the needs of those with whom one shares a common relationship. Hospitality cultivates friendships and promotes harmony and unity.

---

79. Magesa, *African Religion*, 67.
80. Ibid., 66.
81. John S. Mbiti, *African Religions and Philosophy* (New York: Frederick A. Praeger, 1969), 108-9.
82. Ibid., 263-64.
83. Ibid., 68.

In a world more and more dependent on written communication and information gathering, many of the beliefs of African indigenous religions continue to be transmitted by oral tradition. This too has significance not only as an aspect of anthropological curiosity but because such oral communication also enhances relationships. Storytelling, for example, not only communicates the narratives of a community, but it also transmits moral codes from one generation to the next. In addition to the spoken word, African indigenous religions have learned to respect the words of nature, like thunder, which reveal the divine presence in the world.

The sacredness of life includes respect for the natural environment, which also is understood as a gift that flows from a creating God. African indigenous religions believe that creation, which includes not only what is visible but also what is invisible, bears the marks of goodness and godliness. Even though they dedicate specific locations for worship and sacrifice, they believe all space is sacred and that God's presence permeates all of creation.[84]

Because the earth and its resources are seen as part of a common human patrimony, African religious thought shuns the idea of private ownership. African religious principles promote the idea that everything comes from God as a gift for all human beings. Land, in particular, is regarded as an essential source of sustenance for the community, which must be held in trust for the present and future. A community may use a piece of land to cultivate crops, but in the end they are not its final owners.[85] As Julius Nyerere, first president of Tanzania, noted, "It is not God's intention that we should use his free gifts to us—land and air and water—by permission of our fellow human beings."[86] Natural resources, as part of the sacred creation, are a free gift from God for the common use and good of all people, which is an ever more urgent message as we face a growing ecological crisis.

The characteristics of African religions, such as the sacredness of life and creation, the importance of family and community, the imperative of hospitality, and the value of oral tradition, all provide another way of living, moving, and being in the world. As the West becomes more and more characterized by secularism, science, and technology, these basic values from African religious traditions offer much to a global ethic directed toward cultivating ordered relationships, to a deeper level of intimacy and honesty, and to a renewed vision of respect for God, one another, and for the earth.

---

84. Chris Nwaka Egbulem, "African Spirituality," in *The New Dictionary of Catholic Spirituality*, ed. Downey, 20.

85. Magesa, *African Religion*, 280.

86. Julius K. Nyerere, *Freedom and Unity (Uhuru na Umoja): A Selection from Writings and Speeches 1952-65* (London: Oxford University Press, 1967), 56.

WORLD RELIGIONS AND THE CHALLENGE OF PEACE

If a god is that to which one ultimately gives one's energies, one's resources, and one's heart, then to our discussion of world religions and globalization, we must add "moneytheism."[87] As we noted in chapter 1, moneytheism deals with the idolization of capital, expressed as the worship of the gods of the marketplace, and it is often practiced through the rituals of the stock market and the liturgies of global capitalism. It has a creed of its own, and more and more people live it out with unyielding obedience and religious devotion. Yet, as Karl Polanyi has observed, "To allow the market mechanism to be sole director of human beings and their natural environment . . . would result in the demolition of society."[88] Pope Francis may be suggesting that the demolition has already begun: "The current financial crisis can make us overlook the fact that it originated in a profound human crisis: the denial of the primacy of the human person! We have created new idols. The worship of the ancient golden calf (cf. Ex 32:1-35) has returned in a new and ruthless guise in the idolatry of money and the dictatorship of an impersonal economy lacking a truly human purpose." (EG 55)

While the welfare of humanity is vulnerable to moneytheism as a form of market fundamentalism, it is arguably even more vulnerable to religious fundamentalism. Although religion (from *religio* meaning "to tie together") has the greatest potential to unite people, it can also be used as a weapon to divide, alienate, and even destroy people as never before. History has given us many examples, such as the Crusades, the Inquisition, and suicide bombers, to name a few, of how religion can be a destructive force in human society. Yet, as globalization uproots traditional moorings of society and people feel themselves adrift, many will see fundamentalist interpretations of major world religions as easy solutions to complex problems. It remains to be seen whether we can learn from the mistakes of the past and enable religion to be a reconciling force in the world, or whether it will be a source of destruction that will threaten the human race.

The Parliament of the World's Religions points out that, despite the danger of religious fanatics, the major faith traditions of the world are central to developing a new global ethic that can help create a new global order.[89] It proposes that this ethic should be shaped by these central commitments: (1) a commitment to a culture of nonviolence and respect for life, (2) a commitment to a culture of solidarity and a just economic order, (3) a commitment to a culture of tolerance and a life of truthfulness, and (4) a commitment to

---

87. David Loy first introduced me to the term of "moneytheism."
88. Karl Polanyi, *The Great Transformation*, 2nd ed. (Boston: Beacon, 2001), 73.
89. Ibid., 5.

a culture of equal rights and partnership between men and women. Lastly, it says that the earth cannot be changed unless there is a change in consciousness on the individual and communal level. It argues that what is needed is "a change in the inner orientation, the whole mentality, the hearts of people, and a conversion from a false path to a new orientation for life."[90] Martin Marty adds that what is needed is not simply religious tolerance but "the risk of hospitality" toward those who share different belief systems.[91]

As the members of the human family seek to understand better their interconnection to one another beyond their creedal differences, it is helpful to see how this global ethic is already being realized in our present day. Every year on Thanksgiving Day at San Fernando Cathedral in San Antonio, Texas, leaders from many different religions gather to give thanks according to their own creeds and practices. In prayer, meditation, and song, Protestants, Catholics, Jews, Muslims, Buddhists, Hindus, Bahá'í, native tribal religions, and others gather together for a common prayer service. Fittingly, Native Americans begin the service beating a drum, symbolic of a common heartbeat, a common humanity. Then, a Muslim imam reads from the Qur'an. A Jewish rabbi sings a psalm. A Buddhist monk offers a moment of silence. And so on. At the end of the ceremony, all join in a common procession and offer gifts to aid the poor and vulnerable of the community.

Shortly after the first year he organized this service, Virgil Elizondo remembers well the comment of a quiet, traditional, Catholic woman, who had a veil over her head and prayed the rosary. She came over to him and abruptly said, "Father, I need to talk to you!" Fearing the worst of criticisms, he listened as she said, "I have a reaction to this prayer service. I have to tell you that in my home I have a painting of the Last Supper, and it is one of my favorite paintings. When I saw all these different religions gathered here in the cathedral, thanking God and seeking to become better people through their respective faiths, I felt like I was witnessing the Lord's table at the end of time when God will gather all people to himself." She referred to it as a spiritual feast at a common table of all the major world religions.

Similarly, a Hindu woman also in attendance at the service remarked,

Of all the activities I do during the year, I treasure most the gathering of all of these different religions in this cathedral into one harmonious moment. I feel what we have experienced here is a small hope of what we may all become some day. It is my hope that the peace we experience may be multiplied a thousandfold so that what we experience inside this church may embody what we become outside of it.

90. Parliament of the World's Religions, *Towards a Global Ethic: An Initial Declaration*, 7.
91. Martin E. Marty, *When Faiths Collide* (Malden, Mass.: Blackwell, 2005), 1.

Likewise, a Jewish leader observed,

> When I was sitting inside the church, and I looked at the architecture around me, with the beams above and the nave in front of us, it felt like we were all inside a large ship. Then I thought of all of the different religions that had gathered together into this one place. As I thought about all of the wars, divisions, and arguments that we have with each other, but this one moment of peace and harmony we experienced together, it felt like we were gathered all of us into Noah's ark and we were being led through the waves of change into a new creation which allowed us to see our interconnectedness together.[92]

As the major world religions come to find their place in the new world order and their respective contribution to the global community, this experience at San Fernando is a reminder that learning to live together as a common family does not mean watering down one's beliefs into a bland commonality, but rather allowing each religion to express its own creed and tradition faithfully while at the same time being open to the other. Beyond the differences, the basis of a common global ethic is a unified concern for a more just and peaceful world, and a greater commitment to and solidarity with the poor. If we do not learn how to come to the same table even with our differences, we will self-destruct. As Martin Luther King, Jr., said, "Now the judgment of God is upon us, and we must either learn to live together as brothers [and sisters] or we are all going to perish together as fools."[93]

QUESTIONS FOR REFLECTION

1. How do Christian beliefs parallel other world religions in their view of globalization? How are they different?
2. In what ways have you encountered religious traditions different from your own?
3. In what ways do you see "moneytheism" as a fundamental creed today?
4. What concrete examples have you witnessed of ecumenical collaboration and justice?
5. What are the positive and negative sides of pluralism? Relativism?
6. What central tenets of world religions, in your opinion, are most important to help humanize the process of globalization?
7. Discuss this statement: The major world religions today offer the greatest hope for reconciliation and are the greatest threat to world peace.

---

92. I experienced the Thanksgiving service at San Fernando Cathedral in San Antonio; the quotations from other attendees were told to me (Thanksgiving, 2004).

93. Martin Luther King, Jr., *A Testament of Hope: The Essential Writings and Speeches of Martin Luther King, Jr.*, ed. James M. Washington (New York: HarperCollins, 1986), 253.

SUGGESTIONS FOR FURTHER READING AND STUDY

General

Hawkin, David J., ed. *The Twenty-first Century Confronts Its Gods: Globalization, Technology, and War.* Albany: State University of New York Press, 2004.

Knitter, Paul F., and Chandra Muzaffar, eds. *Subverting Greed: Religious Perspectives on the Global Economy.* Maryknoll, N.Y.: Orbis Books, 2003.

Marty, Martin E. *When Faiths Collide.* Malden, Mass.: Blackwell, 2005.

Polanyi, Karl. *The Great Transformation,* 2nd ed. Boston: Beacon, 2001.

Rifkin, Ira. *Spiritual Perspectives on Globalization: Making Sense of Economic and Cultural Upheaval.* Woodstock, Vt.: Skylight Paths, 2002.

Schweiker, William, Michael A. Johnson, and Kevin Jung, eds. *Humanity before God: Contemporary Faces of Jewish, Christian, and Islamic Ethics.* Minneapolis: Augsburg Fortress, 2006.

Islam

Armstrong, Karen. *Islam: A Short History.* New York: Modern Library, 2000.

Esposito, John L. *Islam: The Straight Path.* Oxford: Oxford University Press, 1998.

Khalid, Fazlun M., and Umar Ibrahim Vadillo. "Trade and Commerce in Islam," in *Islam and Ecology,* edited by Fazlun Khalid and Joanne O'Brien. New York: Cassell, 1992.

Mayer, Ann Elizabeth. "Islamic Law and Human Rights: Conundrums and Equivocations." In *Religion and Human Rights: Competing Claims?* edited by Carrie Gustafson and Peter Juviler. New York: M. E. Sharpe, 1999.

Waardenburg, Jacques. "Reflections on the West." In *Islamic Thought in the Twentieth Century,* edited by Suha Taji-Farouki and Basheer M. Nafi. New York: I. B. Tauris, 2004.

Warde, Ibrahim. *Islamic Finance in the Global Economy.* Edinburgh: Edinburgh University Press, 2000.

Hinduism

Crawford, S. Cromwell. *The Evolution of Hindu Ethical Ideals.* Calcutta: Firma K. L. Mukhopadhyay, 1974.

de Mello, Anthony. *The Song of the Bird.* Anand, India: Gujarat Sahitya Prakash, 1982.

Frawley, David. *Hinduism and the Clash of Civilizations.* New Delhi: Voice of India, 2001.

Jhingran, Sarah. *Aspects of Hindu Morality.* Delhi: Motilal Banarsidass Publishers, 1989.

Perrett, Roy W. *Hindu Ethics: A Philosophical Study.* Honolulu: University of Hawaii Press, 1998.

Smith, Huston. *The Illustrated World's Religions: A Guide to Our Wisdom Traditions,* 2nd ed. New York: HarperSanFrancisco, 1995.

Buddhism

Dalai Lama. *Ethics for the New Millennium.* New York: Riverhead Books, 1999.

de Silva, Padmasiri. *Buddhism, Ethics and Society: The Conflicts and Dilemmas of Our Time.* Victoria: Monash University Press, 2002.

Eppsteiner, Fred. *The Path of Compassion: Writings on Socially Engaged Buddhism.* Berkeley, Calif.: Parallax Press, 1988.

Esposito, John L., Darrell J. Fasching, and Todd Lewis, "Buddhism: Ways to Nirvana," in *World Religions Today.* New York: Oxford University Press, 2002.

Harvey, Peter. *An Introduction to Buddhist Ethics.* Cambridge: Cambridge University Press, 2000.

King, Sallie B. *Being Benevolence: The Social Ethics of Engaged Buddhism.* Honolulu: University of Hawaii Press, 2005.

Loy, David R. *The Great Awakening: A Buddhist Social Theory.* Boston: Wisdom, 2003.

The Bahá'í Faith

Bahá'í International Community. *The Prosperity of Humankind.* Haifa, Israel: Bahá'í International Community Office of Public Information, 1995.

Bahá'u'lláh. *The Hidden Words.* Wilmette, Ill.: Bahá'í Publishing Trust, 1985.

Lerche, Charles, ed. *Emergence: Dimensions of a New World Order.* London: Baha'i Publishing Trust, 1991.

Vick, Holly Hanson. *Social and Economic Development: A Bahá'í Approach.* Oxford: George Ronald, 1989.

The Prosperity of Humankind. Wilmette, Ill.: Bahá'í Publishing Trust, 2005.

African Indigenous Religions

Amadiume, Ifi. "Igbo and African Religious Perspectives on Religious Conscience and the Global Economy." In *Subverting Greed: Religious Perspectives on the Global Economy,* edited by Paul F. Knitter and Chandra Muzaffar. Maryknoll, N.Y.: Orbis Books, 2003.

Magesa, Laurenti. *African Religion: The Moral Traditions of Abundant Life.* Maryknoll, N.Y.: Orbis Books, 1997.

Mbiti, John S. *African Religions and Philosophy.* New York: Frederick A. Praeger, 1969.

Nyerere, Julius K. *Freedom and Unity (Uhuru na Umoja): A Selection from Writings and Speeches 1952-65.* London: Oxford University Press, 1967.

Sindima, Harvey. "Community of Life: Ecological Theology in African Perspective," in *Liberating Life: Contemporary Approaches to Ecological Theology,* edited by Charles Birch, William Eikan, and Jay McDaniel. Maryknoll, N.Y.: Orbis Books, 1990.

6

Images of Mercy, Icons of Justice

Five Contemporary Models

Many years ago, there was a village that had been experiencing terrible drought. There had not been a drop of rain in that territory for five years. In desperation, Catholics made processions, Protestants offered prayers, and the Chinese burned joss sticks and shot off guns to drive away evil spirits, hoping it would eventually rain. But still, nothing happened. The cattle were dying, the vegetation had dried up, and the people's hopes had all but evaporated. Famous rainmakers from all over had been called to remedy the situation, but they all failed to make it rain. In the villagers' last attempt, they called upon a renowned rainmaker from afar. He was an old man with a weathered face, but he had a wise heart. They offered him anything he wanted, hoping he could bring down water from heaven. He said, "All I want is a space where I can be alone and quiet." So they found him a little cave way up in the hills, which was no more than a cleft in the rocks, and he hid away there for four days. There was no movement, no noise, and no action in the cave, and the people began to worry. But then on the fifth day, clouds began to form, and then a heavy rain started to fall and quenched the thirst of the parched earth. When the people saw the water, they were overwhelmed and overjoyed. One of the leaders of the village asked the rainmaker how he accomplished such a miracle. The rainmaker replied, "I have done nothing." Astounded at his explanation, the villagers said, "What do you mean you have done nothing? Five days after you came, the rain started." The rainmaker explained, "I come from a place where everything is in Tao, in balance, and in harmony. Things are in order there, and life is aligned with heaven. When I arrived here, the first thing I noticed was that everything in your village was in disorder and out of harmony with heaven. So I spent four days putting myself into harmony with the Divine. Then the rains came.[1]

---

1. I am grateful to Fr. Joe Boyle of the Trappist Monastery in Snowmass, Colorado, for first introducing me to this story. Its origins are attributed to Carl Jung, and there are various versions of

B EYOND THE IDEAS, INFORMATION, AND INDUSTRY of our modern world, there lies deep within the human heart a profound hunger to know the meaning and purpose of life. Finding the best way to satisfy this hunger has never been an easy task in any generation. Some people deal with it by plunging themselves into a relentless pursuit of pleasure, power, and profit-making, only to discover in the end that these are more like narcotics than nourishment. Others feed it by immersing themselves in various philosophies, ideologies, and even religious practices, only to find out that these too can become empty if they are not grounded in meaningful relationships. When one ignores the transcendent dimensions of human life, the soul withers and undergoes a spiritual famine.

Almost three thousand years ago, the prophet Amos said, "Yes, days are coming, says the LORD God, when I will send famine upon the land: Not a famine of bread, or thirst for water, but for hearing the word of the LORD" (Am 8:11). While the social and economic progress of globalization has fed some of the needs of the human family, it has not remedied the undeniable spiritual hungers within people. Amidst the distractions of contemporary life, which often keep us from identifying this hunger, where can one find genuine sustenance? To whom can one look for guidance on this road of the spiritual life? Where are the rainmakers who can bring justice to the world and bring about harmony and peace in our relationships?

Christians affirm that no one has been completely in harmony with heaven except one person. There has only been one "rainmaker," namely, Jesus Christ. He is the One hoped for in the book of the prophet Isaiah, where it is written: "Let the clouds rain down the Just One, and the earth bring forth a Savior" (Is 45:8). As the incarnation of the justice of God, Jesus is the one who unites the human with the divine, who brings order out of disorder, who rains down justice from heaven by bringing people into right relationships. His life continues in the life of his followers, whose inspiration touches some of the deepest hungers of the human heart.

Because human beings are, by nature, relational creatures, they are moved to change and transformation not so much by abstract ideas and propositional truths as by the witness of exemplary people whose lives give expression to the noblest ideals of human existence. Some individuals, in cooperating with the work of divine grace, have so aligned their lives with the justice of God that they embody what it means to live in harmony with God, others, the environment, and oneself. In this chapter, we will explore some contemporary figures from various cultures and traditions who are images of mercy

---

it in printed and Internet form. The story above is my compilation and synthesis of these versions, including my own additions. See Ronald Hayman, *A Life of Jung* (New York: Norton, 2001), 246.

and icons of justice for the human family. As icons they are windows to the sacred. They manifest an integrity of heart, not because they are perfect but because they have had the courage to embrace the entirety of their existence.[2] Their path to harmony has included coming to terms with their confusions as well as their convictions, hesitation as well as hope, fear as well as fortitude, and sinfulness as well as strength. As rainmakers of the contemporary era, they faced the disorder and discord of our own day and age, aligned themselves with the Just One, and renewed the earth with the waters of hope.

Even though the limitation of space does not allow us to examine these individuals in great detail, here we want to explore the lives of Mahatma Gandhi, Martin Luther King, Jr., Dorothy Day, Blessed Teresa, and Oscar Romero. Because we often see them only as individuals rather than as part of a network of relationships, we will look at them alongside other major figures who lived, worked, and in some cases, died with them. To gain a better picture of their lives, we will examine (1) their historical context, (2) the foundational experience that shaped their vision of life, (3) the major metaphors that describe their understanding of God and/or human life, (4) their operative theology, and (5) their contribution to a just faith legacy.

MAHATMA GANDHI AND KASTURBAI GANDHI: ICONS OF NONVIOLENCE

Summary and historical context. Mohandas Karamchand Gandhi (1869-1948) is recognized as one of the great souls of the twentieth century and the leader of India's independence movement. He defined the modern practice of nonviolence and sought inner transformation and social reform through radical love. His life gives witness to the enduring spiritual power of one man to open up a way for God's reign in history, even in the face of the political power of an empire.

Foundational experience. In 1893, on the train to South Africa to practice law for the first time, Gandhi was quietly reading a book in the first-class compartment when a white conductor, seeing the color of his skin, ordered him to the back of the train and into the third-class compartments. Gandhi refused

---

2. I am grateful to Parker Palmer for his reflections on identity and integrity. He says, "By identity and integrity I do not mean only our noble features, or the good deeds we do, or the brave faces we wear to conceal our confusions and complexities. Identity and integrity have as much to do with our shadows and limits, our wounds and fears, as with our strengths and potentials." See Parker Palmer, *The Courage to Teach* (San Francisco: Jossey-Bass, 1998), 13. I also want to thank Mignon Montpetit, who has helped me understand the deeper meaning of integrity.

to move. The train authorities subsequently removed him from first class, beat him, and threw him off the train. As he lay stranded in the freezing cold, he examined his options and realized he could escape by going back to India, react by joining a violent, revolutionary moment in South Africa, or respond peacefully and prayerfully by means of nonviolent protest.[3] This foundational experience galvanized in him a deep disgust of discrimination along with a strong determination to fight racism and injustice through nonviolent means. After witnessing firsthand the racial prejudice against many other Indian immigrants, Gandhi dedicated himself to fighting for human rights.

Major metaphor. Gandhi's vision was shaped by the great truths of all the major religions, particularly those revealed through the Hindu Scriptures (*Bhagavad Gita*). One major metaphor for Gandhi was friendship. Even when he resisted the oppressive practices of the empire of Great Britain, Gandhi did not want to humiliate England or any other oppressor, but he wanted unconditional love to be a force that would reconcile all people and turn even enemies into friends.[4] Three of Gandhi's closest friends were Charlie Andrews (a Christian), Herman Kallenbach (a Jew), and Abdul Gaffer Kahn (a Muslim), and he even forged a genuine friendship with the leader of South Africa in the 1910s, Jan Christian Smuts, who was the first to jail him.[5]

His vision of friendship was built on his vision of a just human being, which he described as someone

> who is jealous of none; who is a fount of mercy; who is without egotism; who is selfless; who treats alike cold and heat, happiness and misery; who is ever forgiving; who is always contented; whose resolutions are firm; who has dedicated mind and soul to God; who causes no dread; who is not afraid of others; who is free from exultation, sorrow, and fear; who is pure; who is versed in action yet remains unaffected by it; who renounces all fruit, good and bad; who treats friend and foe alike; who is untouched by respect or disrespect; who is not puffed up by praise; who does not go under when people speak ill of him; who loves silence and solitude; and who has a disciplined reason.[6]

Gandhi realized that true friendship, however, was not possible without working toward the conquest of himself and against every trace of selfishness. Only from this inner transformation did he believe that he could work for transformation on a broader scale.

---

3. John Dear, ed., *Mohandas Gandhi: Essential Writings* (Maryknoll, N.Y.: Orbis Books, 2002), 20.

4. T. A. Raman, ed., *What Does Gandhi Want?* (New York: Oxford University Press, 1942), 43.

5. I am grateful to John Dear for this insight into the friendships of Gandhi.

6. Dear, *Mohandas Gandhi*, 36.

One of the places he learned about nonviolent resistance was at home. He had some long-term, problematic relationships with his children, and his wife Kasturbai, in particular, challenged his own initial tendencies toward domination in relationships. Her love and resistance to his own sinfulness taught him the truth of nonviolence as a path to human transformation.[7] He said,

> I learnt the lesson of nonviolence from my wife, when I tried to bend her to my will. Her determined resistance to my will, on the one hand, and her quiet submission to the suffering my stupidity involved on the other, ultimately made me ashamed of myself and cured me of my stupidity . . . in the end, she became my teacher in nonviolence.[8]

Gandhi's greatness must be understood alongside those like his wife who knew him well, not only in his strengths but also in his weaknesses.

Operative theology. Gandhi was once asked to sum up his life in three words or less. He said, "That's easy: renounce and enjoy."[9] His self-denial was not a goal in itself but a pathway toward magnanimity, justice, authenticity, and self-realization. His life was shaped by a five-point program, which he said corresponded to the five fingers of his hand: equality for untouchables, spinning, no alcohol or drugs, Hindu–Muslim friendship, and equality for women. They were all connected to the wrist, which stood for nonviolence. From this theological framework, Gandhi wanted to convert the empire through nonviolence.[10]

In the face of many complex cultural, political, and social issues, Gandhi gave special attention to how people's decisions affected the most vulnerable of society. Towards the end of his life in 1947, he wrote,

> Whenever you are in doubt, or when the self becomes too much, apply the following test. Recall the face of the poorest and the weakest man whom you may have seen, and ask yourself if the step you contemplate is going to be of any use to him. Will he gain anything by it? Will it restore him to a control over his own life and destiny? In other words, will it lead to "swaraj" for the hungry and spiritually starving millions? Then you will find your doubts and yourself melting away.[11]

---

7. Eknath Easwaran, *Gandhi the Man*, 3rd ed. (Tomales, Calif.: Nilgiri, 1997), 15, 34-35, 126.

8. Timothy Flinders (Appendix), in Easwaran, *Gandhi the Man*, 167-68.

9. Easwaran, *Gandhi the Man*, 95.

10. Raman, *What Does Gandhi Want?* 36.

11. Mahatma Gandhi, *The Essential Gandhi: An Anthology of His Writings on His Life, Work, and Ideas.* Edited by Louis Fischer (New York: Vintage Books, 2002), 275.

Especially in the later part of his life, Gandhi grounded his life on the plight of the poor, and he dedicated himself to living in solidarity with them. In seeking their liberation, he first practiced civil disobedience on a massive scale in September 1906. The power of Gandhi's love came from what he called *satyagraha* (Sanskrit), meaning "truth force," which meant resisting untruth by truthful means. Only through these means did he advocate social reform, even when it meant persecution, suffering, and death.

Gandhi's commitment to justice was personally very costly. In his efforts to confront racial injustice in South Africa and India, he was arrested twelve times and spent almost six years behind bars (2,089 days in Indian prisons and 249 days in South African prisons). Jail did not diminish his vision, and in many ways it deepened his trust in God. When he went to prison, he commented: "I am a man of faith. My reliance is solely on God. One step is enough for me. The next He will make clear to me when the time for it comes."[12]

For Gandhi, every action was an "experiment in truth" from which he tried to discern what was real, genuine, and liberating.[13] He believed that God reveals himself not in person but in action, which is the measure of a person's character.[14] The closer he came to the truth, the more he became free, and it was from this freedom that he cultivated love. He once observed:

> Truth and nonviolence are as old as the hills. All I have done is to try experiments in both on as vast a scale as I could. In doing so, I have sometimes erred and learned by my errors. Life and its problems have thus become to me so many experiments in the practice of truth and nonviolence.[15]

One of Gandhi's core goals was to abolish Hindu's untouchable caste system, which had existed for thousands of years. He believed that untouchability was contrary to the Hindu creed and was a serious crime against humanity.[16] On September 20, 1932, he began a fast unto death in his prison cell for "the removal of untouchablility." He believed that if a person "wanted to achieve the heights of divinity, he had to touch the bottom of humanity and become one with the starving millions."[17]

Above all, prayer was critically important for Gandhi. Gandhi's efforts to put himself in harmony with heaven were greatly aided by his strict life

---

12. Raman, *What Does Gandhi Want?* 39.

13. See Robert Inchausti, *The Ignorant Perfection of Ordinary People* (Albany: State University of New York Press, 1991).

14. Erik H. Erikson, *Gandhi's Truth* (New York: Norton, 1969), 410.

15. Dear, *Mohandas Gandhi*, 32.

16. D. S. Sarma, ed., *The Gandhi Sutras* (New York: Devin-Adair, 1949), 44.

17. Dear, *Mohandas Gandhi*, 33.

of prayer, meditation, fasting, and Scripture study. He would spend an hour in prayer before sunrise and an hour in prayer in the evening. During the last two decades of his life, in addition to two hours of daily prayer, he also spent one day a week in solitude, hoping to attain self-realization and divine union. He recognized that humanity spends so much energy trying to master the truths of outer nature but so little time realizing the deeper truths of human nature.[18] He believed that the human heart could be transformed only through a deeper union with God, and to aid him in the process of spiritual transformation, he pronounced lifelong vows of truth, celibacy, poverty, fearlessness, and nonviolence.[19]

Gandhi's spiritual depth enabled him to perceive the disorder and sins of the world, sins that he could name as "wealth without work, pleasure without conscience, knowledge without character, commerce without morality, science without humanity, worship without sacrifice, and politics without principle."[20] The more attentively he listened to his own inner voice, the more his vision was transformed, and the more he could hear the clamor of the poor and their cry for justice.[21] Even as he attained greater harmony with his relationships and justice and liberation for the people of South Africa and India, Gandhi was assassinated on January 30, 1948, by an outraged man from his own Hindu tradition. With his last breath, he chanted the name of God.

Core contribution. Gandhi's enduring legacy resides in a far-reaching witness to nonviolence, which expressed itself in a voluntary decision to undergo suffering and even death in order to effect personal transformation, systemic change, and social reform. He embodied the change he wanted to see in the world, and he encouraged others to do the same. He regarded nonviolence as the most powerful weapon in the world, and it could be put into practice everywhere, in our own hearts, in our families, among our friends, in our nation, and all around the world.[22] More than a tool, tactic, or strategy for social change, he saw nonviolence as a power greater than brute force and as a way of living in harmony with the laws of the universe.[23] In an age when the empires of the world seek to resolve international conflicts with military

18. Dhirendra Datta, *The Philosophy of Mahatma Gandhi* (Madison: University of Wisconsin Press, 1953), 147.

19. Ibid., 42.

20. Various sources attribute this quotation to Gandhi; see especially http://www.mkgandhi. org/mgmnt.htm.

21. Erikson, *Gandhi's Truth*, 291.

22. Sarma, *Gandhi Sutras*, 37.

23. Available online at http://www.gandhiinstitute.org.

might, Gandhi opened up a path to peace that has influenced countless people, including Dorothy Day, the Dalai Lama, Archbishop Desmond Tutu, and Martin Luther King, Jr.

MARTIN LUTHER KING, JR., AND ROSA PARKS: ICONS OF HUMAN RIGHTS

Summary and historical context. Martin Luther King, Jr. (1929-1968) was an American clergyman, a prominent leader in the American Civil Rights movement, and an advocate of nonviolent protest and social change. While he grew up in a middle-class family in Atlanta, his experience of the sting of segregation, which was the lot of many black people in the American South, prompted him to work for a more racially integrated society.[24] Motivated by the teachings of Jesus and the method of Gandhi's nonviolence, King challenged the structures of injustice that degraded people and diminished their God-given dignity.[25] His fight against social injustice deepened in 1955, when a black woman named Rosa Parks was arrested and sent to jail for refusing to give up her bus seat to a white man in Montgomery, Alabama, giving birth to the Civil Rights movement. In the years that followed, King organized large-scale protests and won many over to his vision of a more just and egalitarian society.

Foundational experience. In a speech in 1950, King said, "Even though I have never had an abrupt conversion experience, religion has been real to me and closely knitted to life. In fact, the two cannot be separated; religion for me is life."[26] While many experiences shaped his vision, one of the most significant happened when he was put in the Birmingham jail in April 1963. From there, he wrote his now famous letter, which reveals the ethical contours of a man who was profoundly shaped by the Narrative of the Gospel. From this Narrative he resisted the corrupting influence and unjust laws of the Narrative of the Empire, which enslave rather than liberate black people:

> I am in Birmingham because injustice is here. Just as the eighth century prophets left their little villages and carried their "thus saith the Lord" far

---

24. Richard L. Deats, *Martin Luther King, Jr., Spirit-led Prophet* (New York: New City Press, 2000), 18.

25. William D. Watley, ed., *Roots of Resistance: The Nonviolent Ethic of Martin Luther King, Jr.* (Valley Forge, Pa.: Judson, 1985), 48.

26. Martin Luther King, Jr., "An Autobiography of Religious Development," in *The Papers of Martin Luther King, Jr.*, vol. 1, *Called to Serve January 1929 – June 1951*, ed. Clayborne Carson (Berkeley: University of California Press, 1992), 359-63.

beyond the boundaries of their home towns; and just as the Apostle Paul left his little village of Tarsus and carried the gospel of Jesus Christ to practically every hamlet and city of the Greco-Roman world, I too am compelled to carry the gospel of freedom beyond my particular home town . . . We have waited for more than three hundred and forty years for our constitutional and God-given rights. A just law is a man-made code that squares with the moral law or the law of God. An unjust law is a code that is out of harmony with the moral law. To put it in the terms of Saint Thomas Aquinas, an unjust law is a human law that is not rooted in eternal and natural law. Of course, there is nothing new about this kind of civil disobedience . . . It was practiced superbly by the early Christians who were willing to face hungry lions and the excruciating pain of chopping blocks, before submitting to certain unjust laws of the Roman empire. I'm grateful to God that, through the Negro church, the dimension of nonviolence entered our struggle. Was not Jesus an extremist for love—"Love your enemies, bless them that curse you, pray for them that despitefully use you." Was not Amos an extremist for justice—"Let justice roll down like waters and righteousness like a mighty stream." Was not Paul an extremist for the gospel of Jesus Christ—"I bear in my body the marks of the Lord Jesus" . . . So the question is not whether we will be extremist but what kind of extremist will we be. Will we be extremists for hate or will we be extremists for love? Will we be extremists for the preservation of injustice—or will we be extremists for the cause of justice? . . . In those days the [early] church was not merely a thermometer that recorded the ideas and principles of popular opinion; it was a thermostat that transformed the mores of society.[27]

From behind the bars of this jail, King's vision of justice deepened and expanded as he fought, like Gandhi, for racial equality and the nonviolent transformation of society.

Alongside his growth in virtue, King knew personal faults and failures, which included charges of plagiarism and extramarital affairs.[28] Alongside experiences of enlightenment, he also knew the experience of darkness, and at times he trembled in fear before his own feelings of inadequacy. In this midst of the organized protests against segregation, King and his family received menacing letters, phone calls, and even death threats from various antagonists, some of whom even quoted the Bible. After one of these calls he said,

---

27. Martin Luther King, Jr., *A Testament of Hope: The Essential Writings and Speeches of Martin Luther King, Jr.*, ed. James M. Washington (New York: HarperCollins, 1986), 290-302.

28. For more on the shadow side of King's iconic status, see Michael Eric Dyson, *I May Not Get There with You: The True Martin Luther King, Jr.* (New York: Touchstone, 2000).

I hung up, but I couldn't sleep. It seemed that all of my fears had come down on me at once. I had reached the saturation point. I got out of bed and began to walk on the floor. Finally I went to the kitchen and heated a pot of coffee. I was ready to give up . . . In this state of exhaustion, when my courage had all but gone, I decided to take my problem to God. With my head in my hands, I bowed over the kitchen table and prayed aloud. The words I spoke to God that midnight are still vivid in my memory . . . "I am here taking a stand for what I believe is right. But now I'm afraid. The people are looking to me for leadership, and if I stand before them without strength and courage, they too will falter. I am at the end of my powers. I have nothing left. I've come to the point where I can't face it alone" . . . At that moment I experienced the presence of the Divine as I had never experienced Him before. It seemed as though I could hear the quiet assurance of an inner voice saying: "Stand up for righteousness, stand up for truth; and God will be at your side forever." Almost at once my fears began to go. My uncertainty disappeared. I was ready to face anything.[29]

Three nights later his house was bombed, but it was this "kitchen prayer" that not only kept him from despair but also gave him the courage to tell his followers not to return evil for evil but to return love for hatred.

Major metaphor. In speaking about justice, Martin Luther King's poetic eloquence knows few equals in the history of humankind. The major metaphor for his life can be summed up in his "I Have a Dream" speech, which was delivered on August 28, 1963, from the steps of the Lincoln Memorial in Washington, D.C.:

I have a dream that one day this nation will rise up and live out the true meaning of its creed: "We hold these truths to be self-evident: that all men are created equal." I have a dream that one day on the red hills of Georgia the sons of former slaves and the sons of former slave owners will be able to sit down together at a table of brotherhood. I have a dream that one day even the state of Mississippi, a desert state, sweltering with the heat of injustice and oppression, will be transformed into an oasis of freedom and justice. I have a dream that my four children will one day live in a nation where they will not be judged by the color of their skin but by the content of their character . . . I have a dream that . . . little black boys and black girls will be able to join hands with little white boys and white girls and walk together as sisters and brothers . . . This is our hope. This is the faith with which I return to the South. With this faith we will be able to hew out of

---

29. King, *Testament of Hope,* 509.

the mountain of despair a stone of hope. With this faith we will be able to transform the jangling discords of our nation into a beautiful symphony of brotherhood. With this faith we will be able to work together, to pray together, to struggle together, to go to jail together, to stand up for freedom together, knowing that we will be free one day . . . This will be the day when all of God's children will be able to . . . Let freedom ring . . . When we let freedom ring, when we let it ring from every village and every hamlet, from every state and every city, we will be able to speed up that day when all of God's children, black men and white men, Jews and Gentiles, Protestants and Catholics, will be able to join hands and sing in the words of the old Negro spiritual, "Free at last! Free at last! Thank God Almighty, we are free at last!"[30]

In this dream, King tried to awaken people not only to the reality of social injustice but also to the rich possibilities of seeing our interconnectedness to each other. In an unjust society, he realized that both the oppressed and the oppressors need to undergo conversion, and nonviolence provides a way for both to become friends. He believed that physical slavery also leads many people to mental slavery, and he felt that one of the great challenges of justice begins with helping these same people reimagine themselves and the rightful role of black people in society.[31]

Operative theology. King's understanding of God emerged from the tradition of theological liberalism, which emphasized the social dimension of the Gospel, the moral foundation of reality, the value of every human person, and the call to work for a more just society.[32] He saw in the mission of Moses a mirror of his own mission, and he frequently drew from the well of the exodus story to summon people to move out of the slavery of racial oppression and move toward the promised land of civil rights and economic justice.[33]

In one way or another, his theology pointed to the intimate bonds that all human beings share with each other. In 1967, in a Christmas sermon on peace, King summed up his operative theology in this way:

It really boils down to this: that all life is interrelated. We are all caught in an inescapable network of mutuality, tied into a single garment of destiny. Whatever affects one directly, affects all indirectly. We are made to live

---

30. Ibid., 217-20.

31. Martin Luther King, Jr., and James W. Washington, *I Have a Dream: 24 Writings and Speeches That Changed the World* (New York: HarperCollins, 1992), 17.

32. Ira G. Zepp, Jr., ed., *The Social Vision of Martin Luther King, Jr.* (Brooklyn, N.Y.: Carlson, 1989), 235.

33. Lewis V. Baldwin, *There Is a Balm in Gilead: The Cultural Roots of Martin Luther King, Jr.* (Minneapolis: Fortress, 1991), 247.

together because of the interrelated structure of reality. Did you ever stop to think that you can't leave for your job in the morning without being dependent on most of the world? You get up in the morning and go to the bathroom and reach over for the sponge, and that's handed to you by a Pacific islander. You reach for a bar of soap, and that's given to you at the hands of a Frenchman. And then you go into the kitchen to drink your coffee for the morning, and that's poured into your cup by a South American. And maybe you want tea: that's poured into your cup by a Chinese. Or maybe you're desirous of having cocoa for breakfast, and that's poured into your cup by a West African. And then you reach over for your toast, and that's given to you at the hands of an English-speaking farmer, not to mention the baker. And before you finish eating breakfast in the morning, you've depended on more than half the world. This is the way our universe is structured; this is its interrelated quality. We aren't going to have peace on Earth until we recognize this basic fact of the interrelated structure of all reality.[34]

Because of this interconnectedness, King could say that "injustice anywhere is a threat to justice everywhere"[35] and that segregation, economic injustice, and war desecrated "the image of God" that was etched into every human person.[36]

King recognized that sin limits people's judgment to external appearances and eclipses one's vision of the inner qualities of the heart. "We are prone to judge success by the index of our salaries or the size of our automobiles," King would say, "rather than by the quality of our service and relationship to humanity."[37] In a related way, King also perceived that one of the problems that afflicted the human race was not atheism but idolatry:

There is so much frustration in the world because we have relied on gods rather than God. We have genuflected before the god of science only to find that it has given us the atomic bomb, producing fears and anxieties that science can never mitigate. We have worshipped the god of pleasure only to discover that thrills play out and sensations are short-lived. We have bowed before the god of money only to learn that there are such things as love and friendship that money cannot buy and that in a world of possible depressions, stock market crashes, and bad business investments, money is a rather uncertain deity. These transitory gods are not able to save or bring

---

34. King, *Testament of Hope*, 254.
35. Ibid., 147.
36. Michael G. Long, *Against Us, But for Us* (Macon, Ga.: Mercer University Press, 2002), 92.
37. Martin Luther King, Jr., and Coretta Scott King, *The Words of Martin Luther King, Jr.* (New York: Newmarket, 1987), 19.

happiness to the human heart. Only God is able. It is faith in Him that we must rediscover.[38]

King believed that God, not things, must be the subject of one's ultimate loyalty, and therefore God must be obeyed before any human authority or civil law.[39] As a consequence of this faith, he believed that a person must seek to eradicate all forms of hatred from one's heart and even cultivate a capacity to suffer in order to live the ideal of a radical love or *agapē*.[40] From the experience of his own black culture, King developed a theology of hope aimed at the liberation of all people, both the oppressed and oppressor.[41]

Core contribution. King's great legacy is not only in his prophetic challenge to an oppressive society but also in the way he called all people to realize their human dignity and their divine potential. His rhetorical skill changed much of the American imagination and the way it thought about the issue of equality.[42] Regardless of how a society judges a person, King believed that love is the ultimate measure of the person's greatness:

> If you want to be important, wonderful. If you want to be recognized, wonderful. If you want to be great, wonderful. But recognize that he who is greatest among you shall be your servant. That's a new definition of greatness ... by giving that definition of greatness, it means that everybody can be great, because everybody can serve. You don't have to have a college degree to serve. You don't have to make your subject and verb agree to serve. You don't have to know about Plato and Aristotle to serve. You don't need to know Einstein's theory of relativity to serve. You don't have to know the second theory of thermo-dynamics in Physics to serve. You only need a heart full of grace. A soul generated by love.[43]

Toward the end of his life, King's attention moved from a particular focus on desegregation to a more general focus on human rights, particularly economic rights. He believed that the state should mirror divine justice by seeking to eliminate all forms of poverty.[44] He noted that one of the most agonizing dimensions of human life is that we remain unfinished symphonies, but the poor most of all suffer the pain of not seeing their greatest hopes

---

38. Ibid., 63.
39. Long, *Against Us, But for Us*, 96-97.
40. Watley, *Roots of Resistance*, 57.
41. Lewis V. Baldwin, *To Make the Wounded Whole: The Cultural Legacy of Martin Luther King, Jr.* (Minneapolis: Fortress, 1992), 64.
42. John Louis Lucaites and Carolyn Calloway-Thomas, *Martin Luther King, Jr., and the Sermonic Power of Public Discourse* (Tuscaloosa: University of Alabama Press, 1993), 102.
43. King, *Testament of Hope*, 265-66.
44. Long, *Against Us, But for Us*, 182.

and dreams fulfilled.[45] In one of the last sermons before he was assassinated, Martin Luther King, Jr., summed up in his own words how he wanted to be remembered:

> And every now and then I think about my own death and I think about my own funeral. And I don't think of it in a morbid sense. And every now and then I ask myself, "What is it that I would want said?" . . . If any of you are around when I have to meet my day, I don't want a long funeral. And if you get somebody to deliver the eulogy, tell them not to talk too long. And every now and then I wonder what I want them to say. Tell them not to mention that I have a Nobel Peace Prize—that isn't important. Tell them not to mention that I have three or four hundred other awards—that's not important. Tell them not to mention where I went to school. I'd like somebody to mention that day that Martin Luther King, Jr., tried to give his life serving others. I'd like for somebody to say that day that Martin Luther King, Jr., tried to love somebody. I want you to say that day that I tried to be right on the war question. I want you to be able to say that day that I did try to feed the hungry. And I want you to be able to say that day that I did try in my life to clothe those who were naked. I want you to say on that day that I did try in my life to visit those who were in prison. I want you to say that I tried to love and serve humanity. Yes, if you want to say that I was a drum major, say that I was a drum major for justice. Say that I was a drum major for peace. I was a drum major for righteousness. And all of the other shallow things will not matter. I won't have any money to leave behind. I won't have the fine and luxurious things of life to leave behind. But I just want to leave a committed life behind . . . Yes, Jesus, I want to be on your right or your left side, not for any selfish reason . . . But I just want to be there in love and in justice and in truth and in commitment to others, so that we can make of this old world a new world.[46]

Martin Luther King, Jr., was assassinated on April 4, 1968, in Memphis, Tennessee, where he went to support striking black garbage workers. Moments before he was shot, he was on a balcony of a hotel speaking to some of his aides about the upcoming meeting that evening. Ben Branch, the lead saxophonist and song leader from the band Breadbasket was there, and King called down from above and said to him, "Ben, make sure you play 'Precious Lord, Take My Hand' in the meeting tonight . . . Play it real pretty."[47] King's last words on this earth ended with these words from the Narrative of the

---

45. Martin Luther King, Jr., *Strength to Love* (New York: Harper & Row, 1963), 87.
46. King, *Testament of Hope*, 266-67.
47. Taylor Branch, *At Canaan's Edge: America in the King Years, 1965-68* (New York: Simon & Schuster, 2006), 766.

Gospel. Yet his death gave birth to a new era of civil and human rights, and after his assassination, he became an icon of justice in the struggle for racial equality, leaving others to carry on his legacy.

DOROTHY DAY AND PETER MAURIN: ICONS OF CONTEMPLATIVE ACTIVISM

Summary and historical background. Dorothy Day (1897-1980) cofounded the Catholic Worker movement and was an exemplary activist who, drawing from deep spiritual wells, loved and served some of the poorest and least significant members of society.[48] She did not want people to call her a saint because she said, "I don't want to be dismissed that easily."[49] Not only did she not want to be burdened with admiration, but she wanted others to understand their own call to holiness in everyday life, a call to be lived out by serving all people and doing little things with great love. She and Peter Maurin (1877-1949), the cofounder of the Catholic Worker movement, spoke out for the God of Life against wars, economic depression, class struggle, the arms race, and racial segregation.

Foundational religious experience. In college, Day experimented with various social ideologies. During that time, she had various relationships with men, eventually became pregnant, and had an abortion. For many years she lived together with a man she loved (who wanted nothing to do with religion), but eventually she faced the excruciating decision to leave him. It was then that, "with hesitation and uncertainty," she made the decision to become a Catholic, a decision that mingled loss with her sense of liberation. Worn out by her own moral wandering and the insatiability of her own needs and desires, she was attracted to the order and stability of Catholic life: "I had reached the point where I wanted to obey . . . I was tired of following the devices and desires of my own heart, of doing what I wanted to do, what my desires told me I wanted to do, which always seemed to lead me astray."[50]

In December 1932, while working as a freelance journalist in Washington, D.C., on a communist-led hunger march, she came face to face with the fact that there were so many "comfortable churchgoers" who gave "little heed to

---

48. For more on the Catholic Worker, Dorothy Day, and Peter Maurin, see Mark and Louise Zwick, *The Catholic Worker Movement: Intellectual and Spiritual Origins* (Mahwah, N.J.: Paulist, 2005). For an excellent set of online resources, see http://www.catholicworker.org/dorothyday.

49. Dorothy Day, *Selected Writings*, ed. Robert Ellsberg (Maryknoll, N.Y.: Orbis Books, 1992), xviii.

50. Ibid., xxii-xxiii.

the misery of the needy and the groaning of the poor."[51] After the march, she went to the Shrine of the Immaculate Conception in Washington and in the crypt fell to her knees. Recalling that moment, she wrote, "There I offered up a special prayer, a prayer which came with tears and with anguish, that some way would open for me to use what talent I possessed for my fellow workers, for the poor."[52]

When she returned home, Dorothy Day found, in what she later believed was an answer to her prayers, a bright, passionate yet unkempt man named Peter Maurin waiting for her at her door.[53] He began to share with her a grand vision that would become the foundation for the Catholic Worker movement. Maurin had a three-point program, which consisted of (1) round-table discussions for "clarification of thought"; (2) Houses of Hospitality for the practice of the works of mercy; and (3) "agronomic universities," or farming communes, where "workers could become scholars and scholars could become workers."[54] He wanted the church to rediscover its own social teachings:

> If the Catholic Church is not today the dominant social dynamic force, it is because Catholic scholars have taken the dynamite of the Church, have wrapped it up in nice phraseology, placed it in a hermetic container and sat on the lid. It is about time to blow the lid off so the Catholic Church may again become the dominant social dynamic force.[55]

Maurin wanted to bring Catholic social encyclicals to life, to make them tick, and to realize the church's mission to create a just society.

Major metaphor. Scripture, literature, and life experience shaped Day's understanding of the Gospel. She often referred to the story that Grushenka tells in Dostoevsky's *The Brothers Karamazov:*

> Once upon a time there lived a very nasty, horrible old woman. When she died, she didn't leave behind her one single good deed. So the devils got hold of her and tossed her into the flaming lake. Meantime, her guardian angel stood there, trying hard to think of one good deed of hers that he could mention to God in order to save her. Then he remembered and said to God: "Once," he said, "she pulled up an onion in her garden and gave it to a beggar woman." So God said to him: "Take that onion, hold it out

---

51. Jim Wallis and Joyce Hollyday, eds., *Cloud of Witnesses* (Maryknoll, N.Y.: Orbis Books, 1991), 11.
52. Ibid.
53. Day, *Selected Writings*, xxiii.
54. Ibid., xxvi.
55. Peter Maurin, *Easy Essays* (Chicago: Franciscan Herald Press, 1977), 3.

to her over the lake, let her hold on to it, and try to pull herself out. If she does, let her enter heaven; if the onion breaks, the old woman will just have to stay where she is." So the angel hurried to the woman, held out the onion to her, and told her to take hold of it and pull. Then he himself began to pull her out very carefully and she was almost entirely out of the lake when the other sinners saw she was being pulled out and grabbed on to her so that they'd be pulled out of the flames too. But when she saw them, that wicked, horrible woman started kicking them, saying: "I'm being pulled out, not you, for it's my onion, not yours!" As soon [as] she said that, the onion snapped and the woman fell back into the flaming lake, where she's still burning to this day. And her guardian angel wept and walked away.[56]

Day's own spiritual experience also shaped her loving response to a loving God, expressed in the gift of self for those in need.

Operative theology. Dorothy Day's concern for the individual person and the common good meant protecting human dignity and working for the transformation of the social order.[57] Her faith and activism were nurtured by the teachings of the Catholic Church, the writings of the church fathers, the social encyclicals of modern popes, and above all the Christian Scriptures. While much of culture around her emphasized the bank account as the ultimate measure of a person's worth, Day emphasized the Sermon on the Mount (Mt 5-7) as the ultimate standard of a person's worth. Her life's foundation rested on the corporal works of mercy (Mt 25:31-46): feeding the hungry, giving drink to the thirsty, sheltering the homeless, welcoming the lost, and visiting those in prison framed how she understood and lived out the Gospel Narrative. She wanted to be a living mystery who reached out to the mystery of Christ in the poorest of the world. Quoting Cardinal Emmanuel Suhard, she believed that obedience to Christ meant living "in such a way that one's life would not make sense if God did not exist."[58]

Dorothy Day integrated contemplation and action, combining the "street apostolate" with the "retreat apostolate."[59] She connected political commitment with traditional, conservative theology and tried to match her words with actions. She called herself "a loyal and obedient daughter of the Church,"

---

56. Fyodor Dostoevsky, *The Brothers Karamazov*, trans. Andrew H. MacAndrew (New York: Bantam Books, 1970), 426-27.

57. William Thorn, Phillip Runkel, and Susan Mountin, eds., *Dorothy Day and the Catholic Worker Movement* (Milwaukee: Marquette University Press, 2001), 130.

58. Day, *Selected Writings*, xv.

59. Dorothy Day, *Dorothy Day: Writings from Commonweal*, ed. Jordan Patrick (Collegeville, Minn.: Liturgical Press, 2002), 106.

and said she would close down operations if ordered to do so by the cardinal. Stressing the hard words of the Gospel, she advocated prayer, fasting, penance, taking up the cross daily, and following Christ. Her religious devotion expressed itself in daily Mass, weekly confession, the rosary, and at least two hours a day of meditation on Scripture (at a time when most Catholics did not read the Bible). Through these spiritual disciplines, she sought to transform herself and then society, hoping to create a community where it would be easier for people to be good.

Drawing on the thought of Ignatius of Loyola, Day believed that we must "work as though everything depended on ourselves, and pray as though everything depended on God."[60] She also took from Ignatius a sense of the primacy of God in all things. While she did not regard the goods of the earth as evil, she realized that when our hearts become too wrapped up in material things, we lose both a sense of the One to whom we ultimately belong and our vocation to glorify God. More than our things, she knew God desires our hearts, which demands of us everything. For her, love of neighbor meant voluntary poverty and nonparticipation in the comforts and luxuries gained by exploiting others.[61]

Day believed that a church made up of spiritually dedicated and socially committed people was the antidote for a corrupt capitalist system.[62] "We have all known the long loneliness and we have learned that the only solution is love and that love comes with community."[63] Her convictions about community emerged from her profound belief in the interconnectedness of all peoples. "I became aware that my prayer, my sacrifices, would and could contribute the necessary graces to keep alive the faith of some poor prisoner locked away in a Communist or Fascist concentration camp. My prayers and good works also had the power to convert his captors."[64]

Despite her great desires, Day did not try to save the world. She said we are saved, "by little, by little," even if it seems that we are only getting a little bit done. Her patron saint was Thérèse of Lisieux, a simple nun with a great heart who died at twenty-four within the walls of a little-known monastery. From Thérèse, Dorothy Day learned that living in harmony with God, living in that Presence, and doing even small things with great love, helped unite one with Christ and make present his kingdom.

---

60. Dorothy Day, *On Pilgrimage* (Grand Rapids: Eerdmans, 1999), 22.
61. Rosalie G. Riegle, *Dorothy Day* (Maryknoll, N.Y.: Orbis Books, 2003), 6.
62. Michael O. Garvey, foreword, in Dorothy Day, *On Pilgrimage* (Grand Rapids: Eerdmans, 1999), xi.
63. Dorothy Day, *The Long Loneliness* (New York: HarperSanFrancisco, 1997), 286.
64. Day, *On Pilgrimage*, 17.

Core contribution. Much of Dorothy Day's life is chronicled in her autobiography, *The Long Loneliness*, which is considered one of the best spiritual books of all time.[65] One of her great legacies is the Catholic Worker movement. The first House of Hospitality opened in 1933, and today over "277 Catholic Worker communities remain committed to nonviolence, voluntary poverty, prayer, and hospitality for the homeless, exiled, hungry, and forsaken."[66] Day was also instrumental in inspiring peace movements and founding groups such as Pax Christi, the Catholic Peace Fellowship, and the Association of Catholic Trade Unionists. In 2000, Cardinal John J. O'Connor formally introduced her cause for canonization and, among other things, considered her a model for women who are contemplating an abortion. Her love of the Scriptures, her solidarity with the poor, her prophetic witness to peace and nonviolence, her daily religious devotions, and her love of the eucharist all bore fruit in a spirituality of gratitude.[67] Her desire to give her life to others came out of her belief that all had been given to her as a gift, which is why, fittingly, on her gravestone is engraved a design of loaves and fishes and the words *Deo Gratias*.

BLESSED TERESA AND THE MISSIONARIES OF CHARITY: ICONS OF MERCY

Summary and historical context. In a world marked by secularization and neglect of the poor, Blessed Teresa of Calcutta (1910-1997) founded a traditional Catholic religious community called the Missionaries of Charity and helped turn the world's attention to some of the most neglected members of the global village. She described herself in this way: "By blood, I am Albanian. By citizenship, an Indian. By faith, I am a Catholic nun. As to my calling, I belong to the world. As to my heart, I belong entirely to the Heart of Jesus."[68]

Born Agnes Gonxha Bojaxhiu in Skopje,[69] she entered the Irish Branch of the Institute of the Blessed Virgin Mary in Dublin (the Loreto Sisters) at age eighteen. She received the name Teresa, in honor of Saint Thérèse of Lisieux, who, in addition to being the saint who advocated doing great things for God

---

65. Elaine Murray Stone, *Dorothy Day: Champion of the Poor* (New York: Paulist, 2004), 3.

66. For more on the Catholic Worker movement, see http://www.catholicworker.org/index.cfm.

67. For more on these characteristics of Dorothy Day and her spirituality, see http://www.catholicworker.org.

68. For more information on Blessed Teresa, see www.motherteresa.org.

69. At the time, Skopje was part of the Ottoman Empire and presently it is part of Macedonia.

in little ways, was the patron saint of foreign missions. She professed her final vows in 1937.

Foundational experience. For eighteen years, Blessed Teresa served in India at St. Mary's School as a teacher and principal, but she was very moved by the presence of the sick, begging, and dying people on the streets of Calcutta. On September 10, 1946, during the train ride from Calcutta to Darjeeling for her annual retreat, she received her foundational inspiration, something to which she referred as a "call within a call." Although she could never fully articulate this experience, it inspired her to be Christ's light for the world by following him "into the slums."[70] Flowing from this initial experience, she left Loreto convent on August 16, 1948, and initiated her work among the poor. On October 7, 1950, the Missionaries of Charity were born, whose apostolate is to give wholehearted and free service to the poorest of the poor.

Major metaphor. Despite the strong desire to "radiate God's love on souls," paradoxically Blessed Teresa's spiritual life was marked by times of intense darkness. As John Paul II notes,

> Hidden from all eyes, hidden even from those closest to her, was her interior life marked by an experience of a deep, painful and abiding feeling of being separated from God, even rejected by Him, along with an ever-increasing longing for His love. She called her inner experience, "the darkness."[71]

This darkness started when she began her work with the poor and continued until the end of her life. Purifying and terrifying at times, it deepened her mystical participation in the sufferings of Christ and bound her even more closely to God. At the same time it helped her to understand from the inside the desolate experience of the poor.[72] Welling up from this obscurity came tremendous compassion and love, which enabled her to freely surrender to God. She believed that when we surrender to God unreservedly, God makes us instruments of his love. All of this experience came down to one central metaphor. Evocative of her days as a schoolteacher, she described herself as a little pencil in the hand of God, who is sending a love letter to the world.[73]

---

70. Eileen Egan, *Such a Vision of the Street: Mother Teresa, the Spirit and the Work* (Garden City, N.Y.: Doubleday, 1985), 25.

71. *Mother Teresa of Calcutta (1910-1997)*, biography available online at http://www.vatican.va.

72. Ibid.

73. Franca Zambonini, *Teresa of Calcutta: A Pencil in God's Hand* (New York: Alba House, 1993).

Operative theology. The operative theology of Blessed Teresa was framed by two central biblical passages: John 19:28 ("I thirst") and Matthew 25:31-46 ("Whatever you did for the least . . . you did for me"). In the first, Blessed Teresa wanted to give expression to Jesus' thirst for love and for souls, and human beings' thirst for love and for God. This notion of thirst was so central to Blessed Teresa that the words "I thirst" are placed next to the cross in every convent of the Missionaries of Charity. In the second passage, she wanted to radiate Christ's love for all people, especially the poor and forgotten. While she understood the poor primarily as the economically destitute, she saw the poor in those who were hungry not only for bread, but hungry for love; naked not only for clothing, but for human dignity and respect; homeless not only for want of a home, but for want of love and acceptance.[74] She said, "I have come more and more to realize that it is being unwanted that is the worst disease that any human being can ever experience."[75]

She believed that Christ comes to us especially in the distressing disguise of the disfigured in the world. Blessed Teresa insisted that we are to "believe that He, Jesus, is in the hungry, naked, sick, lonely, unloved, homeless, help-less, and hopeless."[76] Wanting not only to read about the poor or take a tour through the slums and remain at a distance, she sought "to dive into it, live it, share it."[77] She believed that

> The shut-in, the unwanted, the unloved, the alcoholics, the dying destitute, the abandoned and the lonely, the outcasts and untouchables, the leprosy sufferers—all those who are a burden to human society, who have lost all hope and faith in life, who have forgotten how to smile, who have lost the sensibility of the warm hand-touch of love and friendship—they look to us for comfort. If we turn our back on them, we turn it on Christ.[78]

As she tried to align her life with God's Spirit, she sought to let God's love reign in her heart. She believed that "the one most united to Him loves her neighbor the most."[79] She regarded intimate union with God as the greatest treasure of human life, and she did not believe that her mission was to make

---

74. Blessed Teresa, *Words to Love By,* ed. Frank J. Cunningham (Notre Dame, Ind.: Ave Maria, 1999), 80.

75. Malcom Muggeridge, *Something Beautiful for God: Mother Teresa of Calcutta* (San Francisco: Harper & Row, 1986), 98-99.

76. Brian Kolodiejchuk, ed., *Jesus Is My All in All* (Tijuana, Mexico: Mother Teresa Center, 2005), 20.

77. Blessed Teresa, *The Joy of Loving: A Guide to Daily Living with Mother Teresa,* ed. Jaya Chaliha and Edward Le Joly (New York: Viking, 1997), 307.

78. David Scott, *A Revolution of Love: The Meaning of Mother Teresa* (Chicago: Loyola, 2005), 86.

79. Kolodiejchuk, *Jesus Is My All in All,* 21.

converts, but to witness to God's love for the world in Jesus by caring for her neighbor.[80] Regarding every life as precious, she spoke in defense of life in all stages, particularly the unborn and the elderly, the sick and those considered a burden on human society.

She gave witness to the gratuity of God's love by caring for all people, regardless of their race or creed. At the same time, she regarded what she did not as social work but as Christian mission.[81] "We may be doing social work in the eyes of some people, but we must be contemplatives in the heart of the world."[82] Justice for her was more than merely giving people food, clothing, and shelter, although certainly it did entail addressing people's basic needs. Justice meant bringing the joy and love of God to people, helping in some small way to bring people to right relationship with God and to restore the rightful place of their human dignity. After his body was half eaten by worms when Blessed Teresa and the sisters found him, one man said, "I have lived like an animal in the street, but I am going to die as an angel loved and cared for . . . I am going home to God."[83]

Beyond the hunger Blessed Teresa witnessed on the streets of Calcutta and around the world, she also saw the deep hunger of people in affluent areas for love and kindness. She recognized that the hurried pace of modern life left people starving for love because everybody is in such a great rush.[84] Beneath the prosperity of globalization, she saw a spiritual poverty in many people who longed for relational connectedness that would speak to their loneliness and emptiness. She tried to awaken the materially prosperous to the profound spiritual hunger in the human heart that leads us to intimacy with God and service to our brothers and sisters in need. In the end, she recognized that one of the greatest diseases today is to be nobody to anybody.

Even while immersed in the suffering of the world, Blessed Teresa loved life.[85] She constantly reiterated that the impetus to love the poor flowed out of the belief that God is merciful. Echoing the spirituality of Saint Thérèse of Lisieux, she believed that "it is how much love we put in the doing that makes our offering something beautiful for God."[86] Her capacity to love came from a deep life of prayer, which opened her heart to receive the gift of God himself,

---

80. Zambonini, *Teresa of Calcutta*, 113.

81. Blessed Teresa, *Life in the Spirit: Reflections, Meditations, Prayers*, ed. Kathryn Spink (San Francisco: Harper & Row, 1983), 55.

82. Blessed Teresa, *Total Surrender*, ed. Angelo Devananda, rev. ed. (Ann Arbor, Mich.: Servant Publications, 1985), 126.

83. Blessed Teresa, *Joy of Loving*, 75.

84. Blessed Teresa, *Life in the Spirit*, 75.

85. Ibid., 60.

86. Blessed Teresa, *A Gift for God: Prayers and Meditations* (New York: Harper & Row, 1975), 69.

which in turn enabled her to sacrifice for others. She believed that the fruit of silence is prayer, the fruit of prayer is faith, the fruit of faith is love, the fruit of love is service, and the fruit of service is peace. The gift of her life to others contributed to the expansion of her soul. In particular, she believed that her union with Christ in the eucharist enabled her to serve the lepers, the dying, and other unwanted people, and to touch the suffering body of Christ. Her life of prayer and service led her to realize a union with God to such an extent that she could say, "He prays in me, He thinks in me, He works with me and through me. He uses my tongue to speak; He uses my brain to think. He uses my hands to touch Him in the broken body."[87]

Core contribution. Beyond her international fame and winning the Nobel Peace Prize in 1979, Blessed Teresa's lasting legacy lies in her direct service to the poor and the religious community she founded. The Missionaries of Charity Sisters (Active and Contemplative) number over five thousand and are established in more than seven hundred communities in over 130 countries. The order expanded and now includes active brothers, contemplative brothers, priests, and seminarians. There are also hundreds of diocesan priests who embrace the Missionaries of Charity charism through the Corpus Christi movement for Priests. In addition, there are thousands of Co-Workers and Lay Missionaries of Charity who share in Blessed Teresa's spirit and mission. Her life reveals not only the common bonds that all people share but also the common desires of the human heart and the hunger to become living embodiments of God's love and mercy. After a long life of service and dedication, Blessed Teresa died in Calcutta on September 5, 1997. When she passed away, her body was taken through the streets on the same gun carriage that carried Gandhi. Rather than fearing the end of her life, she believed that to die in peace with God is like a coronation.[88]

OSCAR ROMERO AND THE MARTYRS OF EL SALVADOR: ICONS OF HUMAN LIBERATION

Summary and historical background. Archbishop Oscar Arnulfo Romero (1917-1980) was a Catholic priest, a staunch defender of human rights, and an icon of human liberation who suffered martyrdom at the hands of Salvadoran death squads in 1980. In a land where wealth and power reside with a handful of families and reigning business elites, Romero laid down his life

---

87. Egan, *Such a Vision of the Street*, 427.
88. Susan Crimp, *Touched by a Saint: Personal Encounters with Mother Teresa* (Notre Dame, Ind.: Sorin Books, 2000), 37.

for social reform and the hope of creating a society reflective of God's reign in history.[89] In denouncing human rights abuses and announcing the kingdom of God, he gave expression to a spirituality and a church that engaged in the historical dimension of liberation while at the same time giving witness to the transcendent dimension of faith beyond the disorder of society.

Foundational experience. While Romero had concern for the poor throughout his life, the Episcopal Conference of Medellín, his experience of the suffering people of his own country, and his sensitivity to the injustices they experienced deepened his conversion to Christ and to the poor. Within weeks after he was named archbishop on February 22, 1977, one of his good friends who worked closely with the poor, Fr. Rutilio Grande, S.J., was brutally assassinated by Salvadoran death squads.[90] Grande's death would significantly impact Romero's life, but Grande was not the first to be killed, and after this event, as Jon Sobrino observes, "the scales fell" from Romero's eyes, revealing more clearly to him the structures of empire that resulted in the unjust suffering of the people of his country.[91]

In the months and years that followed Grande's death, many other priests, nuns, and pastoral agents were killed. Among these were nuns like Dorothy Kazel, Ita Ford, Maura Clarke, and lay worker Jean Donovan, who were murdered on December 2, 1980. These deaths became very public, but there were also many catechists, labor union organizers, journalists, students, medical care personnel, and over three thousand *campesinos* a month who were martyred. These must be added to the list of icons of justice, even though their deaths were largely unknown, unrecognized, and unpublicized. In the midst of these unjust killings, Romero found himself in the middle of a war waged against the poor.[92]

Major metaphor. The major metaphor that shaped Romero's spiritual vision and his priesthood was the crucified Christ and the crucified peoples of El Salvador. He maintained that

---

89. For more on the life and witness of Romero, see Robert S. Pelton, Robert L. Ball, and Kyle Markham, eds., *Monseñor Romero: A Bishop for the Third Millennium* (Notre Dame, Ind.: University of Notre Dame Press, 2004).

90. In his bedroom in the Divine Providence Hospital, Archbishop Romero hung a drawing of Rutilio Grande, which he looked at each time he either entered or left. He said that on entering his bedroom it reminded him of his commitment to God, and on leaving, his commitment to the people of God.

91. Jon Sobrino, *Archbishop Romero: Memories and Reflections*, trans. Robert Barr (Maryknoll, N.Y.: Orbis Books, 1990), 10.

92. For an excellent article on the meaning of Romero's life in light of Catholic social teaching, see Kevin F. Burke, "Archbishop Oscar Romero: Peacemaker in the Tradition of Catholic Social Thought," *The Journal for Peace and Justice Studies* 13, no. 2 (2003): 105-24.

every time we look upon the poor . . . there is the face of Christ . . . The face of Christ is among the sacks and baskets of the farm worker; the face of Christ is among those who are tortured and mistreated in the prisons; the face of Christ is dying of hunger in the children who have nothing to eat; the face of Christ is in the poor who ask the church for their voice to be heard.[93]

The crucified Christ illuminated Romero's vision, even up until his last breath. On March 24, 1980, inside a church on the grounds of the Divine Providence Hospital, Oscar Romero was shot to death while celebrating Mass. Romero's own life and death, in imitation of Christ, were a sacramental expression of God's sacrificial love for the world on behalf of the suffering people of El Salvador and beyond. This brutal murder would sow the seeds of hope and life for all those who struggled for a more just society and who professed faith in a liberating God whose love cannot be extinguished, not even by death.

Operative theology. The major axis around which Romero's life revolved was the life, death, and resurrection of Jesus Christ, and he believed he was called to *sentir con la iglesia,* or to feel with the church, especially as it suffered in the world. Romero believed that the church's mission was to proclaim the reign of God, which is the reign "of peace and justice, of truth and love, of grace and holiness . . . to achieve a political, social, and economic order conformed to God's plan."[94] He preached that commitment to this kingdom demanded personal and collective conversion. He proclaimed that God's kingdom is at hand, and he challenged people to repent of violence if they are going to understand the good news of the Gospel and be saved. He spoke out against structures that are born and nurtured through "the idolatry of wealth, of the absolute right, within the capitalist system, of private property, of political power in national security regimes."[95]

Beyond his words, he sought to embody the conversion he preached. When visited once by an ecclesial official, he was told that his modest living quarters in Divine Providence Hospital was not "fitting" for an archbishop. He agreed, explaining that since most of his flock lived in cardboard shacks, his quarters were too extravagant by comparison. Conversion for Romero

---

93. Publicaciones Pastorales Arzobispado, ed., *Oscar A. Romero: Su pensamiento*, vol. 5, November 26, 1978, homily (San Salvador: Imprenta Criterio, 1980-1989), 327.

94. James R. Brockman, *The Word Remains: A Life of Oscar Romero* (Maryknoll, N.Y.: Orbis Books, 1982), 5.

95. Archbishop Oscar Romero, "The Political Dimension of the Faith from the Perspective of the Option for the Poor," in *Voice of the Voiceless: The Four Pastoral Letters and Other Statements*, trans. Michael J. Walsh (Maryknoll, N.Y.: Orbis Books, 1985), 183.

meant opening one's life to the poor and being in solidarity with them, not as some superior who gives alms but as a brother or sister who walks with them in solidarity. He insisted that "a church that does not join the poor, in order to speak out from the side of the poor against the injustices committed against them, is not the true church of Jesus Christ."[96] Though some perceived this as a distortion of the church's mission and a contamination of the church with politics, Romero said,

> The church is concerned about the rights of people . . . and about life that is at risk . . . The church is concerned about those who cannot speak, those who suffer, those who are tortured, those who are silenced. This is not getting involved in politics . . . Let this be clear: when the church preaches social justice, equality, and the dignity of people, defending those who suffer and those who are assaulted, this is not subversion; this is not Marxism. This is the authentic teaching of the church.[97]

He believed that "the Christian faith does not cut us off from the world but immerses us in it."[98]

Although Romero faced squarely the political challenges of his day, he was not simply a social activist. He was also a man of deep prayer and meditation, which helped him to look beyond and beneath the surface events to the deeper truths of reality. He would often leave intense and heated discussions with his counselors in order to pray over his decisions.[99] Romero knew that without God, genuine human liberation was not possible. He witnessed to the fact that justice deals with the historical dimensions of this world, but he never lost sight of the transcendent dimension of liberation. Indeed, he affirmed that, "without God, there can be no concept of liberation. Temporary liberations, yes; but definitive, solid liberations—only people of faith can reach them."[100]

Contribution to justice. While during his life Romero tried to keep a violence-ridden society from falling apart, after his death El Salvador plunged into a full-fledged civil war. By conservative estimates, this war led to the death of more than seventy-five thousand people, although many believe the number of actual deaths may be as much as three times that. In the face of tragedy

---

96. Oscar Romero, *The Violence of Love*, comp. and trans. James R. Brockman (Farmington, Pa.: Plough Publishing House, 1998), 189.

97. Publicaciones Pastorales Arzobispado, ed., *Oscar A. Romero: Su pensamiento*, vol. 1-2, May 8, 1977, homily (San Salvador: Imprenta Criterio, 1980-1989), 29.

98. Romero, "Political Dimension of the Faith," 178.

99. Brockman, *Word Remains*, 33.

100. Wallis and Hollyday, *Cloud of Witnesses*, 279.

of such dramatic proportions, and in a global culture increasingly intent on "having more," Romero held out the ideal of "being more."[101] The ultimate legacy of his life was the offering of his own life for the people he loved.[102] Romero taught that "the greatest sign of faith in a God of Life is the witness of those who are willing to give up their own life."[103] Shortly before his death, he remarked,

> Martyrdom is a grace that I don't believe I merit. But if God accepts the sacrifice of my life, may my blood be the seed of liberty and a sign that this hope will soon become a reality. May my death, if it is accepted by God, be for the liberation of my people and a testimony of hope in the future.[104]

At the same time, days before his own death Romero remarked, "I should tell you that, as a Christian, I don't believe in death without resurrection. If they kill me, I will be resurrected in the Salvadoran people."[105]

Romero's faith in the God of Life, even while surrounded by threats of death, inspired countless others who struggled for justice, including six Jesuit priests and two women who were assassinated on November 16, 1989. Today, on the site where they were murdered, is the Oscar Romero Center.

Romero's contribution lies also in the ordinariness of his life. He was a man who feared, sweated, and doubted. His transformation from a safe, conservative churchman to a prophetic defender of the poor gives hope to all who are open to the action of God in one's life and who seek to find God's will amidst the ambiguities and complexities of our contemporary world, and even the uncertainties of navigating our way in the search for peace. He testified to the mercy of God in a merciless world. "In my life," he said, "I have only been a poem of the love of God, and I have become in Him what he has wanted me to be."[106] In standing in solidarity with Christ on the altar and Christ crucified in the poor, Romero, and others like him, came to be known as an *entregado*, one who not only gives one's life for his people but also reveals through faithful witness the life of the Savior, known in Spanish as *El Salvador.*

---

101. Romero, *Voice of the Voiceless*, 133.

102. Oscar A. Romero, *Recordando a Monseñor Romero* (Caracas: Universidad Central de Venezuela, 2000), 58.

103. Romero, "Political Dimension of the Faith," 185.

104. Oscar Romero, *La voz de los sin voz*, March 19, 1980, homily (San Salvador: UCA Editores, 1987), 461.

105. Ibid.

106. "En mi vida solo he sido un poema del amor de Dios . . . y me ha realizado como ha querido." The first part of this quotation is now inscribed on the wall of Romero's bedroom in the Divine Providence Hospital.

THE CHALLENGE OF HOLINESS: BEING ONESELF

Beyond those described above, there are many other images of mercy and icons of justice that we could fittingly discuss in this chapter, people such as César Chávez and Dolores Huerta, Desmond Tutu, Jean Vanier, Nelson Mandela, and Dietrich Bonhoeffer, to name a few. The ones we have discussed above give us but a glimpse of how the ideals of justice are incarnated in a globalized world. They help us recognize and probe the contours of love and integrity, of hope and commitment, of liberation and life. They are people who tried to live in harmony with heaven, even when it brought them into discord with society, even when it cost them their own lives.

Though influenced and inspired by many different people, their common search for integrity not only enabled them to become what they admired, but helped them become more authentically human. They invite us not so much to become like them as to become more truly ourselves in the search for justice. An ancient rabbinic tale perhaps best illustrates the challenging call to holiness: "The Rabbi Zusya said a short time before his death, 'In the world to come, I shall not be asked, Why were you not Moses? Instead, I shall be asked, Why were you not Zusya?'"[107]

QUESTIONS FOR REFLECTION

1. Which icon of justice most speaks to you and why? Which icon of justice and mercy do you least identify with? Why?
2. What do you think are the most challenging social issues in our current social context?
3. What are some foundational experiences that have shaped your vision of life?
4. Do you have a major metaphor that describes your life and its direction?
5. How would you describe your operative theology?
6. What lasting contribution would you want to leave for the world?
7. Do the shortcomings and failures of these icons enhance or diminish how you understand them?
8. Discuss this statement: "Identity and integrity have as much to do with our shadows and limits, our wounds and fears, as with our strengths and potentials."

SUGGESTIONS FOR FURTHER READING AND STUDY

Mahatma Gandhi and Kasturbai Gandhi: Icons of Nonviolence

Datta, Dhirendra. *The Philosophy of Mahatma Gandhi*. Madison: University of Wisconsin Press, 1953.

---

107. Martin Buber, *The Way of Man According to the Teaching of Hasidism* (New York: Citadel, 1966), 17.

Dear, John, ed. *Mohandas Gandhi: Essential Writings.* Maryknoll, N.Y.: Orbis Books, 2002.
Easwaran, Eknath. *Gandhi the Man.* 3rd ed. Tomales, Calif.: Nilgiri, 1997.
Erikson, Erik H. *Gandhi's Truth.* New York: Norton, 1969.
Gandhi, Mahatma. *The Essential Gandhi: An Anthology of His Writings on His Life, Work, and Ideas.* Edited by Louis Fischer. New York: Vintage Books, 2002.

Martin Luther King, Jr., and Rosa Parks: Icons of Human Rights

Branch, Taylor. *At Canaan's Edge: America in the King Years, 1965-68.* New York: Simon & Schuster, 2006.
King, Martin Luther, Jr. *Strength to Love.* New York: Harper & Row, 1963.
————. *A Testament of Hope: The Essential Writings and Speeches of Martin Luther King, Jr.* Edited by James M. Washington. New York: HarperCollins, 1986.
King, Martin Luther, Jr., and Coretta Scott King. *The Words of Martin Luther King, Jr.* New York: Newmarket, 1987.
Zepp, Ira G., Jr., ed. *The Social Vision of Martin Luther King, Jr.* Brooklyn, N.Y.: Carlson, 1989.

Dorothy Day and Peter Maurin: Icons of Contemplative Activism

Day, Dorothy. *Selected Writings: By Little and By Little.* Edited by Robert Ellsberg. Maryknoll, N.Y.: Orbis Books, 1992.
————. *The Long Loneliness.* New York: HarperSanFrancisco, 1997.
————. *Dorothy Day: Writings from Commonweal.* Edited by Jordan Patrick. Collegeville, Minn.: Liturgical Press, 2002.
Riegle, Rosalie G. *Dorothy Day.* Maryknoll, N.Y.: Orbis Books, 2003.
Stone, Elaine Murray. *Dorothy Day: Champion of the Poor.* New York: Paulist, 2004.
Thorn, William, Phillip Runkel, and Susan Mountin, eds. *Dorothy Day and the Catholic Worker Movement.* Milwaukee: Marquette University Press, 2001.
Zwick, Mark, and Louise Zwick. *The Catholic Worker Movement: Intellectual and Spiritual Origins.* Mahwah, N.J.: Paulist, 2005.

Blessed Teresa and the Missionaries of Charity: Icons of Mercy

Egan, Eileen. *Such a Vision of the Street: Mother Teresa, The Spirit and the Work.* Garden City, N.Y.: Doubleday, 1985.
Muggeridge, Malcolm. *Something Beautiful for God: Mother Teresa of Calcutta.* San Francisco: Harper & Row, 1986.
Scott, David. *A Revolution of Love: The Meaning of Mother Teresa.* Chicago: Loyola, 2005.
Blessed [Mother] Teresa. *A Gift for God: Prayers and Meditations.* New York: Harper and Row, 1975.

————. *Words to Love By.* Edited by Frank J. Cunningham. Notre Dame, Ind.: Ave Maria, 1999.

Zambonini, Franca. *Teresa of Calcutta: A Pencil in God's Hand.* New York: Alba House, 1993.

Oscar Romero and the Martyrs of El Salvador: Icons of Human Liberation

Brockman, James R. *The Word Remains: A Life of Oscar Romero.* Maryknoll, N.Y.: Orbis Books, 1982.

Pelton, Robert S., Robert L. Ball, and Kyle Markham, eds. *Monseñor Romero: A Bishop for the Third Millennium.* Notre Dame, Ind.: University of Notre Dame Press, 2004.

Romero, Oscar. "The Political Dimension of the Faith from the Perspective of the Option for the Poor." In *Voice of the Voiceless: The Four Pastoral Letters and Other Statements.* Translated by Michael J. Walsh. Maryknoll, N.Y.: Orbis Books, 1985.

————. *The Violence of Love.* Compiled and translated by James R. Brockman. Farmington, Pa.: Plough Publishing House, 1998.

Sobrino, Jon. *Archbishop Romero: Memories and Reflections.* Translated by Robert Barr. Maryknoll, N.Y.: Orbis Books, 1990.

7

A Social Crisis, A Liberating Theology

Contemporary Reflection on Faith and Justice

D URING GRADUATE STUDIES I LIVED in a large university town located
near San Francisco. I resided in a house on a quiet street at the north end
of campus and had a room located on the basement floor. Throughout these
formative years, I spent many hours in this room reading books, studying
some of the great classical and contemporary thinkers, and expanding my
grasp of theology.

One morning I got out of bed and looked outside the basement window;
sleeping on a ledge was a homeless man. He had spent the night on the
other side of the wall from where I slept. Physically, we were only about eight
inches away from each other. Existentially, however, we lived in two totally
different worlds. While mine was the reality of a comfortable home, a warm
bed, and the life of the mind, his was the reality of homelessness, a brick mat-
tress, and the life of the streets. After that night I never thought about the
task of theology in quite the same way. The more I let his world of poverty
encroach on my world of studies, the more it made entirely new demands on
my life and changed the way I thought about God.

The "irruption"[1] of this poor man's presence into my own history made
me aware of the need for a theology that would help me interpret and respond
to the great social challenges in the world today. Beyond the physical wall
that separated this poor man from me, I also began to recognize other walls
formed by my own social location, training, preconceptions, self-interests,
and resistances to conversion. It became clear that my own theological reflection needed to move to the other side of the cognitive wall, from the comfortableness of my own room, my own library, and my own ideas about God

---

1. See Virginia Fabella and Sergio Torres, eds., *Irruption of the Third World: Challenge to Theol-
ogy* (Maryknoll, N.Y.: Orbis Books, 1983), which includes papers from the Fifth International
Conference of the Ecumenical Association of Third World Theologians, August 17-29, 1981, in
New Delhi, India.

to the uncomfortableness of the world, the living "texts" of the poor, and the challenge of the living God.

Around this time, I began reading what is known as a theology of liberation. I was drawn to the efforts of some theologians to ask questions about the meaning of Christian faith from the perspective of the people the world regards as the least significant in society. I was intrigued by a theological framework that offered a way of understanding how to be Christian in a world of destitution. I was also perplexed about its critics and controversies. Yet in time I saw its significance for doing theology in our current global context.

Though some people misunderstand its central message, and some have distorted its teachings, its contribution cannot be underestimated, and it has had a tremendous influence on the church at both the regional and universal levels, including the writings of Saint John Paul II. Some theologians even believe that liberation theology and the central notion of the preferential option for the poor may be as significant and as controversial for our generation as was justification by faith for previous ones.[2] In this chapter we will examine liberation theology and explore how it can help us navigate our way in this new era of globalization.[3] We will look first at its method and its themes, then its critics and its controversies, and lastly its challenges and its contribution to theological reflection and social transformation.

A THEOLOGY OF LIBERATION: REFLECTING ON GOD FROM THE PERSPECTIVE OF THE POOR

In general terms liberation theology is a way to think about God in our contemporary world from the perspective of those left out of the benefits of the current global economy. It is also a social movement that seeks to live out what it means to be a Christian in a world of poverty.[4] While liberation theology is not a monolithic theology, nor a fully formed one, at its core it seeks to answer some fundamental questions: How can the Gospel be proclaimed in a way that the poor believe God loves them, especially when much of what they

---

2. Norbert F. Lohfink, *Option for the Poor: The Basic Principle of Liberation Theology in the Light of the Bible*, 2nd ed. (North Richland Hills, Tex.: Bibal, 1995).

3. Of the many fine summaries and introductions to liberation theology, see especially Phillip Berryman, *Liberation Theology: Essential Facts about the Revolutionary Movement in Latin America—and Beyond* (Philadelphia, Pa.: Temple University Press, 1987); Leonardo Boff and Clodovis Boff, *Introducing Liberation Theology* (Maryknoll, N.Y.: Orbis Books, 1987); Edward L. Cleary, *Crisis and Change: The Church in Latin America Today* (Maryknoll, N.Y.: Orbis Books, 1985), 51-103; Roberto S. Goizueta, "Liberation Theology, Influence on Spirituality," in *The New Dictionary of Catholic Spirituality*, ed. Michael Downey (Collegeville, Minn.: Liturgical Press, 1993), 597-602.

4. Cleary, "A New Ideology: The Theology of Liberation," in *Crisis and Change*.

experience on a daily basis is in fact the negation of love? What does it mean to be Christian in a world where more than half the planet lives in abject poverty? How can the poor themselves become not simply passive recipients of the church's mission but active participants in it? Before exploring these questions in more depth, it is important to define precisely what we mean by the term "liberation."

In contemporary theological discourse, "liberation" is another word for "salvation." While the terms "salvation" and "liberation" both deal with God's desire to free people from sin, oppression, and ultimately death, the term "salvation" frequently connotes what happens after one dies, in the afterlife. Liberation theology is also concerned with what happens in the next life, but it gives attention as well to what happens in this world, in history. While previously many theologians tended to make sharp distinctions between this world and the next, liberation theologians insist on making the integral connection between God's kingdom on earth and God's kingdom in heaven, between the secular and sacred, and between the Jesus of history and the Christ of faith. They argue that there is only one history, one reign, one God, and one process of salvation.[5] Liberation then deals with God's action in history to free people from all that oppresses them right now and at the end of time.

"The theology of liberation," says Gustavo Gutiérrez, "is about God. God's love and God's life are, ultimately, its only theme."[6] It examines the relationship between salvation and the historical process of human liberation in light of a faith that seeks justice.[7] Recognizing the God of Jesus Christ as the Lord of history and the only one in whom one finds true and lasting freedom, liberation theology is language about God and reflection on human experience, beginning with the poor and insignificant of society.[8] It combines a profound sense of the unmerited, gratuitous gift of God's love with the urgency of solidarity with those society considers the least important.[9] In brief, liberation theology is a way of speaking about God and salvation in a world of poverty.

---

5. In the Lord's Prayer, as Norbert Lohfink observed, "God is addressed in heaven, but what is asked for is to happen on earth . . . God is to hallow his name in *this* world, his will is something which happens in *this* history. His rule is coming, since Jesus, in *this* world" (*Option for the Poor*, 6).

6. Gustavo Gutiérrez, "The Task and Content of Liberation Theology," trans. Judith Condor in *The Cambridge Companion to Liberation Theology*, ed. Christopher Rowland (Cambridge, N.Y.: Cambridge University Press, 1999), 19.

7. Gustavo Gutiérrez, *A Theology of Liberation: History, Politics, and Salvation*, rev. ed., trans. Sister Caridad Inda and John Eagleson (Maryknoll, N.Y.: Orbis Books, 1988), 29.

8. Gustavo Gutiérrez, *On Job: God-Talk and the Suffering of the Innocent*, trans. Matthew J. O'Connell (Maryknoll, N.Y.: Orbis Books, 1987).

9. Gutiérrez, "Task and Content of Liberation Theology," 27.

THREE LEVELS OF LIBERATION

The liberation announced by Jesus Christ can be distinguished on three inter-related levels: the social level, the personal level, and the religious level.

The Social Level

Liberation on the social level deals with the transformation of our relation-ships with others and the structures in society that negatively affect these relationships. It involves eliminating the domination, abuse, and subjugation that degrade human interaction. Discriminating against others because of race, gender, culture, religion, or class not only injures the victim but it dehu-manizes the victimizer. When such injustice becomes woven into the fabric of society in a way that privileges some while excluding others, it threatens the peaceful development of human society.

Liberation on the social level also aims to eliminate poverty and the struc-tural causes of poverty. Because poverty is an inhumane condition that nega-tively affects relationships and impedes the development of human beings, poverty means death, not only final death but also death experienced as the diminishment of life that stems from dehumanizing conditions of misery. Social liberation fosters a vision of society based on human dignity, mutual-ity in relationships, and active concern for the most vulnerable members of community.

The Personal Level

While liberation on the social level focuses on our relationships with oth-ers and external structures and systems that affect them, liberation on the personal level deals with internal structures that affect our relationship with ourselves and consequently others. Liberation here means liberation from the negative cognitive habits and personality patterns that dehumanize oth-ers, such as attitudes of superiority, machismo, racism, and other destructive mentalities.

Sometimes personal liberation involves helping the poor change the way they think about themselves, especially when they see their condition as fate or, worse, as divinely ordained. Paulo Freire speaks in terms of the "consci-entization of the poor," by which he refers to the fact that, if the poor do not change their self-perception, they will never be free.[10] Some liberation

---

10. Paulo Freire, *Pedagogy of the Oppressed*, trans. Myra Bergman Ramos (New York: Con-tinuum, 2000), 43-70.

theologians believe that one of the greatest crimes of poverty is that the poor begin to internalize the negative stereotypes they live with on a daily basis. Conversion on this level means rediscovering the original design of creation in which people are called to be free, dignified, and loving human beings.

The Religious Level

While the social and personal levels deal with our relationship with others and ourselves, liberation on the religious level deals with our relationship with God. Liberation here means freedom from sin, which is the ultimate source of injustice and oppression. Sin is breaking friendship with God and others, and liberation deals with restoring the bonds of friendship that are destroyed by sin. Liberation theology considers any form of oppression sinful, a failure to love. Only God, through the redemptive love of Christ, can accomplish this total liberation in human beings and bring about complete reconciliation in all levels of our relationships. Liberation on the religious level invites not only the oppressed to undergo conversion but also the oppressor. Such liberation, which begins in the heart and transforms the entire person, facilitates the birth of what *Gaudium et Spes* calls "a new humanism." In this new creation people primarily define themselves with respect to their relationship with God and their responsibility to their brothers and sisters (GS 55). Liberation theology, then, is not so much a new theology as a contemporary articulation of an ancient theme, namely, the liberation or salvation of all people on all levels of their existence.

THE ORIGINS OF LIBERATION THEOLOGY

Liberation theology was born in the 1960s in Latin America, but it is the offspring of biblical and patristic parents and a cousin of the social doctrine of the church.[11] Though its content has much in common with traditional Christian teaching, two developments in the second half of the twentieth century contributed to its growth and advancement: (1) ecclesiological developments, especially the Second Vatican Council (1962-1965) and subsequent regional meetings of the Episcopal Conference of Latin American Bishops (CELAM); and (2) historical-social developments, particularly the consciousness of widespread economic misery and its causes.

---

11. For more on the history of liberation theology, see Roberto Oliveros, "History of the Theology of Liberation," in *Mysterium Liberationis: Fundamental Concepts of Liberation Theology*, ed. Ignacio Ellacuría and Jon Sobrino (Maryknoll, N.Y.: Orbis Books, 1993), 3-32.

In many respects liberation theology was a natural outgrowth of the Second Vatican Council. A major focus of this council was to address the relationship of the church to contemporary society, particularly in *Gaudium et Spes.* Moving from a place of defensiveness and even isolation from the world, Vatican II defined the church's mission in terms of service not only to Catholics and Christians but to all people. The church saw itself called as a sacrament of salvation for everyone, which it manifested in helping make the world a better place.[12] The major focus was no longer the church *against* the world or the church *in* the world but the church *for* the world.[13]

One area in which the church reiterated a commitment for the world was in the area of human development. While the council did not address the theme of poverty in great detail, subsequent documents such as Pope Paul VI's *Populorum Progressio* (1967) clarified that it was not enough for the church to speak of morality on simply personal terms. As the church began to address morality on social terms as well, it argued that poverty is not the inevitable fate of human civilization but a social reality that is contrary to the will of God.

CELAM, particularly the meetings at Medellín, Colombia (1968), Puebla, Mexico (1979), Santo Domingo, Dominican Republic (1992), and others, would take this reflection even further. Drawing on Vatican II and *Populorum Progressio,* the church in Latin America went to the other side of its own theological and ecclesial walls and let the massive misery of the people make a claim on its conscience. In their magisterial teachings at Medellín in 1968, the bishops began to speak much more strongly in terms of "liberation":

> The Latin American episcopate cannot remain indifferent in the face of tremendous social injustices existent in Latin America, which keep the majority of our peoples in dismal poverty, which in many cases becomes inhuman wretchedness. A deafening cry pours from the throats of millions of [our people], asking their pastors for a liberation that reaches them nowhere else.[14]

In 1979, the bishops further reiterated that the current social situation in Latin America is a sin that cries out to heaven for remedy and calls society to conversion:

> [T]he situation of inhuman poverty in which millions of Latin Americans live is the most devastating and humiliating kind of scourge. And the

---

12. Ibid., 4.
13. Cleary, "New Ideology," 62.
14. Medellín Document on Poverty of the Church in *The Church in the Present-Day Transformation of Latin America in Light of the Council,* ed. Michael Colonnese (Bogotá: General Secretariat of CELAM, 1968), 1-2.

situation finds expression in such things as a high rate of infant mortality, lack of adequate housing, health problems, starvation wages, unemployment and underemployment, malnutrition, job uncertainty, compulsory mass migrations, etc. Analyzing this situation more deeply, we discover that this poverty is not a passing phase. Instead it is the product of economic, social, and political situations and structures, although there are also other causes for the state of misery.[15]

Moreover, such poverty also calls the church to conversion, and renewal in the church in Latin America begins with listening more attentively to the cries of the poor. At Puebla, the bishops reiterated the challenge of liberation in light of the scandalous social situation of Latin America:

Viewing it in the light of faith, we see the growing gap between rich and poor as a scandal and a contradiction to Christian existence. The luxury of a few becomes an insult to the wretched poverty of the vast masses. This is contrary to the plan of the Creator and to the honor that is due Him. In this anxiety and sorrow the Church sees a situation of social sinfulness, all the more serious because it exists in countries that call themselves Catholic.[16]

Such a position was bold and challenging, and it stirred up controversy inside and outside the church.

Amidst the storm, theological reflection began emerging that spoke directly to the Latin American context.[17] Critics began to argue that such contexuality threatens the universality of Christian doctrine. In response, liberation theologians argued that contexuality does not diminish universality but enriches it because each particular expression of Christianity within a culture has a universal dimension. They said that unity does not mean uniformity—the bland homogenization of everything Christian—but rather a celebration of the richness of diversity that is part of God's creative designs. Gradually, liberation theology began to define itself from its unique social location, and it argued that "pure, classical theology" was in fact "European" and "North American" contextual theology. All theology, liberation theologians contend, is contextual, and there is no theology that emerges independently of its social context. As the hegemony of a Eurocentric theology began to weaken, contextual theologies from different parts of the world like Latin America began to gain new strength and energy.

---

15. Puebla Final Document in *Puebla and Beyond: Documentation and Commentary*, ed. John Eagleson and Philip Sharper, trans. John Drury (Maryknoll, N.Y.: Orbis Books, 1979), 29-30.

16. Ibid., 28.

17. See in particular Stephen B. Bevans, *Models of Contextual Theology*, Faith and Cultures Series (Maryknoll, N.Y.: Orbis Books, 2002); and Stephen B. Bevans and Roger P. Schroeder, *Constants in Context: A Theology of Mission for Today* (Maryknoll, N.Y.: Orbis Books, 2004).

In the decades that followed, liberation theology gained momentum through books, conferences, and various forms of dissemination, especially in Christian base communities that began to form in Latin America. Liberation theology reached an important milestone in the publication of Gustavo Gutiérrez's *A Theology of Liberation* in 1971. In the years that followed, other notable theologians emerged, such as Jon Sobrino, Juan Luis Segundo, Elizabeth Johnson, Edward Cleary, Virgilio Elizondo, María Pilar Aquino, J. Míguez Bonino, Diego Irarrázaval, Teresa Okure, Segundo Galilea, Carlos Mesters, Leonardo and Clodovis Boff, Pablo Richard, Elsa Tamez, and others. From the social location of the poor, these theologians began to rethink traditional categories of Christian faith, including the kingdom of God, Trinity, Christology, spirituality, ecclesiology, biblical theology, and other themes. They did not all agree with each other, but out of this process the contours of a theology of liberation began to emerge, and one element that all share is a common method for doing theology.[18]

THE METHOD OF LIBERATION THEOLOGY

Because liberation theology involves rereading the central categories of the faith from the perspective of the poor, many theologians began to change not just *what* but *how* they thought about God.[19] This is a dramatic shift from earlier generations. Until Vatican II, theological formation took place within the safe confines of seminaries and universities and was largely geared toward the formation of priests and religious. Based largely on scholastic philosophy and theology, particularly the thought of Thomas Aquinas, it offered a tight, systematic understanding of the doctrine of God and Christian life. This system has its advantages, but it also has its limitations. One of the greatest limitations of the scholastic system is that in many ways it built a cognitive wall between the reality of the mind and the reality of the poor and did not adequately speak to the pressing questions of an impoverished continent.

Whereas in Europe and North America theologians largely are preoccupied with the question, How do we speak about God in a world of modern science and an increasingly secularized society?, in Latin America the question is much more basic: How do we speak about a personal God in a world that regards the poor as non-persons? The Second Vatican Council, and *Gaudium et Spes* in particular, not only opened up new ways of asking questions but also new ways of investigating them. As Edward Cleary notes:

---

18. See especially Ellacuría and Sobrino, *Mysterium Liberationis.*
19. Gutiérrez, *On Job,* Introduction.

The methodology used in the document turns traditional theology on its head. Instead of proceeding in the time-honored fashion, discussing theological or biblical principles and then applying them to a present-day situation, *Gaudium et Spes* reverses the process: it begins with a careful analysis of the de facto situation, then turns to sacred scripture and theology for reflection on that situation, and finally, as a third step, makes pastoral applications.[20]

In short, liberation theology has a three-step method of theological reflection: (1) *reality:* the description of the church in the world; (2) *reflection:* biblical and doctrinal elaboration; and (3) *response:* pastoral implications that flow from this reflection.

Reality: The Description of the Church in the World

The first step of liberation theology is grasping the contours of reality in which Christian faith is lived. This context is integrally related to *praxis*. In general terms, *praxis* (Greek, "to do") refers to human activity and ministry in light of God's reign in history and in the end of time. The concern of liberation theologians is not just orthodoxy (right doctrine) but orthopraxis (right living). Orthopraxis pertains to putting into practice the will of God (Mt 7:21; 25:31-46; Jas 2:15-17), through which human beings seek to be instruments of God in the transformation of history. Right living and sustained reflection allow one to accurately perceive the truths of reality.

One of the major shifts of the Second Vatican Council was that it began to do more theology from the reality of people's lives. Theology became more of a serious and critical but also creative reflection on the lived experience of the people of God. Understanding the contours of reality also has led liberation theologians to draw on new disciplines, including economics, sociology, politics, history, and other fields. They also began drawing on various ideologies, which generated controversy, confusion, and even censorship from some circles.

Although integrally related to history, praxis also has a contemplative dimension, which speaks to the transcendence of God that can be encountered only in prayer and worship. This point is significant, especially for social activists who are vulnerable to the temptation of diminishing or discounting the role of spirituality in the process of human liberation, particularly when it seems impractical or ineffective. Contemplation enables one to see faith as a gift and a response to God's free and unconditional offer of love,

---

20. Cleary, "New Ideology," 60-61.

which can be apprehended only by those open to entering the holy ground of divine life and divine providence. From this perspective, faith is a gift and a demand that flows from the gratuity of God and a response of committed discipleship. As brought out in German, the word *Gabe* (grace, gift) is related to the word *Aufgabe* (duty, obligation, commitment). Christian faith is lived between *Gabe* and *Aufgabe*, between grace and duty, between the gift given from God for the believer and the gift given by the disciple for others.[21]

Reflection: Biblical and Doctrinal Elaboration

Because previous chapters have explored in more detail the content of this biblical and doctrinal reflection, our focus here is understanding more of the theological method used in formulating spiritual and religious truths. Because thought can also be used to avoid action, liberation theologians emphasize that God is more than an idea to which intellectual assent is made; God is a profound and primary relationship to which a commitment is made. This commitment takes shape especially as one enters into solidarity with the poor in history.[22]

In liberationist thought, theology is understood as a second step: "[I]t rises only at sundown," Gutiérrez notes.[23] The work of theology begins with pastoral activity. At the same time theology also enriches the pastoral life of the church. Theology does not produce pastoral activity but rather reflects on it. This point is significant, especially for scholars who enter into the task of theology as "professionals" without necessarily believing in God, belonging to a church community, or engaging in an active promotion of a faith that does justice. When theology is divorced from the concrete social reality of the world, it frequently answers questions that few are asking, questions that are peripheral to the deeper hungers and suffering of people's lives.

Biblical and doctrinal reflection also takes into account a certain spiritual blindness that can come from reading the Gospel from centers of power and influence. Liberation theologians ground their reflection first on reading from the perspective of the "crucified peoples" of today's society.[24] They have in mind the excluded, the non-persons, and people of color. As Gutiérrez notes,

---

21. I am grateful to Gustavo Gutiérrez for this penetrating insight.

22. Robert McAfee Brown, *Unexpected News: Reading the Bible with Third World Eyes* (Philadelphia: Westminster, 1984), 107.

23. Gutiérrez, *Theology of Liberation*, 9.

24. Ignacio Ellacuría, "The Crucified People" in *Mysterium Liberationis*, 580-603; Sturla J. Stalsett, *The Crucified and the Crucified: A Study in the Liberation Christology of Jon Sobrino* (Bern: Peter Lang, 2003), 537.

The Gospel read from the point of the view of the poor and the exploited . . . requires . . . a Church which arises from the people, a people who wrest the Gospel from the hands of the great ones of this world and thus prevent it from being used to justify a situation against the will of the liberating God.[25]

While this reflection values rigorous and disciplined thought that comes from advanced, formal education, it eschews any tendency to an intellectual classism, especially that which would undervalue the legitimate and crucial insights that can come from the poor and uneducated, or those who would view "pastoral theology" as a watered-down version of pure, academic theology. Liberation theologians argue that only when the Bible is read from the perspective of the poor can theology be a liberating message for all. The insight of the poor, therefore, should have a favored place alongside the work of biblical exegetes, even though the poor process their theology in different ways:

It would be wrong to believe that the poor have no theology, that they do not reflect on the experience of being Christian, that their reflection includes no protest of their condition of poverty. Much of their theological thinking takes place in community; it is not individualistic. Much of their reflection is geared to the particular and concrete; it is seldom systematized or expressed in abstractions. Much of their thinking bears on their pressing situation and problems; it is seldom ahistorical.[26]

In its formulation of doctrine, liberation theology puts primacy not simply on reading written texts but also on reading living texts, not just the insights from scholars but additionally the insights from the poor.

Response: Pastoral Implications

The third step in liberation theology has to do with evangelization or the pastoral implications of this sustained reflection on the church in the modern world. This evangelization is integrally related to liberation and development. In *Evangelii Nuntiandi*, Paul VI noted:

As the kernel and center of His Good News, Christ proclaims salvation, this great gift of God which is liberation from everything that oppresses

---

25. Quoted in Monika Hellwig, "Good News to the Poor: Do They Understand It Better?" in *Tracing the Spirit: Communities, Social Action, and Theological Reflection*, ed. James E. Hug (New York: Paulist, 1983), 127-28.

26. Julio de Santa Ana, ed., *Towards a Church of the Poor* (Maryknoll, N.Y.: Orbis Books, 1981), 114; see also Ernesto Cardenal, *Gospel in Solentiname*, trans. Donald D. Walsh (Maryknoll, N.Y.: Orbis Books, 1976).

human beings but which is above all liberation from sin and the Evil One, in the joy of knowing God and being known by Him, of seeing Him, and of being given over to Him. All of this is begun during the life of Christ and definitively accomplished by His death and resurrection. But it must be patiently carried on during the course of history, in order to be realized fully on the day of the final coming of Christ. (EN 9)

In general terms pastoral response often means, but is not limited to, working directly with the poor. Because it involves helping lighten the burden of those who suffer because of poverty, pastoral response includes any way through which people try to eliminate the *condition* of poverty and the *causes* of it. For this reason, commitment to the poor can express itself in various ways. In more specific terms, solidarity means tithing time of one hour or more a week, a day a month, a week a year, or some other period of time. It can express itself concretely in terms of lobbying Congress, writing elected officials to correct unjust legislation, visiting prisoners in local jails, assisting migrants in finding jobs and housing, volunteering in a home for battered women, helping out in a local soup kitchen, visiting nursing homes, taking part in a Big Brothers/Big Sisters program, providing transportation for the poor, teaching English to migrant workers, attending meetings of inner-city community organizations, tutoring in local schools, and other ways of assisting vulnerable people.[27]

Solidarity with the poor then inspires and provokes transformative action. While there are many ways of working for a more just society, liberation theologians believe that no one can choose to ignore a commitment to the poor and still claim to be Christian. While much of the trajectory of the global culture tends toward an "upward mobility," liberation theologians see in the Gospel a challenge to a "downward mobility" that expresses itself concretely in "the preferential option for the poor."

THE PREFERENTIAL OPTION FOR THE POOR

The core content of liberation theology comes down to one central and concise concept: the preferential option for the poor. This option can be made by individuals, communities, or the whole church. It means resisting injustice and exploitation of other people and working for a world where people can be free from all that oppresses them. It entails the decision to relinquish privileges and resources in order to walk in greater solidarity with the poor, and the decision to allow the poor to speak for themselves and to be subjects and

---

27. Peter J. Henriot, *Opting for the Poor: A Challenge for North Americans* (Washington, D.C.: Center of Concern, 1990), 61-62.

actors in their own struggle for liberation. If poverty is what divides people from one another, making some rich and leaving others in abject misery, then the option for the poor is a movement toward reconciliation, a sharing of life, spirit, and resources, in an attempt to overcome the forces that divide human beings so that all may have what they need to live, grow, and develop as God intends.

To appreciate better this notion of the option for the poor in light of a faith that does justice, it is helpful to look at the phrase in more detail. This also will allow us to nuance more precisely the ways in which this commitment is lived out through voluntary poverty and spiritual poverty in the face of the material poverty in which so many people live.

Preferential

The preferential option for the poor must first be understood in light of God's universal care for all people. "Preferential" does not mean exclusive, as if God loves only the poor. Liberation theology affirms that God loves all human beings, that God offers salvation to all people, and that all are invited into the kingdom of God. At the same time, it acknowledges that people have the freedom to make choices, and human beings can choose to reject God's offer of salvation. God sides with those who are oppressed even when it brings opposition and conflict with those who oppress.

"Preference" consequently involves making a choice for people over things through voluntary poverty. Voluntary poverty is a conscious protest against poverty by which one chooses to live together with those who are materially poor. Its inspiration comes from the life of Jesus, who entered into solidarity with the human condition in order to help human beings overcome the sin that enslaves and impoverishes them.[28] Voluntary poverty affirms that Christ came to live as a poor person not because poverty itself has any intrinsic value but to criticize and challenge those people and systems that oppress the poor and compromise their God-given dignity.

Theologically the notion of preference says more about the goodness of God than it does about the goodness of the poor. It does not mean that the poor are necessarily more virtuous, more deserving, or more holy than those who are not poor, nor that they themselves are always open to the message of salvation. It means that God reaches out in love to those who have a greater need, to those who are most in pain, to those whose life is most threatened. Consider a story told by Jack Jezreel, founder of JustFaith:

---

28. Gutiérrez, "Task and Content of Liberation Theology," 26.

One Saturday morning I have big plans to spend the day with my three daughters. When I walk into their room I awaken them with the news that we are going to the zoo. Two of them kick off the covers and get dressed as fast they can. The third gets out of bed more slowly, looks a little dazed and wobbly, and then falls to the floor in a faint. Suddenly all of my attention is drawn to the daughter who is unconscious on the floor. I am immediately at her side, devoted to her care. For the next several minutes I forget about the zoo, about the oatmeal I am cooking, and even about my other two girls. I have become completely absorbed with the needs of my daughter who is in trouble. While I am dedicated to the care of my daughter who is ill, it does not mean that I love my other two daughters any less. It is simply that love takes me in the direction of greater need.

This experience helped me understand God's love as it is expressed in the preferential option for the poor. God's love is boundless, but when any of us are hungry, homeless, abandoned, or vulnerable, God is moved by love in the direction of greatest need. The option for the poor is not so much a matter of God loving one group of people over another, but a matter of God choosing to go to where love necessarily is drawn—that is, to those who are most vulnerable.[29]

Option

The word "option" does not mean "optional," as if one could choose not to love the poor and call oneself Christian. "Option" is a way of choosing to prefer first the needs of the poor, even as other needs pull at us individually and collectively. While in the contemporary social order the rich most of the time are given priority over the poor, this option is a conscious effort to invert the existing social order by giving primacy to the concerns and interests of the vulnerable. While this option includes those who choose voluntary poverty, living and working directly with the poor, others will strive for their liberation and empowerment in other ways.

In liberation theology this option is grounded on an inner disposition referred to as spiritual poverty. Spiritual poverty is about a radical openness to the will of God, a radical faith in a provident God, and a radical trust in a loving God. It is also known as spiritual childhood, from which flows the renunciation of material goods. Relinquishing possessions comes from a desire to be more possessed by God alone and to love and serve God

---

29. I am grateful to Jack Jezreel for sharing this with me in personal correspondence.

more completely. Spiritual poverty does not infer that there is something bad about material possessions, or even that poverty in itself is good, or a path to holiness. Rather spiritual poverty refers to becoming more open to God's revelation, action, and guidance in our lives and humbly recognizing our place in the universe as children of God. The experience of spiritual poverty will lead each Christian and the Christian community to want to live voluntary poverty in some way. Some are called to live directly with the poor; others to live simply and work as they can, wherever they are, for human liberation. For all, this option entails living in solidarity with the poor in imitation of Christ.

In contrast to certain liberation movements that tend toward a militant identification with the poor and reactive judgmentalism toward the non-poor, this spiritual dimension of liberation theology, which is born of the heart, is deepened through prayer, and bears fruit in detachment, enables people to see reality more clearly and consequently to hear and live the truths of Scripture more openly. This does not mean that the wealthy cannot hear the message, but liberation theologians point out that it is often more difficult for the wealthy to submit to God's rule over their lives, to understand their own existential poverty before God as creatures, to realize their solidarity with all people, and to respond with absolute gratuity to all, as God does.[30]

Spiritual poverty also has an inevitable dimension of joy and fiesta, which is especially necessary in the struggle for justice. Liberation theologians know from experience that the poor are not always sad, that they know joys of life, of family, of friendship, of the promise of the Gospel, and of trust in the Lord of life. This is why in liberation theology, fiesta and prophecy go together and are two sides of the same coin. Fiesta without prophecy easily degenerates into indulgence, escapism, and drunkenness. But prophecy without fiesta can degenerate into anger, cynicism, spiritual elitism, and a suffocating spiritual seriousness.

For the Poor

While the preferential option for the poor has some connection with voluntary and spiritual poverty, its primary focus deals with material poverty. This poverty is a very complex issue, as are its causes and remedies. Whatever distinctions about poverty need to be made, the preferential option for the poor understands poverty first of all as real poverty. Real poverty means

---

30. Marcello de Carvalho Azevedo, *Vocation for Mission: The Challenge of Religious Life Today*, trans. John W. Diercksmeier (New York: Paulist, 1988).

privation, that is, the lack of goods necessary to meet basic human needs. It means inadequate access to education, health care, public services, living wages, insurance, and other such factors. Liberation theologians reiterate that there is nothing "blessed" about this kind of poverty; it is dehumanizing and contrary to the will of God.

Because material poverty is a complex subject, liberation theologians do not limit their reference point only to the economically poor. For Gustavo Gutiérrez, to be poor, above all, means to be insignificant. It refers to those individuals and groups whose lives count for little or nothing in society because of their race, gender, religion, culture, or economic status. Opting for the poor in this way means protecting the human dignity of all peoples and fostering the conditions necessary for human development of all people in all aspects of their existence.

In summary, liberation theology, its core message of the preferential option for the poor, and its lived expression through voluntary, spiritual, and material poverty, is about the proclamation of the good news of Jesus Christ. This proclamation is not a social ideology with a religious mask but a profound challenge aimed at a *metanoia*—a changing of mind and heart. As a theology at the service of preaching the Gospel, it seeks to give expression to the resurrection of Jesus, which entails being against death in all its forms: physical death, cultural death, and many other kinds of death. Liberation theology is oriented toward a Gospel that denounces death as it announces life. The preferential option for the poor is an old idea with new consequences. "To opt for the poor," says Gutiérrez, "is to make an option for Jesus Christ, who is salvation."

As the forces of globalization create still greater disparities between the rich and the poor, the option for the poor is even more important now than in 1979, when the bishops at Puebla reiterated:

> With renewed hope in the vivifying power of the Spirit, we are going to take up . . . a clear and prophetic option expressing preference for, and solidarity with, the poor.[31]

When the Latin American bishops first issued this statement, it stirred up much controversy and still does, especially among Christians who believe that the church has no business commenting on the affairs of the world. Anticipating and experiencing this controversy, the bishops of Latin America at Puebla nonetheless affirmed with conviction:

> We do this despite the distortions and interpretations of some, who vitiate the spirit of Medellín, and despite the disregard and even hostility of others.

---

31. Puebla Final Document, in *Puebla and Beyond: Documentation and Commentary* no. 1134.

We affirm the need for conversion on the part of the whole Church to a preferential option for the poor, an option aimed at their integral liberation.[32]

THE VATICAN AND LIBERATION THEOLOGY

Because of the controversy it engenders, some believe that the Vatican in general, and John Paul II and Pope Benedict XVI in particular, have condemned liberation theology. Such a perception neither adequately understands liberation theology nor the two statements issued on the subject. Not only did the Vatican not censure liberation theology, but it actually affirmed its immense "promise" and importance in the whole of Christian theology. At the same time the Vatican sought to address and correct some of the abuses of liberation theology. In order to avoid confusing the content of liberation theology with its distortions, and in order to appreciate its undeniable influence on the church and especially on papal teachings, it is important to take some time to examine some of the objections and challenges to liberation theology.

The Vatican's Congregation for the Doctrine of the Faith, under the leadership of Cardinal Joseph Ratzinger (elected Pope Benedict XVI in 2005), issued two letters regarding liberation theology. The first is called "Instruction on Certain Aspects of the Theology of Liberation" (*Libertatis Nuntius,* 1984) and the second is the "Instruction on Christian Freedom and Liberation" (*Libertatis Conscientia,* 1986). The purpose of the first letter was to address "deviations, and risks of deviations" that are "damaging to the faith and to Christian living, that are brought about by certain forms of liberation theology" (LN Intro). The purpose of the second was to "highlight the main elements of the Christian doctrine on freedom and liberation" (LC 2). The two documents are meant to be read together, and they seek to clarify what it means when the church affirms that "the Gospel of Jesus Christ is a message of freedom and a force for liberation" (LN Intro). These instructions offer a way of thinking about Christian freedom and responsibility in political and social arenas.[33]

The second document speaks very favorably in terms of the importance of liberation theology, and when it was issued John Paul II spoke to the bishops of Brazil and said that the theology of liberation was "not only opportune, but useful and necessary."[34] The major concern of the first document, however,

---

32. Ibid.

33. Gustavo Gutiérrez, *The Truth Shall Make You Free*, trans. Matthew J. O'Connell (Maryknoll, N.Y.: Orbis Books, 1990), 87.

34. John Paul II, "Giant Brazil at a Crossroads" (Opening Address to Brazilian Bishops, March 13, 1986), *Origins* 15, no. 42 (April 3, 1986): 684.

is tendencies toward reductionism in liberation theology, that is, reducing human liberation to what happens in this world, reducing the notion of sin to social sin, reducing the kingdom of God to political changes and human timelines, and especially reducing Christian theology to social ideology. While they do not mention any theologian by name, these documents address "certain forms of liberation theology which use, in an insufficiently critical manner, concepts borrowed from various currents of Marxist thought" (LN Intro). The corruption or distortion of Christian doctrine by Marxist ideology is a genuine issue of concern that needs careful examination.

Part of the confusion and conflict comes from the fact that Marxism does have something in common with Christianity. Marx, too, sought to remedy the problem of injustice in the world, and he offered certain scholarly tools that help in that process. Some liberation theologians have recognized the value of these tools when analyzing issues related to dependency, class analysis, structural sin, the spiral of violence, and injustices of capitalism.[35] The fact that Marxist notions are present in the theory of dependency, for example, does not mean that liberation theologians subscribe to Marxist thought, Marxist solutions, or Marxist ideology.[36] Not every liberation theologian embraced the use of Marxist tools; most rejected them completely. Gustavo Gutiérrez has affirmed consistently that the first and last line of liberation theology is against Marxism. For Marx, religion was oppressive and alienating. For liberation theologians, religion is liberating and reconciling. When critics too quickly dismiss liberation theology as Marxist, they understand neither liberation theology nor the social teaching of the church. As Archbishop Dom Hélder Câmara once remarked, "When I give food to the hungry, they call me a saint; when I ask why the poor are hungry, they call me a communist."[37]

In order to clarify the confusion between Marxism and liberation theology, a distinction needs to be made between Marxism as an ideological program for social change and Marxism as a tool for social analysis. Drawing on Marxist tools is not equivalent to subscribing to the Marxist system or Marxist conclusions, any more than one who speaks of the subconscious subscribes to all of Freudian thought. To speak about class struggle, for example, is not an ideological statement but a statement about reality. Vatican documents also speak of class struggle (QA 113-14; CA 14). The problem is not mentioning class struggle but making class struggle—rather than God—the driving force of history (LN X, 3) or making class struggle a rationale for hatred and

---

35. Cleary, "New Ideology," 84.

36. Pedro Arrupe, "Marxist Analysis by Christians," in *Liberation Theology: A Documentary History*, ed. and trans. Alfred T. Hennelly (Maryknoll, N.Y.: Orbis Books, 1990), 307-13.

37. Robert Ellsberg, "The Centenary of Dorothy Day's Birth," *Origins* 27, no. 27 (December 18, 1997): 457.

violence (LN VIII, 7-9). Not only does such an approach unravel the bonds of community, but it can give rise to totalitarian regimes, undermine church (hierarchal) authority, and distort core Christian doctrine.

While the Vatican instructions bring out that the quest for social change must not involve causing other injustices, they positively assert that love for the poor, the struggle for justice, and the hope of human liberation are at the heart of the Gospel message.[38] John Paul II speaks about "the positive value of an authentic theology of integral human liberation" (CA 26), and he addresses the issue of class conflict in *Laborem Exercens* (11). He speaks of the struggle for worker's rights and the need to meet their just needs, and his words leave no doubt that justice and human liberation must begin in this world:

> The needs of the poor must take priority over the desires of the rich, the rights of workers over the maximization of profits, the preservation of the environment over uncontrolled industrial expansion, production to meet social needs over production for military purposes . . . The poor people and poor nations . . . will judge those people who take these goods away from them, amassing to themselves the imperialistic monopoly of economic and political supremacy at the expense of others.[39]

At the same time, he believed that true liberation can come only from the love of Christ, in whom we are set free from all alienation, doubt, and ultimately sin and death (RM 11). In *Redemptoris Missio*, he notes that, even while we await the fullness of redemption in Christ at the end of time, it is accomplished through a true conversion of heart and mind, which leads to the recognition of the worth and dignity of every human being, the fostering of solidarity, and the deepening of commitment and service to one's neighbor, which in turn leads to a kingdom of peace and justice (RM 59).

Although the Vatican instructions seek to correct abuses in liberation theology, they expressly state that they should in "no way be interpreted as a disavowal of all those who want to respond generously and with an authentic evangelical spirit to the 'preferential option for the poor'" (LN Intro). Neither, the magisterium cautions, should they be used as a theological weapon to justify the existing social dis-order. The fact that some take liberation theology in problematic directions does not discount the whole of liberation theology nor nullify its validity. The instructions are as much a challenge to those who benefit from the current world order and baptize unjust structures as to those

---

38. John Paul II, "Liberation and Commitment to the Poor," *Origins* 20, no. 2 (May 24, 1990): 31.

39. John Paul II, "Address on Christian Unity in a Technological Age" (Toronto, September 14, 1984), *Origins* 14, no. 16 (October 4, 1984): 248ff.

who take liberation theology out of context and use it to justify actions that contradict it. In both instances it is clear that any teaching can be taken out of context and be used to justify actions that contradict it. This is true not only for liberation theology but for any theology and even the Scriptures. Having justified slavery on biblical grounds, Christians are not immune from the temptation to quote the Bible for unjust ends.

As the challenge of justice makes demands on the self-interest of individuals, organizations, and nations, and calls all to conversion, it is intellectually and spiritually responsible to assess critically not only the writings of liberation theologians but also the positions of those who find liberation theology objectionable. Because there is always a temptation to read the Gospel message out of the framework of centers of influence, from those arguably connected to the interests of empire, serious effort must be made to avoid reading the Gospel on human terms and making God into our own image and likeness. As Archbishop Dom Hélder Câmara observed, "The more we have to lose, the more weighty becomes our decision to respond to God's call, and the more fiercely and subtly we resist."[40]

Liberation theology and Vatican teachings insist that, as Benedict XVI notes, "the Church cannot and must not remain on the sidelines in the fight for justice" (DCE 28). To challenge a system of inequity does not confuse faith with politics. Rather, it reveals political implications of Christian commitment. "Christian faith," as Donal Dorr notes, "necessarily has a political aspect; those who allow it to be privatized are not really eliminating this political aspect but are making an option for the present unjust status quo; they are colluding with the rich and the powerful by failing to challenge the injustice of society."[41] The authentic commitment to human liberation is a graced effort to unmask the idols of prosperity, power, prestige, and pride, and to break down the walls between the powerful and the poor and ultimately between human beings and God.

LIBERATION THEOLOGY IN GLOBAL PERSPECTIVE

Along with the development of liberation theology in Latin America—and often in dialogue and relationship with it—other regions and other groups around the world began to develop similar theologies with "a similar frame-

---

40. Dom Hélder Câmara, *The Desert Is Fertile*, trans. Dinah Livingstone (Maryknoll, N.Y.: Orbis Books, 1974), 35.

41. Donal Dorr, "The Preferential Option for the Poor" in *The New Dictionary of Catholic Social Thought*, ed. J. A. Dwyer (Collegeville, Minn.: Liturgical Press, 1994), 755.

work" to Latin American liberation theology.[42] These theologians also do theological reflection that begins with social analysis and critical reflection on experience, then explore the Gospels and the Christian tradition to discern an evangelical response to existing conditions, and move finally to concrete action for social and personal transformation. As a result, we can say today that there is not simply a liberation theology but liberating theologies. Such theological reflection can now be distinguished by regions—such as Latin America, Africa, Asia—and by social groups—the poor, Hispanics, Dalits, women, indigenous peoples, and others. All of these groups share a common experience of perceived oppression because of class, race, gender, religion, or global economic dimensions. While space does not permit a more thorough elaboration on this important development, I want to touch briefly upon liberation theology as it has emerged in a few areas, namely, black, Hispanic, feminist, and Asian liberation theologies.

Black Theology: The Challenge of Freedom

Black theology arose out of the civil rights and black power movements of the 1960s. It has taken shape primarily in the United States and South Africa but also in the Caribbean, South America, and in greater Africa.[43] It began with an analysis of the situation in which black people find themselves, particularly in light of oppression by white people. In 1969, James Cone published *Black Theology and Black Power,*[44] which became one of the foundational texts of a black theology of liberation. That same year, a group of black church leaders formulated some of the contours of this theology, saying,

> Black Theology is a theology of black liberation. It seeks to plumb the black condition in the light of God's revelation in Jesus Christ, so that the black community can see that the gospel is commensurate with the achievement of black humanity. Black Theology is a theology of "blackness." It is the affirmation of black humanity that emancipates black people from white racism, thus providing authentic freedom for both white and black people. It affirms the humanity of white people in that it says "No" to the encroachment of white oppression.[45]

---

42. Allan Aubrey Boesak, *Farewell to Innocence: A Socio-ethical Study on Black Theology and Black Power* (Maryknoll, N.Y.: Orbis Books, 1977).

43. Shawn Copeland, "Black Theology" in *The New Dictionary of Catholic Social Thought*, ed. Dwyer, 91.

44. James H. Cone, *Black Theology and Black Power* (Maryknoll, N.Y.: Orbis Books, 1997).

45. Statement by the National Committee of Black Churchmen, June 13, 1969, in *Black Theology: A Documentary History, 1966-1979*, ed. Gayraud S. Wilmore and James H. Cone (Maryknoll, N.Y.: Orbis Books, 1979), 101.

Cone and others assert that "Christ is black," meaning that "the biblical God is related to the black struggle for liberation. This means that God has joined in the oppressed condition of black people and is known wherever people experience humiliation and suffering."[46] Black theology affirms that God is united with the oppressed and their rightful cause for justice. At its core, this theology challenges the sin of racism. Drawing on the Bible as a primary source of inspiration, and challenging any misuses of that inspiration—especially where it justifies the subordination of black people—this theology proclaims Jesus is the liberator, and freedom as the ultimate message of the Gospel. Other theologians are examining womanist theology and black theology within the global context.[47]

Hispanic Theology: The Challenge of Culture

Alongside black theology, Hispanic theology also came to birth and addressed the challenge of cultural oppression. While sharing similar challenges of the economic marginalization and racial discrimination of Latin America with its African/African American counterparts in the United States, Hispanic theology has given expression to the challenge of cultural identity. Although Hispanics include a wide range of cultural identities among themselves, ranging from Mexico to Cuba to all of Latin America, a foundational work in Hispanic liberation theology is Virgilio Elizondo's *Galilean Journey: The Mexican American Promise.*[48] In this work Elizondo does a cultural reading of the Gospel and a Gospel reading of culture, especially a reading of the oppressed Mexican American culture in the United States. He sees Galilee of the Scriptures not simply as a geographical category but as a theological one, with immense potential for human liberation. He sees in Jesus' Galilean identity many similarities with the identity of Mexican Americans. As a Galilean, Jesus was a marginal Jew coming from a marginal province, who shared

---

46. Stanley J. Grenz and Roger E. Olson, *20ᵗʰ Century Theology* (Downers Grove, Ill.: Inter-Varsity, 1992), 207.

47. See Traci C. West, *Disruptive Christian Ethics: When Racism and Women's Lives Matter* (Louisville: Westminster John Knox, 2006); Stephanie Y. Mitchem, *Introducing Womanist Theology* (Maryknoll, N.Y.: Orbis Books, 2002). See also Dwight N. Hopkins, *Being Human: Race, Culture, and Religions* (Minneapolis: Fortress, 2005); idem, *Introducing Black Theology of Liberation* (Maryknoll, N.Y.: Orbis Books, 1999); Linda E. Thomas, ed., *Living Stones in the Household of God: The Legacy and Future of Black Theology* (Minneapolis: Fortress, 2004); eadem, *A Black Theology of Liberation* (Maryknoll, N.Y.: Orbis Books, 1990); Cone and Wilmore, *Black Theology: A Documentary History 1966-1979*; and *Black Theology: A Documentary History 1980-1992*, vol. 2 (Maryknoll, N.Y.: Orbis Books, 1993).

48. See Virgilio Elizondo, *Galilean Journey: The Mexican American Promise* (Maryknoll, N.Y.: Orbis Books, 2000).

many common struggles with Mexican Americans, who live on the margins of society. Like Jesus, the Mexican Americans, frequently held in contempt by the prevailing white Anglo U.S. culture, are called to confront the centers of power that oppress them. Elizondo's purpose is not simply to criticize U.S. society or the current global economy but to validate the experience of Mexican Americans and to affirm the unique contribution their culture has made to the larger human society.

Feminist Theology: The Challenge of Gender

Feminist theology emerged out of the women's movement of the 1970s, and it views the principal problem of oppression not simply in terms of economics, race, or culture, but in terms of gender. It challenges all forms of male patriarchy and sexism. Sandra Schneiders asserts, "If we truly believe that the word of God is not bound (cf. 2 Tim 2:10) and that the God of universal liberation and *shalom* cannot endorse the oppression of any of God's creatures, then we must find a way to allow God's word to promote and enhance the full personhood of women."[49] The ultimate hope of "radical feminists (where radical means not 'fanatical' but 'going to the root, *radix*, of the problem') is accordingly a society in which all persons, regardless of their sex, can be self-determining."[50]

In broad terms, feminist theology seeks to reflect on the problems of a patriarchal culture in which God has been viewed as male and women have been perceived as less than human, even as the source of sin and the fall of humanity. In particular terms, feminist theology has taken different forms on different continents and in different cultures. Womanist theology is a black feminist theology that goes beyond gender dualism and sees oppression linked to a more pervasive race, gender, and class oppression.[51] *Mujerista* theology looks at the preferential option for the poor in light of Latina women, although even among Latina theologians there are differences and nuances.[52]

49. Sandra M. Schneiders, *Beyond Patching: Faith and Feminism in the Catholic Church*, rev. ed. (New York: Paulist, 2004), 71. Works of other leading feminist theologians include: Elisabeth Schüssler Fiorenza, *Wisdom Ways: Introducing Feminist Biblical Interpretation* (Maryknoll, N.Y.: Orbis Books, 2001); and Elizabeth A. Johnson, *She Who Is: The Mystery of God in Feminist Theological Discourse* (New York: Crossroad, 1992).

50. James A. Wiseman, *Spirituality and Mysticism: A Global View*, Theology in Global Perspective (Maryknoll, N.Y.: Orbis Books, 2006), 217.

51. Emilie M. Townes, "Womanist Theology," in *Introduction to Christian Theology: Contemporary North American Perspectives*, ed. Roger A. Badham (Louisville: Westminster John Knox, 1998), 214.

52. Ada María Isasi-Díaz, *Mujerista Theology* (Maryknoll, N.Y.: Orbis Books, 1996); Isasi-Díaz, *En la Lucha In the Struggle: A Hispanic Women's Liberation Theology* (Minneapolis: Fortress, 2004); Isasi-Díaz, *La Lucha Continues* (Maryknoll, N.Y.: Orbis Books, 2004).

Believing that the scriptural texts, though inspired, have a patriarchal basis, women have sought to do a rereading of them from their situation of oppression, which has given rise to new insight and new interpretations of these biblical documents. In the process, women sometimes refer to their situation as being doubly or triply oppressed (because of their economic condition, because of their culture, and because of their gender), and they give expression to a hope of greater equality with men and greater participation in church and society.

Asian Theology: The Challenge of Religious Plurality

Asian liberation theology takes shape out of not only vast poverty and oppression on the continent but also a pluralized religious landscape intimately connected to the great world religious traditions, particularly Hinduism, Buddhism, and Confucianism. The foremost Asian liberation theologians include Peter Phan and Aloysius Pieris.[53]

With a population that is less than 13 percent Christian, Asia is a radically different context from Latin America, even while they share the common experience of poverty and oppression. Whereas Latin America shares a common history, language, and even religious heritage, Asia has a diverse history that defies easy categorization about any topic, let alone liberation theology. Nonetheless, the pluralized religious landscape has led many Asian liberation theologians to look at what these traditions share in common as they unite together in seeking liberation for those who are poor and insignificant. Peter Phan articulates both the common culture and the challenges of applying liberation theology in Asia:

> Asia is characterized not only by the abject poverty of the teeming masses but also by their profound religiousness. How can the proclamation of the reign of God embrace both the poor and the religious? . . . Many contemporary liberation theologians . . . insist that the gratuitousness of God's kingdom is not opposed to human action but requires it as a response to God's free gift. How can this tension between gift and task be conveyed in the Asian context in which salvation is seen to be the outcome of both pure grace from a compassionate being (for example, the Amida Buddha in Pure Land Buddhism) and of personal self-cultivation (for example, according to Zen Buddhism and Confucianism)?[54]

---

53. See Peter C. Phan, *Christianity with an Asian Face: Asian American Theology in the Making* (Maryknoll, N.Y.: Orbis Books, 2003); Aloysius Pieris, *An Asian Theology of Liberation* (Maryknoll, N.Y.: Orbis Books, 1988).

54. Phan, *Christianity with an Asian Face*, 79.

Some of the other notable schools of Asian liberation theology are found in Minjung theology of Korea, Dalit theology of India, and the theology of struggle in the Philippines, as well as in other theologies emerging from tribal groups in Taiwan, India, Japan, and others throughout Asia.[55] The liberation theologies coming out of these areas are very diverse, but some of the major themes addressed in Asian liberation theology are massive poverty, democratic rights, and the ecological crisis.[56] As Christians in Asia seek greater solidarity with the poor, and even risk imprisonment, torture, and death in the process, the people of Asia begin to speak of a God of Life that is with them, even when the threat of death afflicts them on many levels.[57]

As the church seeks to understand the distinctiveness of Christian revelation in the face of a pluralized religious landscape, such statements will also generate controversy as the church struggles to distinguish between the uniqueness of Christian revelation and the problem of religious relativism. It will also open up new doors to human solidarity and ecumenism as all the major religions find a common concern in the liberation of the poor.

In summary, all of these theologies of liberation seek to give expression to the irruption of exploited classes, marginalized cultures, and humiliated races around the world.[58] Black liberation theology in its work for racial equality, Hispanic theology in its insistence on cultural values, feminist theologies in their stress on the full human dignity of women, and Asian theologies with their emphasis on interreligious dialogue are but a few examples of the various liberationist theological initiatives. In all of them, liberation theology seeks to be a humanizing force in a global environment that for many is becoming increasingly more dehumanized.

LIBERATION THEOLOGY AND THE EUCHARIST

In the end, liberation theologians are the first to affirm that what matters most is not liberation theology but the liberation of people. In the midst of a complex globalization agenda, driven largely by Western values that homogenize cultures, generate elitist structures, and widen the gap between the rich

---

55. See Kim Yong Bock, ed., *Minjung Theology: People as the Subjects of History* (Maryknoll, N.Y.: Orbis Books, 1983); A. P. Nirmal, "Toward a Christian Dalit Theology," in *Frontiers in Asian Christian Theology* (Maryknoll, N.Y.: Orbis Books, 1994), 27-40; see also Xavier Irudayaraj, *Emerging Dalit Theology* (Madras: Jesuit Theological Secretariate, 1990).

56. Bastiaan Wielenga, "Liberation Theology in Asia," in Christopher Rowland, ed., *Cambridge Companion to Liberation Theology*, 2nd ed. (New York: Cambridge University Press, 2007), 55.

57. Ibid., 47.

58. From 1981 New Delhi Conference of the Ecumenical Conference of Third World Theologians; see also Berryman, *Liberation Theology*, 163.

and the poor, liberation theology proclaims a Gospel of freedom and life that leads to the integral development of all human beings. As the church seeks to liberate those who are oppressed—even at the cost of the lives of its members—it seeks to be a sign and sacrament to the world, "the efficacious revelation of the call to communion with God and to the unity of all humankind."[59] The church celebrates this sacramental calling in living out a faith that does justice and in its celebration of the eucharist, which, as Gustavo Gutiérrez notes, is at the heart of liberation theology.

The eucharist is central to liberation theology because it is a résumé of the entire Christian message. It is a memory of the life, teachings, death, and resurrection of Jesus. As the church celebrates the eucharist in memory of Jesus, it remembers all that Jesus did and all he stood for in the proclamation of the reign of God.[60] This eucharist is both an act of memory and an act of thanksgiving. It celebrates God's gift to humanity and humanity's response in gratitude.

Moreover, to remember Jesus is to remember his preference for the least ones of society. The church recalls how God acted in history and God's commitment to those considered by society as the most insignificant. As God seeks to free people from all that oppresses them, the eucharist is set in the context of the Passover meal, the memorial of God's liberating activity in the life of Israel. The eucharist is the church's hope in the Lord of Life who overcame death and who still struggles for liberation in the lives of the crucified peoples of today. We see this sacramental life at work in all people who work for a more just world and even give their lives for it, as was the case with Archbishop Oscar Romero, assassinated in El Salvador while celebrating the eucharist. He proclaimed the hope of liberation, even though only a fraction of it would be accomplished in his lifetime. The following prayer reflects the spirit of those who know that even their best efforts are but the beginning of transformation, and complete liberation will happen only when Christ comes again:[61]

> It helps, now and then, to step back
> and take a long view.
>
> The kingdom is not only beyond our efforts,
> it is even beyond our vision.

---

59. Gutiérrez, *Theology of Liberation*, 146.
60. Ibid., 148.
61. This prayer, often attributed to Archbishop Oscar Romero, was written by Bishop Ken Untener for Cardinal John Dearden. See "The Peace Pulpit by Bishop Thomas J. Gumbleton, March 28, 2004," *National Catholic Reporter*, available at http://www.nationalcatholicreporter.org.

We accomplish in our lifetime only a tiny fraction
of the magnificent enterprise that is God's work.
Nothing we do is complete, which is a way of saying
that the kingdom always lies beyond us.
No statement says all that could be said.
No prayer fully expresses our faith.
No confession brings perfection.
No pastoral visit brings wholeness.
No program accomplishes the church's mission.
No set of goals and objectives includes everything.

This is what we are about.
We plant the seeds that one day will grow.
We water seeds already planted,
knowing that they hold future promise.

We lay foundations that will need further development.
We provide yeast that produces far beyond our capabilities.

We cannot do everything, and there is a sense of liberation
in realizing that. This enables us to do something,
and to do it very well. It may be incomplete,
but it is a beginning, a step along the way,
an opportunity for the Lord's grace to enter and do the
    rest.

We may never see the end results, but that is the difference
between the master builder and the worker.

We are workers, not master builders; ministers, not
    messiahs.

We are prophets of a future not our own.

QUESTIONS FOR REFLECTION

1. What have you heard about, or what has been your understanding of, liberation theology before reading this chapter? Do you think liberation theology is an adequate articulation of the Gospel message? Why or why not?
2. What are the three levels of liberation?
3. What do you see as the major challenges of proclaiming the Gospel to those who are poor and oppressed? If you were pope, how would you preach the Gospel as good news to the poor?
4. What is the relationship between Catholic social teaching and liberation theology?

5. In what ways have you seen lived out voluntary poverty, spiritual poverty, and material poverty?
6. Discuss this statement: "Oppression cannot take place without the participation of the oppressed."
7. What are the particular emphases of different liberation theologies around the world? What do they all have in common?
8. In what ways are the social teaching of the church, liberation theology, and Marxism similar and different?
9. What does "option for the poor" mean to you in your life?

SUGGESTIONS FOR FURTHER READING AND STUDY

Aquino, María Pilar. *Our Cry for Life.* Maryknoll, N.Y.: Orbis Books, 1993.

Berryman, Phillip. *Liberation Theology: Essential Facts about the Revolutionary Movement in Latin America—and Beyond.* New York: Pantheon, 1987.

Boesak, Allan Aubrey. *Farewell to Innocence: A Socio-ethical Study on Black Theology and Black Power.* Maryknoll, N.Y.: Orbis Books, 1977.

Boff, Clodovis. *Theology and Praxis.* Maryknoll, N.Y.: Orbis Books, 1987.

Boff, Leonardo. *Jesus Christ Liberator.* Maryknoll, N.Y.: Orbis Books, 1978.

———. *St. Francis: A Model for Human Liberation.* New York: Crossroad, 1982.

Boff, Leonardo, and Clodovis Boff. *Introducing Liberation Theology.* Maryknoll, N.Y.: Orbis Books, 1987.

Brown, Robert McAfee. *Liberation Theology.* Louisville, Ky.: Westminster John Knox, 1993.

Cleary, Edward L. *Crisis and Change: The Church in Latin America Today.* Maryknoll, N.Y.: Orbis Books, 1985.

Clifford, Ann. *Introducing Feminist Theology.* Maryknoll, N.Y.: Orbis Books, 2001.

Cone, James. *A Black Theology of Liberation.* Maryknoll, N.Y.: Orbis Books, 1990.

Conferencia General del Episcopado Latinoamericano (CELAM II: Medellín, Colombia, 1968). 1970-73. *Medellín Conference: Final Document. The Church in the Present-Day Transformation of Latin America in Light of the Council.* 2 vols. Bogotá: General Secretariat of CELAM.

Conferencia General del Episcopado Latinoamericano (CELAM III: Puebla, Mexico, 1979). 1978. *Puebla Conference—Final Document. Visión Pastoral de America Latina: Equipo de Reflexión, Departamentos y Secciones de CELAM.* Bogotá: Consejo Episcopal Latinoamericano.

Conferencia General del Episcopado Latinoamericano (CELAM IV: Santo Domingo, Dominican Republic, 1992). 1993. *Conclusions: New Evangelization, Human Development, Christian Culture.* Washington, D.C.: U.S. Catholic Conference.

Elizondo, Virgilio. *Galilean Journey: The Mexican American Promise.* Maryknoll, N.Y.: Orbis Books, 2000.

Ellacuría, Ignacio, and Jon Sobrino, eds. *Mysterium Liberationis: Fundamental Concepts of Liberation Theology.* Maryknoll, N.Y.: Orbis Books, 1993.

Floristán, Casiano, and Juan-José Tamayo, eds. *Conceptos fundamentales del cristianismo.* Madrid: Trotta, 1993.

Groody, Daniel G., ed. *The Option for the Poor in Christian Theology.* Notre Dame, Ind.: University of Notre Dame Press, 2007.

Groody, Daniel G., ed. *The Option for the Poor beyond Theology.* Notre Dame, Ind.: University of Notre Dame Press, 2014.

Gutiérrez, Gustavo. *On Job: God-Talk and the Suffering of the Innocent.* Maryknoll, N.Y.: Orbis Books, 1987.

———. *A Theology of Liberation: History, Politics, and Salvation.* Maryknoll, N.Y.: Orbis Books, 1988.

———. *We Drink from Our Own Wells: The Spiritual Journey of a People.* Maryknoll, N.Y.: Orbis Books, 1984.

Hennelly, Alfred. *Liberation Theologies: The Global Pursuit of Justice.* Mystic, Conn.: Twenty-Third Publications, 1995.

Irarrázaval, Diego. *Inculturation: New Dawn of the Church in Latin America.* Maryknoll, N.Y.: Orbis Books, 2000.

Johnson, Elizabeth A. *Consider Jesus: Waves of Renewal in Christology.* New York: Crossroad, 1996.

Míguez Bonino, José. *Toward a Christian Political Ethics.* Philadelphia, Pa.: Fortress, 1983.

Petrella, Ivan, ed. *Latin American Liberation Theology: The Next Generation.* Maryknoll, N.Y.: Orbis Books, 2005.

Phan, Peter. *Christianity with an Asian Face: Asian American Theology in the Making.* Maryknoll, N.Y.: Orbis Books, 2003.

Pieris, Aloysius. *An Asian Theology of Liberation.* Maryknoll, N.Y.: Orbis Books, 1988.

Schüssler Fiorenza, Elisabeth. *In Memory of Her: A Feminist Theological Reconstruction of Christian Origins,* 10th anniversary ed. New York: Crossroad, 1994.

Segundo, Juan Luis. *Liberation of Theology.* Maryknoll, N.Y.: Orbis Books, 1976.

Sobrino, Jon. *Christ the Liberator.* Maryknoll, N.Y.: Orbis Books, 2001.

Tamez, Elsa. *Bible of the Oppressed.* Maryknoll, N.Y.: Orbis Books, 1982.

Torres, Sergio, and Virginia Fabella. *Irruption of the Third World.* Maryknoll, N.Y.: Orbis Books, 1983.

8

Worshiping in Spirit, Living in Truth

Liturgy and Justice

A NUMBER OF YEARS AGO ON NOVEMBER 1, I attended a eucharistic celebration in El Paso, Texas, along the United States–Mexico border. The Mass was celebrated outside, in the open air, in the dry, rugged, and sun-scorched terrain where the United States meets Mexico. It was a time to remember the life of Jesus, the lives of all the saints and souls of history, and the lives of thousands of undocumented Mexican immigrants who died crossing the border in recent years. As with other liturgies, a large crowd gathered to pray and worship together. Unlike other liturgies, however, a sixteen-foot iron fence divided this community in half, with one side in Mexico and the other side in the United States.

During the eucharist, border patrol agents in helicopters and SUVs kept a strict watch over the crowd. As they ensured that no undocumented persons would pass over from Mexico to the United States, the gathered people praised God for Christ's Passover from death to life. Each part of this eucharistic celebration testified to the bonds that united the people of God beyond the political constructions that divided them. The aspersion of holy water at the beginning of Mass gave expression to a common baptism and a common faith in a common Lord that brought people from all nations into one body. The Scripture readings from Isaiah spoke of God's promise to "destroy the veil that veils all peoples" (Is 25:7), and the Gospel alluded to God's promise to bring people across all borders, even the border of death, into the eternal kingdom of life (Jn 11:32-44). The joining of a common altar at the fence testified to the unity of the community, and the greeting of peace spoke of a common solidarity, even though we could only touch fingers through small holes in the fence. The giving of the Bread of Life at communion, and the sending forth of the community at the end of the liturgy spoke of the gift and challenge of Christian faith and the call to feed the world's hunger for reconciliation amidst the fractured reality of the present moment. In a global reality that often sets up walls and barriers, this eucharist witnessed to the primacy of God's universal, undivided, and unrestricted love. It also made us more aware not only of the walls separating one country from another but of the walls that separate contemplation from action, devotion from discipleship, and liturgy from justice.

In this chapter we will look at the eucharistic liturgy as a privileged place where God breaks down the walls that divide the human family in order to bring about personal, social, and even environmental reconciliation. First, we will look at liturgy and justice as the celebration of right relationships. Second, we will look at ritual as the structuring of this celebration and sacramentality as the way God comes to us through this celebration. Third, we will examine how this celebration becomes rooted in local cultures and communicates its spiritual theology through its biblical texts, songs, and prayers. Fourth, we will examine the eucharist as a graced event that celebrates God's transformative activity in the world and the Christian calling to participate in that transformation.

LITURGY AND JUSTICE:
CELEBRATING RIGHT RELATIONSHIPS

In the words of Dom Virgil Michel, one of the forerunners of the liturgical renewal movement, "No person has really entered into the heart of the liturgical spirit if he has not been seized also with a veritable passion for the re-establishment of social justice."[1] Despite these words, many people make no connection between what happens inside of church and what happens outside of it. In the minds of many, there is a great wall between personal piety and social responsibility. As Cardinal Roger Mahony has pointed out,

> At one extreme, there are those who very readily identify issues of justice and peace with politics, and demand that we keep politics out of liturgy . . . At the other extreme are those who perceive the Eucharist and liturgy to be a forum for the promotion of some special cause or concern . . . and the liturgy can be "used" to validate some particular action or strategy on behalf of a laudable justice or peace issue.[2]

Kevin Seasoltz adds:

> The temptation on the part of liturgists is to retreat from the world's problems into a safe, comfortable, aesthetically pleasing past and to convert

---

1. Virgil George Michel, "Timely Tracts: Social Justice," *Orate Fratres* 12, no. 3 (January 1938): 132.
2. Roger Mahony, "The Eucharist and Social Justice," *Worship* 57, no. 1 (January 1983): 53.

liturgical worship into thematic celebrations of abstract universals that supposedly please God but have little to do with responsible life in the world. The temptation on the part of social activists is to reject the liturgy as totally irrelevant, as a distraction of valuable time and energy which should be spent solving the world's problems.[3]

To overcome this recurring divide between justice and liturgy, it is helpful if we recall what we mean by justice and clarify what we mean by liturgy.

Justice in the Scriptures refers to God's overflowing and uncalculating love, which brings people into right relationship again with God, others, self, and the environment. In the New Testament, Jesus—who is revealed as the Justice of God—acts in the world through the transformative power of the Spirit. If evil and sin have put us in wrong relationships, then God's salvific action in Christ and the Spirit works in us the grace of new creation by bringing about righteousness or right relationships. Through this process God brings healing, order, peace, and reconciliation to our lives.[4] One of the special places where this reconciliation takes place is in the liturgy.

If justice is about the establishment of right relationships, then liturgy is about the celebration of these relationships.[5] The word "liturgy" comes from the Greek word *leitourgia*, which combines two other Greek words, *laos* (people) and *ergon* (work). Originally coined in civil society, liturgy referred to work on behalf of the people or "public service," but over time, the early church adopted the term to speak about liturgy as "service to God."[6] Gradually, liturgy became known as the work of Christ on behalf of the people and the work of people in service to God. In its civil and ecclesial usage, however, liturgy, by nature, was understood as a social event directed toward the common good. When lived as a private affair with God without connection to the larger gathering of believers, or when any person is absent from the celebration, all liturgy is diminished. For these reasons and many others, as Anne Koester notes, "The intrinsic relationship between liturgy and justice is critical to the ongoing renewal of Church life and the created world."[7]

---

3. Kevin Seasoltz, "Justice and the Eucharist," *Worship* 58, no. 6 (November 1984): 509.

4. Jay Freel-Landry, "Becoming What We Celebrate in the Eucharist: The Body of Christ Loving This Suffering World" (Master's thesis, University of Notre Dame, Notre Dame, Indiana, 1997).

5. Kathleen Hughes and Mark Francis, *Living No Longer for Ourselves: Liturgy and Justice in the Nineties* (Collegeville, Minn.: Liturgical Press, 1991).

6. I am especially indebted to Anne Koester for her extraordinary work on the subject of liturgy and justice. See especially Anne Y. Koester, ed., *Liturgy and Justice: To Worship God in Spirit and Truth* (Collegeville, Minn.: Liturgical Press, 2002).

7. Koester, *Liturgy and Justice,* ix.

RITUAL AND SACRAMENTALITY:
STRUCTURING REVELATORY CELEBRATIONS

If liturgy is about building and celebrating right relationships, then ritual is about how that celebration is structured. In recent years, psychologists, anthropologists, sociologists, and theologians alike have come to appreciate the role that ritual plays in the formation, development, and integration of the human person in community.[8] Ritual is a structured, purposeful, interpersonal activity directed toward the internalization of certain values and beliefs. While Roman Catholics have a rich liturgical tradition composed of varied ritual structures, other Christian traditions, other religions, and civil society also use ritual to inculcate core beliefs and principles. The purpose of Christian liturgy is to enter more deeply into the meaning of who we are, to whom we belong, and where we are going. It also gives us a framework that better enables us to relate to the One in whom we have ultimate hope. Our focus here will be on Roman Catholic eucharistic liturgy, especially as it opens us up to a profound spiritual undercurrent that gives meaning, sustenance, and shape to our lives and helps us discover and embrace the deeper, divine dimensions of human existence.

If ritual structures the liturgical celebration, then sacramentality deals with how God touches us through this celebration. In its varied components, Roman Catholic liturgy gives expression to the inexpressible mystery of the living God. Sacramentality speaks of the way God's presence meets us in our daily lives and is experienced in both formal and informal ways.[9] Formally, sacraments deal with the seven major liturgical celebrations of the church (baptism, confirmation, eucharist, matrimony, holy orders, reconciliation, and anointing the sick). Informally, sacramentality refers to any way in which we encounter God and the values of the kingdom in our daily lives. Sacramentality includes the seven sacraments but is not limited to them, because it refers to any way God's presence meets us and is mediated to us through our relationships and the created world.[10]

While sacramentality helps us understand that God's action in the world is never limited to what happens inside church buildings, the sacrament of the eucharist is the usual place where the people of God experience the extraordinary event of divine–human encounter. In this liturgy, people

---

8. George S. Worgul, Jr., "Ritual," in *The New Dictionary of Sacramental Worship*, ed. Peter Fink (Collegeville, Minn.: Liturgical Press, 1990), 1101-6.

9. For more on this subject, see Bernard J. Cooke, *Sacraments & Sacramentality* (Mystic, Conn.: Twenty-Third Publications, 1994).

10. Leonardo Boff, *Los Sacramentos de la Vida*, my translation (Santander: Editorial Sal Terrae, 1978), 24.

celebrate the work of God in Christ (expressed as internal justice or justification), and promote good works (expressed as external justice) that facilitate the transformation of the world. This liturgy integrates word, sacraments, and social doctrine into a rich cycle of feasts and seasons, at the service of human redemption, as outlined in table 6 below.

INCULTURATION AND HYMNODY:
GLOCALIZING AND GLOBALIZING WORSHIP

While the church places much emphasis on its fundamental unity, it also promotes the diverse ways that people in various cultures worship and praise God. Contemporary theological reflection reiterates that globalization should not entail a westernization that weakens local cultures, and evangelization should not mean homogenization that undermines legitimate, varied expressions of its liturgy. Globalization necessitates glocalization, and this means that the universal dimension of worship is celebrated in very particular, local, cultural ways.[11] The liturgy is one of the few places in the contemporary world that seeks to safeguard the integrity of local cultures in a global society that increasingly threatens them. Here we want to look at culture and song in the liturgy. Inculturation deals with how the unique qualities of various races and nations enrich our understanding of God's action in the world (SC 37), and hymnody gives us a unique, poetic window into the spirituality and theology of a people.

Music is one of the primary ways through which the liturgy is inculturated, and it is often one of the ways in which oppressed groups in particular resist the cultures that dominate them.[12] Many African slaves in America, for example, created hymns that were liberating utterances sung in the face of the enormous power of the empire. Slaves, through song, could truly claim their freedom in their churches. In those places of worship slave masters did not own them—indeed, could not own them—because, while singing, the African slaves reaffirmed their freedom in the Spirit as children of God.[13] Their hymns gave them power to reimagine their relationship to the world, and it

---

11. The term "glocalization" was coined in Japan, in reference to marketing issues, to describe local reactions to attempts to bring the global, in the sense of the macroscopic aspect of contemporary life, into conjunction with the local, in the sense of the microscopic side of life in the late twentieth century. See Roland Robertson, *Globalization: Social Theory and Global Culture* (London: Sage, 1992).

12. Paul Westermeyer, *Let Justice Sing: Hymnody and Justice* (Collegeville, Minn.: Liturgical Press, 1994).

13. Joseph A. Brown, *To Stand on the Rock* (Maryknoll, N.Y.: Orbis Books, 1998).

defied the society that typecast them. No longer defined by the Narrative of the Empire, owned by God and not by any human being, slaves could sing and affirm the true freedom of their own narratives made possible through the Narrative of the Gospel.[14]

Song is not only an important expression of culture; it is an integral component of liturgy. From the entrance rite to the concluding rite, the rich tradition of hymnody carries many themes of justice, blending the Narratives of the Scriptures and the power of the Spirit into a harmonious whole. Like sacrament, song is a doorway to the sacred, offering poetic imagery and melody that give people a glimpse of divine mystery and allow a taste of far greater spiritual realities, whose fulfillment is promised in the end of time. Song helps shape the dispositions of people's hearts, which inspires them to give thanks to God and to respond through a loving concern for their neighbor in need, who is also made in the image of the just God.[15]

THE EUCHARIST AND SOCIAL JUSTICE: TRANSFORMING THE WORLD THROUGH CHRIST

In *Sacrosanctum Concilium* the church affirms that the Liturgy of the Eucharist is "the summit toward which the activity of the Church is directed [and] it is also the source from which all her power flows" (SC 8). As such, the eucharist is the most important work of the church. It is the point from which to gain a panoramic vision of the rest of life and to discover and rediscover what it means to be Christian and enter into the life, death, and resurrection of Christ. While in one sense the eucharist is about a liturgical celebration that takes place in a church building, more generally speaking the eucharist pertains to the church's overall participation in the transformation of the world. When the eucharistic celebration is not understood in light of the larger context of this transforming mission, the liturgy can be reduced to an excessive concern for rubrics or a monotonous routine that does little to inspire people, change hearts, or renew communities. Liturgy, then, becomes more about the mere fulfillment of religious obligations than about the celebration of life and salvation.

---

14. Don E. Saliers, "Singing Our Lives," in *Practicing Our Faith*, ed. Dorothy C. Bass (San Francisco: Jossey-Bass, 1997), 179-93.

15. David A. Stosur, "Bread of Life, Justice of God: Economic Structures and the Transformation to Christian Justice," *Liturgical Ministry* 7 (Fall 1998): 182-89.

Table 6. Integration of Liturgy, Sacraments, and Social Doctrine[16]

LITURGY	LITURGICAL ELEMENTS	CATHOLIC SOCIAL TEACHING LINKS	POSSIBLE ISSUES TO EXPLORE
BAPTISM AND CONFIRMATION	Exorcisms	Rejection of "the sin of the world" or "structures of sin"	Social laws/realities that violate human life and dignity
	Blessings of Baptismal Water	Passing through waters of Red Sea places us on journey from slavery to freedom (human rights)	Respect for basic human rights (e.g., religious freedom, immigration, non-discrimination)
	Baptism with Water	Water: symbol of new birth and life; essential to all life (care of the earth)	Respect for life (abortion, euthanasia, capital punishment); ecology
	Reception of the Lighted Candle	Light: symbol of our mission to be "the light of the world" (Mt 5:14)	Our mission is to enlighten debates of public and corporate policies
	Anointing with Sacred Chrism	Anointed to "bring glad tidings to the poor, release to captives" (Lk 4:18)	Called to take up Christ's mission to the world with all its social implications
EUCHARISTIC CELEBRATION	Penitential Rite	Participation in "the sin of the world" or "structures of sin"	Unjust laws, social prejudices, unfair business practices
	Liturgy of the Word	Scriptural narratives that deal with justice	Address the full range of the Church's social concerns
	Creed	Faith in "one God" recognizes unity and dignity of all people	Global solidarity, racism, ethnic cleansing, war, and peace
	Offertory	Gifts for those in need remind us of the option for the poor	Poverty, living wages, health care, international development
	Communion Rite	The body of Christ commits us to the poor; sharing bread with all	Hunger (worldwide); unity of human family (solidarity, world peace)
	Sign of Peace	The peace of Christ calls us to be peace for one another	World peace, arms trade, solidarity, violence
	Concluding Rite	Sent forth in mission to the world; "Mass" (Latin *missa*, to send)	Our mission is to act on social teaching in families, work, public

16. United States Catholic Conference, *Leader's Guide to Sharing Catholic Social Teaching* (Washington, D.C.: United States Catholic Conference, 2000), 40.

LITURGY	LITURGICAL ELEMENTS	CATHOLIC SOCIAL TEACHING LINKS	POSSIBLE ISSUES TO EXPLORE
LITURGICAL YEAR	Advent	Expectation of Messiah; preparation for the reign of God	Building a society that mirrors the values of reign of God, Prince of Peace
	Christmas	Incarnation divinizes humanity and affirms human dignity	Human life and dignity; human rights
	Feast of the Holy Innocents	This slaughter highlights need to protect vulnerable children	Abortion, child abuse, childhood hunger and disease
	Lent	Penitential prayer, alms-giving, fasting; solidarity with poor	Poverty, world hunger, global development, simple lifestyle
	Easter Season	The risen Lord conquers death and enters into his reign	Issues of life and death; example of early Church's serving the poor
	Solemnity of Christ the King	Nothing lies outside the scope of Christ's concern or mission	All political, social, and cultural forces are accountable to God
	Memorial of Francis of Assisi	Simplicity of life and poverty call us to live in harmony with nature	Care of God's creation and option for the poor

The word "eucharist" comes from the Greek *eucharistein*, meaning "to give thanks." In celebrating the eucharist, the church gives thanks for God's action in the world, especially through the life, death, and resurrection of Christ. It is not just a noun but a verb, and not only a physical element but a transformative action.

The eucharist has been understood in various ways throughout history. It is understood as a meal that commemorates the Last Supper. It is understood as a sacrifice that reflects how Jesus laid down his life for the good of others. It is understood as communion that unites others with Christ and binds people together in community. It is understood as a Mass, which comes from the Latin *missa*, meaning "sent." It is understood as a memorial of Jesus that recalls Jesus' life-giving mission. In brief, the eucharist recapitulates all that Jesus taught and stood for in his earthly life, and also all he was in himself, that is, the living presence of God among us. Among all of these important understandings of the eucharist, one in particular stands out in terms of our focus on social justice: the eucharist remembers those for whom Jesus had particular affinity, especially the poor and rejected.

As a memorial of Jesus that includes the excluded and announces good news to the poor, however, the eucharist is not simply some kind of nostalgic, spiritual theater that remembers the earthly life of Jesus while the audience passively observes. Still less is the eucharist an hour-long obligation that provides a "fire insurance" policy at the last judgment. Rather, the eucharist is a grace that invites people to partake actively in and be transformed by the very life-giving relationship they are celebrating. Celebrating the eucharist means not only witnessing bread and wine change into the body and blood of Christ, but also it means becoming what one receives: a sacrament of love for the world. In summary, the transubstantiation of the bread and wine into the body and blood of Christ, as Benedict XVI notes, is the beginning of the transformation of believers, which should lead to the transformation of the world until Christ becomes all in all.[17]

THE RITE OF THE EUCHARIST: MAKING RITE RELATIONSHIPS

Understanding more about how the liturgy is structured helps us better understand the relationship between the eucharist and social justice. The eucharistic celebration has two main parts or rites, the Liturgy of the Word and the Liturgy of the Eucharist, which form one single act of worship.[18] There are also two smaller parts that open and close the celebration called the Introductory Rite and the Concluding Rite. These four parts are in turn broken down into smaller rites, each of which has symbolic and sacramental importance. Here we want to examine in more detail these four principal rites and explore in what ways they facilitate the restructuring and redeeming of our relationships and shape us into becoming a more just and loving community.

The Introductory Rite: Gathering the Believing Community and Ritualizing the Christian Journey

In a time when more and more emphasis is placed on individual freedom and autonomy, one of the most countercultural symbols of the eucharistic liturgy is simply the gathering of the believing community. In a world where it is becoming rare for a family to eat a meal together, the Liturgy of the

---

17. Benedict XVI, "Eucharist: Setting Transformations in Motion" (XX World Youth Day, Cologne, Germany, August 21, 2005), *Origins* 35, no. 12 (September 1, 2005): 202.

18. United States Conference of Catholic Bishops, *General Instruction of the Roman Missal*, no. 28, http://www.usccb.org.

Eucharist brings the family of God together into one place for a common spiritual banquet. Breaking down the walls of personal isolation and reminding us of our fundamental interconnection with each other, the liturgy recalls that it is not good to be alone (see Gn 2:18; Heb 10:25), that we are on a journey together, and that we come to understand our deepest identity not as independent individuals but in our relationships with others.

The Introductory Rite consists of the gathering hymn, the procession, the sign of the cross, the presider's greeting, the act of penitence, the *Kyrie* (or alternative sprinkling rite), *Gloria,* and opening prayer. During the initial hymn, the movement of the ministers from the back of the church to the sanctuary is more than an exercise of liturgical administration. Rather, the procession is a ritual that expresses the church's belief that Christian faith is a journey, and it is a sacramental event that expresses people's deepest hope for life in the context of their deepest fear of death. Especially within our contemporary context, this part of the liturgy is significant and merits further reflection.

Although today we have the capacity to move from place to place with greater facility and efficiency than at any point in human history, some people today still feel unable to discern the deeper dimensions of who they are and where they are going. Feeling sometimes adrift in a sea of apparent meaninglessness, many find themselves drowning underneath waves of contemporary distractions. Many people feel internally fragmented and scattered, even at liturgy. Amidst the hyperstimulation and constant noise of the modern world, the Introductory Rite focuses people's energies toward the hope and promise of their baptismal calling. It has a twofold significance: to gather people together and to prepare them to hear the Word of God.

The journey of Christian life begins with spiritual birth in baptism and reaches its climax in one's physical death with Christ on the altar, which is a symbol of the new Jerusalem and one's heavenly home. The church sees the celebration of liturgy on earth as a foretaste of the celebration of the liturgy in heaven, toward which the church journeys as a pilgrim people. Committed Christians are not meant to be stationary, nor aimlessly drifting through life, without purpose, without meaning, without a mission, and without a destination. Rather, as a pilgrim people, they are meant to be in the process of a spiritual migration from this world to the next. This processional journey at the beginning of the liturgy ritualizes the Christian journey as a movement from injustice to justice, sin to holiness, and ultimately from death to life.

As pilgrims, however, the church recognizes that its journey is imperfect, that the road is rocky, that it sometimes loses direction, and that individually and collectively its members stumble and fall in their attempts to find the right path in life. This is why after the entrance ritual the liturgy includes a penitential rite. It recognizes that, in its labor for the new world, the church struggles to embody the right relationships that it celebrates. As a community of saints *and* a school for sinners, it commemorates liturgy not because it always embodies justice as right relationships, but because it builds these relationships in hope as the church waits for the One who will bring reconciliation and renew the earth. In Christ, the community anticipates God's promise to restore all the bonds of human life that will one day make the human family whole again.

This penitential rite, properly understood, is not a fault-finding exercise of a God who has trouble seeing good in human beings and requires that people rebuke themselves before being acceptable. Rather, the penitential rite is a way of dealing with human selfishness, which, when left unaddressed, creates a wall between one's life and God, others, and even the environment. Nonetheless, while the humble acknowledgment of the wrong that one has done and the good that one has failed to do is an important part of this ritual, this component of the Mass is less about human failures than about God's love and mercy. After confessing its sins, the community gives expression to its conviction that God's love is greater than human weakness and sinfulness, and it is this unconditional love that leads the community to praise and worship in the *Gloria*. In liturgy the church celebrates the liberating news of the loving God who died for sinners (Rom 5:8), of the physician who has come to heal the sick (Mt 9:12), and the just God who has come for the unrighteous (1 Pt 3:18). In light of this mercy, people do not come to the liturgy because they are good, but they become good because of God's love for them.

The Liturgy of the Word: Proclaiming the Scriptural Narratives and Forming a Just Community

If the entrance rite helps people become more conscious of their personal stories as pilgrims on a journey, the Liturgy of the Word helps bring these stories into greater interaction with the ongoing story of God's action in history. In chapter 2, we identified five key metanarratives in the Judeo-Christian Scriptures: the Narrative of the Poor, the Narrative of the Empire, the Narrative of Yahweh, the Narrative of Idolatry, and the Narrative of the Gospel. We also acknowledged the Passover Narrative as the central integrating Narrative of the Scriptures. The Liturgy of the Word is a time to read from these narratives, engage these narratives, and be transformed by these narratives.

Understanding more about how these readings are selected and arranged into a lectionary helps us appreciate more of the contours of the Liturgy of the

Word. A lectionary (Latin *lectio*, meaning "reading") is an orderly arrange-
ment of biblical passages which, if read day by day, week by week, or for two
years (the weekday readings), or three years (the Sunday readings), presents
the main themes and stories of the Old and New Testaments.[19] The Catholic
Church and many of the mainline Protestant churches (Episcopal, Lutheran,
and others) use the lectionary as the basis for their worship services, their
preaching, and their Bible studies.[20] While there is some variation among the
lectionaries used in churches of different denominations, in recent years more
effort has been made to have a common lectionary: in Protestant churches the
Revised Common Lectionary, and in Catholic churches the Roman Catholic
Lectionary for Mass.[21]

The lectionary is read during the church's liturgical year, which differs to
some extent from the civil calendar year. Each liturgical year begins with the
first Sunday of Advent and ends a week after the feast of Christ the King, just
before first vespers on the first Sunday of Advent a year later.[22] In its calendar of saints, or sanctoral cycle, it offers models of Christian virtue, some of
whom embody the exemplary ideals of justice. The church also celebrates the
seasons of Advent, Christmas, Lent, Easter, Pentecost, and Ordinary Time,
which emphasize different aspects of the Christian mystery.

As we look at the lectionary readings during the season of Advent, we see
one example of how the theme of justice comes through the Liturgy of the
Word.[23] The readings during this season come from prophets like Isaiah,
Jeremiah, Baruch, Zephaniah, Micah, and others who speak about the coming of the Just One, the promise of a just world, the legacy of David as the
"just shoot," the anticipated savior with a band of justice around his waist,

---

19. The lectionary has three readings on Sundays and two on weekdays. Both Sundays and
weekdays also have a responsorial psalm, which is either recited or sung. These lectionary readings are drawn from one of four parts of the Bible: the Old Testament (first reading), the Psalms
(responsorial psalm), the New Testament—apart from the Gospel—(second reading), and one of
the four Gospels (Gospel reading). For more on the lectionary and justice, see Larry Hollar, ed.,
Hunger for the Word: Lectionary Reflections on Food and Justice, Year A (Collegeville, Minn.: Liturgical
Press, 2004).

20. Throughout its history, the church has used a variety of approaches in creating lectionaries.
The two main approaches are called *lectio selecta* and *lectio continua*. *Lectio selecta* is arranged according to particular themes or calendar events, whereas *lectio continua* presents the readings book by
book in more or less sequential fashion.

21. For more on the lectionary and its development, see Horace T. Allen, Jr., and Joseph P.
Russell, *On Common Ground: The Story of the Revised Common Lectionary* (Norwich, England: Can-
terbury, 1998); and Fritz West, *Scripture and Memory: The Ecumenical Hermeneutic of the Three-Year
Lectionaries* (Collegeville, Minn.: Liturgical Press, 1997).

22. On Sundays, the lectionary has a three-year cycle (Year A, Year B, and Year C). During the
week, the lectionary has a two-year cycle (Year 1 and Year 2).

23. See especially James L. Empereur and Christopher G. Kiesling, *The Liturgy That Does
Justice* (Collegeville, Minn.: Liturgical Press, 1990), 61-81.

the just judge, the new Jerusalem wrapped in a cloak of justice, and Jesus as the Justice of God.[24] Even the Psalms of this season are the poetic grammar of transformation, promising a time when "justice and peace shall kiss" (Ps 85:11) and "justice shall flourish . . . and fullness of peace for ever" (Ps 72:7). Advent is a time for preparing the way for the Lord and waiting in hope for "a new heaven and a new earth." In the other seasons of the church year and the lectionary readings that correspond to them, we see other ways in which people are called to be formed into a just community.

Another part of the Liturgy of the Word is the homily. The homily connects the written text of Scripture with the living text of one's life. It is meant to break open the meaning of the Scriptures and lead people to live out the Gospel Narrative that involves both an ongoing turning to Christ and an ongoing commitment to love as Christ loved.[25] Preaching justice means preaching Christ and calling people beyond ethical and legal justice to a sense of social justice, marked by fidelity to God, to others, to creation, and especially to the poor. Only after a community has named its injustices and committed itself to doing something about them, can it authentically proclaim "The Word of the Lord."

The Liturgy of the Eucharist: Transforming Bread and Wine and Transforming the People of God

In the early days of the church, after the intercessory prayers for the church, the world, and the poor, the members of the community brought to the altar food, drink, or other material necessities for the poor in their midst.[26] This offering was not just a tithe but an expression of human solidarity welling up from the conviction that worship of God is intimately related to care for the needy. Although in time this became a monetary collection, its purpose was not just to support ecclesial personnel and cover the physical costs of church maintenance, but it was a practical gesture of charity. This offering of gifts is the first part of the Liturgy of the Eucharist, and it is called the Preparation Rite. The Liturgy of the Eucharist also includes the Eucharistic Prayer and the Communion Rite. The Communion Rite includes the Our Father, the gesture of peace, the Lamb of God, the breaking of bread (or the fraction rite) and distribution of communion. These rituals of reconciliation

---

24. John Haughey, "Jesus as the Justice of God," in *Faith That Does Justice: Examining the Christian Sources for Social Change*, ed. John C. Haughey, Woodstock Studies 2 (New York: Paulist, 1977), 264-90.

25. Walter Burghardt, *Preaching the Just Word* (New Haven: Yale University Press, 1996), 18.

26. See Robert Hovda, "Money or Gifts for the Poor and the Church," *Worship* 59, no. 1 (January 1985): 65-71; and Paul Turner, "Gifts for the Poor," *Assembly* 24, no. 1 (January 1998): 34-35.

are directed toward the transformation of the community on the local and global levels.

In the eucharistic celebration as a whole, the community gathers around two principal tables: the table of the Word and the table of the eucharist. In the Liturgy of the Word, the ambo or the pulpit is the table on which the food of the Scriptures is shared. In the Liturgy of the Eucharist, the altar is the table on which the body and blood of Christ are shared. These tables are the most central symbols in the worship service, and they have great theological significance. To understand better the meaning of the Liturgy of the Eucharist, it is helpful to look more closely at the meaning of tables in the time of Jesus.

Tables are an integral part of liturgy because important events in the life of Jesus took place around tables. In the Narrative of the Gospel, one of the central expressions of the reign of God was Jesus' openness to invite all people to the table, including the poor, the excluded, and the spiritually and socially rejected. Jesus conducted much of his ministry and teaching around tables (Mt 26:7; Lk 5:29-32; 7:36-50; 14:1-24). As in our own day, in biblical times tables were the places where relationships were forged, business was conducted, and commerce was transacted. Because of its power to restore people to right relationships, table fellowship is a symbol of reconciliation, a symbol of fellowship with God and others, and a symbol of God's justice.[27]

Through table fellowship Jesus fulfills the message of the prophets, invites all people to salvation, and promises his disciples a place "at table" in God's kingdom (Lk 22:30). While this invitation to the table was good news for the poor and others who were marginalized or rejected from society, it confused some and scandalized others. Jesus' table fellowship with sinners, in Norman Perrin's words, "must have been most meaningful to his followers and most offensive to his critics."[28] Jesus' rejection of social and religious categories of inclusion/exclusion was probably what prompted his critics to want to crucify him, because it affronted their religious vision. Jesus challenged people to look beyond the walls of their own mind-sets in order to realize a higher law based on God's uncalculating mercy rather than their limited notions of worthiness and unworthiness. Such radical inclusiveness proved to be too much for those in authority, even though Jesus challenged them to relinquish their power in favor of a more radical and welcoming power of love.

---

27. See Eugene LaVerdiere, *Dining in the Kingdom of God* (Chicago: Liturgy Training Publications, 1994); and Michael Joncas, "Tasting the Kingdom of God: The Meal Ministry of Jesus and Its Implications for Contemporary Worship and Life," *Worship* 74, no. 4 (July 2000): 329-65.

28. See Norman Perrin, *Rediscovering the Teaching of Jesus* (1967; San Francisco: Harper & Row, 1976), 102.

As Robert J. Karris asserts, "Jesus was crucified because of how he ate."[29] In bringing scribe, tax collector, fisherman, and zealot into one community, Jesus challenged his hearers to a new kind of relationship, one based not on social status, the empire's rules, or religious self-righteousness but instead on a common hope for the coming of God's reign (Mt 8:11; 11:16-19). The early Christians put great emphasis, even to the point of excess, on continuing the Jesus tradition of festive table fellowship, which makes concrete God's offer of salvation and the promises of God's reign.[30] Table fellowship reveals a God who welcomes and invites all to the table and reveals a God who serves and gives himself for all, regardless of their social, economic, or moral standing. The Liturgy of the Eucharist makes present this promise of the universal and all-embracing love revealed in the ministry of Jesus and his life-giving death.

During the Liturgy of the Eucharist, the priest, in union with the whole community, invokes the Spirit to come upon the bread and wine (*epiclesis*) to transform them into the body and blood of Christ (transubstantiation). The changing of these ordinary elements of life, bread and wine, into the real presence of Christ is one of the most significant parts of the liturgy and a central dimension of Catholic faith, and the doxology is the high point of the Eucharistic Prayer. It is not, however, a "magic show" at which the congregation passively observes. Rather it is a sacramental event that invites the involvement of the entire gathered community, so that, locally and globally, God might transform through Christ the entire way human beings relate to each other.[31] As Kathleen Hughes suggests,

> Participation in the liturgy means participation in the life, death, and rising of Jesus, *truly* dying and rising with him, *truly* laying down our lives. Participation means working mightily for the establishment of the reign of God by letting the spirit of God work in us to complete Christ's work on earth. Participation means living Christ's life: pouring ourselves out for the poor and the imprisoned and the suffering, wherever we encounter these realities in our every day. Participation means "living no longer for ourselves but for God." Otherwise, how can we say "Amen" to such a prayer?[32]

---

29. Robert J. Karris, *Luke: Artist and Theologian* (New York: Paulist, 1985), 47.

30. Casiano Floristán, "The Place of the Poor in the Eucharistic Assembly," in *The Option for the Poor in Christian Theology*, ed. Daniel G. Groody (Notre Dame, Ind.: University of Notre Dame Press, 2007), 240-43.

31. Nathan Mitchell, "Who Is at the Table? Reclaiming Real Presence?" *Commonweal* (January 27, 1995): 10-15.

32. Kathleen Hughes, "Liturgy and Justice: An Intrinsic Relationship," in *Living No Longer for Ourselves*, 50-51.

In other words, some liturgists speak of a *double epiclesis*, which emphasizes not only the changing of the bread and wine into the body and blood of Christ but also changing the gathered community into Christ's real presence in the world.[33]

The rite of the Liturgy of the Eucharist is built on the Last Supper that Jesus had with his disciples, which, according to the Synoptic Gospels, was a Passover meal. The Passover Narrative takes on a deeper meaning at the moment of the Last Supper when Jesus invites his own disciples to share in his Passover from this world to the next, from the narrow confines of an empire mentality (Lk 22:25-27) to the freedom of the reign of God (Lk 22:15-30). When Jesus celebrates the Passover with his disciples the night before he dies, he invites his disciples to "pass-over" with him from injustice to justice, from alienation to reconciliation, from death to life. So significant is this last event that Jesus calls his disciples to celebrate this meal in memory of him, for he lived as he died, and he died as he lived. The church structures that memory in the Liturgy of the Eucharist, as indicated in the Eucharistic Prayer:

> Before he was given up to death, a death he freely accepted, he took bread and gave you thanks. He broke the bread, gave it to his disciples, and said, "Take this, all of you, and eat it: this is my body which will be given up for you." When supper was ended, he took the cup. Again he gave you thanks and praise, gave the cup to his disciples, and said: "Take this, all of you, and drink from it: this is the cup of my blood, the blood of the new and everlasting covenant. It will be shed for you and for all so that sins may be forgiven. Do this in memory of me."

This meal, these words, and this memory are at the heart of God's ongoing action in history through Christ. At the heart of the eucharist is God's love revealed in Christ and his command to remember him in the offering of his own life for the salvation of the world.

Above all, the eucharist is a way of understanding God's love for the world. Jesus' death on the cross reveals not only that Jesus paid the debt of sin but also that God's love for humankind cannot be extinguished. Through Jesus, God so totally loves the human race that nothing is capable of killing this love, not rejection, insults, betrayal, mockery, or even death. The church is born of mercy, through the pouring out of God's life for us. God in Christ loves sinful humanity even to the point of pouring out the blood and water

---

33. John H. McKenna, "The Epiclesis Revisited," in *New Eucharistic Prayers: An Ecumenical Study of Their Development and Structure,* ed. Frank C. Senn (New York: Paulist, 1987), 169-94.

of his own body, which symbolize the birth of the church in baptism and eucharist (Jn 19:34).

Pope Benedict XVI explains the deeply significant relationship between Christ's death and the eucharist when he says, "By making the bread into his body and the wine into his blood, he anticipates his death, he accepts it in his heart, and he transforms it into an action of love. What on the outside is simply brutal violence [the Crucifixion] from within becomes an act of total self-giving love."[34] He goes on to say that this act of love celebrated in the eucharist is the initial transubstantiation that sets in motion a series of transformations in us, which call us forth to renew and transform the world until God becomes all in all (1 Cor 15:28). In this act of radical love, Jesus in the eucharist binds the world more closely to himself and accomplishes the work of right relationship or reconciliation, even in the face of the world's darkest moment, even when human beings sentenced the Son of God to death!

The Liturgy of Eucharist ritualizes the memory of the life of Jesus, which is a dangerous memory because it is a memory of reconciliation.[35] Reconciliation is dangerous because it breaks down walls and disturbs established patterns of sin and injustice. It is the memory of solidarity that breaks down the walls of exclusion. It is the memory of his love that breaks down the walls of hatred. It is the memory of his teachings that breaks down the walls of ignorance. "Do this in memory of me" means remembering Jesus' concern for the poor and suffering and his desire for reconciliation on all levels of human existence. The Our Father, the gesture of peace, the Lamb of God, and the breaking of bread are prayers and rituals that mark the beginning of this reconciliation because they give expression to breaking down walls that are created by sin and result in alienating our relationships. In the end, the memory of Jesus' death breaks down the walls of mortality and reveals the God of Life.

The climax of the Liturgy of the Eucharist is the distribution and reception of communion, when believers share in the body and blood of Christ and become united with him in the sacrament. Communion is the ultimate sacramental expression of reconciliation. While Ireneaus observed, "That which is not assumed is not redeemed," in the eucharist we might say that which is not consumed and enacted does not transform. But the eucharist is not simply a matter of physical digestion or passive reception of a material food.

---

34. Benedict XVI, "Eucharist: Setting Transformations in Motion," 202.

35. Johannes Baptist Metz, "The Future in the Memory of Suffering," in *New Questions on God,* ed. Johannes Baptist Metz, New Concilium Series 76 (New York: Herder & Herder, 1972), 15. See also Bruce T. Morrill, *Anamnesis as Dangerous Memory: Political and Liturgical Theology in Dialogue* (Collegeville, Minn.: Liturgical Press, 2000).

Rather, the eucharist is a matter of spiritual digestion through which Christ penetrates into every cell of human beings, possesses them so completely, and draws them so totally into his own life that they become, through this grace, another Christ. In the process, Christians hope to become that which they eat. Augustine summarizes the significance of this dynamic at the eucharistic table in his instruction to his newly baptized catechumens at the Easter vigil:

> If you are the body and members of Christ, then what is laid on the Lord's table is the sacrament of what you yourselves are, and it is the sacrament of what you are that you receive. It is to what you yourselves are that you answer "Amen," and this answer is your affidavit. Be a member of Christ's body, so that your "Amen" may be authentic.[36]

Through communion Christians seek to become an embodiment of the self-giving love of God they receive.

The Concluding Rite: Sending Forth the Community and Ritualizing Christian Mission

The Concluding Rite consists of the blessing of the faithful, the dismissal of the community, and the ritual recession from church. For the most part, this rite centers on the final blessing and the commissioning words of the priest, who says, "The Mass is ended. Go in peace to love and serve the Lord." While these words mark the end of the church service, they do not signal the end of the Liturgy of the Eucharist.[37] Rather, they are the beginning of the liturgy of the church as the body of Christ in service to the reign of God.

The closing recession ritualizes Jesus' command to his disciples to "Go . . . and make disciples of all nations" (Mt 28:19), each according to his or her gifts, abilities, and vocations. During this rite the ministers do not walk out with the lectionary or the book of the Gospels. Nor do they recess out with the consecrated hosts. This time they walk out with the cross and the people of God, who, having been nourished by Word and sacrament, are now called to embody Christ's life in the world.

John Paul II insisted that the authenticity of the eucharistic celebrations can be measured only by the community's commitment to the poorest among

---

36. Quoted in Robert Cabié, "The Eucharist," in *The Church at Prayer*, vol. 2, ed. A. G. Martimort (Collegeville, Minn.: Liturgical Press, 1968), 118.

37. Michael Driscoll notes that this closing rite could be developed more in such a way that it gives better expression to the sending forth of ministers of various kinds to respond to the many needs of the church and the world. Michael S. Driscoll, "Sending Us Forth," *America* 193, no. 9 (October 3, 2005): 20-22.

us and therefore must be used "as an occasion to make a serious commit-ment to fight the tragedy of hunger, the affliction of illness, the loneliness of the elderly, the hardships of the unemployed and the struggles of the immi-grants" (MND 28). In this sense, we can say that the real presence of Christ is "confected" not only in the changing of bread and wine but in caring for the "least" of society (Mt 25:31-46). What Martin Luther King, Jr., said about religion in general could also be said about the eucharist:

> I say to you that religion must be concerned not merely about mansions in the sky, but about the slums and the ghettos in the world. A proper religion will be concerned not merely about the streets flowing with milk and honey, but about the millions of God's children in Asia, Africa, and South America and in our nation who go to bed hungry at night. It will be concerned [not only] about a long white robe over yonder but about [people] having some clothes down here. It will be concerned not merely about silver slippers in heaven but about men and women having some shoes to wear on earth.[38]

The church's liturgy as the work of God, then, is not just to celebrate the sacraments of the church but, as noted in *Lumen Gentium*, to become a sac-rament to the world (LG 1). This means giving oneself for the needs of the world and healing it through love amidst all its (and one's own) brokenness, fragility, and vulnerability. Active participation in the liturgy offers a gift and then lays down a challenge; it calls people to become something new as a result of the story they have heard, celebrated, and enacted.[39] Liturgy as a sacrifice is not only about Christ in the eucharist offering himself on the altar in the church, but about Christians offering themselves to others on the altar of the world.

THE LITURGY OF THE WORLD:
FINDING GOD IN ALL THINGS

While the eucharistic liturgy celebrates in a special way God's action in the church, its purpose is to draw people's attention to God's all-pervading activ-ity in the world. The goal of the eucharist is not to take people out of the world but to help them better see what is going on in the world all the time. Gerard Manley Hopkins wrote,

---

38. Martin Luther King, Jr., Sermon Preached at Ebenezer Baptist Church, Atlanta, July 7, 1963, quoted in Frederick Trost, *Confessing Christ Newsletter*, DeForest, Wisconsin (May 18, 1995). Quoted in Westermeyer, *Let Justice Sing*, 110.

39. Stosur, "Bread of Life, Justice of God," 182-89.

The world is charged with the grandeur of God
It will flame out, like shining from shook foil.[40]

He had a mystical sense that there are ceaseless opportunities in daily life to be moved to prayer, to thank and praise God, and to find Christ in all things. In a similar manner, Karl Rahner noted that the central purpose of the eucharistic liturgy is to help people better grasp what he calls the "Liturgy of the World."[41] For Rahner the "Liturgy of the World" is about God's action in history and gives expression to the fact that God's grace permeates the earth and meets us constantly in our daily lives: through our relationships, in the created world, and in the events of our lives. The outpouring of the Holy Spirit on all of creation meets us in all we do, even in our limitations, sins, and failures.[42] In order better to discern God's activity in the world, it is helpful here, as a final note, to explore the Liturgy of the World, especially as it relates to the liturgies of globalization, the liturgy of creation, and the liturgy of final consummation.

The Liturgies of Globalization

Alongside the eucharist, contemporary society has its own liturgies, which are less obvious but nonetheless must be identified and discerned. Human life in reality takes shape within structures and rituals of all kinds, and some of these include the liturgies of globalization. Some of these liturgies compete for our attention and can keep us from apprehending the Liturgy of the World. They can unravel our own inner peace and become destructive to our relationships even when they appear to us as ways to progress. Some rituals in this liturgy diminish and suffocate the spirit while others expand and liberate it; some deepen our relationships with God and each other, and others make them superficial; some lead us to a deeper engagement with reality, whereas others anesthetize and distract us from the world and others around us. Like church rituals, global rituals without a sense of relationships and justice leave one feeling hollow and empty in the end. As John Hogan remarks,

---

40. Gerard Manley Hopkins, "God's Grandeur" in *Gerard Manley Hopkins: Major Works*, ed. Catherine Phillips (New York: Oxford University Press, 2002), 128.

41. See Karl Rahner, "Considerations on the Active Role of the Person in the Sacramental Event," in *Theological Investigations* 14 (New York: Seabury, 1976), 161-84, especially 169-70. See also Michael Skelley, *The Liturgy of the World: Karl Rahner's Theology of Worship* (Collegeville, Minn.: Liturgical Press, 1991).

42. See also Nathan Mitchell, "The Spirituality of Christian Worship," *Spirituality Today* 34, no. 1 (March 1982): 5-17.

The jury is still out as to whether globalization will prove a blessing or a curse to humanity. Thus far, however, it has had a killing effect on the world's poor, local cultures, and the environment. In a sense globalization has become a liturgy writ-large—with matching vestments, rituals, music, drama, food and text. It has its rubrics, hierarchy, acolytes, and parishioners—only the poor are left out.[43]

If ritual structures exist not only in the eucharistic liturgy but in the liturgies of contemporary society, then the central issue is not whether we participate in liturgy but in which liturgies we participate and what kind of people we become as a result of that participation. In a culture where global rituals pressure people to have and to possess, the Liturgy of the Eucharist invites us to realize the primacy of our call to be more connected to others and to be more and more possessed by God and God alone.

The Liturgy of Creation

The Liturgy of the Eucharist is also intimately connected to our relationship to creation. The elements of water and wine in the Mass bind the eucharistic celebration not only to people but also to the created world. The bread that is changed into the body of Christ and the wine that becomes his blood are "the sign of the transformation of creation to meet the needs of humanity and the safeguarding of resources necessary for future generations" (IL 3). The eucharist as a means of transforming the world is related to the hope of Christians, who await "new heavens and a new earth" (2 Pt 3:13), when all things will be reconciled to Christ, even the things of the earth.

Pierre Teilhard de Chardin sensed that the whole created world was in the process of transformation by the light and fire of God's Spirit at work in the world. For Teilhard, the eucharist was at the heart of this transformation, and its meaning not only encompassed but also surpassed the material elements. In 1923, while on a scientific expedition in the Ordos Desert in China, he found it impossible to celebrate Mass because he did not have any bread or wine. Some accounts indicate that this was on the Feast of the Transfiguration. The sun was rising, and he had a mystical vision of the transformation of the whole world. This experience led him at that moment to make an offering of the entire cosmos to the energy, fire, and power of the Holy Spirit. At this time he wrote "The Mass on the World."

---

43. John P. Hogan, "People of Faith and Global Citizens: Eucharist and Globalization," in *Liturgy and Justice*, ed. Koester, 57-58.

THE MASS ON THE WORLD
PIERRE TEILHARD DE CHARDIN

Since once again, Lord . . . I have neither bread, nor wine, nor altar, I will raise myself beyond these symbols, up to the pure majesty of the real itself; I your priest, will make the whole earth my altar and on it will offer you all the labors and sufferings of the world . . .

I will place on my paten, O God, the harvest to be won by this renewal of labour. Into my chalice I shall pour all the sap which is to be pressed out this day from the earth's fruits.

My paten and my chalice are the depths of a soul laid widely open to all the forces which in a moment will rise up from every corner of the earth and converge upon the Spirit . . .

One by one, Lord, I see and I love all those whom you have given me to sustain and charm my life. One by one also I number all those who make up that other beloved family which has gradually surrounded me, its unity fashioned out of the most disparate elements, with affinities of the heart, of scientific research, and of thought. And again one by one—more vaguely it is true, yet all-inclusively—I call before me the whole vast anonymous army of living humanity; those who surround me and support me though I do not know them; those who come and those who go; above all, those who in office, laboratory, and factory, through their vision of truth or despite their error, truly believe in the progress of earthly reality and who today will take up again their impassioned pursuit of the light . . .

[T]his ocean of humanity whose slow, monotonous wave-flows trouble the hearts even of those whose faith is most firm: it is to this deep that I thus desire all the fibers of my being should respond . . . This is the material of my sacrifice, the only material you desire.

Once upon a time men took into your temple the first fruits of their harvests, the flower of their flocks. But the offering you really want, the offering you mysteriously need every day to appease your hunger, to slake your thirst is nothing less than the growth of the world borne ever onward in the stream of universal becoming.

Receive, O Lord, this all-embracing host which your whole creation, moved by your magnetism, offers you at this dawn of a new day.

This bread, our toil, is of itself, I know, but an immense fragmentation; this wine, our pain, is no more, I know, than a draught that dissolves. Yet in the very depths of this formless mass you have implanted—and this I am sure of, for I sense it—a desire irresistible, hallowing, which makes us cry out, believer and unbeliever alike: "Lord, make us *one*."[44]

44. Pierre Teilhard de Chardin, *The Heart of Matter*, trans. René Hague (New York: Harcourt Brace Jovanovich, 1979), 119-21. See also *Pierre Teilhard de Chardin: Writings* (Maryknoll, N.Y.: Orbis Books, 1999), 80-81.

Teilhard perceived in this experience that the structures of the eucharistic celebration are central to transforming the human heart and even transforming the entire universe. He believed that the heart of God was found in the heart of the world.[45] Such a vision, in light of globalization, sees the current historical developments as part of a spiritual evolution by which the world is gradually being transformed into Christ.

The Liturgy of Final Consummation

While the eucharist has much to do with the memory of the past and the application of that memory in the present, Teilhard's vision also illustrates that the eucharist has to do with the future and the culmination of history in Jesus Christ. As the church waits for the fullness of God's reign in the *parousia*, the church lives in this time between the first and second coming, between the inauguration of the reign of God in Jesus' earthly life and its promised fulfillment in the end of time.

Vatican II's Constitution on the Sacred Liturgy (*Sacrosanctum Concilium*) brings out that the liturgy we celebrate today is intimately intertwined with the liturgy that will take place when Christ comes again: "In the earthly liturgy we take part in a foretaste of that heavenly liturgy which is celebrated in the holy city of Jerusalem toward which we journey as pilgrims" (SC 8). Even while the world constructs walls and divisions that separate people from one another, the liturgy fundamentally celebrates a unity that is already being realized in Christ. The liturgy helps us realize that on this side of heaven we are all immigrants; migration is part of the church's very self-definition. As William Cavanaugh says,

> The Christian wanders among the earthly nations on the way to her eternal *patria* [homeland], the Kingdom of God. The Eucharist makes clear, however, that this Kingdom does not simply stand outside of history, nor is heaven simply a goal for the individual to achieve at death. Under the sign of the Eucharist the Kingdom becomes present in history through the action of Christ.[46]

In other words, according to Cavanaugh, any walls that we construct on earth will ultimately be torn down when Christ comes again. The liturgy provides an opportunity to reshape the secular imagination that constructs walls and borders with a radically new Christian imagination, which is based on com-

---

45. See also Ursula King, introduction to *Pierre Teilhard de Chardin: Writings*, 14.
46. William T. Cavanaugh, *Torture and Eucharist: Theology, Politics, and the Body of Christ* (Malden, Mass.: Blackwell, 1998), 224-25.

mon bonds as a people of God. To receive communion means to allow God to break down the walls within people's minds and hearts that cause discrimination, exclusion, and division in our society. As Kevin Seasoltz notes,

> To follow Christ and live through the power of his Spirit means that one must share his life not only with other committed disciples but with all those who are excluded from communion. The scandal of the rich in the gospel is not that they are rich and others are poor, implying that life would be just if everyone were equally well off. The scandal is that wealth gives the rich a false sense of security which walls them off from the demands of others, thus creating an essentially divisive situation. To attempt to live with the justice of God implies facing not only the problems of the poor but also the problems of the rich.[47]

"To participate in the Eucharist," Cavanaugh adds, "is to live inside God's imagination. It is to be caught up into what is really real, the body of Christ. As human persons, body and soul, are incorporated into the performance of Christ's *corpus verum*, they resist the state's ability to define what is real."[48] The walls and fences we set up, which we think will protect us from outsiders, are barriers that imprison us and keep us from realizing our common interconnection with each other. The eucharistic celebration affirms that breaking down walls and bringing together the world is already happening in the liturgy, and when the world is consummated in Christ, the reconciliation of all people will be complete. As the writer of the letter to the Ephesians says, "For [Christ] is our peace, he who made both one and broke down the dividing wall of enmity, through his flesh" (Eph 2:14).

In the end, the celebration of the eucharist is intimately interconnected with the call to give thanks to God for all the blessings of one's life, even amidst life's trials and sufferings. Typically, we believe that such gratitude is something that wells up in us in times of prosperity. Yet many people who are materially prosperous today never feel happy because they never feel they have enough. Yet on the night before Jesus died, at the moment his passion began, he gave thanks and praise to God. As a memorial of Jesus, the eucharist is a ritual of gratitude, and one of the most mysterious manifestations of the God of Life is the capacity to give thanks to the God of Life amidst life's most godless moments.

While in the desert of Arizona, near the place where many immigrants die attempting to cross into the United States, I got a glimpse of what Teilhard de Chardin spoke of in the desert and what Jesus said in the midst of his trials. I met a woman named Maria, who was forced to cross the United States–

---

47. Seasoltz, "Justice and the Eucharist," 513.
48. Cavanaugh, *Torture and Eucharist*, 279.

Mexico border without papers. She came north from Guatemala, looking for work so she could provide food and medicine for her family. After stowing away on a freight train for a week, she tried to cross the border three times. The first time her *coyote*-guide tried to rape her. The second time bandito gangs mugged her and took everything she had. The third time she walked across the treacherous desert in 120-degree heat, ran out of food and water, suffered heat exhaustion, and began to vomit. Border patrol agents arrested her, put her in a detention center, then sent her back over the border. After listening to her story, I asked her what she would say if she had fifteen minutes to talk with God. She said, "First of all, I do not have fifteen minutes to talk with God. In my journey I have felt that God is always with me, and I am always talking with him. But if I could see him face to face, the first thing I would do is thank him for having given me so much and for having been so good to me." Maria's clear, sincere, and penetrating words gave powerful expression to what it means to give thanks, to worship in Spirit, to live in truth, and above all to celebrate the eucharist in the world.

QUESTIONS FOR REFLECTION

1. Why does social justice need liturgy, and why does liturgy need social justice?
2. What is the relationship between the Liturgy of the Word, the Liturgy of the Eucharist, and the Liturgy of the World?
3. Discuss this statement: "The transubstantiation of the bread and wine into the body and blood of Christ is the beginning of the transformation of believers, which should lead to the transformation of the world until Christ becomes all in all."
4. What walls do you see between liturgy and life?
5. Discuss this statement: "[W]hen any person is absent from the celebration, all liturgy is diminished."
6. Discuss this statement: "Sacraments are not limited to the seven formal sacraments, but can include any way in which God's presence is revealed to us."
7. What are the liturgies of globalization? How are they related to the Liturgy of the Eucharist?
8. How does the fraction rite (Lamb of God/breaking bread) implicate Christians for sharing wealth and the world's goods?
9. How can the closing rite be organized in a more effective way to emphasize mission and commission?

SUGGESTIONS FOR FURTHER READING AND STUDY

Balasuriya, Tissa. *The Eucharist and Human Liberation.* Maryknoll, N.Y.: Orbis Books, 1979.

Boff, Leonardo. *Sacraments of Life, Life of the Sacraments.* Washington, D.C.: Pastoral Press, 1987.

Boureau, Christophe, Janet Martin Soskice, and Luiz Carlos Susin, eds. "Hunger, Bread and Eucharist." *Concilium* (2005/2): 7-8.

Burghardt, Walter J. *Let Justice Roll Down like Waters: Biblical Justice Homilies Throughout the Year.* New York: Paulist, 1998.

Cavanaugh, William T. *Torture and Eucharist: Theology, Politics, and the Body of Christ.* Malden, Mass.: Blackwell, 1998.

Crockett, William R. *Eucharist: Symbol of Transformation.* New York: Pueblo, 1989.

Dallen, James. "Liturgy and Justice for All." *Worship* 65, no. 4 (July 1991): 290-306.

Dussel, Enrique. "The Bread of the Eucharistic Celebration as a Sign of Justice in the Community." In *Can We Always Celebrate the Eucharist?* Edited by Mary Collins and David Power. Concilium 152. New York: Seabury, 1982.

Empereur, James L., and Christopher G. Kiesling. *The Liturgy That Does Justice.* Collegeville, Minn.: Liturgical Press, 1990.

Gelpi, Donald L. *Committed Worship: A Sacramental Theology for Converting Christians.* 2 vols. Collegeville, Minn.: Liturgical Press, 1993.

Grassi, Joseph A. *Broken Bread and Broken Bodies: The Lord's Supper and World Hunger.* Maryknoll, N.Y.: Orbis Books, 1985.

Groaz, Edward M., ed. *Liturgy and Social Justice: Celebrating Rites—Proclaiming Rights.* Collegeville, Minn.: Liturgical Press, 1989.

Hellwig, Monika K. *The Eucharist and the Hunger of the World.* 2nd rev. ed. Kansas City, Mo.: Sheed & Ward, 1992.

Henderson, J. Frank, Stephen Larson, and Kathleen Quinn. *Liturgy, Justice, and the Reign of God: Integrating Vision and Practice.* Mahwah, N.J.: Paulist, 1989.

Hessel, Dieter T. *Social Themes of the Christian Year: A Commentary on the Lectionary.* Philadelphia, Pa.: Geneva, 1983.

Hughes, Kathleen, and Mark R. Francis. *Living No Longer for Ourselves: Liturgy and Justice in the Nineties.* Collegeville, Minn.: Liturgical Press, 1991.

John Paul II, Apostolic Letter, *Mane Nobiscum Domine,* October 7, 2004.

Koester, Anne Y., ed. *Liturgy and Justice: To Worship God in Spirit and Truth.* Collegeville, Minn.: Liturgical Press, 2002.

Mahony, Roger. "The Eucharist and Social Justice." *Worship* 57, no. 1 (January 1983): 52-61.

McKenna, Megan. *Rites of Justice: The Sacraments and Liturgy as Ethical Imperatives.* Maryknoll, N.Y.: Orbis Books, 1997.

Moore, Gerard. *Eucharist and Justice.* North Sydney, Australia: Australian Catholic Social Justice Council, 2000.

Pecklers, Keith F. *The Unread Vision: The Liturgical Movement in the United States of America: 1926-1955.* Collegeville, Minn.: Liturgical Press, 1998.

Power, David. "The Song of the Lord in an Alien Land." In *Politics and Liturgy.* Edited by Herman Schmidt and David Power. New York: Herder & Herder, 1974.

Ramshaw, Gail. *God's Food: The Relationship Between Holy Communion and World Hunger.* Philadelphia: Fortress, 1986.

Searle, Barbara, and Anne Koester. *Vision: The Scholarly Contribution of Mark Searle to Liturgical Renewal.* Collegeville, Minn.: Liturgical Press, 2004.

Seasoltz, R. Kevin. "Justice and the Eucharist." *Worship* 58, no. 6 (November 1984): 507-25.

Stamps, Mary E., ed. *To Do Justice and Right upon the Earth: Papers from the Virgil Michel Symposium on Liturgy and Social Justice.* Collegeville, Minn.: Liturgical Press, 1993.

Westermeyer, Paul. *Let Justice Sing: Hymnody and Justice.* Collegeville, Minn.: Liturgical Press, 1998.

9

A Loving Heart, A Just Faith

Spirituality and Transformation

A NUMBER OF YEARS AGO I WAS HIKING alone in the backcountry of Yosemite National Park in California. On the last day of the trip, I wanted to climb its signature peak called Half Dome. It is a massive granite monolith that majestically juts almost a mile above the valley floor. The first part of the hike to the summit entails an eight-mile climb to the backside of the mountain. The second part of the hike, which is the most difficult, involves climbing a seventy-degree vertical ascent of bare rock. Its sheer steepness makes it impossible to reach the top without ropes or cables. Yet even with them, I had to face the prospect of falling to my death thousands of feet below.

When I came to the final part of the climb, I stood there in both awe and terror. While my heart wanted to grasp the world from the top of this peak, my mind wanted me to run as far as I could in the other direction. In the shadow of this immense mountain, I deliberated carefully about making this final, dangerous trek, and I was completely intimidated.

After some time I took my first step forward. Then I started to walk up the long, steep incline, grabbing the cables on either side of me and hiking upwards in what felt like a perpendicular line. After about one hundred feet I could see down to the valley floor, thousands of feet below. Suddenly, my knees began to shake uncontrollably. I then looked above at the rock wall in front of me, and I suddenly had trouble breathing. My courage began to give out, so I hiked back down to the base of the final section. I stayed there awhile, wondering whether or not to try again.

On my next attempt I made it about one hundred feet further, but I still became overwhelmed. I descended a second time and thought about the climb and the risks. Not knowing if or when I would have this opportunity again, I realized this was a decisive moment, a moment of choice. To reach the summit, something had to change. More than anything else, my vision had to be transformed. I did not know what this meant exactly, only that my current framework had broken down and was inadequate to reach the new heights that beckoned me.

Amidst my fears and hopes, I began praying and meditating at the base of the peak. I also began reimagining my whole approach to the climb. From this prayer and new vision, I began to look differently at what I was doing, which gave me a new strength to risk. Gradually, through a series of careful steps, I set out on the path up the mountain again and eventually arrived at the summit of Half Dome, unharmed and elated. From above I encountered a beauty that to this day rivals any I have ever seen, and it gave me a whole new perspective on the world. It was a true peak experience.

In the last chapter we spoke of the eucharist as "the summit toward which the activity of the Church is directed [and] . . . the source from which all her power flows" (SC 10). As a way of entering more deeply into the life, death, and resurrection of Jesus Christ, the eucharist is the peak from which to gain perspective on the whole of life and a panoramic vision of our spiritual journey. In this final chapter, we will explore more fully the spirituality at the heart of the eucharistic celebration that animates the journey of justice. First we will consider the path of Christian spirituality as an ascent up the mountain of God. Then we will explore how spirituality transfigures one's vision, enabling one to see with the "eyes of the heart." Third we will examine discipleship as a descent into the valley of injustice. Finally, we will examine some spiritual disciplines and spiritual exercises that help strengthen us for our journey with God as we search for a better world.

SPIRITUALITY: ASCENDING THE MOUNTAIN OF GOD

While globalization and technological developments have given us more and more control over the external world, they have given us little grasp of the inner world of the human person and the ultimate questions of human existence. Beyond the discord and disorder of the world, the bruised and broken dimensions of human relationships, and the emptiness and ennui of the consumer culture, there are enduring human questions that globalization has largely ignored and left unexplored. These questions deal with loneliness and belonging, good and evil, peace and division, healing and suffering, meaning and meaninglessness, hope and despair, love and apathy, justice and injustice, freedom and slavery, and ultimately, life and death. These issues can be worked out only in the inner depths of the human heart, where we forge the metal of what we most value. These values are the concern of spirituality. While spirituality in general deals with what people most value, Christian spirituality involves living out what Jesus most valued. In other words Christian spirituality is about following Jesus, living out the values of the kingdom of God, and generating a community transformed by the love of God and others. Lived out in its personal and public dimensions, Christian spirituality is the way in which the invisible heart of God is made visible to the world.

While there are many metaphors to describe the spiritual life, some of the finest writings about the spiritual life speak of the soul's ascent to God, which is a response to God's descent to human beings in Jesus Christ. The imagery of ascending and descending the mountain of God has its roots in the Scriptures, where many important events took place on the mountains (Ex 3:1-12; Nm 33:38; Dt 34:1-8; 1 Kgs 18:15-40; Mt 4:8; 5-7; Mk 5:11; Lk 6:12). Mountains are often a symbol for God's stability (Ps 30:7), God's power (Ps 121:2), and joy and abundance (Is 44:23; 55:12; Am 9:13). Above all mountains are holy places. In Isaiah we read,

> The mountain of the Lord's house shall be established as the highest mountain and raised above the hills. All nations shall stream toward it; many peoples shall come and say: "Come, let us climb the Lord's mountain, to the house of the God of Jacob, that he may instruct us in his ways, and we may walk in his paths." (Is 2:2-3)

The psalmist adds,

> Who may go up the mountain of the Lord? Who can stand in his holy place? The clean of hand and pure of heart, who are not devoted to idols, who have not sworn falsely. They will receive blessings from the Lord, and justice from their saving God. (Ps 24:3)

In the Gospels, one of the most illuminating moments the disciples had with Jesus takes place on a mountain:

> After six days Jesus took Peter, James, and John and led them up a high mountain apart by themselves. And he was transfigured before them, and his clothes became dazzling white, such as no fuller on earth could bleach them. Then Elijah appeared to them along with Moses, and they were conversing with Jesus. Then Peter said to Jesus in reply, "Rabbi, it is good that we are here! Let us make three tents: one for you, one for Moses, and one for Elijah." He hardly knew what to say, they were so terrified. Then a cloud came, casting a shadow over them; then from the cloud came a voice, "This is my beloved Son. Listen to him." Suddenly, looking around, they no longer saw anyone but Jesus alone with them. (Mk 9:2-8)

The mountain here is a place of revelation and transformation. As a place of revelation, it involves Jesus as the promised Messiah, who proclaims the kingdom of God, confronts the powers of injustice, and reconciles the world to himself (Dt 18:15; Mal 4:5-6). As a place of transformation, it offers the disciples an entirely new way of seeing who Jesus is, how they will follow him, and how they will face trials and suffering.

In Mark's Gospel we learn what Jesus values by seeing what he does. He casts out demons (Mk 1:26, 34, 39; 5:13; 7:30); he cures sicknesses and infirmities (Mk 1:30, 32-34, 42; 2:12; 3:5, 10; 5:29; 6:5, 56; 7:35; 8:23-25); he raises the dead (Mk 5:41-42); he is Lord over nature (Mk 4:39; 6:48-51); he provides bread in a deserted place for the crowds (Mk 6:41-44; 8:6-9), he forgives sins (Mk 2:10); he welcomes sinners (Mk 2:17), and through all these actions, he calls people to repent and believe that the kingdom of God is at hand (Mk 1:15).

A central moment in the disciples' journey with Jesus comes when Peter confesses that Jesus is the Messiah (Mk 8:29), the Promised One of God who will bring justice to the earth. Here Peter offers the right answer about Jesus' identity, but he does not yet understand Jesus or his mission (8:31-33). Despite their physical proximity to Jesus, the disciples are slow learners. Especially in Mark they are often portrayed as hard of hearing and near-sighted (Mk 4:10-13), fearful and lacking in faith (Mk 4:40); they often do not understand Jesus words, and their vision is frequently limited to changes that deal with the social and political economy of this world and their own status in it (Mk 9:33-35; 10:35-45).

Immediately after Peter's profession, Jesus says, "The Son of Man must suffer greatly and be rejected by the elders, the chief priests, and the scribes, and be killed, and rise after three days" (Mk 8:31). This is a prediction that the disciples do not understand, least of all Peter. Unable to hear and see clearly, Peter rebukes Jesus. But Jesus, in turn, rebukes Peter and says, "Get behind me, Satan. You are thinking not as God does, but as human beings do" (Mk 8:31-33). Indicating that there is something wrong with Peter's vision, Jesus reveals that following him demands ascending to the values, ideals, and ethical demands of the kingdom of God. In order to see the world as God sees it, they must begin to see with the eyes of the heart (Eph 1:15-21).

TRANSFIGURATION: SEEING WITH THE EYES OF THE HEART

Like mountains, the human heart has always been understood metaphorically as well as biologically, and it is integrally related to the soul's ascent to God. In the Scriptures, the heart is more than the sentimental and emotional center of a person but is the symbol of one's whole being.[1] Although it

---

1. Jean de Fraine and Albert Vanhoye, "Heart," in *Dictionary of Biblical Theology*, ed. Xavier Léon-Dufour (Paris: Desclée, 1967), 200-202.

includes reason, it also transcends and transforms it, integrating and informing all aspects of a person. The heart is the place from which one does one's
deepest searching, discovers one's most authentic desires, finds one's ultimate
identity, and perceives accurately the deepest realities. Because Christian
spirituality deals with the highest aspirations of the human life, it deals with
the heart. It reveals what one values (Mk 10:17-25), how one spends one's
time (Lk 10:38-42), where one stores one's treasure (Mt 6:19-21), how one
lives out one's relationships (Rom 12:18), and ultimately how one loves (1 Cor
13:4-8a). In other words, the heart is the place of divine–human encounter.
The challenge of Christian spirituality, lived as following Jesus, deals with
making the mind and heart of Christ one's own.

Only after much trial and error do the disciples begin to understand the
mind and heart of Jesus. The structure of Mark's Gospel in general and the
account of the transfiguration in particular help us understand that the conversion process for the disciples was gradual, even though it had its moments
of illumination. One key section is Mark's account of Jesus' road to Jerusalem
(8:27-10:52). This section is preceded by the healing of a blind man (8:22-26)
and ends with the healing of a blind man (10:46-52). In between we read
the story of the transfiguration. While this redaction leaves much room for
interpretation, one plausible reading is that Mark indicates that following
Jesus demands more than simply confessing Jesus as the Messiah: the disciples must be healed of the spiritual blindness that keeps them from seeing
the demanding realities of love that will summon them to sacrifice for the
kingdom. While they learn that obeying the commandments, fulfilling the
law, and confessing faith in Jesus as Lord are important aspects of the ascent
up the mountain of God, the second and more difficult part of the climb, like
scaling Half Dome, involves undergoing a radical transformation of vision
and learning to see the world as God sees it.

While on one level the transfiguration on the mountain may be understood
as something that happened to Jesus, on another level it can be understood as
something that happened to the disciples. Through this experience the eyes
of their hearts are opened, enabling the disciples to behold Jesus in all his
glory and—at least for a moment—to see reality as God sees it. It is likely that
this event also enables them to have a different perception of other people as
well. No longer judging people by external appearances, they are able to see
deeper into the heart of other people, as if to begin to behold others as God
does (1 Sm 16:7), as if to see the glory that resides within each and every person. While this event is an important moment in changing the outlook of the
disciples, we also learn that seeing the world in a new way will continue to be
a problem even after the transfiguration. We can infer, then, that conversion
for the disciples is an ongoing challenge that goes beyond any mountaintop

experiences of divine–human encounter. The story of the second healing of a blind man (Mk 10:46-52) brings out that the path of discipleship requires an ongoing transformation of vision.

While there is every indication that the disciples wanted to stay up on the mountain and savor this spiritual experience, even in all its terror and wonder (Mk 9:6), they regretfully discover that such peak experiences are momentary. To this day on the top of Mt. Tabor (where tradition says the transfiguration happened),[2] as well as on the top of Half Dome, there are signs that say "No camping." Beyond the practical reasons for these signs, the spiritual implications are noteworthy. While the disciples appear to want to hold on to their spiritual experiences, they begin to discover that this grace of spiritual illumination is not an end in itself but a gift given to strengthen them for the difficult road ahead. Eventually, they have to come down the mountain (Mk 9:9). They must go back with Jesus into the world they left and return to the suffering and injustice of the valley.

DISCIPLESHIP: DESCENDING INTO THE VALLEY OF INJUSTICE

In mountain climbing, one of the more dramatic ways to scale down a mountain peak is by rappelling, which involves ropes, nylon harnesses, and metal devices called carabineers and figure 8s. It is more demanding and riskier than the ascent and sometimes more frightening, but its rewards are infinitely greater. Rappelling is a paradoxical process. Because of the friction and tension created between the ropes and the figure 8, when one lets go of the rope, it holds the climber securely in place. When one holds on to the rope, one becomes dependent on one's own power and begins to fall. While I had seen other climbers before me successfully navigate this process, it was a different story when it was my turn.

The first time I ever rappelled down the face of a mountain, I was wrapped in a matrix of ropes and climbing gear, and an experienced climber at the top guided me through the process and "spotted" me in case I fell. He instructed me to take the rope in my hands and to walk backwards until I got to the edge of the cliff. After nervously following his instruction, he then said, "Now lean backwards until you are parallel to the ground."

As I was dangling over the side of the mountain and as my knuckles

---

2. Tradition says that the transfiguration took place on Mt. Tabor, but its elevation is only 1,850 feet, and in Jesus' day it was probably fortified and inaccessible. Some scholars believe—and it may be more likely—that the transfiguration took place on Mt. Hermon, at 9,100 feet, near Caesarea Philippi, where there would have been more opportunity for solitude. Trent C. Butler, ed., *Holman Bible Dictionary* (Nashville: Holman Bible Publishers, 1991), 639, 1362.

turned white from holding the rope in a virtual death grip, my heart sank as the next words came from above: "Now let go of the rope!" I was paralyzed with fright and my knees began to shake uncontrollably. Sensing my fear and hesitation, the guide reminded me again, "The rope will hold you, but you have to let go!" Never in my life did a decision of faith have such decisive stakes. But as I let go of the rope I discovered a power to uphold me I never even knew existed. I began to learn that the movement down the mountain has its moments of holding on and letting go, yet the more demanding and challenging part of the process is learning to surrender, because it is counter-instinctual to everything I had learned up to that point.

Mark's Gospel speaks of a dramatic descent down the mountain. Jesus indicates that following him on the road to Jerusalem and trusting God as they descend into the valley of injustice requires them to surrender every-thing and relearn almost everything they have known. Unless they surrender they will neither perceive nor understand; they will be neither informed nor transformed. They must learn to put their lives in the hands of God, who promises to uphold, guide, and protect them, even as evil threatens to crush them. Following Jesus will mean letting go of everything as they descend down the mountain into the valley of injustice.

Descending into the valley begins with a conviction of the power of love in a world driven by the love of power. Guided by love and the vision of the kingdom, Jesus' own heart draws him downward toward those who suffer. Saint Paul describes the downward mobility of God in this way:

> Christ Jesus . . . though he was in the form of God, did not regard equality with God something to be grasped. Rather, he emptied himself, taking the form of a slave, coming in human likeness; and found human in appearance, he humbled himself, becoming obedient to death, even death on a cross. (Phil 2:5-8)

In this self-emptying (*kenōsis*), Jesus empties himself of everything but love, a love that reaches its greatest self-giving expression on the cross. As Jon Sobrino describes it,

> On the cross of Jesus God himself is crucified. The Father suffers the death of the Son and takes upon himself all the pain and suffering of history. In this ultimate solidarity with humanity he reveals himself as the God of love, who opens up a hope and a future through the most negative side of history. Thus Christian existence is nothing else but a process of participating in this same process whereby God loves the world and hence is the very life of God.[3]

---

3. Jon Sobrino, *Christology at the Crossroads* (Maryknoll, N.Y.: Orbis Books, 1994), 224.

Through his death and resurrection, Jesus unites heaven with earth, divinity with humanity, mountain with valley. Cross and resurrection, then, are part of one inseparable mystery whereby God reconciles the world to himself and restores human beings to right relationships.

Pierre Teilhard de Chardin explained that, "from the very origins of humankind as we know it, the Cross was placed on the crest of the road which leads to the highest peaks of creation . . . The Christian is not asked to swoon in the shadow, but to climb in the light of the Cross."[4] It takes time to understand the meaning of these words, to understand them with the eyes of the heart. But throughout the centuries, Christian mystics have echoed Teilhard de Chardin's insights on the cross as a means of spiritual ascent and transformation. The cross is at the core of any authentic Christian spirituality, so much so that it is often referred to in tradition as our only hope.

The transfiguration experience given to the disciples on top of the mountain, then, is not an end in itself but a grace to strengthen them to face the challenge of the valley and the scandal of the cross. Jesus did not seek the cross. He sought the kingdom and accepted the cross as part of it. In a similar way, the night before he was assassinated, Martin Luther King, Jr., in the context of his own fears, accepted the cross in light of what he had seen on the mountain:

> We've got some difficult days ahead. But it doesn't matter with me now. Because I've been to the mountaintop. And I don't mind. Like anybody, I would like to live a long life. Longevity has its place. But I'm not concerned about that now. I just want to do God's will. And He's allowed me to go up to the mountain. And I've looked over. And I've seen the Promised Land. I may not get there with you. But I want you to know tonight, that we, as a people, will get to the Promised Land. And I'm happy, tonight. I'm not worried about anything. I'm not fearing any man. Mine eyes have seen the glory of the coming of the Lord.[5]

For King, and those of us who follow Christ in the power of the Spirit, the vision of the promised land, the hope of right relationships, and ultimately union with God and one another, animate the journey even as they lead us back into the valley to heal a broken world.

---

4. Pierre Teilhard de Chardin, *Le Milieu Divin: Essai de Vie Intérieure* (Paris: Éditions du Seuil, 1957), 108-9. "Dès la origine de l'Humanité actuelle nous comprenons qu'elle était dressée en avant de la route qui mène aux plus hautes cimes de la création . . . Pour le Chrétien, il n'est pas question de s'évanouir dans l'ombre, mais de monter dans la lumière, de la Croix."

5. Martin Luther King, Jr., *A Testament of Hope: The Essential Writings and Speeches of Martin Luther King, Jr.*, ed. James M. Washington (New York: HarperCollins, 1986), 286.

THE SPIRITUAL DISCIPLINES: STRENGTH FOR THE JOURNEY

Following Jesus through the power of the Spirit involves entering more fully into Christ's death and resurrection. It means accepting the gifts and responsibilities of Christian love expressed in a faith that does justice. Though rewarding, the journey is arduous, making significant demands on one's strength, one's energies, and ultimately one's heart. Like hiking, the spiritual journey entails weathering difficult conditions, facing the limits of strength, encountering ever-present temptations to give up, paying the costs of the climb, and bearing the heavy wood of the cross. The journey of ascending and descending the mountain, in the end, is not a journey for the faint of heart. Yet there are tools that promote spiritual growth, strengthen us for the journey, and help rebuild and renew our relationship with God, others, the environment, and ourselves. They include fasting and prayer, community and solidarity, nature and simplicity, and recollection and the Sabbath.

Renewing Our Relationship with God

Fasting

The discipline of fasting reminds us of the positive role of self-denial in the process of self-realization.[6] In a world more and more shaped by the commercial agendas of the modern media, fasting helps us distinguish between what we really need and what our consumer culture tells us we need and what it will sell us for a profit.[7] While it seeks to fill the God-shaped void in the human heart through a new car, a bigger house, a larger paycheck, a faster computer, a fancier vacation, or some other new commodity, fasting enables us to recall that we have hungers within for more enduring values that can be fed only through the path of discipline and sacrifice.

Fasting strengthens our relationship with God by disciplining our passions, consolidating our energies, and directing our hearts to our bedrock, God-given desires rather than dissipating them on superfluous wants.[8] C. S. Lewis put it this way:

---

6. Among books that detail the spiritual and physical benefits of fasting, as well as the different approaches, see Thomas Ryan, *Fasting Rediscovered* (New York: Paulist, 1981); idem, *The Sacred Art of Fasting* (Woodstock, Vt.: Skylight Paths, 2005); and Richard J. Foster, *Celebration of Discipline: The Path to Spiritual Growth*, rev. ed. (San Francisco: Harper & Row, 1988).

7. See "Facts and Figures About Our TV Habit," available at www.letsgo.org.

8. E. Edward Kinerk, "Eliciting Great Desires: Their Place in the Spirituality of the Society of Jesus," in *Studies in the Spirituality of Jesuits* (St. Louis: Institute of Jesuit Sources, 1984).

Indeed, if we consider the unblushing promises of reward and the staggering nature of the rewards promised in the gospels, it would seem that Our Lord finds our desires, not too strong, but too weak. We are half-hearted creatures, fooling about with drink and sex and ambition when infinite joy is offered to us, like an ignorant child who wants to go on making mud pies in a slum because he cannot imagine what is meant by the offer of a holiday at sea. We are far too easily pleased.[9]

From the perspective of Christian spirituality, fasting does not mean desiring less but desiring more: its goal is not to eliminate desire but to intensify it and orient it toward flourishing human relationships and the prospering of human life.

Fasting as fidelity, fasting for justice, fasting from food and drink, and fasting from electronics are four ways this discipline can be practiced today. Fasting as fidelity is difficult, and giving oneself generously and wholeheartedly to one's primary relationships and the ordinary demands of one's family, community, and work is a form of asceticism. It involves relinquishing certain inclinations that can lead us off the trail and requires dying to self, renouncing some desires, and giving up some things that are even good in themselves. In a culture that more and more proffers cheap grace,[10] which is grace without discipleship or grace without the cross, fasting highlights the role of trusting surrender that is part of the path of an authentic spirituality.

Isaiah also reminds us that fasting and justice go together:

> This, rather, is the fasting that I wish:
> releasing those bound unjustly,
> untying the thongs of the yoke;
> Setting free the oppressed,
> breaking every yoke.
> Sharing your bread with the hungry,
> sheltering the oppressed and the homeless;
> Clothing the naked when you see them,
> and not turning your back on your own. (Is 58:6-7)

According to the church fathers, fasting that is not connected to nourishing the poor is not fasting at all. Augustine believed that fasting meant sharing with others; otherwise it is useless and self-serving.[11] Fasting can open

---

9. C. S. Lewis, "The Business of Heaven," in *The Inspirational Writings of C. S. Lewis* (New York: Inspirational Press, 1984), 299-300.

10. Dietrich Bonhoeffer reminds us that grace is free but it is not cheap, because it involves the cross. See *The Cost of Discipleship* (1948; New York: Touchstone, 1995).

11. Augustine, *St. Augustine: Sermon on the Mount; Harmony of the Gospels; Homilies on the Gospels*, ed. Philip Schaff (Grand Rapids: Christian Classics Ethereal Library, 1886), 101.

us up to the needs and suffering of others, and it can also express itself by participating in organizations that work for social transformation.[12] Joining individual efforts with collective responses to injustice is an effective means of addressing social problems and keeps us from getting overwhelmed by our inner blindness, the enormity of the problems of injustice, and the seeming insignificance of our personal labors.

Third, fasting from food or drink for a period of time also strengthens us on our journey. When done properly fasting can even be enjoyable, especially as one begins to experience its positive effects, including spiritual growth and increased physical vitality.[13] It purifies the body of toxins and teaches us to savor realities greater than our physical hungers. It not only helps free us from the tyranny of our unending wants but also helps create a sense of solidarity with those who hunger involuntarily because of poverty. In a more radical form, some choose an extended hunger fast for the sake of correcting a specific injustice in the world, and various icons of justice like Gandhi undertook such fasts from time to time.

A fourth kind of fasting is simply fasting from electronics. Our need to be wired to gadgets of every kind has taken a toll on our relationships and fostered new kinds of addictions. One of the most troubling examples of this addiction happened when I was attending a graveside funeral service. At the end of the liturgy each person was invited to take a handful of dirt and put it in the grave. As he was waiting in line, one man got a call on his cell phone, and instead of ignoring it, he continued talking on the phone even as he paid his last respects to the deceased. When not even death can break such addictive habits, it is time to fast. As a way of enhancing relationships, some people refrain from computers, televisions, and other electronics for at least one day a week. Such electronic detox helps break the growing compulsive habit that comes from always having to be connected to life through a machine, and given the amount of time we spend on computers, answering e-mail, watching television, and the like, periodic fasting from electronics is a decision for freedom.

Prayer
One of the primary benefits of fasting is that it deepens our prayer life. As many people today find themselves paralyzed by fear, anxiety, and even terror, prayer opens up the door to the one unchanging relationship that promises stability amid the vicissitudes of life and the uncertainties of the contempo-

---

12. See in particular the organizations listed at *Social Justice Organizations*, available online at http://www.freechild.org.

13. While fasting in general terms is a valuable spiritual discipline, fasting from food is not suitable for everyone, especially those already susceptible to eating disorders.

rary world. Tapping into some of the deepest places of loneliness and long-ing lodged in the human heart, prayer allows us to develop that intimate conversation with Christ that enables us to abide with him and know each other as intimate friends (Jn 15:4; NMI 32). It is the doorway to spiritual depth, human meaning, and genuine intimacy and allows us to perceive more clearly the truths of life. Exercised in private and in community, prayer builds and nourishes our relationships on all levels and is expressed in many forms. More than simply reciting formal structured utterances, prayer is an ongoing conversation from heart to Heart.

Prayer helps us understand God's gratuity, and it is deepened through par-ticipation in the sacraments. The sacraments of reconciliation and the eucha-rist, in particular, greatly facilitate the work of rebuilding, restoring, and reconciling our relationships. The gratuity of God's grace in prayer became clearer to me a few years ago when I was at a small eucharistic celebration with Saint John Paul II in his private chapel in the Vatican. There were about thirty of us present, and we joined him after he had been at prayer for about an hour in silent meditation before the Blessed Sacrament. When the Mass began, there was a period of silence after the first reading. After the Psalm, there was another long pause. Then still longer periods of quiet after the Gospel reading and communion. At first I welcomed the space to pray, but after an extended period of time I began to grow quite uncomfortable. I knew I had many tasks that day to attend to, and I could not even imagine what was on the pope's agenda. In the silence I feared we were wasting time, time that could be used for productive output, even ministerial service. As my own compulsions and attachments to work became more evident, I looked over at the pope. Kneeling in stillness, a part of me thought, "you have one bil-lion people to shepherd . . . with a workload I cannot even begin to imagine . . . isn't it time to get moving?" The pope's attentiveness to God's presence, even amidst the demands of daily life, made me realize that prayer cannot be reduced to one task among others but indeed must be the pipeline through which the love of God flows into us.

Recognizing its vital importance, Martin Luther said, "I have so much business I cannot get on without spending three hours daily in prayer." For most of us, however, when we get busy, prayer is often the first discipline we relinquish. Yet as our relationship with God falters, so too does our effective-ness in ministry. Prayer is not just a psychological tool for self-actualization but a spiritual grace that facilitates human transformation. It is a fundamen-tal human need and is especially important for those involved in the work of justice. Prayer and justice are two sides of the same spiritual coin: justice without prayer quickly degenerates into frenetic social activism, but prayer without justice is hollow and empty.

While justice often motivates us to want to change the world, prayer also challenges us to change ourselves. If we are unwilling to change, we will abandon prayer as a regular practice in our lives.[14] Prayer opens us up to the Spirit, who alone can change all that which does not conform to the mind and heart of Christ (Rom 12:2). The desire to change the world begins with a commitment to change ourselves.

Because we are constantly bombarded by noise and external stimuli in contemporary society, prayer requires carving out a space of silence in daily life. We frequently have difficulty finding moments of silence that help us read our inner lives, but silence allows the soul to breathe, the heart to listen, and the Spirit to speak. Prayer is the doorway to self-knowledge, and it gives us a place to listen to God speaking to us in the depths of our hearts, in the events of our daily lives and in the contemporary world, and in the Scriptures. It is also a profound way of entrusting our lives into the heart of a God who cares for us, a way of unburdening our lives to a God who waits for us, and a practical way to allow the peace of Christ to reign in our hearts. Part of this exercise of trust involves identifying and cultivating "holy desires" that God inspires within us.[15] Desires for forgiveness, justice in the world, peace of mind, a sense of mission, guidance in decisions, a renewed spirit, and help for loved ones are concrete ways in which we invite the Spirit of God to complete God's work within us. As it grounds and connects us to God, prayer informs, reforms, and transforms us and all other relationships, allowing God to guide, shape, and influence our decisions, and accomplish in us some of the highest work of the human heart.

Renewing Our Relationship with Others

Community

When we begin to see with the eyes of the heart, we realize that prayer, even when done in solitude, connects us with other people. Not only is the notion of a private Christian a contradiction in terms, but it also keeps us from understanding that God did not come to save individuals but rather a community.[16] Not only are we not strong enough to journey alone, but Christian faith draws us into relationship, reminding us that we need not only God but each other. We are not atomistic individuals pursuing our own interests but a spiritual body through baptism into Christ's death and resurrection.

---

14. Foster, *Celebration of Discipline*, 31.
15. See Kinerk, "Eliciting Great Desires."
16. Norbert Lohfink, *Option for the Poor: The Basic Principle of Liberation Theology in the Light of the Bible* (Berkeley, Calif.: Bibal, 1995), 8.

The purpose of Christian community, as Catholic Worker cofounder Peter Maurin said, is to create a place "where it is easier for people to be good."[17] More than a faceless institution, a social club, or a political action organization, Christian community offers an alternative way to live, move, and be in the world. Amidst the trials of the valley, community gives witness to the enduring values of the Gospel in cultures that frequently contradict those values and even foster doubts about transcendent realities. It also helps us to not become overwhelmed or discouraged in the fight against injustice.

Community most thrives when it gathers together generous people. Magnanimous individuals are those whose hearts gradually expand, through the work of grace and choice, until they are capable of loving everyone, even their enemies (Mt 5:43-44). Only those capable of great love are capable of understanding the Gospel message. They are the most able to penetrate the superficialities of our contemporary era and see the deeper dimensions of reality. The small-hearted do not understand, and to them the good news is threatening, not liberating. Settling for lesser treasures, they content themselves with titles, positions of authority, and even a sense of self-righteousness, only to neglect the weightier matters of the law of love and the call to social righteousness (Mt 23). More often than not, the small-hearted are scandalized by what matters little and not scandalized by what matters most.

Because love grounds our existence, the bigger the heart, the clearer the vision. Love, because it is nonviolent, not only testifies to the truth that violence is never a solution to conflict and division, but also that love is the greatest, most transforming power in the world. The big-hearted know that true power resides in touching the lives of others, serving them in their needs, and even forgiving enemies. The magnanimous believe that no matter what the trial, love is stronger than those forces which seek to extinguish it. Love is the greatest of all virtues (1 Cor 13:13); it leaves the most lasting legacy and is what binds us together (Col 3:12-14).

Because Christian community is rooted in Christ, it opens up a space to love even those whom the world considers the most unlovable. Nourished and strengthened by a relationship greater than itself, Christian community is a way of learning to love others as Christ first loved us. In contrast to a society that frequently discriminates based on race, ethnicity, religion, and social class, Christian community opens the door to all, offering hospitality in an increasingly inhospitable world.[18]

Even among the big-hearted, however, community is difficult. Gathering together imperfect people with imperfect vision, the church as a community

---

17. Dorothy Day, *The Long Loneliness* (San Francisco: Harper & Row, 1981), 170.
18. Eberhard Arnold, *Why We Live in Community* (Farmington, Pa.: Plough Publishing House, 1995), 24.

is not only a gathering of the holy people of God but also a school for sinners. Those who avoid Christian community because they are deterred by the hypocritical practices of its members fail to recognize that the miracle of the church is that it survives. By all human standards it should have ceased to exist long ago. As a notable archbishop once observed, "The surest proof of the Church's divinity is its own stupidity, because by all rational accounts it should have destroyed itself." The church survives not because it is perfect, nor because its members always agree with each other, but because it believes that its Redeemer lives (Jb 19:25). As it tries to conform itself to the life of Christ, it holds out the challenge of conversion, not only for others but for each and every one of its members.

Christian community, then, is not simply about living together with like-minded people but learning to love with the mind and heart of Christ. When Christ alone is our sole focus, the frictions and tensions of everyday life do not negate the possibility of community but create opportunities to love each other even when we do not like each other. Difficulties in community can create opportunities to go deeper into the mystery of dying and rising with Christ on a daily basis. As a noted Scripture scholar once said to me, "I used to think that loving one's enemies [Mt 5:44 and par.] was the great challenge of a Christian. Now that I have lived in community for a while, I think the greater challenge in everyday life is simply learning to 'love one another' [Jn 15:12]." Sometimes the romantic ideals of serving Christ in far-off mission territories or fighting global injustices in the world can preempt the more radical and demanding challenge to love those God has already put in our path and who live in our very own homes.

Because we are built for love, the greatest gift of community is the experience of connection, especially as this takes shape in genuine friendship. Aristotle observed that perfect friendship happens between two people who are good and alike in virtue.[19] Spiritual friendship takes interconnectedness to another level because it binds a person not only to another but to God. Jesus claimed friendship as the crowning gift of his ministry and indeed the model for perfect discipleship (Jn 15:15). So deep does such friendship penetrate the heart that it is like the coming together of one soul in two bodies, and the closer each grows in relationship with God, the closer they are to each other. Because we are made for each other and we are made to share with each other, such spiritual friendship feeds the infinite longing of the heart in a way that nothing else can. As a gift received, sustained, and nurtured in freedom, it satisfies in a way greater than any other material possession. To the awak-

---

19. Richard McKeon, ed., *The Basic Works of Aristotle*, "Nicomachean Ethics" (New York: Random House, 1941), 1061.

ened heart, spiritual friendship is one of the lasting treasures of the human life and a foretaste of the final communion we will have with each other in the end of time. In learning to care for one another, community helps make visible the invisible heart of God.[20]

Solidarity

Because we are all interrelated, solidarity connects us with those most disconnected from the human family. In a time when there is such emphasis on upward mobility, solidarity, as an expression of Christian charity, is a form of downward mobility that expresses itself concretely in the preferential option for the poor. Downward mobility puts its emphasis on people rather than possessions, on action on behalf of justice rather than accomplishments on behalf of the ego, and on the God of hope rather than the god of greed.

Solidarity lived as an option for the poor is not only a statement about the God of Jesus Christ but a statement of our human nature. Solidarity unveils the humbling truth of our broken human condition, which enables us to see at the same time our own poverty before God. In a society that spends billions of dollars annually on cosmetics, we do a good job of covering up our imperfections and existential poverty. This becomes problematic when we put more energy into developing an image of ourselves than into dealing with the reality of who we truly are. Gross expenditures for plastic surgeries of every kind often are pursued at the cost and neglect of the far deeper beauties of the human heart, which can be cultivated without financial expenditure. Precisely because we are often attached to superficiality, the poor can unmask who we are deep down and show us how needy we really are as human beings. While this truth can be liberating, our own imperfections, insecurities, and needs frighten us at the same time. Reluctantly we ask for help, yet our inability to ask gets in the way of our spiritual growth.[21] We often do not realize how poor we are, how much we need each other, and how deep is our need for God (Rv 3:17). Johannes Baptist Metz puts it this way:

> We are all beggars. We are all members of a species that is not sufficient unto itself. We are all creatures plagued by unending doubts and restless, unsatisfied hearts. Of all creatures, we are the poorest and the most incomplete. Our needs are always beyond our capacities, and we can only find ourselves when we lose ourselves.[22]

---

20. I am grateful to Mary J. Miller for this insight.
21. I am grateful to Rob Ercoline from Catholic Charities of South Bend, Indiana, for this insight.
22. Johannes B. Metz, *Poverty of Spirit* (New York: Paulist, 1968), 27.

Solidarity entails sociopolitical conversion, and Donald Gelpi believes that this involves a commitment to change at least one significant issue of injustice in our world, such as world hunger, the death penalty, abortion, human rights, immigration, Africa and other areas of economic underdevelopment, debt relief, the environment, gender inequality, natural disasters, HIV/AIDS, genocide, homelessness, militarism, trade inequities, corporate accountability, consumption, and many other issues.[23] While practically we cannot address all the issues of injustice that face the world, we can do something, and because we are interconnected, our personal efforts for justice are integrally linked to the search for justice on a global scale.

Solidarity with the poor does not mean helping the poor from a privileged position of economic superiority or even ministerial power. It involves cultivating relationships with the poor that are marked by mutual receptivity and reciprocity. It means that one can always receive something of value from the poor, even a simple morsel of food, or most of all, the offer of friendship. Broadening our circle of friends enlarges the heart and deepens our spirituality because it makes love boundless. While those with wealth can help alleviate the suffering of the poor, in the end, because of the intimate connection between Christ and the poor, it is not that the church saves the poor but, paradoxically, it is the poor who save the church.

The option for the poor, then, is at the same time a radical decision to imitate Christ, a radical call to solidarity with all people, and radical realization of our true selves. No Christian is exempt from this option, not even the poor, and indeed our final salvation is integrally related to it.

The Gospel of Matthew speaks of the judgment at the end of time as integrally related to what one has done for the least of one's brothers and sisters (Mt 25:31–46). To offer food, drink, hospitality, clothing, medical care, and liberation to all who are crucified today is not only an act of charity but an act of solidarity with Christ himself, who is present in a real way in the poor. The face of Christ, in which we shall one day read our judgment, already mysteriously gazes on us from every human face, particularly those who suffer and are excluded.

Renewing Our Relationship with the Environment

Nature

The call to solidarity extends not only to people but also to creation. Especially as society becomes more technological and urbanized, and as we face

---

23. For more from Donald Gelpi on forms of conversion, see "The Converting Jesuit," *Studies in the Spirituality of Jesuits* 18, no. 1 (January 1986), http://ejournals.bc.edu.

environmental dangers that put the whole human family at risk, renewing our relationship with the earth is not simply a matter of recreation but a vital need, personally and collectively. As John Muir observed in 1898, "Thousands of tired, nerve-shaken, over-civilized people are beginning to find out that going to the mountains is going home; that wilderness is a necessity; and that mountain parks and reservations are useful not only as fountains of timber and irrigating rivers, but as fountains of life."[24] All who have felt the ocean waters wash across their bare feet, beheld the mystery of the sun setting over the sea, or hiked to the peak of a mountain know the power of nature to revitalize, energize, and humanize.

When we forget our fundamental connection to the earth, we lose something of ourselves. Extended periods of time in the outdoors help renew our relationship with the earth, such as a backpacking trip or other such excursions, but since practically such trips are not possible or even desirable for everyone, connection with nature also can develop though a walk around a park, working in a garden, or even the simple act of smelling a rose. Such moments remind us that we are more than our ideas, our possessions, and most of all, our work and its pressures for productive output.

Throughout history some theologians have referred to nature as one of the great "texts" of God. Yet because of sin, as Bonaventure points out, it is as if it were written in a foreign language.[25] John Calvin believed that the legibility of this text for a fallen world is so blurry that it can be likened to that of "old or bleary-eyed men and those with weak vision" who stand before a beautiful volume and can scarcely construe two words.[26] As we learn to see with the eyes of the heart, however, we become more capable of perceiving the fingerprint of God in nature and the intimate bond between the Creator, creatures, and creation. As the first sacrament of God, nature is one of the primary ways that God's life, creativity, and beauty are revealed to us.

The Native Americans also understand the sacredness of the earth, as Seneca Indian philosopher and activist John Mohawk observes:

> The natural world is our bible. We don't have chapters and verses; we have trees and fish and animals. The world-view that Indian people live by is spiritual. Our attention to the creation is our spiritual seeking of it. The Indian sense of natural law is that nature informs us and it is our obligation to read nature as you would a book, to feel nature as you would a poem,

---

24. John Muir, *Our National Parks* (San Francisco: Sierra Club Books, 1991), 1.
25. See Saint Bonaventure, *Collations on the Six Days*, 2, no. 20, trans. José da Vinck (Patterson, N.J.: St. Anthony Guild Press, 1970), 32.
26. John Calvin, *Institutes of Christian Religion*, 1, ed. John T. McNeill (Philadelphia: Westminster, 1960), 70.

to touch nature as you would yourself, to be a part of that and step into its cycles as much as you can.[27]

While science has greatly contributed to subduing the earth and understanding its intrinsic properties, it has not even begun to understand the mystical communion humanity shares with it. It is a point not only of intellectual hubris but of theological ignorance and postmodern naiveté to think that it is only a matter of time before science will be able to explain the truths of the world, which have been shrouded under the superstitious veil of "religion." Without understanding science within the larger context of a creating, loving God, our journey ends at the base of a cognitive "foothill" rather than at the peak of spiritual Everest. As Robert Jastrow notes,

At this moment it seems as though science will never be able to raise the curtain on the mystery of creation. For the scientist who has lived by his faith in the power of reason, the story ends like a bad dream. He has scaled the mountains of ignorance; he is about to conquer the highest peak; as he pulls himself over the final rock, he is greeted by a band of theologians who have been sitting there for centuries.[28]

In addition to being an object to be studied, creation is a gift to be contemplated in a spirit of reverence and respect. Without a humble recognition of our intimate bond with the earth, and practical ways to nurture and protect it, not only will we become a more violent society, but we will engineer our own demise as a civilization.

The current trajectory of consumption raises very serious questions about environmental sustainability as well as the consequences we are now facing because of environmental irresponsibility. Not only do 20 percent of the population in developed nations consume 86 percent of the earth's goods, but according to a spokesperson of the World Wildlife Fund, "If all the people consumed natural resources at the same rate as the average US and UK citizen we would require at least two extra planets like Earth" by 2050.[29] Even with the potential discovery of new resources, it is clear that up until now the free-market economy has not proved to be a reliable or sustainable system, especially for the environment, and given the potential catastrophic consequences, justice demands greater fidelity to our relationship with nature. We cannot continue to exploit nature without serious consequences for our own

---

27. John Mohawk, "A Native View of Nature," *Resurgence* 178 (September-October 1996): 11.
28. Robert Jastrow, *God and the Astronomers*, 2nd ed. (New York: Norton, 2000), 107.
29. *Human Development Report 1998* (Oxford: Oxford University Press, 1998), 2; Mark Townsend and Jason Burke, "The World's Ticking Timebomb: Earth Will Expire by 2050," *London Observer*, July 7, 2002.

self-preservation and well-being. To put it succinctly, in destroying the environment we destroy ourselves.

Simplicity

Simplicity is a practical way of trying to live more and more in harmony with the earth.[30] As a lifestyle of responsible stewardship for God's creation, it is also an act of solidarity with those who come after us.[31] Few lifestyles swim more upstream against the current of contemporary society than simplicity. In a world where we are consistently told that more is better, simplicity seeks to free us from the slavery of inordinate human want.

Focused more on being than having, on the quality of one's heart rather than the quantity of one's possessions, and on the value of inner beauty rather than outer appearance, those committed to a Gospel-motivated simplicity seek to look beyond the consumer creeds of contemporary culture in order find what truly liberates. Questioning all the premises of the global marketplace, a simple lifestyle recognizes that material prosperity, paradoxically, has not necessarily made us better people, nor has it made us happier, leaving many with questions about how to evaluate the material gains, human costs, and ethical losses in the current world order.[32]

A Paradox of Our Times

The paradox of our time in history is that we have taller buildings but shorter tempers, wider freeways but narrower viewpoints. We spend more but have less. We buy more but enjoy less. We have bigger houses and smaller families, more conveniences but less time. We have more degrees but less sense, more knowledge but less judgment, more experts yet more problems, more medicine but less wellness.

We drink too much, smoke too much, spend too recklessly, laugh too little, drive too fast, get too angry, stay up too late, get up too tired, read too little, watch TV too much, and pray too seldom. We have multiplied our possessions but reduced our values. We talk too much, love too seldom, and hate too often. We've learned how to make a living but not a life. We've added years to life, not life to years.

---

30. Y. de Andia, V. Desprez, and M. Dupuy, "Simplicité," in *Dictionnaire de Spiritualité ascéti-que et mystique*, ed. Marcel Viller et al., vol. 14, cols. 892-921; J. Bauer, "Simplicity," in *Sacramentum Verbi: An Encyclopedia of Biblical Theology*, vol. 3, ed. J. Bauer (New York: Herder & Herder, 1970), 847-48; R. Plus, *Simplicity* (Westminster, Md.: Newman, 1951); and D. Shi, *The Simple Life: Plain Living and High Thinking in American Culture* (New York: Oxford University Press, 1985). See also Steven Payne, "Simplicity," in *The New Dictionary of Catholic Spirituality*, ed. Michael Downey (Collegeville, Minn.: Liturgical Press, 1993), 885-89.

31. Payne, "Simplicity," 889.

32. Tibor Scitovsky, *The Joyless Economy: The Psychology of Human Satisfaction* (Oxford: Oxford University Press, 1992).

We've been all the way to the moon and back, but have trouble crossing the street to meet a new neighbor. We conquered outer space but not inner space. We've done larger things but not better things. We've cleaned up the air but polluted the soul. We've conquered the atom but not our prejudice. We write more but learn less. We plan more but accomplish less. We've learned to rush but not to wait. We build more computers to hold more information to produce more copies than ever, but we communicate less and less.

These are the times of fast foods and slow digestion, big men and small character, steep profits and shallow relationships. These are the days of two incomes but more divorce, fancier houses but broken homes. These are the days of quick trips, disposable diapers, throwaway morality, one night stands, overweight bodies, and pills that do everything from cheer, to quiet, to kill. It is a time when there is much in the showroom window and nothing in the stockroom. . . .[33]

Although many of us in more economically prosperous parts of the world live with the modern illusion that we are more "advanced" than previous generations, the paradox of the present moment stems in many ways from a spiritual impoverishment; it brings us to the realization that there are not only developed and underdeveloped countries but developed and underdeveloped people. Simplicity helps us sort out this often paradoxical relationship between economic development and spiritual development, between the cravings of the body and the hunger of the soul, between the invisible hand of the economy and the invisible heart of the human person. In helping clear our vision, simplicity is a way of trying to judge wisely the things of earth and choose life rather than death in our daily decisions.

While related to material possessions, simplicity has more to do with clarity of heart and intention than with simply not having "things." Simplicity is above all a spiritual disposition, grounded in the desire for wholehearted commitment to live in relationship with God and respond fully to God's revelation in one's life. Simplicity in food, dress, possessions, and speech flows from a more fundamental desire to live in complete dedication to God. As the kingdom of God more and more governs one's life, everything else is reprioritized and revalued, and one begins to see the things of the earth in a different way. Less prone to grasp, more open to hold in freedom, simplicity gives expression to the truth that in God alone we find our ultimate worth and value, and love received through humble openness is the greatest possession of human life.

---

33. "A Paradox of Our Times," is attributed to numerous sources and is available in many forms on the Internet.

Simplicity potentially opens us up to more and more people, especially the poor, from whom it is often easier to learn that human life is first of all about relationships. The simple and open-hearted often learn more quickly than the rich the radical interconnectedness of people and that relationships are the real treasure of life. They understand more readily that we are not ultimate masters of our own destiny, and there is much to learn about the limitations of life, about our deepest needs, and about hope in greater things. They give expression to the radical nakedness of our lives beyond the titles, accomplishments, and degrees we often hide behind; they also allow us to see a truth about God and about the reality of our lives as they are unmasked transparently before God, even while such revelation directly contradicts many of the established norms, values, and conventions of society.

The simple and the poor often have learned how to be patient, how to be humble, how to endure. They have also learned how to share generously from the scarcity of their resources and to choose hope in the midst of their suffering. Even when everything is taken away, many realize the one thing that cannot be taken is the freedom to choose what kind of person one will become. Living in such poverty, either voluntarily or involuntarily, can dispose people to respond to the call of the Gospel with a total abandonment because they have so little to lose and are ready for anything.[34]

Renewing Our Relationship with Ourselves

Recollection

Because simplicity has more to do with the quality of the heart than the quantity of possessions, the discipline of "recollection" is a way of consolidating the conflicting and scattered energies of our lives and focusing them on "the one thing necessary (Lk 10:42)," namely, simple loving attention to God and surrender to the transforming action of the Spirit. Recollection helps ground the intensity with which we can interact with the world and helps us mellow our response to the accelerating pace of contemporary society, which frequently fragments our lives with centrifugal force. Through various methods and disciplines, recollection is a way of "collecting" our scattered lives around a spiritual center, which helps renew our lives by bringing us to a place of inner peace and wholeness. The more we practice this discipline, the more we can anchor our lives in the truth of our existence as it unfolds before God.

The long story of human history indicates that the inner fragmentation we

---

34. Monika Hellwig, "Good News to the Poor: Do They Understand It Better?" in *Tracing the Spirit: Communities, Social Action and Theological Reflection*, ed. James. E. Hug (New York: Paulist, 1983), 145.

experience is part of life in a broken world, even though its intensity may be greater now than in previous generations. Various spiritual masters believe that the task of integration is directly related to spiritual progress. Gregory the Great saw recollection as the first stage of the contemplative ascent up the mountain of God.[35] Francisco de Osuna thought that recollection calms the intellect, the will, and the memory and allows one to advance in the spiritual journey.[36] Teresa of Avila felt that recollecting the human faculties enables the soul to center itself on its true core, the indwelling Spirit of God in Christ.

Especially when we have trouble "reading" what is going on inside our hearts and our bodies, recollection is a valuable way to begin prayer. Yet for many people their inner lives are a foreign land. Driven by compulsion and often controlled by external stimuli, recollection helps ground our lives in the liberating truth of self-knowledge. Without self-knowledge, our relationships begin to unravel on the most basic level, namely, with ourselves. The discipline of recollection helps reconcile our own inner lives and our interactions with the outer world.

Research in various spiritual and psychological practices have reaffirmed the value of recollection. As Thomas McKenna notes,

On the one hand, these techniques consist in efforts to create a tranquil outer and especially inner space so that the heart can unburden itself of the compulsivities of modern life and become a quiet cell where God can dwell. On the other, they recognize the gentle receptivity needed to let the Father of Jesus Christ be reborn into the consciousness of the believer.[37]

One particular way of rediscovering the practice of recollection is through what Eugene Gendlin calls "focusing" and what Peter McMahon and Edwin Campbell have referred to as "bio-spirituality."[38] Focusing and bio-spirituality are contemporary names and nuanced approaches to this ancient practice of recollection, and they provide various approaches through which people find practical ways to come to a sense of inner wholeness, beginning with naming the truth of what one is experiencing in the present moment.

Focusing and bio-spirituality involve a series of steps that help one understand what is going on inside the heart, which includes the input from the emotions and the body, so that dispersed, repressed, and scattered energy

---

35. Pope Saint Gregory the Great, *Homily on Ezekiel*, II: 5, 8-9.Francisco de Osuna, *The Third Spiritual Alphabet*, trans. M. Giles (New York: Paulist, 1981).

36. Francisco de Osuna, *The Third Spiritual Alphabet*, trans. M. Giles (New York: Paulist, 1981).

37. Thomas F. McKenna, "Recollection," in *The New Dictionary of Catholic Spirituality*, ed. Downey, 806.

38. Eugene T. Gendlin, *Focusing*, 2nd ed. (New York: Bantam Books, 1981); Peter A. McMahon and Edwin M. Campbell, *Bio-Spirituality* (Chicago: Loyola University Press, 1985).

can be recollected, released, and integrated into one's system in a wholesome way.[39] While space does not permit a detailed discussion of this prayer form, the methods and practices of this approach involve trusting one's biological, affective, and intuitive dimensions as an inherent source of wisdom and understanding, not as a threat and a danger. In contrast to some spiritual schools of thought that totally reject and mistrust the body and emotions as capricious and unreliable, recollection helps people tune in to the emotional and biological wisdom of our system. Such recollection requires practice, experience, and discipline, but it helps people find an inner reference point that emerges the more one is thoroughly honest with who one is in the world.

Focusing, bio-spirituality, and other forms of recollection then help us read the whole range of one's responses to reality. They help us deal particularly with challenging and uncomfortable feelings that often go unacknowledged or unrecognized yet exist below the surface of our consciousness. The endless demands of work can cause burnout in people when they do not take the time for healthy self-maintenance and a periodic self-inventory about what they are honestly feeling and experiencing. Practicing recollection is particularly important for those involved in social ministries, which can generate a range of feelings, including being overwhelmed, feeling powerless, guilty, exhausted, and frustrated. Ignoring or rejecting these feelings at the conscious level, because they do not fit the image of who we think we are, can control and dominate people's lives and leave people with a sense that they are unfree, constrained, and even depressed without knowing why. Recollection enables us to accept and allow these feelings as normal and indeed a natural part of the landscape of life. A healthy acknowledgment of them actually helps release, liberate, and integrate the energy of these emotions. The fruit of such recollection is that it helps us come to a greater sense of "at home-ness" with ourselves, and from this base we are better able to navigate the path to peace in a natural way.

Sabbath

In the context of feeling frequently overextended, constantly pressured, and seldom rested, the Sabbath in an important path to personal renewal and spiritual growth. In addition to being a divine command and a divine institution (Gn 2:3; Ex 20:11; 31:17), the Sabbath is a human need. It is a gift of God that reminds us we are worth more than the work of our hands, the effectiveness of our ministry, and the efficiency-mindedness that often controls us.[40] When observed as a regular part of the week, the Sabbath teaches

---

39. For more on the steps of focusing, see *Six Steps (en)*, http://www.focusing.org/sixsteps.html.

40. For more on biblical understanding of Sabbath, see Michael D. Guinan, *To Be Human before God: Insights from Biblical Spirituality* (Collegeville, Minn.: Liturgical Press, 1994), 75-85. For more

us that the longing of our hearts is beyond our best accomplishments, that our lives rely on the gratuity of God more than our own strength and effort, and that our ministries are more about the Lord of the work than the work of the Lord.

Sabbath celebrates time and makes it holy. In Genesis we read that "God blessed the seventh day and made it holy" (Gn 2:3). While for six days a week human beings live under the pressures and demands of work, on the Sabbath, Abraham Heschel observes, "We are called upon to share in what is eternal in time, to turn from the results of creation to the mystery of creation; from the world of creation to the creation of the world."[41]

The word Sabbath comes from the Hebrew *shabbat*, which means to "cease" or "desist." It is not a day to catch up on work but a time to stop working in order to rest and worship God. As Heschel eloquently states,

> Six days a week we wrestle with the world, wringing profit from the earth; on the Sabbath we especially care for the seed of eternity planted in the soul. The world has our hands, but our soul belongs to Someone Else. Six days a week we seek to dominate the world, on the seventh we try to dominate the self.[42]

Addicted to a culture of productivity and consumerism, however, we rarely cease from work or shopping, and we break the command to observe the Sabbath so regularly that we do not even think of it as disobedience. Defined more by efficiency and a 24/7 schedule, we drive ourselves to run like machines, but without periodic rests our biological-spiritual system breaks down. Recent studies have confirmed how the pace of the current global economy is taking its physical toll on the human heart. In economically prosperous areas like Europe, Japan, and the United States, researchers have documented a greater increase in heart disease, which they believe is linked to the global push for greater productivity.[43] Longer hours, more pressure, increased job insecurity, and a faster pace of life are causing a greater incidence of coronary diseases.

These physical ailments may also be indicative of a larger inner problem. When the deeper aspirations of the human heart are not addressed, they can manifest themselves in our bodies. Because there is an integral relationship between the body and the spirit, physical sicknesses can oftentimes be indicative of a spiritual sickness that has largely been undiagnosed and untreated.[44]

---

on how ritual helps restore the integrity of creation, see Frank Gorman, *The Ideology of Ritual: Space, Time, and Status in the Priestly Theology* (Sheffield: Sheffield Academic Press, 1990), 39-60.

41. Abraham Heschel, *The Sabbath* (New York: Farrar, Straus & Giroux, 2005), 10.

42. Ibid., 13.

43. Nancy Cleeland, "Job Stress Taking Its Toll: Workers' Hearts Pay Price of New Global Economy," *The Palm Beach Post*, April 2, 2005, p. 2f.

44. The Hebrew word *nephesh*, often translated as "soul," is understood in the Jewish Kabbalistic

While in previous generations much energy has gone into the problems associated with sexual repression, the increasing secularization of society, which often denies the transcendent dimensions of the human heart, will mean that greater attention will need to be given to problems that stem from spiritual repression.[45]

If in biblical times Jesus challenged religious leaders for adhering to a narrow understanding of the Sabbath, today he likely would challenge our global society for losing a sense of its role all together. We forget that the Sabbath is not something that we do for God but something that God does for us (Mk 2:27). We rest not only because it will enable us to be more effective in the week to come but to remind us that our deepest hope lies in God, who is creator and redeemer. The Sabbath also helps us understand the gratuity of God and how our lives are not earned or achieved but are gifts that flow from a God of love. The Sabbath helps strengthen our journey, especially as we struggle on our way up and down the mountain. As the Jewish people have often observed, more than they have kept the Sabbath, the Sabbath has kept them.[46] In the midst of labor, trials, and struggle, the Sabbath is a symbol of the divine rest to come (Heb 4:1-11). Someday we will inherit the fullness of divine rest, when all relationships will be restored and our hearts will possess at last what we have longed for all our lives.

A NEW MIND, A NEW HEART:
LEARNING TO LIVE AND LOVE LIKE CHRIST

While there are many other spiritual disciplines that can help restore our relationships and navigate the path to peace, their purpose in the end is not to restrict our lives but to free them, to empower us to climb, as Richard Foster says, the "Himalayas of the Spirit."[47] The more we are guided from the vision on the mountaintop, and the more we realize that the challenges of ascent and descent are daily demands, the more we will see that disciplines are liberating because they help us change. In helping us change, they lead us to freedom. In leading us to freedom they bring us joy. In bringing us joy they enable us to find life. In guiding us to life, they lead us to God, who alone renews our relationships and reveals to us the love our hearts most desire.

---

tradition as having to do with one's physicality. To Jewish Kabbalistic thinkers, *nephesh* is not just the soul but actually comprises the physical component of the human being, an insight that supports the idea of the body-soul unity.

45. Gerald G. May, *Will and Spirit: A Contemplative Psychology* (San Francisco: HarperCollins, 1987).

46. See Heschel, *Sabbath*.

47. Foster, *Celebration of Discipline*, 201.

As we bring the vision from the mountaintop to the valley, and as we look at the immense problems of the world that we want to change, it helps every now and again to remember that the challenge of global change begins on the most local level. Discipleship challenges us to behold and love the world as God loves us in Christ. Only as we leave our baggage behind can our blindness be healed and our hearts transformed. The more we do so, the more we can make the arduous but rewarding climb that leads us to the promising views from the mountaintop. Then even our view of the valley is transformed by what we have seen from above.

A number of years ago I was in New York City, passing through Grand Central Station. While there I noticed a woman sitting beside a wall near one of the trains. Her head was slumped over her knees, and her gray, straggly hair dangled on either side of them. She wore a faded blue, nylon coat, and just sat there, like an empty, lifeless shell. Nearby was a coffee shop, so I bought two cups of coffee and then went over to her. I sat down beside her and then offered her the drink. I said, "How are you doing?" As she lifted up her head from her knees, she looked over at me guardedly, suspiciously, and said, "Fine!" Then she looked away. I then asked, "How has the day been?" "Good!" she quipped, defensively and definitively. Unsure if I should say anything else, I asked, "What's new?" and she said, "Nothing!" With that word, she completely turned away and shut me down, as if a wall had come between us.

I realized our conversation would probably go nowhere. So I just sat next to her, drinking my coffee, while thousands rushed by us, without even noticing we were sitting there. This was about as low as I had ever descended into the valley: we were nobody to anybody. After about twenty minutes, she finally turned my way and said, "Who the hell are you anyways and what are you doing here?" Wanting to keep my words brief, I said, "I'm a priest and I just thought you needed a cup of coffee."

Then something unexpected happened. She looked at me and started to cry, sobbing so intensely that her tears could have flooded Grand Central Station. I did not know what to do at first, and the moment was too profound to touch with words. Not wanting to get in the way of the Spirit, I just stayed there with her in silence, wondering what stories lay beneath her tears. After a while she began to calm down, and we began to move into another kind of emotional space. I looked over at her and gently asked, "What is your name?" And she said, "Sara." For the next few moments we talked about her life, her struggles, and her broken relationships.

Then I asked her, "Sara if you could change anything in the world today, what would it be?" She hesitated, and there was a long moment of silence. I anticipated that she might say, "the mayor," "the president," or the social structures that contributed to her oppression, all of which would have made sense. But she looked over at me and said, "If I could change anything in the world . . . I would change . . . my mind." She revealed that her mind held her heart in prison and the possibility of conversion held out the hope for genuine freedom. As I sat on the floor and drank my coffee with Sara, it was as if I could hear Jesus' words, "You are not far from the Kingdom of God" (Mk 12:34).

QUESTIONS FOR REFLECTION

1. How would you distinguish needs from wants in your own life?
2. In what ways has your spiritual life seemed like an uphill climb?
3. Have you ever had a "peak experience"?
4. Have you ever had an experience of descending into the "valley of injustice"?
5. What keeps us from being reconciled to others?
6. Which spiritual discipline do you find yourself most drawn to practice? Which do you find the most difficult? Why?
7. When the last chapter of your life is written, how do you want to be remembered?

SUGGESTIONS FOR FURTHER READING AND STUDY

Arnold, Eberhard. *Why We Live in Community.* Farmington, Pa.: Plough Publishing House, 1995.

Au, Wilkie. *By Way of the Heart: Toward a Holistic Christian Spirituality.* Mahwah, N.J.: Paulist, 1989.

Augustine. *The Confessions of St. Augustine.* Translated by John K. Ryan. Garden City, N.Y.: Doubleday, 1960.

Bonhoeffer, Dietrich. *The Cost of Discipleship.* 1948. New York: Touchstone, 1995.

Burton-Christie, Douglas. *The Word in the Desert: Scripture and the Quest for Holiness in Early Christian Monasticism.* New York: Oxford University Press, 1993.

Callahan, Annice, ed. *Spiritualities of the Heart: Approaches to Personal Wholeness in Christian Tradition.* New York: Paulist, 1990.

Campbell, Peter A., and Edwin M. McMahon. *Bio-Spirituality: Focusing as a Way to Grow.* Chicago: Loyola University Press, 1985.

Collins, Kenneth J., ed. *Exploring Christian Spirituality: An Ecumenical Reader.* Grand Rapids: Baker Books, 2000.

De Sales, Francis. *Introduction to the Devout Life.* Translated and edited by John K. Ryan. New York: Doubleday, 1989.

Downey, Michael. *Understanding Christian Spirituality.* New York: Paulist, 1997.

Foster, Richard J. *Celebration of Discipline: The Path to Spiritual Growth.* Rev. ed. San Francisco: Harper & Row, 1988.

Frankl, Viktor. *Man's Search for Meaning.* Rev. ed. Translated by Ilse Lasch. New York: Simon & Schuster, 1962.

Gelpi, Donald L. *Committed Worship: A Sacramental Theology for Converting Christians.* Vols. 1 and 2. Collegeville, Minn.: Liturgical Press, 1993.

Gendlin, Eugene T. *Focusing.* 2nd ed. New York: Bantam Books, 1981.

Green, Thomas H. *Weeds among the Wheat: Discernment Where Prayer and Action Meet.* Notre Dame, Ind.: Ave Maria, 1984.

Guinan, Michael D. *To Be Human before God: Insights from Biblical Spirituality.* Collegeville, Minn.: Liturgical Press, 1994.

Habito, Ruben. *Living Zen, Loving God.* Somerville, Mass.: Wisdom Publications, 2004.

Heschel, Abraham. *The Sabbath.* New York: Farrar, Straus & Giroux, 2005.

Houdek, Frank J. *Guided by the Spirit: A Jesuit Perspective on Spiritual Direction.* Chicago, Ill.: Loyola Press, 1996.

May, Gerald G. *Will and Spirit: A Contemplative Psychology.* San Francisco: Harper-Collins, 1987.

Metz, Johannes B. *Poverty of Spirit.* New York: Paulist, 1968.

Nouwen, Henri. *The Way of the Heart.* New York: Seabury, 1981.

Pascal, Blaise. *The Provincial Letters.* Translated by A. J. Krailsheimer. London: Penguin Books, 1967.

Rolheiser, Ronald. *The Holy Longing: The Search for a Christian Spirituality.* New York: Doubleday, 1999.

Ryan, Thomas. *The Sacred Art of Fasting: Preparing to Practice.* Woodstock, Vt.: Skylight Paths, 2005.

Teresa of Avila. *The Interior Castle.* Translated by Kieran Kavanaugh and Otillio Rodriguez. New York: Paulist, 1979.

Waaijman, Kees. *Spirituality: Forms, Foundations, Methods.* Leuven: Peeters, 2002.

Ward, Benedicta, trans. *The Sayings of the Desert Fathers.* Kalamazoo, Mich.: Cistercian Publications, 1975.

Warren, Rick. *The Purpose Driven Life.* Grand Rapids: Zondervan, 2002.

Afterword

Theodore M. Hesburgh, CSC

A number of years ago I was visiting a small village in the Altiplano of Peru where there lived a number of indigenous communities. Many of these people tilled the soil, planted seeds, and harvested crops in this beautiful yet barren landscape. Among them lived a generous and wise priest, and one night when we sat down for supper, he prayed the following prayer: *Da pan a los que tienen hambre, y a los que tienen pan, da hambre para la justicia,* "Give bread to those who hunger, and to those who have bread, give them a hunger for justice." This prayer is a fitting description of what Daniel Groody has tried to do in his profound and much needed book. He has tried to awaken us once again to the hungers of the people of the world, and for those who have resources, he has sought to awaken a collective sense of responsibility to transform our world into one that is reflective of a God of Life who created us to live in his image and likeness.

Groody's keen and perceptive analysis of the world situation is enough to make anyone ponder. His over-view, under-view, and inner-view of the complex world today are not only thoroughly researched but accessible to a wide audience. While grounded on a solid understanding of our current socioeconomic "reality," Groody asks probing questions about the role of theological reflection in this new age of globalization. Alongside the work of eminent political scientists, economists, sociologists, and other scholars, he points to the central need to look at the theological and spiritual dimensions of globalization. His premise is that theology and spirituality are important academic disciplines that can help build bridges with other areas of scholarship and offer unique insight into global transformation. His theological reading of globalization and global reading of theology make an important and unique scholarly contribution in understanding this era of widespread change.

An important contribution of this book is that it helps us rediscover the wealth of the Christian tradition as we confront the difficult challenge of poverty, a challenge we must take up. Throughout this book Groody makes the point that the one constant in the church's history is the call to care for and empower the poor. Especially as the gap between rich and poor continues to widen, this message is as relevant now as ever. The difference today is that the stakes are higher now than ever. As we reflect on our relationship with God, others, and the environment, we recognize that unless we move our efforts in the right direction we put the survival of humanity at risk.

Like nuclear energy, this time of global change can be used constructively or destructively. A number of years ago I was asked to be part of the International Atomic Energy Agency. The United Nations assembled noted leaders from around the world to sit on this commission and deal with the challenging questions regarding the peaceful use of nuclear energy. Some questioned what role a theologian could play in the midst of such a complex issue. My response at the time was that theology helps us deal with crucial human questions, not the least of which relates to the issue of good and evil. Theology also confronts us with the imperative of moral decision making amidst the complex and difficult issues of our own day and age.

I remember a number of years ago when the late Jesuit Superior General Pedro Arrupe reiterated how in this time of great change, we must in fact deepen rather than retreat from the challenge of faith. He said,

> We live in the atomic age. It is as though an insane brat had got hold of a loaded pistol. Journalists have tried to give prominence these days to a period of my life when Providence willed that I should find myself in the zone blasted by the atomic bomb of Hiroshima and that I should escape unhurt. Well then, I remember that when I was still under the terrible impression of the catastrophe, in a conversation with some young students we were commenting on the power of the weapon employed, and calculated the thousands of casualties in our neighbourhood and those which might be expected as a consequence. I remember how, after a pessimistic diagnosis by the youths, a spontaneous observation occurred to me which impressed them profoundly: "And after all, my dear friends, in spite of this new powerful weapon and any others that may still come, you must know that we have a power much greater than the atomic energy: we have the Heart of Christ. But while the atomic energy is destined to destroy and atomize everything, in the Heart of Christ we have an invincible weapon whose power will destroy every evil and unite the minds and hearts of the whole of mankind in one central bond, his love and the love of the Father.[1]

This book is not only a book of great scholarship but a work of profound prayer. Etched out in the library but weaved together in the soul, it educates not only the mind but the heart. It is spiritual in its approach but political in

---

1. Pedro Arrupe, *In Him Alone Is Our Hope: Texts on the Heart of Christ (1965-1983)* (St. Louis: Institute of Jesuit Sources, 1984), 114-15.

its implications as it explores the social dimensions of Christian faith. This book names the deeper truths of life that liberate, empower, and inspire us to live authentically and embrace our human family. Groody does not just look at the world as it is, but he looks at who God is and then asks what kind of world our loving Creator calls us to co-create.

While Groody writes with clarity on global poverty, he does not cast a cynical, foreboding shadow over the future. His book contains profound hope rooted in a vision of the kingdom of God, a kingdom of life and love, freedom and justice. It illustrates how concern for the poor is at the heart of the message of the Gospel, and even as we struggle to find the right course of action, Groody reminds us that justice has been and will remain, like the North Star, the one fixed reference point on the horizon as we seek to create a more peaceful world.

While we know that we are called to use every ounce of heart, mind, and soul in the service of justice and peace, it is God's Spirit who leads us on the right path, transforms our vision, and inspires us to action. This book moves me to pray what has been the guiding prayer of my life, the path to renewal, and the cry of justice: "Come, Holy Spirit. Guide us in this time of global challenge and global opportunity. Renew the face of the earth. Renew the heart of humanity."

Index